THE EVERYDAY DAIRY-FREE COOKBOOK

THE
EVERYDAY
DAIRY-FREE
COOKBOOK

Over 180 Delicious Recipes to Make Eating a Pleasure

MILLER ROGERS AND EMILY WHITE

KEY PORTER  BOOKS

National Library of Canada Cataloguing in Publication
Rogers, Miller
   The everyday dairy-free cookbook : recipes for lactose intolerants /
Miller Rogers and Emily White

ISBN 1-55263-216-4

   1. Milk-free diet—Recipes. 2. Lactose intolerance—Diet Therapy—
Recipes. I. White, Emily II. Title

RM234.5.R64 2003   641.5'63   C2002-905638-1

The publisher gratefully acknowledges the support of the Canada
Council for the Arts and the Ontario Arts Council for its publishing
program. We acknowledge the support of the Government of Ontario
through the Ontario Media Development Corporation's Ontario Book
Initiative. We acknowledge the financial support of the Government of
Canada through the Book Publishing Industry Development Program
(BPIDP) for our publishing activities.

Key Porter Books Limited
70 The Esplanade
Toronto, Ontario
Canada M5E 1R2

www.keyporter.com

Cover design: Joan Sommers Design
Electronic formatting: Joan Sommers Design

Printed and bound in the United States

03 04 05 06 07 08 6 5 4 3 2 1

Note: When making any of the recipes in this book, only
follow one set of measures at a time (i.e. metric or imperial).

Contents

FOREWORD

Between 30 and 50 million North Americans are lactose intolerant. A shocking figure—until you consider lactose intolerance for what it really is: a natural condition, a biological trait as unremarkable as olive skin or blue eyes.

Lactose, the sugar found in milk, is broken down by the enzyme lactase. In most of the world's population, lactase is produced only by infants, to aid in the digestion of mother's milk. The exception is people of northern European descent, whose diet for generations has been heavy in milk, cheese and cream—resulting in the production of lactase in adulthood. This group's influence is obvious in North American dietary culture: ice cream is a favorite dessert, children learn that milk builds strong bones and you can order almost anything with extra cheese.

Fortunately for the many people who come from different cultural traditions, times are changing. The demand for dairy-free cuisine will continue to grow with our diversifying population. For the 75% to 90% of North Americans with African, Asian or Native heritage who are lactose intolerant, relief is in sight as more grocery stores and restaurants address the growing market gap.

Ethical concerns over animal treatment and the impact of agricultural practices on the environment are causing more and more people to find alternatives to dairy products. National rates of obesity, coronary artery disease and diabetes are skyrocketing as well, and foods low in cholesterol and saturated animal fat are urgently needed.

Whether it's a matter of preference or necessity, *The Everyday Dairy-Free Cookbook* provides many simple and delicious solutions to dairy-free eating. From Mushroom and Walnut Strudel to Blueberry Muffins and Apple Pie, there is something for everyone who wants good-tasting, easy-to-prepare recipes free of milk and milk products.

As understanding of the condition increases, lactose intolerance becomes a far less distressing diagnosis. With *The Everyday Dairy-Free Cookbook*, lactose intolerance loses even its nuisance status. This recipe collection finally provides a satisfying answer to the dairy-free eater's enduring question "What foods can I enjoy?"

Suzanne Havala Hobbs, Dr. PH, MS, RD
Adjunct Assistant Professor
Department of Health Policy and Administration
School of Public Health
The University of North Carolina at Chapel Hill

INTRODUCTION

The word "allergy" is bandied around so often and appears to be the cause of so many health problems that it seems we have been overtaken by an epidemic of allergies. People claim to be allergic to almost anything, including sunlight, pollution, cell phones, most foods, the buildings they work in and even their boss or spouse!

By definition, an allergy is a hypersensitivity to a specific substance, such as insect stings, food, pollen, mold or dust. The substance causing the reaction is called an allergen. For most people insect stings, food, pollen, mold or dust are harmless. For the allergic person, reactions can range from mild symptoms, such as sneezing and itchy, red eyes in the case of pollen-induced hay fever, to life-threatening anaphylactic shock caused by eating peanuts or being stung by a bee.

While many North Americans have probably experienced the minor discomfort of seasonal hay fever, far fewer have ever experienced a true food allergy. In the United States, only 2 to 2 1/2 percent of the population suffers from food allergies, about 6 to 7 million Americans, according to the Food Allergy & Anaphylaxis Network, a nonprofit organization dedicated to increasing awareness about food allergies. Of the Americans with food allergies, nearly 3 million suffer from peanut or tree nut allergies. In Canada, 0.3% to 7.5% of children and 1% to 3% of adults are affected by food allergies, according to the National Institute of Nutrition.

Food allergy is the leading cause of anaphylactic shock outside of the hospital, accounting for an estimated 30,000 emergency room visits and 2,000 hospitalizations annually. It is estimated that 150 to 200 people die each year from food allergy reactions; approximately 50 people die annually from insect sting reactions.

When it comes to food allergies, eight foods account for 90 percent of the allergic reactions:
- Peanuts
- Tree nuts (walnuts, pecans, cashews, etc.)
- Shellfish
- Eggs
- Fish
- Milk
- Soy
- Wheat

Peanuts are the leading cause of severe allergic reactions, followed by shellfish, tree nuts and eggs.

A food allergy is an immune system response to a food that the body mistakenly believes is harmful. Once the immune system decides that a particular food is harmful, it creates specific antibodies to it. The next time the person eats the food, the immune system releases massive amounts of chemicals, including histamine, in order to protect the body. These chemicals trigger a cascade of allergic symptoms that can affect the respiratory system, gastrointestinal tract, skin or cardiovascular system. In the most severe cases, anaphylactic shock can result. Epinephrine, also called adrenaline, is the medication of choice for controlling a severe reaction. The drug is available by prescription in a quick-inject pen that can be self-administered.

For the millions of North Americans suffering from food allergies, there is help but no cure. Avoiding the suspect food is the easiest way to prevent an allergic reaction. Although an individual could be allergic to any food, such as fruits, vegetables and meats, allergies to those foods are not as common as to the eight foods listed above.

Milk allergy is relatively common among those with food allergies, although its effects are not usually as severe as allergies to shellfish, nuts and eggs. There is also a great deal of confusion and misinformation about milk allergy and lactose intolerance.

This book has been designed to help anyone with a milk allergy or lactose intolerance begin and maintain a dairy- or lactose-free diet. We will explain what a milk allergy is and how it differs from lactose intolerance; then we will describe the different symptoms and how to follow a dairy- and lactose-free diet. We will look at foods that can replace dairy products and give helpful tips for getting enough calcium and protein in your diet without using dairy products. We've included handy hints for eating out as well as cooking and preparing dairy-free recipes.

The recipes in this book can be classified into two types: those that have been adapted to be dairy-free, and recipes that have traditionally, and deliciously, been dairy-free. So in addition to learning how to make some of your favorite dishes dairy-free, we'll introduce you to wonderful dishes from around the world that stand on their own merit, no dairy needed or wanted.

If you have any concerns about following a dairy-free diet or have a condition such as pregnancy or lactation that may be affected by what you choose to eat, please consult your health-care provider before starting any diet.

So what is a milk allergy?

An allergy is an abnormal reaction by the immune system to a specific substance, called an allergen. An allergy to milk is caused by a reaction to proteins in milk, such as casein.

And lactose intolerance?

Lactose intolerance is an inability to digest lactose fully. Lactose is the primary carbohydrate in milk. Lactose is digested by the enzyme lactase. If the lactose is not broken down properly by lactase, components of the lactose remain in the intestinal tract, where it feeds bacteria, which then multiply, causing the characteristic symptoms of lactose intolerance, which include digestive-tract distress in the form of cramps, flatulence and/or diarrhea.

Sometime between weaning and young adulthood, many people begin losing their ability to produce lactase, the enzyme responsible for digesting lactose. Having a milk allergy or a deficiency in producing lactase doesn't mean you can't drink milk or eat other dairy products. Some sensitivity to milk is dose-related, with symptoms more likely to occur if milk is consumed frequently, if it is consumed in large amounts, or depending on what other dairy products are consumed with it. Many people who are lactose-intolerant are able to digest small amounts of dairy, thanks to friendly intestinal bacteria.

Lactose intolerance occurs in four forms: primary, secondary, congenital and galactosaemia. Primary lactose intolerance is a complete lack of lactase production, rather than diminished production; it tends to occur in early adolescence and stays throughout life.

Secondary lactose intolerance is usually short term and occurs if the lining in the intestines has become damaged as a result of illness or infection. Diarrhea and some medicines such as nonsteroidal anti-inflammatories, antibiotics and aspirin can inhibit lactase production for a few weeks.

Congenital lactose intolerance occurs in children born with no lactase production. These children cannot tolerate any amount of milk or milk products.

Galactosaemia is a rare hereditary disease and prevents the person with the ailment from metabolizing galactose, a component of lactose.

Allergy symptoms
Food allergy symptoms can range from a tingling sensation in the mouth to swelling of the tongue and throat, difficulty breathing, hives, vomiting, abdominal cramps, diarrhea, drop in blood pressure, loss of consciousness and death. Food allergy symptoms typically appear within minutes to two hours after the person has eaten the food to which he or she is allergic.

Food allergy symptoms appear in three categories: skin reactions; stomach and intestinal reactions; and nose, throat and lung reactions. The following symptoms are *not* specific to a milk allergy—they indicate an immune-system reaction to *any* allergen. If any of these symptoms persist *after* eliminating milk from your diet, consult a professional health-care provider who can help you identify any other allergies that you might have.

Skin reactions:
- Itchy, red rash
- Hives
- Eczema
- Swollen lips, tongue, mouth, face and/or throat
- Allergic eyes, black eyes ("shiners")

Stomach and intestinal reactions:
- Abdominal pain
- Abdominal bloating
- Gas or wind
- Cramps
- Diarrhea (usually very runny)
- Vomiting

Nose, throat and lung reactions:
- Coughing
- Wheezing
- Runny nose
- Sneezing
- Watery or itchy eyes
- Shortness of breath

Lactose-intolerance symptoms
The symptoms of lactose intolerance can resemble some of the stomach and intestinal reactions experienced as a result of milk or other food allergies. These symptoms include:
- Abdominal pain and bloating
- Stomach cramps
- Cramps
- Gas or wind

- Diarrhea (starting $1/2$ to 2 hours after lactose consumption)
- Nausea and vomiting

Usually there is a correlation between the amount of lactose consumed and the severity of the symptoms. Someone suffering severe lactose intolerance could also experience malnutrition and weight loss.

Diagnosis
If you suspect you are allergic to milk or are lactose intolerant, you should have your health-care provider confirm a diagnosis. A blood test will verify an allergy; breath and stool tests will determine if you are lactose intolerant.

Once diagnosed, you may wish to consult with a registered dietitian or nutritional therapist. With a thorough health and lifestyle history, and by keeping a food and symptoms diary, your dietitian or therapist will be able to help you decide which foods, if any, might need to be reduced, substituted or eliminated from your diet. Never reduce, substitute or eliminate foods from a child's diet without professional advice.

Treatment
If you have a milk allergy, you will want to begin eating a diet that is milk-free and contains no milk products. As soon as you start to eat fewer foods containing the milk protein casein, and other triggers, your allergy symptoms should improve. If your allergy resulted from a weakened immune system, your symptoms may fade as your immune system becomes stronger. Generally, though, the treatment for a food allergy means eliminating the offending food long term.

If you have lactose intolerance, you may find that you can alleviate your symptoms by simply taking one of a number of products containing lactase that are available over the counter. The products, such as Lactaid™ and Dairy Ease™, provide the missing lactase enzyme needed to digest lactose. They can either be added to milk in droplet form or be taken with a meal or beverage as capsules.

What is a dairy-free diet?
A dairy-free diet excludes any food or product that is made with animal's milk. Strictly speaking, this is not just cow's milk but goat's and sheep's milk too. Milk-based foods include cream, butter, yogurt, cheese, cottage cheese, ice cream, milk chocolate and, in some cases, margarine.

Less obvious milk derivatives used by food manufacturers include whey, the thin fluid remnants of cheese making; casein, a milk protein; and lactose, a milk carbohydrate. These milk derivatives are often added to store-bought breads, cereals, sandwich spreads, salad dressings, cakes, cookies and fresh or frozen prepared meals.

If you have been diagnosed with a milk allergy or lactose intolerance, the first thing you need to do is learn to read labels. Until legislation governing food labels in the United States is simplified, you'll have to become something of a food detective. The following list of off-limits foods should help you avoid any milk or milk derivatives:
- Artificial butter flavor
- Butter, butter fat, butter oil
- Buttermilk
- Casein (casein hydrolysate)

- Caseinates (in all forms)
- Cheese
- Cottage cheese
- Cream
- Curds
- Custard
- Ghee (clarified butter used in Indian cooking)
- Half & half
- Lactalbumin, lacta albumin phosphate
- Lactulose
- Milk (in all forms, including condensed, derivative, dry, evaporated, goat's milk and milk from other animals, low-fat, malted, milkfat, non-fat, powder, protein, skimmed, solids, whole)
- Nougat
- Pudding
- Rennet casein
- Sour cream, sour cream solids
- Sour milk solids
- Whey (in all forms)
- Yogurt

The following may contain milk protein:
- Caramel candies
- Chocolate
- Flavorings (including natural and artificial)
- High-protein flour
- Lactic acid starter culture
- Lactose
- Luncheon meat, hot dogs, sausages
- Margarine
- Non-dairy products

The above list is available on a sturdy, wallet-sized plastic card from the Food Allergy & Anaphylaxis Network (FAAN). The card can be ordered by calling (800) 929-4040 or visiting www.foodallergy.org. The price is $2.00.

In Canada, a list of programs and services for adults and kids is available at Anaphylaxis Canada's website: www.anaphylaxis.org.

If a food does not have a label, the person with a milk allergy should not eat that food. If the label contains unfamiliar terms, the shopper should call the manufacturer and ask for detailed information about the ingredients, or avoid eating that food.

In addition to the above list, be aware that there are some unexpected sources of dairy. These include:
- Deli meat slicers, which are frequently used for both meat and cheese products.
- Some brands of canned tuna fish that contain casein, a milk protein.
- Many non-dairy products that contain casein (a milk derivative), listed on the ingredient labels.

- Some meats that may contain casein as a binder. Check all labels carefully.
- Many restaurants that put butter on steaks after they have been grilled to add extra flavor. The butter is not visible after it melts.

Don't despair!

The lists and "don'ts" might at first look overwhelming, but don't despair. Fortunately, milk is a very easy ingredient to substitute for in most cooking and baking, plus there are many delicious and healthful milk substitutes such as lactose-free milk, soy milk, rice milk and nut milks available at supermarkets and health food stores.

Although people with milk allergies will not be able to use sheep's or goat's milk, there are some chemical differences between goat's and cow's milk, and some people with lactose intolerance have found that they can tolerate goat's milk. This is probably due to the fact that casein, one of the milk proteins, occurs in different forms, and the one most prevalent in cow's milk is absent in goat's milk. The casein in goat's milk also groups together in smaller clusters, making it easier to tolerate.

Sheep's milk might also be tolerated by those with lactose intolerance who cannot eat cow's milk and its derivatives. Sheep's milk is available fresh and powdered. Buffalo mozzarella, however, should probably be avoided. In the U.S. and Canada, it is most likely made from cow's milk, not buffalo's milk, as it is in Italy. However, buffalo are in the bovine family, so buffalo mozzarella should be avoided if you have a milk allergy, although it might be all right if you have lactose intolerance.

People who are lactose-intolerant can sometimes eat yogurt. This is because the bacteria culture added to milk to turn it into yogurt breaks down some of the lactose before it is eaten. You'll have to experiment to see if cow, sheep or goat yogurt works best for you. Anyone with a milk allergy should avoid yogurt.

Hard cheeses can also sometimes be tolerated by people who are lactose intolerant because much of the lactose is removed during production. Aged Gouda and Edam cheeses and cottage cheese have the least amount of lactose.

What about kosher food?

Observant Jews use a system of product markings to indicate whether a food is kosher, or prepared in accordance with Jewish dietary rules. There are two kosher symbols that can be of help to those with a milk allergy: a "D," or the word dairy, on a label next to "K" or "U" (usually found near the product name) indicates presence of milk protein, and a "DE" on a label indicates the food was produced on equipment shared with dairy.

If the product contains neither meat nor dairy products, it is pareve (parev, parve). Pareve-labeling indicates that the products are considered milk-free according to religious specifications. Be aware that under Jewish law, a food product may be considered pareve even if it contains a very small amount of milk. Therefore, a product labeled as pareve could potentially have enough milk protein in it to cause a reaction in a person with a milk allergy.

Substituting with soy

Fortunately, milk is one of the most easily substituted ingredients in cooking and baking. You can easily modify existing recipes by substituting water or fruit juice measure for measure for milk.

In addition to water or juice, there are many excellent dairy-free ingredients that can replace milk. These include soy milk and cream, rice milk and nut and seed milks. In terms of availability, taste, appearance and nutrition, plain soy milk fortified with calcium (not calcium carbonate) is probably the closest approximation to milk, containing about the same amount of protein and calcium. It also has milk's creamy color and consistency.

But first, a little background on soy. It is a member of the legume family that has been cultivated for human consumption for thousands of years. Unlike most other legumes, soy is relatively low in carbohydrates and high in protein. Soy is the only member of the bean family that contains all eight essential amino acids. Although relatively high in fat compared with other beans, soybeans are cholesterol free, and the fat is mostly unsaturated, resulting in less of a potential concern about cholesterol buildup associated with animal foods such as dairy and meat. In addition, soy milk is thought to contain valuable plant estrogens that are linked to reduced rates of breast and prostate cancers, and it is a good source of Omega 3 fatty acids, the "good" fat that has been shown to reduce the risk of heart attack and stroke. It is also a good source of iron and B vitamins.

Soybeans are eaten fresh, boiled, sprouted, and dried and roasted. In addition, they are pressed into oil and made into a multitude of further-processed foods including tofu, a traditional Asian food made from ground soybeans that have been curdled and pressed into blocks like cheese. Soybeans also form the bases of soy cheese, soy yogurt, soy sour cream, soy ice cream, soy margarine, soy mayonnaise, soy flour, soy nut butter, soy sauce, textured vegetable protein, soy burgers, soy sausage and miso, a fermented soybean paste.

Rice milk is similar in appearance to milk and soy milk, but it contains less protein and calcium and has a milder flavor. Like soy milk, it is available at most supermarkets. Nut and seed milks can be used like milk but provide minimal calcium. Blanched almonds, cashews and sesame seeds make the best nut milks. A tablespoon of flaxseed ground with the nuts or a teaspoon of lecithin granules mixed with water will help blend the mixture to help keep the fats and liquid in suspension. Pour the nut milk through a strainer to remove any coarse pieces that could make the liquid grainy. Nut milks are available at natural foods stores.

But before adding any new food such as soy foods, soy milk or nut and seed milks to your diet, check with your health-care provider, registered dietitian or nutritional therapist. Some people are allergic to nuts and soy. Like milk, allergies to soy are generally not as severe as those to shellfish, tree nuts and eggs.

If you are not allergic to soy, a wide array of soy foods are available at supermarkets, natural foods stores and ethnic markets. As with any new product, read the label carefully. While soy itself is dairy-free, other ingredients may have been added to packaged products during processing.

The calcium question
Because milk and milk products such as yogurt are high in calcium, it is often thought that a dairy-free diet will leave people with low or inadequate amounts of this important mineral in their diet. In fact, calcium is quite common in food. What is important is the amount of calcium that is absorbed and retained by our bodies.

Calcium is used for building and maintaining healthy bones and teeth, as well as being necessary for muscle contraction, transmission and interpretation of nerve impulses and maintenance of cell membranes. Inadequate calcium has been linked to deformed bones, retarded growth and bone thinning, the precursor to osteoporosis.

Calcium is especially important during the years when bones grow larger and heavier. Pregnant and lactating women must also eat adequate amounts to help fetal bones calcify and produce mother's milk, while keeping their own bones strong.

In the Western diet, the current daily recommended amount for calcium is 1,000 mg, with the elderly and pregnant and lactating women needing even more. However, in countries where there is not a strong tradition of dairy and red meat consumption, people do very well on calcium levels of around 300 mg a day.

There are two reasons for the disparity in calcium levels in the Asian and Western diets. One reason is the absorption or malabsorption of calcium in our bodies; the other reason is the amount of calcium leeched from our bodies. Both malabsorption and leeching are effected by the foods we eat. In Asian diets, where far less animal protein in the form of dairy and red meat is consumed, people eat less calcium in their diet but absorb more of it. In the Western diet, high in dairy and red meat, we eat more calcium but do not efficiently absorb or utilize it. The primary culprit in calcium loss is protein, something the average American eats far too much of.

When too much animal protein is eaten, excess nitrogen and sulfur are produced in the blood, leading to an acid condition. To neutralize the acid, calcium is leeched from the bones and then excreted in the urine. Leeching is also caused by foods and drinks high in phosphorus. These include items processed with sodium phosphates and carbonated soft drinks. Foods containing oxalic acid, such as spinach, also decease absorption. Diets extremely high in fiber from whole grains containing phytic acid can also cause calcium to bind up, deceasing its absorption.

There are four simple steps you can take to ensure that you are getting adequate amounts of calcium: eat moderate, not excessive, amounts of animal protein; spend a little time in sunlight each day to get vitamin D, which helps utilize calcium; eat a variety of plant foods containing calcium; and add calcium supplements to your diet, if necessary.

If you have any concerns about the amount or sources of calcium in your diet, or whether you are absorbing it properly or need to use supplements, consult with your health-care provider, registered dietitian or nutritional therapist.

The table below lists various dairy-free foods and their calcium content.

Food	Calcium content mg per 3½ ounces
Oatmeal	52
All-purpose flour	130–140
Tomato sauce	48
Watercress, raw	170
Spinach, raw	170
Celery, raw	41
Garbanzo beans, cooked	43
Baked beans	53
Shrimp	150
Mussels	200
Anchovies	300
Sardines	300
Apricots	73
Oranges	47
Tahini	680
Egg	57

The protein paradox

Foods such as meat, fish and milk are prized for their high protein content, but the reality is that Western diets are rarely short of protein. In recent years the recommended daily amount for protein has been downgraded, and it is currently set at an average of about 45 grams per day. Some nutritionists recommend even lower amounts, closer to 30 to 35 grams per day, believing that animal protein and its associated cholesterol, saturated fat and undesirable Omega 6 fatty acids are responsible for a host of health problems, especially heart disease.

Because milk and its derivatives are often relied upon as a source of protein, it is important to make sure that the dairy-free diet provides enough protein. Fortunately, this is easy to accomplish using a rich variety of vegetable sources of protein such as soy foods, beans and legumes, along with moderate amounts of lean red meat, skinless poultry and seafood.

Anyone choosing a strict vegetarian diet that eschews all forms of animal food, including milk, cheese, yogurt, eggs, meat, poultry and seafood, should consult with a health-care professional to discuss their daily protein needs as well as the need to supplement their diet with B12 and other important vitamins and minerals.

Eating out

Eating out with a food allergy or a severe intolerance can at times be stressful. However, with a little forethought, patience and a simple explanation, you should be able to make your needs known with a minimum of fuss. A sense of humor helps as well.

If at all possible, call the restaurant ahead of time and explain to the manager or host that you have an allergy or severe intolerance. Ask what dishes on the menu are dairy-free. As eclectic and multi-ethnic as menus are today, chances are there are dishes made without dairy already listed. If a dish you would like to order contains dairy, ask the manager, hosts or chef if it is possible for the dish to be modified with non-dairy ingredients. If your menu questions are answered satisfactorily, make a reservation at the restaurant, giving the chef time to think about a dish and modify it, if necessary. Call the restaurant before your reservation to remind the staff that you are arriving and have special dietary needs. Do not call the restaurant during prime service hours and expect to speak to the chef. Instead, call during off hours and start with the manager or host.

If you do not have the opportunity to check out the restaurant or menu in advance, mention to the manager or host on the way to your table that you have a food allergy or severe intolerance. Ask if there is a server who is familiar with allergies, or a server who can answer detailed food questions, such as those concerning ingredients. Ask the server to point out to you menu items that are dairy-free. If the server seems unsure, ask to speak to the manager. During peak service hours, it is unlikely that the chef will be able to leave the kitchen to speak with you. Taking a moment to quietly explain your allergy to the manager or server will achieve better results than being fussy, difficult or loud. Please keep in mind that when restaurants are "slammed" with hungry diners during peak service hours, your special request puts extra strain on an already stressed kitchen and staff. If at all possible, make your needs known in advance, by telephone, during off-peak serving hours.

The restaurant you choose can also lessen the pitfalls of eating out. If the restaurant is French or Continental, you can assume that the sauces are cream and/or butter based. At an Italian restaurant, while there are still cream-based sauces, you will have a larger selection of tomato-based sauces. If you choose a Japanese, Thai or Chinese restaurant, you will likely find a large selection of dairy-free dishes.

At a French-style restaurant, you can order your dish with no sauce, or ask for the meat or fish to be grilled with oil instead of butter. In general, chefs tend to respond better to a specific request, such as "no sauce or butter, please," rather than a blanket "no dairy."

In Indian restaurants, most dishes are cooked in ghee, which is butter that has been clarified to remove most of the milk solids. While ghee is still off limits for people with milk allergies, many people with lactose intolerance find that they can eat ghee. Indian dishes might also contain yogurt, which many people with lactose intolerance can eat, although people with milk allergies should not.

When it comes to fast food, pizzas can be ordered with just the tomato sauce and other dairy-free toppings such as pepperoni, mushrooms, olives or pineapple.

Other reasons to be dairy-free

Not all people choose to be dairy-free as a result of allergies or intolerance. They choose a dairy-free diet for health reasons; for weight loss; for ethical reasons such as opposition to animal cruelty; for environmental reasons such as the wasteful use of water to grow grain to feed animals or the pollution resulting from factory farming techniques. Some people just don't feel quite right and suspect that dairy foods may be the cause; others prefer to avoid using products that might contain traces of the growth hormones and antibiotics that are routinely used to treat cows. Still others avoid meat and dairy products out of concern over mad cow disease.

For whatever reason you choose to eliminate dairy from your diet, the result can benefit your health, and the health of the planet, in many ways.

- *Lower cholesterol and fat intake:* High levels of cholesterol and fat in milk have been linked to heart disease, stroke and other circulatory diseases.
- *Fewer mucus problems:* Congestion, hay fever, and sinus problems often occur where there is high dairy consumption. This is because milk tends to produce mucus in the intestines and other parts of the body.
- *Better protein digestion:* Milk neutralizes stomach acids, and since proteins are digested in the acid stomach environment, this results in proteins being only partially digested, often causing discomfort.
- *Better nutrient absorption:* Milk tends to build up mucus in the intestines, and when it mixes with food residue it forms a hard material coating the intestinal wall. This blocks movement through the intestinal wall, affecting both nutrient absorption and enzyme secretion that aids digestion. Excluding dairy from your diet will also discourage "unfriendly" bacteria that inhibit mineral absorption from colonizing in your intestines.
- *Healthier cells, potassium balance:* Our bodies have a mechanism to maintain the correct balance of potassium and sodium ions within our cells. It is known as the sodium-potassium pump and works to drive the sodium ions out while holding on to the potassium ions and keeping cells healthy. In babies the requirements in the cell are reversed, and milk has the capability of encouraging sodium into the cells against the force of the sodium-potassium pump. As the baby changes into a child, the body requires less intracellular sodium. By continuing to drink milk, too much sodium enters the cells, causing increased susceptibility to chronic disease.
- *Healthier cells, magnesium balance:* Despite containing high levels of calcium, milk and milk products can actually deplete the body of calcium. This is because magnesium is needed to regulate calcium metabolism and keep the body's calcium in the right places,

such as the bones. Milk contains a low ratio of magnesium to calcium (1=10). Unless we eat foods with high levels of magnesium to counteract the low level of magnesium in milk, we cannot utilize the calcium properly. A dairy-free diet will help you achieve a better calcium-magnesium ratio.

- *Less colic in babies:* Studies have shown that bottle-fed babies with colic tend to improve if dairy is removed from their diets. Lactating mothers who eat and drink dairy products pass along cow's proteins and antibodies to their babies, also causing colic.
- *Healthier arteries:* By skipping dairy you will avoid the enzyme xanthine oxidase in milk, which is believed to attack the coronary arteries. The enzyme is a particular concern in homogenized milk.
- *Other concerns:* Increasing research is finding links between diseases and dairy consumption. Some of these concerns include insulin-dependent diabetes, autism, hyperactivity, learning difficulties, insomnia, pulmonary disease and eczema.

Healthy eating and living
Dairy-free or not, the general guidelines for healthy eating remain the same: low-fat, no added salt, at least five portions of fresh vegetables and fruits a day, and replacement of refined foods with whole-grain versions whenever possible.

And don't neglect exercise as part of your plan for healthy eating and living. Too many calories, no matter how good they are for you, are still too many calories and will result in unwanted extra pounds. Extra weight, even a relatively small amount, is associated with a number of chronic diseases.

Cooking and preparing recipes
If you pick up a cookbook and find a recipe that you would like to make, but it includes dairy products, don't feel that you can't make it. As you get used to your new dairy-free way of eating, you will find that you are easily able to spot substitutions. There are a few basic replacements that will make your life easier, such as replacing butter with dairy-free margarine for spreading, frying or baking. In many cases, a mild-flavored oil such as canola or olive can be used to replace butter. Try the many milk substitutes such as soy milk, rice milk and nut and seed milks with different recipes.

You will see that hummus has been added to a number of recipes. It creates a creamy feel and texture without adding dairy. Soy yogurt and soy sour cream can also be experimented with.

If you are cooking for someone who has a milk allergy or lactose intolerance, *do not* experiment on them. If you are in doubt about any ingredient, check with the person first. It is not worth risking any possible harm or discomfort to another person.

If you do not already have one, a blender, food processor or wand (immersion) blender is a worthwhile investment, as the texture of almost any pureed food can add a creamy look and feel to many dishes.

Unless otherwise noted, all recipes have been made with medium eggs, and all measures are level. The nutritional data are based on the lower number of servings indicated, if a range is given, and the first ingredient listed where an alternative is mentioned. Optional and "to taste" ingredients are not included in the nutritional data. In the list of ingredients, North American measurements are given in the left-hand column and metric in the right-hand; in many cases, exact conversions were not possible.

The information contained in this book is correct at the time of writing and is intended as a general reference only. It is not suitable for professional medical advice or as a substitution for a medical exam. Always seek the advice of your health-care provider if you believe you are suffering from the symptoms of a milk allergy or lactose intolerance, or any other medical condition. No information in this book should be used to diagnose, treat, cure or prevent a dairy allergy or lactose intolerance or any other medical condition without the supervision of a health-care provider.

Food Allergy & Anaphylaxis Network (U.S.)

Via Mail
10400 Eaton Place, Suite 107
Fairfax, VA 22030-2208

Via Phone
(800) 929-4040

Via Fax
(703) 691-2713

Via Email
faan@foodallergy.org

Anaphylaxis Canada

Via Mail
416 Moore Avenue, Suite 306
Toronto, ON M4G1C9

Via Phone
(416) 785-5666

Via Fax
(416) 785-0458

Via Email and Internet
info@anaphylaxis.ca
www.anaphylaxis.org

Additional information (also see "Helpful Organizations," page 195)

For a list of doctors in your area, please contact one of the following organizations:

United States

American Academy of Allergy, Asthma & Immunology
(800) 822-ASMA
www.aaaai.org

American College of Allergy, Asthma & Immunology
(800) 842-7777
www.allergy.mcg.edu

American Academy of Pediatrics
(800) 433-9016
www.aap.org

Canada

College of Family Physicians of Canada
(905) 629-0900
www.cfpc.ca

Dietitians of Canada
(416) 596-0857
www.dietitians.ca

National Institute of Nutrition
(613) 235-3355
www.nin.ca

—*Miller Rogers and Emily White*

Soups, Dips, Starters and Snacks

Chunky Leek, Potato and Lentil Soup

Cream of Spinach and Nutmeg Soup

Smoked Trout Chowder

Creamy Carrot and Cilantro Soup

Miso Soup with Tofu, Noodles
and Wakame Seaweed

Hummus Dip

Chive Cream Cheese Dip

Tahini and Lemon Dip

Herbed Olive and Tuna Dip

Avocado and Shrimp Empañadas

Crab Cakes

Crispy Garlic- and Leek-Stuffed Mussels

Seafood Fritto Misto

Herb-Crumbed Catfish Fillets

Niçoise Tartlets

Smoked Salmon Roulade with Smoked Trout Mousse

Squid with Chilies and Tomatoes

Chinese-Style Crispy Pork Strips

Marinated Lime and Sesame Chicken Sticks

Smoked Duck Salad with Spiced Walnuts

Mushroom and Nut Pâté

Roasted Cherry Tomato Bruschetta

Crispy Spinach and Pine Nut Filo Parcels

Hummus, Chili and Crisp Vegetable Wrap

Bacon, Tomato and Watercress Wrap

Never cook legumes in salted water. They will become tough. Try this recipe using red lentils or brown lentils, varying the cooking time accordingly.

Garam masala is an Indian spice that may be found in ethnic aisles or at Indian grocery stores.

Chunky Leek, Potato and Lentil Soup

Serves 4–6

Lentils are easy to cook and do not require pre-soaking. They also provide an excellent source of protein and fiber. I usually have plenty of onions, potatoes and lentils in my cupboard and quite often make this recipe when everything else has run out and I want a quick and nutritious soup for lunch.

1 cup	lentils (7 oz)	196 g
2	medium leeks	2
5/8 lb	potatoes (weight after peeling)	280 g
1 tbsp	sunflower oil	15 ml
1	large onion, finely chopped	1
3	cloves garlic, crushed	3
1 tsp	garam masala	1 tsp
1 1/2 qts	boiling water	1 1/2 liters
2–3 tbsps	vegan (dairy-free) bouillon	2–3 tbsps
	salt and freshly ground pepper	
1 tbsp	chopped fresh parsley	25 g

First rinse the lentils. Cover with plenty of cold water in a large saucepan. Bring this to a boil and simmer for 10 minutes, drain well.

Wash, trim and chop the leeks, and cut the potatoes into small cubes. Heat the oil in a large saucepan, and fry the onion and garlic for about 4 minutes until soft. Next add the garam masala and drained lentils and stir well.

Pour over the boiling water, and cook for a further 15 minutes.

Mix in the potatoes, leeks and bouillon powder, and cook this uncovered, stirring occasionally, for a further 10 minutes until soft but not mushy.

Season with salt and freshly ground pepper.

Spoon the soup into warmed bowls, and sprinkle with chopped parsley.

PER SERVING	
Calories	291
% Calories from fat	13
Fat (g)	4.3
Saturated fat (g)	0.4
Cholesterol (mg)	0
Sodium (mg)	506
Protein (g)	16
Carbohydrate (g)	49.3
Calcium (mg)	82.4

EXCHANGES	
Milk	0.0
Vegetable	0.0
Fruit	0.0
Bread	3.0
Meat	1.0
Fat	0.5

This soup can also be made with watercress and produces a wonderful nutritious dish.

Cream of Spinach and Nutmeg Soup

Serves 4–6

This should be a lovely fresh-looking green soup. To make it more impressive, pour a swirl of soy cream onto the top before serving. The less you cook the spinach, the more the color and nutrients are retained.

1 tbsp	vegetable oil	1 tbsp
1	large onion, roughly chopped	1
2	ribs celery, washed and chopped	2
4 cups	diced potatoes (weight after peeling 1lb)	450 g
1 qt	vegan vegetable stock	1 liter
5–6 cups	spinach (7 oz)	5–6 cups
1/4 tsp	freshly grated nutmeg	1/4 tsp
	salt and freshly ground pepper	

Heat a large saucepan with the oil. Gently cook the onion and celery for about 5 minutes until soft, taking care not to let them brown. Add the diced potato and stir well.

Pour in the stock, bring this up to a boil and simmer about 20 minutes until the potato is beginning to fall apart and the onion is tender. Wash the spinach well; remove any tough stalks but keep the tender ones.

Put the spinach in the pan and push down, cover with lid and allow to cook for about 4 minutes, with all spinach submerged. It should not be cooked for too long or the soup will become gray; cool slightly.

Purée in a blender or food processor until smooth and creamy. Season with nutmeg, salt and freshly ground pepper. To serve, heat the soup through gently.

PER SERVING	
Calories	172
% Calories from fat	23
Fat (g)	4.9
Saturated fat (g)	0.5
Cholesterol (mg)	0
Sodium (mg)	1077
Protein (g)	7.7
Carbohydrate (g)	28.7
Calcium (mg)	74

EXCHANGES	
Milk	0.0
Vegetable	0.0
Fruit	0.0
Bread	2.0
Meat	0.0
Fat	1.0

For a different variation, try this recipe with crab, clams or shrimp. Or for a vegan chowder, omit fish stock and use vegetable stock. The potato and sweetcorn alone provide a tasty, nourishing soup.

Smoked Trout Chowder

Serves 6

A chowder is a cream-based chunky fish soup that originated in North America. We often have this nourishing soup as a meal in itself. The potatoes should just be beginning to break down and slightly thicken the soup. The addition of sweetcorn is not only traditional, but it also provides added milkiness to the dish.

1	medium leek	1
1 tbsp	vegetable oil	1 tbsp
1	large onion, finely chopped	1
4 cups	cubed potatoes (weight after peeling 1 lb)	450 g
2½ cups	vegetable, fish or chicken stock	570 ml
1 lb	fillet of smoked trout, skinned, boned and cut into small cubes	450 g
1 cup	frozen, fresh or canned, drained, sweetcorn kernels (1 cup)	170 g
1 tbsp	arrowroot	1 tbsp
1¾ cups	coconut milk	400 ml
2 tbsps	chopped fresh cilantro to serve	2 tbsps

Wash, trim and thinly slice the leek. In a large pan, heat oil and gently cook the onion and leek for about 5 minutes until soft but not brown.

Add the potatoes and cook for about 3 minutes, stirring regularly. Pour in the stock, mix well and simmer for 20 minutes until the potatoes and leeks are both tender.

Add the cubed trout, sweetcorn and arrowroot (if using fresh corn off the cob, add to the soup after potatoes have been cooking for 5 minutes) and simmer for 5 minutes.

Pour in the coconut milk and warm through. Serve in warm bowls garnished with fresh cilantro.

PER SERVING

Calories	370
% Calories from fat	47
Fat (g)	20.4
Saturated fat (g)	15.3
Cholesterol (mg)	24.9
Sodium (mg)	1200
Protein (g)	23.7
Carbohydrate (g)	27.4
Calcium (mg)	44.5

EXCHANGES

Milk	0.0
Vegetable	0.0
Fruit	0.0
Bread	2.0
Meat	2.0
Fat	2.5

Use parsnips, cauliflower, broccoli or celery for a variation.

Creamy Carrot and Cilantro Soup

Serves 6–8

This rich, creamy soup is delicious as a lunch dish with hot crusty bread. It is also delicious with a sprinkling of crispy bacon and parsley on top instead of cilantro. This forms the basis of many creamy-style vegetable soups.

2 tsps	vegan margarine	16 g
1	large onion, chopped	1
3 cups	chopped potatoes (weight after peeling 10 oz)	280 g
4 cups	chopped carrots (weight after peeling 12 oz)	340 g
1½ qts	vegetable stock	1.5 liters
	small bunch fresh cilantro	

Melt margarine in a large saucepan over medium heat. Add the onion and gently cook for about 4 minutes until soft but not brown.

Stir in the chopped potatoes and carrots and pour the stock over. Bring the soup to a boil and gently simmer for about 30–40 minutes or until vegetables are soft.

Purée in a blender or food processor until smooth and creamy. Season with salt and freshly ground pepper.

Gently reheat. Serve the soup in hot bowls with freshly chopped cilantro sprinkled on top.

PER SERVING

Calories	112
% Calories from fat	18
Fat (g)	2.5
Saturated fat (g)	0.3
Cholesterol (mg)	0
Sodium (mg)	1041
Protein (g)	4.6
Carbohydrate (g)	21.3
Calcium (mg)	32.8

EXCHANGES

Milk	0.0
Vegetable	0.0
Fruit	0.0
Bread	1.5
Meat	0.0
Fat	0.0

This could also be made without noodles for a lighter soup. I included them to make it a little more substantial and therefore also suitable as a light meal.

Miso Soup with Tofu, Noodles and Wakame Seaweed

Serves 4

This soup is very nourishing and high in protein. Miso is readily available in health food shops. The wakame seaweed is widely used in Japanese soups and salads and has no calories. It is very high in minerals and calcium. Try experimenting with Japanese foods if you enjoy this soup.

1	piece dried wakame seaweed (about 4 inches)	10–15 g
1	pack firm tofu (about 10 oz)	280 g
1 qt	weak vegetable stock (could use fish stock)	1.2 liters
1 cup	medium or thin noodles (1 cup)	110 g
4 tsps	low-salt miso	4 tsps
2	green onions, trimmed and cut into fine rounds (save the green ends for garnish)	2

Soak wakame in cold water until it softens (about 10 minutes); don't oversoak. Drain and trim away any tough sections, then cut into 1-inch lengths.

Cut the tofu into 1/2-inch cubes. Heat stock over medium heat until very hot, add noodles and cook for half their required cooking time (about 2 minutes).

Turn heat down and allow to cool slightly. Add the miso and stir well. Then stir in the green onions and tofu and allow the soup to heat through, but do not boil.

Lastly, add the wakame and remove from heat just before soup boils. Serve in pre-heated bowls garnished with the green ends of the onions.

PER SERVING	
Calories	188
% Calories from fat	22
Fat (g)	5
Saturated fat (g)	0.5
Cholesterol (mg)	0
Sodium (mg)	1275
Protein (g)	12.5
Carbohydrate (g)	27.3
Calcium (mg)	124

EXCHANGES	
Milk	0.0
Vegetable	0.0
Fruit	0.0
Bread	2.0
Meat	1.0
Fat	0.0

Try making this with soaked and cooked yellow split peas for an interesting alternative.

Hummus Dip

Serves 16 (1 heaping tablespoon per serving)

Hummus is a popular dip that originates in Lebanon. The texture is often deliciously creamy, yet the ingredients are all extremely nutritious. Hummus will store well for several weeks in the fridge, making it a useful food to have for quick nutritious snacks. Try using it in sandwiches with crisp salad or sprouted alfalfa.

Many supermarkets now stock hummus. However, making it at home is certainly more economical, and also you can monitor the salt content, as the bought product can be deceptively high in salt.

2	15-oz cans chick peas, drained (or 4 cups cooked from dried)	2
1/4 cup	tahini (puréed sesame seeds)	1/4 cup
	juice from 2–3 lemons	
3	cloves garlic	3
3 tbsps	olive oil	45 ml
2–3 tsps	salt	2–3 tsps
	paprika to garnish	

Blend the chick peas, tahini, lemon juice and garlic in a food processor until it has a creamy and smooth consistency.

Gradually add the olive oil; if mixture is too thick add water spoon by spoon until smooth-dropping consistency. Blend in the salt a teaspoon at a time, tasting for seasoning.

Spoon some into a serving dish and sprinkle the top with paprika if desired. Store the remaining hummus in sealed jars in the fridge. This recipe above makes about 3 jars (24 ounces) of hummus.

PER SERVING	
Calories	76
% Calories from fat	55
Fat (g)	4.8
Saturated fat (g)	0.6
Cholesterol (mg)	0
Sodium (mg)	367
Protein (g)	1.9
Carbohydrate (g)	7
Calcium (mg)	14.8

EXCHANGES	
Milk	0.0
Vegetable	0.0
Fruit	0.0
Bread	0.5
Meat	0.0
Fat	1.0

Try this served on small squares of pumpernickel as a smart canapé topped with smoked salmon, gravlax or mock caviar. Challenge anyone to guess it is dairy free.
 Also delicious as a dip with crudités.

PER SERVING	
Calories	68
% Calories from fat	83
Fat (g)	6.3
Saturated fat (g)	1.3
Cholesterol (mg)	0
Sodium (mg)	90
Protein (g)	0.7
Carbohydrate (g)	2.2
Calcium (mg)	1.7
EXCHANGES	
Milk	0.0
Vegetable	0.0
Fruit	0.0
Bread	0.0
Meat	0.0
Fat	1.5

Add Dijon mustard and use as a coleslaw dressing.

Chive Cream Cheese Dip

Serves 6 (2 tablespoons per serving)

Soy cream cheese can be bought from most health food shops and tastes very similar to normal cream cheese but actually contains less fat. By adding lemon and chives you can make a quick and easy dip, which will store well for up to a week.

1/2 cup	soy cream cheese	110 g
1/4 cup	soy cream	60 ml
2 tsps	lemon juice	10 ml
10	strands of chives, chopped	10

   Beat the soy cream cheese and soy cream together in a bowl until smooth.
   Add the lemon juice and chives, mixing well. Store in sealed container in the fridge until required. Makes about 3/4 cup.

PER SERVING	
Calories	53
% Calories from fat	87
Fat (g)	5.4
Saturated fat (g)	0.6
Cholesterol (mg)	0
Sodium (mg)	44
Protein (g)	0.7
Carbohydrate (g)	1
Calcium (mg)	5.5
EXCHANGES	
Milk	0.0
Vegetable	0.0
Fruit	0.0
Bread	0.0
Meat	0.0
Fat	1.0

Tahini and Lemon Dip

Serves 8 (1 tablespoon per serving)

This makes a smooth and creamy dip suitable for crudités.
The tahini and other ingredients form a thick emulsion, so it can be used as a substitute for egg-based mayonnaise. Serve with crisp raw carrots, celery, cauliflower florets and cucumber sticks.

2 tbsps	tahini	2 tbsps
3 tbsps	water	45 ml
2 tbsps	mild oil (sunflower or vegetable)	30 ml
	juice of 1/2 lemon	
1 tsp	soy sauce	5 ml
1/2 tsp	honey (optional)	1/2 tsp

   Mix the tahini with half the water and whisk well until smooth. Continue whisking and gradually drizzle in the oil until the mixture thickens, then stir in the remaining water.
   Season with the lemon juice, soy sauce and honey. Chill in a sealed container until required. Makes about 1/2 cup.

Herbed Olive and Tuna Dip

Serves 10 (1 tablespoon per serving)
This is a Mediterranean-style dip that is full of flavor. Delicious served as a dip with crudités or on hot grilled toast.

1	5-oz can tuna, in water, drained	1
¹/₄ cup	pitted black olives	55 g
1	slice white bread, crusts removed	1
1	clove garlic, crushed	1
2 tbsps	capers, drained and rinsed	2 tbsps
2 tsps	wine vinegar	10 ml
1 tbsp	lemon juice	15 ml
2 tbsps	olive oil	30 ml
2 tbsps	low-fat mayonnaise (optional)	2 tbsps
2 tbsps	chopped parsley	2 tbsps
1 tsp	chopped fresh thyme leaves	1 tsp

Process the tuna, olives, bread, garlic, capers, vinegar and lemon juice until well combined.

While motor is running, drizzle in the olive oil until the mixture becomes smooth.

Finally, stir in mayonnaise, if using, and herbs and store in the fridge. Makes about ³/₄ cup.

PER SERVING

Calories	57
% Calories from fat	58
Fat (g)	3.7
Saturated fat (g)	0.5
Cholesterol (mg)	4.2
Sodium (mg)	177
Protein (g)	3.9
Carbohydrate (g)	2.1
Calcium (mg)	13.6

EXCHANGES

Milk	0.0
Vegetable	0.0
Fruit	0.0
Bread	0.0
Meat	1.0
Fat	0.0

For vegetarians, try other fillings such as mushroom and eggplant. These could also be deep-fried for a light and crispy texture.

Avocado and Shrimp Empañadas

Serves 8

These crisp Mexican-style parcels are perfect to serve as a starter or a light main course with some crisp salad. They are delicious served with either the Tomato and Mint Salsa on page 120 or Roasted Sweetcorn and Lime Salsa on page 118.

1	beaten egg for glazing	1
1 tbsp	vegetable oil	15 ml
1	medium onion, finely chopped	1
2	cloves garlic, crushed	2
1	heaping teaspoon ground cumin	1
2 tbsps	tomato purée	2 tbsps
3	bottled jalapeño peppers, drained, chopped	3
1 tsp	dried oregano	1 tsp
2	medium tomatoes, quartered, seeds removed, chopped	2
3/4 lb	cooked, peeled large shrimp (cut into thirds)	337 g
1	large, firm but ripe avocado or 2 smaller ones	1
	salt and freshly ground pepper	
1 recipe	Cornmeal Pastry on page 185	1 recipe
1	egg, beaten	1

Pre-heat the oven to 375F. Grease a large baking sheet.

Heat the oil in a large saucepan and gently fry the onion and garlic for about 5 minutes until soft. Stir in the ground cumin and cook for about 2 minutes. Mix in the tomato purée, peppers, oregano and chopped tomatoes.

Remove this mixture from the heat and allow to cool slightly before adding the shrimp and the peeled, diced avocado. Season well.

Divide the cornmeal pastry into 8 portions. Roll portions into 6-inch rounds.

Divide the filling and spoon onto the rounds; brush edges with beaten egg. Fold rounds in half, enclosing filling. Press edges together firmly, trim with knife and decorate edges with fork. Place the parcels onto the prepared baking sheet. Brush the pastry with beaten egg.

Bake in a hot oven for about 20 minutes until browned and heated through.

PER SERVING	
Calories	335
% Calories from fat	48
Fat (g)	18.1
Saturated fat (g)	3
Cholesterol (mg)	165
Sodium (mg)	478
Protein (g)	15.3
Carbohydrate (g)	28
Calcium (mg)	47.1

EXCHANGES	
Milk	0.0
Vegetable	0.0
Fruit	0.0
Bread	2.0
Meat	1.0
Fat	3.0

If using fresh whole crab, make sure you discard the small grayish-white stomach sac just behind the mouth and the long white-pointed "dead man's fingers." These can be easily distinguished, and it is a quick and easy job to remove them.

Crab Cakes

Serves 4 (1 cake each)

These crab cakes make an impressive starter or light main course with lemon dressing. The grated half-cooked potato holds the cakes together, unlike traditional fish cakes which use mashed potato to bind the fish and are coated in breadcrumbs. The result is a much lighter and tastier fish cake.

Try to use fresh crabmeat if possible; otherwise, defrosted frozen crabmeat would be a good alternative. Delicious served accompanied with the Creamy Lemon Dressing on page 140.

5–6	small boiling potatoes (10 oz)	280 g
10 oz	mixed fresh crabmeat (try and use mainly white crabmeat)	280 g
1 tbsp	chopped fresh dill	1 tbsp
2	green onions, finely chopped	2
	zest and juice of one large lemon	
1/2 tsp	cayenne pepper	1/2 tsp
	salt and freshly ground pepper	
	oil for frying	
	sprigs of fresh cilantro or parsley to garnish	

First peel the potatoes, then steam or boil them in boiling salted water for about 10 minutes. They should be slightly uncooked in the middle. Allow the potatoes to cool.

Shred the potatoes into a large bowl using a cheese grater. In another bowl, carefully mix together the crabmeat, dill, green onion, zest and juice of lemon with the seasonings.

Now carefully combine the grated potato with the crab mixture, mixing well without breaking up the potatoes too much.

Have a large baking sheet handy, and divide the mixture into four for a light main course. Squeeze each portion into a ball and then slightly flatten each ball into a small round cake. When the cakes are all made, cover with plastic wrap and refrigerate for 1–2 hours to become firmer.

To cook the crab cakes, heat a large frying pan (preferably non-stick) with 1 tablespoon of oil. When the oil is hot but not smoking, pan-fry the crab cakes for about 4 minutes, then turn the crab cakes carefully with a spatula, and repeat on the other side (depending on size) until heated through and golden.

Transfer to a warm serving plate. Garnish with cilantro or parsley.

PER SERVING	
Calories	134
% Calories from fat	9
Fat (g)	1.3
Saturated fat (g)	0.1
Cholesterol (mg)	37.5
Sodium (mg)	761
Protein (g)	16.2
Carbohydrate (g)	14.3
Calcium (mg)	60.2
EXCHANGES	
Milk	0.0
Vegetable	0.0
Fruit	0.0
Bread	1.0
Meat	2.0
Fat	0.0

Mussels are at their best in the cold weather, usually from October to March. A sign of freshness is that most when raw are tightly closed; if there are too many with open shells don't buy them. Buy extra to account for any that may be discarded. To wash, put in a sink full of cold water. First, throw away any that float to the top, then leave the tap running and scrape off barnacles with a knife, pulling off the hairy beards. Discard any broken mussels and those that are open and refuse to close tight when given a sharp tap with a knife. Once sorted and cleaned, place in a bowl of clean water. Once cooked, discard any whose shells haven't opened.

Crispy Garlic- and Leek-Stuffed Mussels

Serves 6

Mussels go very well cooked with leeks, which, combined with breadcrumbs and garlic, make a delicious starter. The dish may be prepared up to a day before, and the final broiling done just before serving. Serve with crusty fresh bread and a squeeze of fresh lemon.

	about 30 mussels	
1 cup	dry white wine (or stock if preferred)	240 ml
1	small onion, finely chopped	1
1	large leek	1
1 tbsp	olive oil	15 ml
4	cloves garlic, peeled and crushed	4
3–4 slices	crusty white bread	3–4 slices
1 tbsp	chopped fresh tarragon	1 tbsp
1	bunch of parsley, finely chopped	1
3 tbsps	vegan margarine	75 g
	more olive oil and wedges of lemon to garnish	

PER SERVING	
Calories	229
% Calories from fat	41
Fat (g)	10.4
Saturated fat (g)	1.8
Cholesterol (mg)	20
Sodium (mg)	379
Protein (g)	10.9
Carbohydrate (g)	16.8
Calcium (mg)	77.2

EXCHANGES	
Milk	0.0
Vegetable	0.0
Fruit	0.0
Bread	1.0
Meat	1.0
Fat	2.0

Begin by washing and scrubbing the mussels (see sidebar).

Pour the wine into a large pan with the chopped onion and bring this to a boil. Tip in the prepared mussels, and cover with a lid. After about 4 minutes, shake pan to ensure that the mussels are moved about.

The mussels are cooked when they have all opened up, which should take about 8 minutes altogether. Remove the pan from the heat and allow to cool. Next, clean and chop the leek finely, discarding any tough outer leaves.

In a large frying pan, heat the olive oil and gently cook the leek and garlic, stirring occasionally, for about 5 minutes until soft but not brown. Tip into a large bowl and allow to cool slightly. Process the bread into crumbs.

When leek mixture is slightly cool, add the tarragon, parsley and breadcrumbs, mixing thoroughly.

Stir in the margarine and press the mixture together with a spoon. Season with salt and pepper.

Open the mussels, leaving one half-shell with the mussel inside, discarding the other half-shell which will be empty.

Using your hands, stuff the mixture into the mussel shell, smoothing down and covering the mussel completely. Place on a large tray.

Either store stuffed mussels in fridge for use within 2 days or to cook; place under a hot broiler for about 5 minutes until golden and crispy.

Drizzle with some more olive oil and serve garnished with lemon wedges.

Try to use a fairly good quality vegetable or peanut oil. The fish is also good if it is fried in a mild-flavored light olive oil.

Seafood Fritto Misto

Serves 8–10 as starter

Fritto Misto originated in Italy, where there are many different versions. In some cases a yeast or beer batter is made to coat the fish or shellfish. The version below is much more straightforward and, providing fresh shellfish is used, equally as delicious. Serve hot with mayonnaise mixed with a squeeze of lemon and some salad.

½ lb	peeled shrimp	225 g
½ lb	small squid (buy ready cleaned)	225 g
½ lb	haddock or mahi-mahi	225 g
	plenty of all-purpose flour for dusting	
	oil for deep-frying	
	salt and freshly ground pepper	
	lemon wedges and parsley to garnish	

Remove veins from the back of shrimp if necessary, and cut in half lengthways.

Cut the squid into rings and pat dry using absorbent paper. Wash the haddock and dry thoroughly. On a large plate, dust all the seafood with plenty of flour, shaking off any surplus.

Heat the oil in large saucepan or a deep-fat fryer. To determine whether the oil is hot enough for frying, drop a tiny amount of fish into the oil: it should stiffen and instantly come to the surface.

Deep-fry the seafood in hot oil, a few pieces at a time, until it has formed a rich, golden crust on one side; using a slotted spoon, turn the seafood over to cook the other side.

Remove from the oil, drain on absorbent paper and season with salt and pepper.

Serve hot garnished with wedges of lemon and sprigs of fresh parsley.

PER SERVING	
Calories	80
% Calories from fat	13
Fat (g)	1.1
Saturated fat (g)	0.2
Cholesterol (mg)	124.3
Sodium (mg)	69
Protein (g)	15.4
Carbohydrate (g)	1.1
Calcium (mg)	31.1
EXCHANGES	
Milk	0.0
Vegetable	0.0
Fruit	0.0
Bread	0.0
Meat	2.0
Fat	0.0

Herb-Crumbed Catfish Fillets

Serves 4

Ideal as a starter or light supper. Serve with a spoonful of warmed Roasted Tomato Sauce on page 119.

4	fresh catfish fillets (about 1 lb)	4
	all-purpose flour	
	salt and freshly ground pepper	
1	egg, beaten	1
2 tbsps	soy milk	30 ml
1 cup	breadcrumbs	220 g
1 tbsp	finely chopped parsley	1 tbsp
1 tbsp	finely chopped oregano	1 tbsp
	peanut oil for shallow frying	
	lemon wedges to garnish	

Rinse catfish and scrape off any loose scales. Fillet by using a sharp knife and beginning at tail. Cut down against backbone until you reach the head, cutting off fillet at that point. Repeat on the other side, and tidy the fillets up pulling out larger pin bones.

Alternatively, ask the fish market to fillet the fish for you. To coat the fillets you will need 3 large plates. On the first plate season the flour with salt and freshly ground pepper. On the second plate mix the beaten egg with the soy milk. And on the third, combine the breadcrumbs with the fresh herbs.

Dip each fillet first in the seasoned flour, then the beaten egg and finally roll them in the breadcrumbs.

Place fillets on a tray sprinkled with a few of the breadcrumbs to stop them from sticking together.

In a large frying pan, pour about 2 tablespoons of peanut oil. When hot, fry several fillets at a time for about 3 minutes until golden brown. Turn over and repeat on the other side. Keep these warm while you cook the remaining fillets. You may need to wipe out the pan with paper towels to remove any burnt crumbs before adding another 2 tablespoons of oil. Serve on a warm serving platter garnished with lemon wedges.

PER SERVING	
Calories	281
% Calories from fat	37
Fat (g)	11.4
Saturated fat (g)	2.7
Cholesterol (mg)	106
Sodium (mg)	310
Protein (g)	22.8
Carbohydrate (g)	20
Calcium (mg)	83

EXCHANGES	
Milk	0.0
Vegetable	0.0
Fruit	0.0
Bread	1.5
Meat	2.0
Fat	1.0

Change the filling if you are cooking for a vegan. Omit the anchovies and the tuna and use marinated artichoke hearts, peppers or mushrooms.

Niçoise Tartlets

Serves 6

These tartlets have a wonderful Mediterranean theme. I tend to keep most of the ingredients in my cupboard and often have puff pastry in the freezer, thus making it a great and impressive dish for an unexpected visitor. For a lunchtime dish you could make one large tart and serve it with a crisp salad. Easy to prepare in advance and keep in the fridge until ready to cook.

1 tbsp	olive oil	15 ml
1	small red onion, finely sliced	1
2	cloves garlic, crushed	2
1	13-oz pack frozen puff pastry (or see Quick Flaky Pastry recipe, p. 187)	1
2 tbsps	sun-dried tomato paste	2 tsps
1	8-oz can tuna, water-packed, drained	1
12	cherry tomatoes, cut into quarters	12
18	capers, drained	18
12	black olives	12
	fresh basil leaves to garnish	

Pre-heat the oven to 425F. Heat the olive oil in a small pan and sauté the onion and garlic for about 5 minutes, until soft.

Roll pastry until large enough to allow for six, 6 x 6-inch squares. Cut 3/4-inch strips off sides of each square.

Cut these strips to the same length as the squares, wet one side of each strip and stick strips along edges of squares, overlapping at corners. Place the pastry cases on a baking sheet. Prick the inside of each case with a fork.

Spread the sun-dried tomato paste over the inside of the uncooked pastry cases, taking care not to put anything over the side strips.

Spoon one-sixth of the tuna into each pastry case, cover with 8 quarters of tomatoes, 3 capers and some red onion mix. Top with 2 olives.

Bake for 10–15 minutes, until pastry has risen and is golden. Serve hot or warm, garnished with basil leaves.

PER SERVING

Calories	430
% Calories from fat	56
Fat (g)	27.1
Saturated fat (g)	6.5
Cholesterol (mg)	11.3
Sodium (mg)	489
Protein (g)	14.9
Carbohydrate (g)	32.2
Calcium (mg)	26.5

EXCHANGES

Milk	0.0
Vegetable	0.0
Fruit	0.0
Bread	2.0
Meat	1.0
Fat	5.0

The filling could be made with other fish such as fresh cooked salmon, cooked smoked haddock, smoked mackerel, smoked salmon, etc.

Smoked Salmon Roulade with Smoked Trout Mousse

Serves 8

This recipe uses mayonnaise and smoked fish to produce a deliciously creamy mousse rolled up in smoked salmon. The end result is extremely impressive and suitable for any occasion, whether it be a summer lunch with salad and French bread or an extremely eye-catching starter. The roulade can be made well in advance and will last for several days in the fridge.

6 oz	smoked salmon, in thin slices	170 g
1	package (¼ oz) gelatin	1
½ cup	soy milk	120 ml
½ cup	low-fat mayonnaise	110 ml
1	smoked trout (weight when skinned and boned about 6 oz)	1
3 tbsps	lemon juice	45 ml
	freshly ground mace	
	sprig fresh dill	
	freshly ground pepper	
	lemon wedges and watercress to garnish	

You will need a rectangular platter about 5 inches by 9 inches, covered with plastic wrap, overlapping the edges. Lay out thin layers of the smoked salmon evenly over the plastic wrap.

Next, soak the gelatin in a bowl of cold water until softened (about 5 minutes). Place the soy milk, mayonnaise and smoked trout in the blender and process quickly until almost smooth.

Heat the lemon juice in a small pan and when hot, remove the pan from the heat and add the gelatin, stirring well until melted. Pour the melted gelatin into the blender with the smoked trout mixture. Process again fairly briefly until thoroughly dispersed.

Mix in ground mace, dill and pepper (you should not need salt because of the saltiness of smoked fish). Spread evenly over the smoked salmon, and chill until set. When the mousse is set, using the plastic wrap, lift the salmon along the long edge of the platter and roll it over and over, pulling away the plastic wrap as it rolls. Secure firmly in place by wrapping the roll in plastic wrap (it should resemble a fat sausage) and chill. To serve, unwrap the roulade and slice it with a sharp knife.

Garnish with lemon wedges and watercress. Serve with hot bread or toast.

PER SERVING	
Calories	114
% Calories from fat	52
Fat (g)	6.7
Saturated fat (g)	1.1
Cholesterol (mg)	12
Sodium (mg)	310
Protein (g)	11.1
Carbohydrate (g)	3
Calcium (mg)	18.1

EXCHANGES	
Milk	0.0
Vegetable	0.0
Fruit	0.0
Bread	0.0
Meat	2.0
Fat	0.0

This dish could also be made with shrimp (freshly shelled even better).

The smaller the squid, the more tender it should be. Take care not to overcook squid, as it becomes tough and rubbery.

Squid with Chilies and Tomatoes

Serves 6 as starter

There was a time when squid was generally only available in an unprepared way, which meant lots of inky mess and strange things to be pulled out of the squid. Not a job for the squeamish cook! Nowadays, it is usually available ready prepared from most fish markets and supermarkets. Squid is quite economical, and the combination of tomatoes and chili peppers makes for an exceptional dish. Serve this with hot Italian bread.

2 tbsps	olive oil (or use the oil from the drained sun-dried tomatoes)	30 ml
2	green onions, finely chopped	2
1	large red chili pepper, de-seeded and finely chopped	1
2	tomatoes, finely chopped	2
1 tbsp	tomato purée	1 tbsp
8	sun-dried tomatoes, oil packed, finely chopped	8
1 tbsp	chopped parsley	1 tbsp
1 tbsp	chopped fresh oregano (could use 1 teaspoon dried)	1 tbsp
1 lb	fresh prepared squid, cut into rings	450 g
	salt and freshly ground pepper	

Heat 1 tablespoon of the oil in a large wok or frying pan until medium hot. Add the green onions, chilies, tomatoes, tomato purée and sun-dried tomatoes and stir quickly for 4 minutes.

Stir the parsley and oregano into the sauce and pour out into a separate dish.

Wash out the wok or pan and add remaining oil. When very hot, add the squid. Toss the squid in the pan quickly for 30 seconds.

Pour in the tomato sauce and mix well with the squid. Season with salt and freshly ground pepper.

Serve hot.

PER SERVING	
Calories	133
% Calories from fat	42
Fat (g)	6.3
Saturated fat (g)	1
Cholesterol (mg)	176.1
Sodium (mg)	53.4
Protein (g)	12.7
Carbohydrate (g)	6.6
Calcium (mg)	37.4

EXCHANGES	
Milk	0.0
Vegetable	1.0
Fruit	0.0
Bread	0.0
Meat	2.0
Fat	0.0

Chinese-Style Crispy Pork Strips

Serves 8 as starter
These are very easy and very tasty. Try barbecuing instead of broiling for a fabulous dish.

For the Pork Strips

1½ lb	pork loin	675 g
2 tsps	Chinese 5 spice powder	2 tsps
1	red chili pepper, deseeded and chopped	1
2	cloves garlic, peeled and crushed	2
1 inch	piece ginger, finely chopped	2½ cm
	pinch salt	
1 cup	water	240 ml

For the Sauce

2 tbsps	soy sauce	30 ml
1 tbsp	dry sherry	15 ml
1 tbsp	dark brown sugar	25 g
1 tsp	cornstarch	1 tsp

Pre-heat the oven to 350F. Using a sharp knife, cut the meat into about 8 strips.

Lay the pork strips in a large baking dish and cover with the Chinese 5 spice, chili, crushed garlic and chopped ginger and salt.

Pour the water into the dish, cover with aluminum foil and bake for about 1 hour.

Pour off the remaining juice into a small saucepan. Skim off any excess pork fat that may be floating at the top and discard. Place the pork strips on a suitable pan for grilling.

Into the pork juice, stir the soy sauce, sherry and dark brown sugar. Bring to a boil and cook for about 1 minute.

Mix the cornstarch with 1 tbsp water until smooth, and add to the sauce, stirring well. Bring the sauce to a boil and stir until the sauce begins to thicken (if it is too thick add dash of water).

Heat the broiler. Spoon a little of the sauce over the pork strips and broil for about 3 minutes on each side until the strips become crisp.

Heat the sauce and serve with the pork strips.

PER SERVING	
Calories	138
% Calories from fat	31
Fat (g)	4.6
Saturated fat (g)	1.6
Cholesterol (mg)	49.9
Sodium (mg)	303
Protein (g)	18.7
Carbohydrate (g)	3.7
Calcium (mg)	23.8

EXCHANGES	
Milk	0.0
Vegetable	0.0
Fruit	0.0
Bread	0.0
Meat	2.0
Fat	0.0

The longer you marinate the kebabs, the more flavor the chicken will have.

If you are using wooden skewers, soak them in water first to stop them from charring.

Marinated Lime and Sesame Chicken Sticks

Serves 6 as starter

These chicken sticks are quick and easy to prepare and have a delicate Thai flavor. Served simply with a wedge of lime, they provide a nutritious low-fat starter. However, if you want more of a special dish, serve with my hot Peanut and Coconut Chili Sauce.

2	boneless chicken breasts (about 1 lb)	2
2	limes	2
1 tsp	sweet paprika	1 tsp
1 tbsp	sesame oil	15 ml
2	cloves garlic, crushed	2
6	wooden skewers	6
1	red bell pepper, de-seeded and cut into cubes	1
1 tbsp	sesame seeds	1 tbsp
	arugula leaves or salad to garnish	

Remove the skin of the chicken breasts and cut each breast into about 12 cubes.

In a bowl, mix the cubed chicken with the zest and juice of one lime, paprika, sesame oil and garlic. Leave for several hours to marinate in the fridge. Pre-heat broiler.

Spike the cubed chicken onto the skewers alternating with the red pepper.

Lay the chicken sticks under the hot broiler for about 15 minutes, turning from time to time to ensure even cooking. Halfway through the cooking, drizzle over any remaining sesame and lime marinade.

Sprinkle the chicken sticks all over with the sesame seeds. Serve each chicken stick on a small warm plate and drizzle over any cooking juices.

Garnish with some arugula leaves and a wedge of lime.

PER SERVING	
Calories	129
% Calories from fat	28
Fat (g)	4
Saturated fat (g)	0.7
Cholesterol (mg)	45.6
Sodium (mg)	42
Protein (g)	18.9
Carbohydrate (g)	4.5
Calcium (mg)	34.6

EXCHANGES	
Milk	0.0
Vegetable	0.0
Fruit	0.0
Bread	0.0
Meat	2.0
Fat	0.0

This salad may also be made with smoked chicken breast.

Smoked Duck Salad with Spiced Walnuts

Serves 6 as starter

This starter is a real treat and easy to prepare in advance, without spooning over the dressing. The smoked duck tastes wonderful with the sweet and sour flavor of the onion marmalade and the spiciness of the walnuts.

Smoked duck is quite a luxury ingredient and fairly expensive, but cut thinly it goes quite a long way. You should find it in your local delicatessen or buy it mail order from a smokery.

2	bunches crisp romaine lettuce leaves	2
¹/₂ recipe	Spiced Walnuts (see page 125)	¹/₂ recipe
1	smoked duck breast, skin and fat removed (about 8 oz)	1
³/₈ cup	Tarragon French Dressing (see page 139)	90 ml
4 tbsps	Onion Marmalade (see page 124)	100 g

Wash and dry the lettuce, and break it into pieces. Distribute the lettuce onto six individual plates. Sprinkle the spiced walnuts over the lettuce.

Next, slice the smoked duck into thin strips. Lay thin slices of the smoked duck over the top of each salad.

Drizzle a couple of spoonfuls of dressing over each plate.

Finally, dollop a teaspoon of the onion marmalade onto the sliced duck.

Serve with crisp warm French bread.

PER SERVING	
Calories	321
% Calories from fat	76
Fat (g)	27.9
Saturated fat (g)	3.9
Cholesterol (mg)	33.6
Sodium (mg)	226
Protein (g)	13
Carbohydrate (g)	6.7
Calcium (mg)	50.2

EXCHANGES	
Milk	0.0
Vegetable	0.0
Fruit	0.0
Bread	0.0
Meat	2.0
Fat	5.0

Vary the nuts according to what you have in your cupboard. For a much creamier texture, increase the quantity of peanut butter. Also, almond butter is a nice substitute for peanut butter.

Mushroom and Nut Pâté

Serves 10

This tasty vegetarian pâté is made with a mixture of lentils and nuts. The addition of peanut butter enables the pâté to become rich and creamy in texture. It will keep well up to about 8 days in the fridge and makes a quick and nutritious snack. Try spreading it on hot toast or with grated carrot in a crispy sandwich.

³/₄ cup	uncooked red lentils (6 oz)	170 g
3 cups	water for cooking lentils	700 ml
1 tbsp	olive oil	1 tbsp
1	large or 2 medium onions, finely chopped	1
2	cloves garlic, crushed	2
3 cups	button mushrooms, wiped and very finely chopped (7 oz)	200 g
1 tsp	vegan bouillon powder	1 tsp
1 tsp	ground cumin	1 tsp
¹/₂ tsp	ground turmeric	¹/₂ tsp
1 tsp	ground cilantro	1 tsp
¹/₂ tsp	chili powder	¹/₂ tsp
1 tsp	Dijon mustard	1 tsp
3 tbsps	crunchy peanut butter	3 tbsps
	juice of ¹/₂ lemon	
³/₄ cup	ground, roasted hazelnuts (2¹/₂ oz)	³/₄ cup
1 tbsp	chopped fresh cilantro (save a few leaves for garnish)	1 tbsp
	salt and freshly ground pepper	

PER SERVING	
Calories	217
% Calories from fat	56
Fat (g)	14.2
Saturated fat (g)	1.5
Cholesterol (mg)	0
Sodium (mg)	132
Protein (g)	9.5
Carbohydrate (g)	15.9
Calcium (mg)	37.4
EXCHANGES	
Milk	0.0
Vegetable	0.0
Fruit	0.0
Bread	1.0
Meat	1.0
Fat	2.0

Rinse the lentils in a sieve under cold water. Put the lentils in a large saucepan with the water and bring to a boil. Skim off any scum that forms.

Boil gently for 10–15 minutes until soft, but not completely mushy. Strain through a sieve and leave to dry.

Next, heat a large frying pan with the oil, add the onion and garlic and cook for about 5 minutes until beginning to soften.

Mix in the mushrooms, stir well and cook for several minutes. Add bouillon powder and spices and sauté for about 4 minutes until mixture dries out. Transfer to a large bowl. Add the cooked lentils, mustard, peanut butter, lemon juice, roasted nuts, cilantro and seasonings. Refrigerate for at least 1 hour. Serve, smoothed into individual ramekins, each garnished with a cilantro leaf.

Omit anchovies for a vegan alternative. Try using different toppings, such as grilled eggplant, bell peppers, asparagus or marinated artichoke hearts. For the meat eater, thin slices of ham or bacon would be delicious with the tomatoes.

Important note—try to use fresh young garlic, as some older garlic becomes bitter and unpleasant in taste.

Roasted Cherry Tomato Bruschetta

Serves 4

Bruschetta are little Italian toasts, an excellent way of using up any leftover stale French or Italian bread. The combination of flavors and the olive oil on crisp toasts make a delicious Mediterranean-style dish also suitable for a light summer lunch, especially when you have a glut of small tomatoes.

Do not be alarmed by the amount of garlic used, as the cooking process takes away the strong taste associated with raw garlic. Boiling the garlic beforehand allows easy peeling and begins to cook it slightly.

8	cloves garlic, unpeeled	8
1	medium red onion, cut in half and sliced	1
1/4 cup	olive oil	60 ml
2 tbsps	capers, rinsed	2 tbsps
1	2-oz can anchovy fillets in oil, drained	1
24	cherry tomatoes	24
	freshly ground pepper	
1 tbsp	balsamic vinegar	15 ml
1	demi-baguette French bread (about 8 inches)	1
2 tbsps	vegan pesto (found in health food shops; alternatively you can use sun-dried tomato paste)	2 tbsps
	garnish with fresh basil leaves	

Pre-heat the oven to 400F. Put garlic cloves in small pan of cold water, bring to boil and cook for 2–3 minutes; drain and peel.

In a large oven dish, roast the red onion and garlic cloves mixed with 1/8 cup of the olive oil in the oven for about 10 minutes. Remove from the oven and stir in the capers, halved anchovy fillets, cherry tomatoes and freshly ground pepper. Return to the oven and roast for a further 15 minutes. Stir in the balsamic vinegar.

Meanwhile, slice the bread into about 8 slices and place them on a baking sheet. Drizzle with the remaining olive oil and some more pepper. Bake for about 5 minutes, turn the bread slices over and repeat for several minutes until golden and crisp.

Spread pesto onto the crisp bruschettas and spoon over the hot tomato mix and any remaining roasting juices. Garnish with fresh basil leaves.

PER SERVING	
Calories	366
% Calories from fat	45
Fat (g)	18.5
Saturated fat (g)	2.9
Cholesterol (mg)	13.9
Sodium (mg)	1063
Protein (g)	11.4
Carbohydrate (g)	39.5
Calcium (mg)	115.1
EXCHANGES	
Milk	0.0
Vegetable	2.0
Fruit	0.0
Bread	2.0
Meat	0.0
Fat	4.0

If it is easier, use about 6 oz frozen, defrosted spinach. Squeeze out excess water and add to onions while still frying. Also delicious with chopped sun-dried tomatoes added to the filling. If you are unable to buy pine nuts, you could use flaked almonds for an interesting texture and flavor.

Crispy Spinach and Pine Nut Filo Parcels

Serves 8 (1 parcel per serving)

These are a great way to start a meal. You can serve them with the Sun-Dried Tomato, Basil and Garlic Dressing on page 143. Or serve as a light meal with Tomato and Pimiento Coulis on page 121.

If made slightly smaller by cutting the sheets into 3, they are a great idea for canapés. The addition of mustard gives them more of a savory flavor.

6–7 cups	fresh spinach leaves (about 10 oz)	280 g
1	medium onion, finely chopped	1
2	cloves garlic, crushed	2
1 tbsp	olive oil	15 ml
2/3 cup	soy cream cheese	150 g
1 tbsp	Dijon mustard	1 tbsp
2 tbsps	pine nuts	2 tbsps
	good pinch of grated nutmeg	
	salt and freshly ground pepper	
4	sheets of filo pastry, thawed if frozen	4
1 1/2 tbsps	vegan margarine, melted	37 g

Pre-heat the oven to 400F. Wash and trim stalks from the spinach. Put the spinach leaves into a large saucepan, covered, over a medium heat and cook for approximately 5 minutes.

Drain, rinse under cold water and press down in a sieve to drain off any excess water. Chop the spinach once it is drained of excess water.

In a frying pan, gently cook the onion and garlic in the olive oil for about 8 minutes or until soft and beginning to caramelize. Mix in the chopped spinach, cream cheese, mustard, pine nuts and seasonings.

Keep the filo pastry under a damp tea cloth until required.

Taking one sheet at a time, cut in half lengthways and brush with melted margarine.

Spoon an eighth of the filling onto one end of the pastry strip. Fold diagonally and again until you reach the end, having made a triangular parcel.

Place parcels on an oiled baking sheet. Bake for 15–20 minutes until crisp and golden brown. Serve hot.

PER SERVING	
Calories	140
% Calories from fat	70
Fat (g)	10.9
Saturated fat (g)	2.3
Cholesterol (mg)	0
Sodium (mg)	247
Protein (g)	3.1
Carbohydrate (g)	7.5
Calcium (mg)	34.2

EXCHANGES	
Milk	0.0
Vegetable	0.0
Fruit	0.0
Bread	0.5
Meat	0.0
Fat	2.0

You could use warm pita bread instead of tortillas.

Hummus, Chili and Crisp Vegetable Wrap

Serves 4 (1 wrap per serving)

This is an ideal vegan snack that can be taken to work and eaten cold or warmed up slightly in the oven or microwave.

4	flour tortillas, about 8 inch diameter	4
¼ cup	hummus (shop bought or homemade)	¼ cup
4 tsps	sweet chili sauce (or hot chili sauce if desired)	4 tsps
1 cup	finely shredded red or green cabbage	110 g
2	medium carrots, peeled and grated	2
	freshly ground pepper	

Warm the tortillas according to manufacturer's instructions. Spread 1 tablespoon hummus, followed by 1 teaspoon of chili sauce on each tortilla. Sprinkle over cabbage, carrot and pepper. Roll up each tortilla into a roll and serve.

VEGAN

PER SERVING

Calories	157
% Calories from fat	21
Fat (g)	3.7
Saturated fat (g)	0.8
Cholesterol (mg)	0
Sodium (mg)	364
Protein (g)	4.2
Carbohydrate (g)	27.3
Calcium (mg)	69.9

EXCHANGES

Milk	0.0
Vegetable	0.0
Fruit	0.0
Bread	2.0
Meat	0.0
Fat	0.5

Bacon, Tomato and Watercress Wrap

Serves 4 (1 wrap per serving)

This wrap has a hot filling and is best assembled just before serving. The roasted tomatoes prevent the filling from becoming dry and make a mouth-watering combination with the bacon and watercress.

6	slices smoked or unsmoked bacon	6
4	medium tomatoes, quartered	4
2	green onions, chopped	2
	drizzle of olive oil	
2 tsps	balsamic vinegar	10 ml
4	flour tortillas, about 8 inch diameter	4
1 tbsp	sun-dried tomato paste	1 tbsp
1	small bunch of watercress	1
	freshly ground pepper	

   Pre-heat the oven to 400F. In a large baking dish, arrange the bacon at one end. At other end place the quartered tomatoes, sprinkled with green onions.
   Drizzle over a little olive oil and the balsamic vinegar. Grind on some black pepper.
   Roast in the oven for 10 minutes, until the tomatoes are soft and the bacon is cooked.
   Warm tortillas slightly according to manufacturer's instructions. Spread a little sun-dried tomato paste over each tortilla.
   Spoon tomato and onion mixture onto each tortilla and spread around.
   Sprinkle the roughly chopped bacon and watercress over the tomatoes.
   Roll up each tortilla and serve immediately.

PER SERVING	
Calories	207
% Calories from fat	37
Fat (g)	8.6
Saturated fat (g)	2.7
Cholesterol (mg)	10.2
Sodium (mg)	393
Protein (g)	8
Carbohydrate (g)	25.4
Calcium (mg)	64.6

EXCHANGES	
Milk	0.0
Vegetable	0.0
Fruit	0.0
Bread	2.0
Meat	0.0
Fat	1.5

Light Meals and Lunches

Caribbean-Style Spare Ribs

Moroccan Lamb Burgers

Smoked Ham and Lentil Pie

Baked Eggs in Pancetta and Mushroom Tartlets

*Risotto of Artichoke Hearts and
Mushrooms Topped with Parma Ham*

Caramelized Onion, Bacon and Red Lentil Quiche

Spaghetti, Carbonara Style

*Sautéed Chicken Livers in Wine and
Sage Sauce on Garlic Bread Croutons*

Spicy Chicken Quesadillas

Grilled Fresh Tuna on Potato Niçoise

Smoked Salmon and Spinach Quiche

Potato Pancakes

Eggplant and Red Lentil Loaf

Baked Stuffed Mushrooms

Chick Peas with Tomatoes and Cilantro

Curried Spinach and Eggs

Potato, Bean and Corn Frittata

Sweet Potato and Chick Pea Cakes

Caribbean-Style Spare Ribs

Serves 8

Pork ribs are an affordable cut of meat. These deliciously messy ribs make an ideal meal for summer barbecues and should be popular with all the family.

1	onion, peeled and roughly chopped	1
2	small or 1 large red chili peppers, de-seeded and quartered	2
3	garlic cloves	3
1 tsp	ground allspice	1 tsp
1/2 tsp	ground cinnamon	1/2 tsp
1 inch	piece of fresh gingerroot, peeled and roughly chopped	2.5 cm
	handful fresh thyme sprigs, leaves removed or 1 teaspoon dried	
1/4 tsp	ground black pepper	1/4 tsp
	juice and grated zest of 1 lime	
5 tbsps	cider vinegar or white wine vinegar	75 ml
1/2 cup	dark soy sauce	120 ml
2 tbsps	dark superfine sugar	50 g
3 tbsps	peanut or sunflower oil	45 ml
4 lb	pork ribs	1.8 kg

Place the onion, chilies, garlic, allspice, cinnamon, ginger, thyme and black pepper in food processor and purée for about 30 seconds until well blended.

Add the lime juice and zest, vinegar, soy sauce, sugar and oil and process again until it becomes a purée consistency.

Lay the pork ribs in a large glass or ceramic (non-metallic) baking dish. Pour the marinade over the ribs.

Marinate in the fridge for 4–24 hours, basting occasionally.

Cook on a barbecue grill, basting occasionally with marinade; cook the remaining sauce in a pan and serve with the ribs.

Alternatively, grill under a low to medium pre-heated broiler for about 25–30 minutes turning occasionally and brushing with marinade, until tender inside but beginning to char on the edges.

PER SERVING	
Calories	730
% Calories from fat	72
Fat (g)	56.4
Saturated fat (g)	20.1
Cholesterol (mg)	115.2
Sodium (mg)	1106
Protein (g)	40.7
Carbohydrate (g)	8.6
Calcium (mg)	31.5
EXCHANGES	
Milk	0.0
Vegetable	0.0
Fruit	0.0
Bread	0.5
Meat	6.0
Fat	9.0

Add fresh chili for a hot and fiery touch. Moroccan dishes sometimes use prunes—try them instead of the apricots for a different taste.

Moroccan Lamb Burgers

Serves 4

Moroccan dishes are becoming increasingly popular. The balance of fruit and spices makes these burgers an interesting addition to a barbecue or a light lunch.

The stickiness of the chopped apricots holds the burger together surprisingly well, and they also add a sweetness that may appeal to children. Serve with Harissa Dressing (see page 141) and Spiced Rice (see page 109).

1	small onion, peeled and quartered	1
1 inch	piece fresh gingerroot, peeled and chopped	2.5 cm
2	cloves garlic	2
1	small bunch cilantro, washed	1
1 tsp	ground cinnamon	1 tsp
1½ tsps	ground cilantro	1½ tsps
1½ tsps	ground cumin	1½ tsps
½ cup	dried apricots, finely chopped	½ cup
1 lb	lean ground lamb	450 g
	salt and freshly ground pepper	

Place the onion, ginger, garlic and cilantro in a food processor and finely chop.

Add the spices, apricots, lamb and salt and pepper, and pulse briefly, keeping the mixture chunky.

Shape into four burgers; refrigerate until required.

Heat a large non-stick frying pan. Cook the burgers for about 5 minutes on either side, and press down with a spatula occasionally to cook through.

Alternatively, cook on a barbecue grill or under a hot broiler on an oiled baking sheet.

Burgers should be dark golden brown and just cooked through.

PER SERVING

Calories	337
% Calories from fat	57
Fat (g)	21.6
Saturated fat (g)	9.1
Cholesterol (mg)	77.4
Sodium (mg)	60
Protein (g)	20.2
Carbohydrate (g)	15.8
Calcium (mg)	49.6

EXCHANGES

Milk	0.0
Vegetable	0.0
Fruit	1.0
Bread	0.0
Meat	3.0
Fat	2.0

For a vegan (dairy- and egg-free vegetarian) dish, substitute chopped mushrooms for the ham and saute with the onion.

Smoked Ham and Lentil Pie

Serves 4

This is an inexpensive and hearty pie. The nutty lentils mixed with the ham are particularly tasty with the wholegrain mustard mashed potato topping. Try serving this with lightly steamed green vegetables or a crisp salad.

3/4 cup	brown lentils (6 oz)	170 g
1 tbsp	olive oil or sunflower oil	15 ml
1	medium onion, finely chopped	1
2	cloves garlic, crushed	2
3/4 lb	ham hock, weight of meat off the bone and diced (smoked or unsmoked)	337 g
1	14-oz can chopped tomatoes	1
1 tbsp	tomato purée	1 tbsp
	sprig of fresh thyme	
	freshly ground pepper	
1 recipe	Wholegrain Mustard Mashed Potatoes (see page 103)	1 recipe

Pre-heat the oven to 400F. Rinse the lentils. Cover with plenty of cold water in a large saucepan, bring to a boil, cover and simmer gently for about 20–25 minutes until the lentils are soft. Drain well.

In a large saucepan, heat the oil and cook the onion and garlic for about 5 minutes until soft.

Stir in the diced ham and cook for a further 5 minutes.

Tip in the chopped tomatoes and tomato purée, and mix well. Cover the pan and simmer for about 15 minutes. Season with thyme and ground pepper.

You will probably not need salt, as the ham will make the dish salty enough.

Pour into a large baking dish. Cover with wholegrain mustard mashed potatoes and smooth down with a fork.

Put into the hot oven and cook for about 25 minutes until golden, broiling the top if necessary to make a crisp golden topping before serving.

PER SERVING	
Calories	544
% Calories from fat	25
Fat (g)	15
Saturated fat (g)	3.5
Cholesterol (mg)	49.3
Sodium (mg)	1537
Protein (g)	38.6
Carbohydrate (g)	65.3
Calcium (mg)	78.7

EXCHANGES	
Milk	0.0
Vegetable	1.0
Fruit	0.0
Bread	4.0
Meat	3.0
Fat	1.0

For a vegetarian alternative, substitute the pancetta with freshly steamed, drained and chopped spinach well seasoned with freshly ground nutmeg.

Baked Eggs in Pancetta and Mushroom Tartlets

Serves 6

These make a wonderful light meal. The tartlets can be prepared in advance and up to the stage before the egg is added. The baked egg in the middle gives the tartlet a lovely richness, especially if the yolk remains slightly runny. Serve with a dressed salad.

1 recipe	Shortcrust Pastry (see recipe on page 187 or use a suitable bought pastry)	1 recipe
1	large onion, finely chopped	1
2	cloves garlic, crushed	2
1 tbsp	vegetable oil	15 ml
2 cups	mushrooms, finely chopped (6 oz)	170 g
5–6 slices	pancetta (or smoked back bacon), chopped (about 4 oz)	112 g
1 tbsp	chopped parsley (or French tarragon if available)	1 tbsp
	salt and freshly ground pepper	
6	eggs (free range if possible)	6

You will also need 6 quiche pans with 4 inch base diameter, 1/2 inch deep, and a 51/2-inch-diameter round cookie cutter

Pre-heat the oven to 350F. Roll out the pastry on a floured surface to a thickness of about 1/8 inch and large enough to cut out six 51/2-inch rounds.

Grease the pans and line each with the pastry; prick the base with a fork. Allow pastry cases to relax in the fridge for about 30 minutes.

Then place the pans on a solid baking sheet in the hot oven for about 10–15 minutes until golden. Remove from oven. Sauté the chopped onion and garlic in the oil for about 5 minutes until soft.

Add the mushrooms, and cook for several minutes; if the mixture becomes wet, increase temperature and cook out the liquid. Remove from heat and add pancetta, parsley and seasonings.

Spoon this mushroom mixture into the tartlet cases, making a well in the center. Then break an egg into a small cup, and tip this into center of tartlet. Repeat with remaining tartlets.

Return to oven for 12–15 minutes or until just set and yolks are still soft and creamy. Remove from the pans and serve immediately, as the eggs will continue cooking.

PER SERVING	
Calories	287
% Calories from fat	57
Fat (g)	18.2
Saturated fat (g)	5.2
Cholesterol (mg)	221
Sodium (mg)	194
Protein (g)	11
Carbohydrate (g)	19.5
Calcium (mg)	37.2

EXCHANGES	
Milk	0.0
Vegetable	1.0
Fruit	0.0
Bread	1.0
Meat	1.0
Fat	3.0

Omit ham for vegans and use a good vegetable stock. Alternatively, try using smoked salmon instead of ham.

If you have fresh artichokes, you may wish to cook these and remove the hearts, which is quite a time-consuming job, but well worth it.

Risotto of Artichoke Hearts and Mushrooms Topped with Parma Ham

Serves 4

Many people are now realizing that risottos are actually quite simple to make and can be tackled at home. The combination of artichokes, mushrooms and Parma ham makes this creamy risotto extremely appetizing. Serve with a crisp salad.

2 tbsps	olive oil	30 ml
1¼ cups	button mushrooms, wiped and sliced (about 8 oz)	225 g
8	marinated artichoke hearts, drained and quartered	8
1	red onion, finely chopped	1
2	cloves garlic, crushed	2
1 cup	(scant) Arborio rice (7 oz)	196 g
5 tbsps	dry white wine	75 ml
2¾ cups	chicken stock, heated	660 ml
1 tbsp	soy cream	15 ml
	salt and freshly ground pepper	
4 oz	thinly sliced Parma ham, cut in thin strips	112 g
	whole chives cut in half to garnish	

Heat frying pan with 1 tablespoon olive oil, and sauté the sliced mushrooms. After about 4 minutes add the artichoke hearts; cook briefly, then tip into a bowl and set aside.

Meanwhile, heat remaining oil in a large saucepan, and sauté the red onion and garlic for about 5 minutes until soft.

Add the rice, remove from heat and stir until rice is coated. Return the pan to the heat, add all the wine and then 2 ladlefuls of stock. Simmer, stirring constantly until the rice has absorbed nearly all the liquid; add more stock and repeat.

After 20–25 minutes, nearly all the stock will have been absorbed by the rice, and each grain will have a creamy coating but remain al dente.

Add the artichokes and mushrooms to the rice, and heat through. Just before serving, add the soy cream and seasonings.

Spoon onto four warm plates garnished with strips of Parma ham and chives.

PER SERVING	
Calories	384
% Calories from fat	37
Fat (g)	15.5
Saturated fat (g)	2.7
Cholesterol (mg)	33.6
Sodium (mg)	695
Protein (g)	15.2
Carbohydrate (g)	42.2
Calcium (mg)	13.2

EXCHANGES	
Milk	0.0
Vegetable	2.0
Fruit	0.0
Bread	2.0
Meat	1.0
Fat	3.0

Omit bacon for a vegetarian version. The whole wheat pastry in this recipe does not require much pre-cooking.

Caramelized Onion, Bacon and Red Lentil Quiche

Serves 6

This is not your typical creamy quiche filling, although the red lentils break down enough to give it a smooth, wholesome texture, which is very nutritious, and the mustard gives added flavor. Serve warm or cold with a crisp salad.

1 recipe	Whole Wheat Pastry (see page 188)	1 recipe
½ cup	dried red lentils (3 oz)	84 g
2	medium to large onions, peeled and sliced in half rings	2
1 tbsp	olive oil	15 ml
5–6 slices	unsmoked or smoked back bacon, rind removed, diced (about 4 oz)	112 g
1 tsp	vegan bouillon powder	1 tsp
1 cup	(scant) soy milk	200 ml
1 tbsp	Dijon mustard	1 tbsp
	2 eggs plus 2 egg whites, beaten together	
	salt and freshly ground pepper	
1 tbsp	chopped parsley	1 tbsp
1	sprig of fresh thyme	1

Pre-heat the oven to 350F. Lightly grease a 9-inch flan or quiche dish (a deeper dish is preferable, as this has quite a substantial amount of filling).

Roll out the pastry and line the baking dish, easing any overlapping pastry back into the sides. Prick the base with a fork, and bake in the oven for 5 minutes to set the pastry.

Meanwhile, rinse the lentils and place in a small pan covered with plenty of water. Bring to a boil, then simmer for 8–10 minutes until almost cooked but not mushy; drain well.

In a large frying pan, sauté the onions with the olive oil over medium heat for about 10 minutes, stirring well. Remove from heat when soft and beginning to caramelize.

Add the bacon to the onions, and cook over medium heat for a further 4 minutes until just cooked. Stir in the lentils. Set aside.

In a large bowl, blend the bouillon powder with 2 tablespoons of boiling water, add the soy milk, mustard and eggs and season with salt and freshly ground pepper. Mix well, then finally stir in the chopped parsley and thyme leaves.

Spoon the onion and lentil mixture into the half-cooked pastry case. Carefully pour the egg mixture into the pastry case so that all the filling is well covered. Return to oven and cook for about 35 minutes until risen, firm and golden.

PER SERVING	
Calories	390
% Calories from fat	55
Fat (g)	23.2
Saturated fat (g)	6
Cholesterol (mg)	78.6
Sodium (mg)	600
Protein (g)	13.7
Carbohydrate (g)	29.3
Calcium (mg)	131.8

EXCHANGES	
Milk	0.0
Vegetable	0.0
Fruit	0.0
Bread	2.0
Meat	1.0
Fat	4.0

For a vegetarian dish, omit bacon. You could add walnuts for a more nutritious meal.

For a vegan dish, omit both bacon and egg.

Spaghetti, Carbonara Style

Serves 4

The idea of adding hummus to hot spaghetti may seem a bit strange. The result, however, is surprisingly delicious and creamy, with a slightly grainy texture not too dissimilar to Parmesan. Serve an arugula or lettuce salad with this pasta dish.

1 tbsp	olive oil	15 ml
1	medium onion, peeled and finely chopped	1
2	cloves garlic, crushed	2
5–6 slices	smoked bacon, diced (about 4 oz)	112 g
2/3 cup	button mushrooms, wiped and sliced (about 4 oz)	112 g
12 oz	dried spaghetti or tagliatelle	340 g
1/2 cup	hummus (the bought variety is excellent for this dish)	1/2 cup
1 tbsp	mild Dijon mustard	1 tbsp
2	egg yolks	2
2 tbsps	finely chopped parsley	2 tbsps
	salt and freshly ground pepper	

Heat the oil in a saucepan, add onions and garlic and sauté gently for 5 minutes, stirring continuously.

Next, add the diced bacon and, stirring well, cook for 2 minutes; then add the mushrooms and cook for a further 4 minutes on a slightly higher heat.

Set aside while you cook pasta. Don't worry if the mushrooms become slightly wet, as the pasta will absorb any liquid.

Cook the pasta in boiling salted water for 8–10 minutes or until al dente (tender but still firm to the bite). Drain well.

Immediately toss the pasta with the mushroom and bacon mixture, return to low heat, add hummus, mustard, egg yolks and half the parsley and season well. Stir the pasta well over a low heat for several minutes to cook the yolks, although not too hot or you will curdle the yolks.

To serve: tip on to warm plates and sprinkle over the remaining parsley.

PER SERVING	
Calories	506
% Calories from fat	27
Fat (g)	14.9
Saturated fat (g)	3.6
Cholesterol (mg)	114.8
Sodium (mg)	333
Protein (g)	17.6
Carbohydrate (g)	73.5
Calcium (mg)	54.7

EXCHANGES	
Milk	0.0
Vegetable	3.0
Fruit	0.0
Bread	4.0
Meat	0.0
Fat	3.0

Try this dish with mushrooms for a delicious vegan alternative. It can also be served as a starter for 8 with one crouton each.

Sautéed Chicken Livers in Wine and Sage Sauce on Garlic Bread Croutons

Serves 4

Chicken livers are extremely economical and nutritious. They can usually be bought in tubs frozen from the butcher. This recipe incorporates them in a fairly sophisticated dish. The croutons add to the texture and appearance of the dish.

For the croutons		
8	slices thick-cut white bread	8
4	cloves garlic, crushed to a smooth paste	4
2 tbsps	olive oil	30 ml
For the chicken livers		
1 lb	chicken livers, defrosted if frozen	450 g
1 tbsp	olive oil	15 ml
2	small shallots, finely chopped	2
12	fresh sage leaves	12
1/4 cup	dry white wine	60 ml
1/4 cup	fat-free chicken stock or vegetable stock	60 ml
1/4 cup	soy cream	60 ml
	salt and freshly ground black pepper	
	chopped parsley to garnish	

Pre-heat the oven to 375F. Using a large round cutter, or a cup, cut out 8 discs from the slices of bread. You can use the remainder for breadcrumbs.

Lay the bread on a large baking sheet and spread each bread disc with garlic, coating them well.

Drizzle the olive oil over the garlic bread discs and bake them in the oven for 10–15 minutes, until golden and crisp. Keep warm when cooked.

Meanwhile, prepare the chicken livers. Examine livers carefully for green spots, and cut these away and remove any bits of fat.

Rinse the livers in cold water, then gently pat dry with paper towels.

Next, heat the oil in a large frying pan and sauté the shallots for about 4 minutes.

Turn the heat up high and add the chicken livers and sage leaves.

Cook for about 2 minutes, turning frequently, until the livers lose their raw, red color.

Transfer the chicken livers and sage to a warm plate, using a slotted spoon.

Pour the wine and stock into the hot pan, and simmer for about 1 minute, scraping the pan well to remove cooking residues.

Return the livers to the pan and heat thoroughly.

Lower the heat, stir in the soy cream and season well.

Place a crouton on each of the four plates, and spoon the livers and sauce over each crouton.

Top with another crouton placed at an angle. Sprinkle with chopped parsley and serve immediately.

PER SERVING	
Calories	402
% Calories from fat	40
Fat (g)	17.5
Saturated fat (g)	3.1
Cholesterol (mg)	499.9
Sodium (mg)	382
Protein (g)	25.4
Carbohydrate (g)	31.7
Calcium (mg)	93.6
EXCHANGES	
Milk	0.0
Vegetable	0.0
Fruit	0.0
Bread	2.0
Meat	3.0
Fat	2.0

Use bought tortillas or follow recipe on page 127 for homemade Flour Tortillas.

If you are unable to get soy mozzarella and want a touch of something resembling sour cream, try spooning onto the tortillas a dollop of Tofu and Almond Cream on page 170.

Serve with Chili Bean Salsa (see page 114) or Roasted Sweetcorn and Lime Salsa (see page 118).

Spicy Chicken Quesadillas

Serves 4

Mexican food is always extremely popular. It is a fun way of cooking, with lots of diverse and interesting flavors. These quesadillas can be kept in the fridge, rolled and ready to cook, so when your friends arrive there is very little work left to do. What's so good about this dish is that if you are cooking for lots of people, some of whom may eat dairy, you can vary the cheese accordingly.

1 lb	skinned chicken breast	450 g
2 tsps	ground cumin	2 tsps
2	cloves garlic, crushed	2
2 tsps	ground cilantro	2 tsps
1/2 tsp	chili powder	1/2 tsp
2 tbsps	peanut oil	30 ml
8	flour (or corn) tortillas	8
4	green onions, sliced	4
1	red bell pepper, de-seeded and thinly sliced	1
2	jalapeño green chilies, thinly sliced	2
8	slices of soy mozzarella	8

Cut the chicken into thin strips and place in bowl with cumin, garlic, cilantro and chili powder. Mix well, then leave to marinate in the fridge for 2 hours.

Heat half a tablespoon of the oil and fry the chicken strips in batches, until golden and just cooked through.

Soften the tortillas in a microwave or follow manufacturer's instructions.

Mix the green onions, red bell pepper, chilies and chicken in a bowl.

Divide chicken mixture among tortillas, folding and rolling each to enclose filling.

To re-heat, cook in batches seam-sides down in a large, hot frying pan with the remaining oil, turning occasionally until golden.

Cover each quesadilla with a slice of soy mozzarella and place under a hot broiler until the mozzarella just starts to melt. Serve immediately.

PER SERVING	
Calories	549
% Calories from fat	35
Fat (g)	21
Saturated fat (g)	3.6
Cholesterol (mg)	65.7
Sodium (mg)	756
Protein (g)	44.7
Carbohydrate (g)	42.5
Calcium (mg)	420.6
EXCHANGES	
Milk	0.0
Vegetable	0.0
Fruit	0.0
Bread	3.0
Meat	5.0
Fat	1.0

If fresh tuna is unavailable, or for a picnic, use canned tuna steak, drained and mixed with the potato salad.

Plunging cooked vegetables into cold water helps retain a good green color and prevents further cooking.

Grilled Fresh Tuna on Potato Niçoise

Serves 4

This well-balanced light meal is great for barbecues if you make salad and dressing in advance, then barbecue the fish to order.

Fresh tuna is now readily available in most supermarkets, and being an oily fish, it contains the essential fatty acids.

5–6	small new potatoes (about 8 oz)	225 g
3/4 cup	stringbeans (about 4 oz)	112 g
2 tbsp	capers, drained	2 tbsp
8	sun-dried tomatoes, oil packed, drained and chopped	8
1/4 cup	pitted black olives	1/4 cup
14	cherry tomatoes, washed and halved	14
4	6-oz tuna loin steaks cut about 3/4 inch thick	4
	double recipe of the Sun-Dried Tomato, Basil and Garlic Dressing (see page 143)	
	fresh basil to garnish	

Boil or steam the new potatoes until cooked but not too soft.

Steam the stringbeans, and when cooked but still crisp, refresh by running cold water over them.

Mix potatoes, beans, capers, sun-dried tomatoes, olives and tomatoes in bowl, and refrigerate.

To cook the tuna, lightly oil a non-stick skillet, place over a high heat, and when hot put in tuna steaks for about 1 minute.

When the tuna steaks have changed to a white color two-thirds of the way through, carefully turn the steaks and cook for a few more seconds.

Spoon the potato salad mixture onto 4 plates.

Arrange the tuna on top of the potato salad and drizzle about 2 tablespoons of dressing over the top of each plate; garnish with fresh basil leaves.

PER SERVING	
Calories	406
% Calories from fat	38
Fat (g)	17.2
Saturated fat (g)	2.5
Cholesterol (mg)	75.8
Sodium (mg)	351
Protein (g)	43.5
Carbohydrate (g)	20
Calcium (mg)	70.6
EXCHANGES	
Milk	0.0
Vegetable	1.0
Fruit	0.0
Bread	1.0
Meat	1.0
Fat	2.0

Try making this quiche with smoked haddock for another delicious combination.

Smoked Salmon and Spinach Quiche

Serves 4

Most savory quiches contain cheese; however, the combination of spinach and smoked salmon is so delicious that you forget about the missing cheese completely. Quite often fish markets will have inexpensive salmon offcuts. These are ideal for this quiche, as the salmon is chopped up. This quiche may be served hot, warm or cold with a mixed leaf or tomato salad.

4–5 cups	fresh spinach (5 oz)	140 g
1 recipe	Shortcrust Pastry (see recipe on page 187 or use a suitable bought pastry)	1 recipe
1/2 cup	soy cream cheese	110 g
2/3 cup	soy milk	160 ml
1	large egg plus 1 egg yolk, beaten	1
1 tbsp	Dijon mustard	1 tbsp
	freshly grated nutmeg	
	salt and freshly ground pepper	
1/2 cup	chopped smoked salmon (4 oz)	112 g

Pre-heat the oven to 350F. To prepare the spinach, wash well and either steam for 2 minutes or place in a large covered pan and heat until wilted; refresh by running it under cold water. Squeeze dry and chop.

Roll out the pastry on a floured surface and line a greased 8-inch quiche dish, easing any overlapping pastry back into the sides; prick base with a fork. Bake the pastry case blind, using greaseproof paper and dried beans, for 15 minutes on the center shelf.

Remove from the oven, and take out the paper and beans. Return to the oven for a few more minutes to dry.

Beat the cream cheese with the soy milk until smooth. Add the eggs, mustard, nutmeg and seasonings, stirring well.

Arrange the chopped spinach and the smoked salmon evenly on the pastry base. Pour the egg mixture over the spinach and salmon.

Bake at 350F for 25–30 minutes until the center is set and the filling golden and puffy.

PER SERVING	
Calories	374
% Calories from fat	58
Fat (g)	23.6
Saturated fat (g)	6.4
Cholesterol (mg)	65.7
Sodium (mg)	569
Protein (g)	13
Carbohydrate (g)	25.8
Calcium (mg)	42.7
EXCHANGES	
Milk	0.0
Vegetable	0.0
Fruit	0.0
Bread	2.0
Meat	1.0
Fat	4.0

You can make these and freeze them, but allow them to cool first. When thawed just heat through, covered with foil, in a warm oven.

Potato Pancakes

Serves 6 (2 pancakes per serving)

Here are some of the different toppings you could try:
– slices of smoked salmon topped with chive soy cream cheese and decorated with whole chives
– warm crispy bacon and sun-dried tomatoes sprinkled on a dollop of chive soy cream cheese
– quick-fried diced smoked salmon, capers and parsley
– for the vegan, try roasting garlic, peppers and eggplant
– mushrooms tossed in garlic, parsley and olive oil.

3 cups	quartered potatoes (weight peeled 10 oz)	280 g
3/4 cup	soy cream	180 ml
2 tbsps	vegan margarine	50 g
3 1/2 tbsps	all-purpose flour	3 1/2 tbsps
4	eggs, beaten	4
	oil for frying	
	salt, pepper and nutmeg	

Steam or boil potatoes until tender but not wet and mushy. Drain well.

In a large bowl, mash the hot potatoes with the soy cream and margarine until smooth.

Beat in the sifted flour and eggs, which should result in a thick pouring consistency. Season well with salt, pepper and nutmeg.

Heat a large lightly oiled non-stick frying pan.

Drop about half a ladle full of the mixture into the frying pan. It should spread slightly; make as many pancakes as you can fit in the pan.

Cook for about 1 minute, turn and heat the other side. They should be golden and spongy to touch when cooked.

Serve warm with different toppings. Makes about 12.

PER SERVING	
Calories	172
% Calories from fat	49
Fat (g)	9.3
Saturated fat (g)	1.8
Cholesterol (mg)	141.7
Sodium (mg)	96
Protein (g)	6.2
Carbohydrate (g)	15.1
Calcium (mg)	27.1
EXCHANGES	
Milk	0.0
Vegetable	0.0
Fruit	0.0
Bread	1.0
Meat	0.0
Fat	2.0

Many of the ingredients may be changed for a different variation. Mushrooms could be used instead of eggplant. Cashew nuts or Brazil nuts could be used instead of the hazelnuts. Yellow split peas could be used instead of the lentils.

Eggplant and Red Lentil Loaf

Serves 4–6

Savory loaves made out of nuts and legumes were one of the first dishes introduced when vegetarianism became popular. They are not really so popular now, as many other more sophisticated vegetarian dishes are the fashion. However, this type of loaf is very nutritious and often very tasty.

This loaf has the interesting addition of spices and eggplant as well as the nuts and legumes. I find the eggplant prevents the loaf from being too dry. Made in advance, it reheats very well, or have it cold the next day with a tomato salad and mixed greens and perhaps some warm brown rice. If serving this loaf hot, try serving it with the Tomato and Pimiento Coulis on page 121 and the Cucumber, Mint and Soy Yogurt Salad on page 134.

²/₃ cup	dried red lentils	150 g
2	medium onions, finely chopped	2
2 tbsps	olive oil	30 ml
1	small eggplant, cut into small cubes	1
2	cloves garlic, crushed	2
1 tbsp	mild curry powder	1 tbsp
1 tsp	cumin powder	1 tsp
1 tsp	turmeric	1 tsp
¹/₂ tsp	cilantro powder	¹/₂ tsp
1 tsp	vegan bouillon powder	1 tsp
¹/₂ cup	breadcrumbs	110 g
2 oz	hazelnuts, finely chopped	56 g
1	egg, beaten	1
2 tbsps	chopped fresh cilantro	2 tbsps
	salt and freshly ground pepper	

Pre-heat the oven to 350F. Grease and line the base of a 1 quart loaf pan.

Rinse the lentils and tip into a small saucepan. Cover with plenty of water, bring to a boil then simmer for 8–10 minutes until tender; drain and leave to dry out.

In a large saucepan, sauté the onion in the olive oil for about 3 minutes.

Add the eggplant and garlic, and continue cooking, stirring well, for about 6 minutes until soft.

VEGETARIAN

PER SERVING	
Calories	399
% Calories from fat	40
Fat (g)	18.4
Saturated fat (g)	2.3
Cholesterol (mg)	53.1
Sodium (mg)	389
Protein (g)	16.9
Carbohydrate (g)	45.8
Calcium (mg)	106.6

EXCHANGES	
Milk	0.0
Vegetable	0.0
Fruit	0.0
Bread	3.0
Meat	1.0
Fat	3.0

Stir in the curry powder, cumin, turmeric, cilantro and bouillon and sauté for several minutes to cook the spices.

Mix in the lentils, breadcrumbs and hazelnuts, until well blended.

Add the beaten egg and fresh cilantro and season well.

Pour into the prepared loaf pan and smooth down.

Bake for about 40 minutes until the top is crisp and golden and the loaf feels firm to the touch in the center. Insert a toothpick in the center of the loaf, and if it comes out very wet, cook longer.

Allow to cool for a few minutes, then turn out onto a warm plate to serve.

Larger field mushrooms have a more intense flavor than the small cup variety.

Baked Stuffed Mushrooms

Serves 4 (4 mushrooms per serving)

This is one of my favorite vegetarian dishes, especially as it is so incredibly easy to prepare with the mushrooms requiring no pre-cooking. They can be made in advance and cooked when required.

This would also be suitable as part of a buffet lunch or as a starter, using small mushrooms.

Delicious served with the Roasted Tomato Sauce on page 119 and a green salad, or as a hot main meal with the Tomato and Pimiento Coulis on page 121.

16	large brown or white mushrooms	16
1	large onion, finely chopped	1
1 tbsp	olive oil	15 ml
3	cloves garlic, crushed	3
2	ribs celery, finely chopped	2
1/2 cup	breadcrumbs	110 g
1	bunch parsley (the greener, the tastier the stuffing)	1
2	sprigs fresh thyme	2
2 oz	flaked almonds (2 tbsps)	56 g
1/2 cup	soy cheese	110 g
	salt and freshly ground pepper	
	a little extra olive oil to drizzle	

VEGAN

PER SERVING

Calories	247
% Calories from fat	51
Fat (g)	14.8
Saturated fat (g)	1.6
Cholesterol (mg)	0
Sodium (mg)	242
Protein (g)	11.1
Carbohydrate (g)	20.8
Calcium (mg)	190.1

EXCHANGES

Milk	0.0
Vegetable	1.0
Fruit	0.0
Bread	1.0
Meat	1.0
Fat	2.0

Pre-heat the oven to 375F. Wipe the mushrooms and remove the stalks; place the mushrooms in a suitable baking dish.

In a large frying pan, sauté the onion in the olive oil over medium heat for about 5 minutes until fairly soft.

Stir in the garlic and celery and sauté gently for a further 4 minutes, stirring regularly.

If making breadcrumbs in a processor, add the herbs while processing the bread. If you already have breadcrumbs, chop the herbs finely and mix them with the breadcrumbs.

Under the broiler, grill the flaked almonds until golden, turning regularly to prevent them from blackening.

In a large bowl, combine the breadcrumbs, onion mixture and almonds. Then crumble or grate in the soy cheese; mix well and season.

If the mixture seems very dry, add an extra tablespoon of olive oil to moisten it (this will hold it together better for stuffing).

Fill the mushrooms, packing the mixture in well, and drizzle with extra olive oil.

Bake in the oven for about 20–25 minutes until the mushrooms are soft and the tops are golden brown. Transfer to warm plates to serve.

Some washed and finely sliced spinach could be stirred into the hot mixture just before serving.

Garam masala is an Indian spice that may be found in ethnic aisles or at Indian grocery stores.

PER SERVING

Calories	437
% Calories from fat	22
Fat (g)	11.4
Saturated fat (g)	1.2
Cholesterol (mg)	0
Sodium (mg)	634
Protein (g)	15.3
Carbohydrate (g)	73.2
Calcium (mg)	173.2

EXCHANGES

Milk	0.0
Vegetable	0.0
Fruit	0.0
Bread	0.0
Meat	0.0
Fat	0.0

Chick Peas with Tomatoes and Cilantro

Serves 2–3

This is a nutritious and satisfying dish using chick peas, which have a distinctive nutty flavor and are one of the most versatile beans. I sometimes like to cook them so they are slightly more crunchy than the canned variety, although having a can available in the cupboard is extremely handy. Serve this with brown rice and a crisp salad or as an accompaniment to Indian dishes.

1 tbsp	vegetable oil	15 ml
1	medium onion, finely chopped	1
3	cloves garlic, crushed	3
2	small green chili peppers, de-seeded and finely chopped	2
1/2 tsp	ground paprika	1/2 tsp
1 tsp	ground cumin	1 tsp
1 tsp	ground cilantro	1 tsp
1/2 tsp	garam masala	1/2 tsp
4	large ripe tomatoes, roughly chopped	4
1 tsp	brown sugar	8 g
1	14-oz can of chick peas, drained (about 2 cups cooked from dried)	1
2 tbsps	chopped fresh cilantro	2 tbsps
	salt and pepper	

Heat the oil in a medium saucepan, add the onion and sauté gently for about 4 minutes.

Stir in the garlic, chilies and spices and continue cooking for several minutes.

Next, add the tomatoes and sugar, and simmer gently for about 10 minutes until tomatoes turn to a purée.

Stir in the chick peas and the fresh cilantro and heat for about 3 minutes until chick peas are heated through.

Season well and serve in a warm dish.

Try to use free-range eggs whenever possible.

Curried Spinach and Eggs

Serves 4

This is a very tasty, quick and nutritious supper. Serve hot with either brown rice or hot Indian naan bread.

10 cups	fresh spinach or 10 oz pkg frozen leaf spinach	280 g
1 tbsp	peanut oil	15 ml
1	medium onion, finely chopped	1
2	cloves garlic, crushed	2
1 tsp	black mustard seeds	1 tsp
2 tsps	medium curry powder	2 tsps
1 tsp	turmeric	1 tsp
1/2 tsp	chili powder	1/2 tsp
1 cup	vegetable stock	240 ml
1/2 cup	low-fat coconut milk	120 ml
	salt and freshly ground pepper	
	pinch of nutmeg	
1 tbsp	chopped fresh cilantro	1 tbsp
6	fresh eggs	6

Wash and prepare spinach. Put into a pan without water, cover and cook gently (or you could steam it above some rice). After about 5 minutes the spinach will have reduced by two-thirds (it should be just under-cooked).

Drain, rinse with cold water to retain color, squeeze all water out and roughly chop.

In a large frying pan, heat the oil and sauté onion and garlic for about 5 minutes until soft. Add the mustard seeds and powdered spices and cook, stirring well, for a further 5 minutes.

Next, mix in the stock and coconut milk and bring to a boil. Stir in the spinach, season, heat through and keep warm.

Put the eggs in a small saucepan of cold water, bring up to a boil, then gently simmer for 6–7 minutes until just hard boiled. Remove shells, and cut in half while still hot.

Serve spinach in a large warm dish and place the halved eggs on top. Sprinkle with cilantro to serve.

VEGETARIAN

PER SERVING

Calories	203
% Calories from fat	59
Fat (g)	13.4
Saturated fat (g)	4
Cholesterol (mg)	318.7
Sodium (mg)	334
Protein (g)	13
Carbohydrate (g)	8.2
Calcium (mg)	123.4

EXCHANGES

Milk	0.0
Vegetable	2.0
Fruit	0.0
Bread	0.0
Meat	1.0
Fat	2.0

I often cook this with any combination of fillings, such as peppers, mushrooms, ham, bacon, broccoli, asparagus, etc.

Potato, Bean and Corn Frittata

Serves 4

A frittata is an open Italian omelette. Unlike many omelettes, which may be creamy or runny, a frittata is set firm but not stiff and dry. It is not folded as is a conventional omelette, but consists of a single thin layer at the bottom of the pan in which it is made. Also, the filling ingredients are added to the eggs while they are uncooked, and the frittata is then cooked slowly over a low heat.

1 tbsp	olive oil	15 ml
4	green onions, washed and sliced	4
1	clove garlic, crushed	1
2 cups	cooked, diced new potatoes (1/2 lb)	225 g
3/4 cup	cooked fresh sweetcorn (scraped off the cob)	165 g
1/2 cup	stringbeans, blanched and refreshed, cut into 1/2-inch lengths (about 4 oz)	112 g
6	eggs, beaten and seasoned with salt and pepper	6
1 tbsp	chopped fresh parsley	1 tbsp
1 tbsp	vegan margarine	25 g

Using a large, heavy-based omelette pan, heat the oil and gently sauté the green onions, garlic and new potatoes for about 8 minutes until the potatoes begin to turn golden. Then add in the sweetcorn and the beans and mix well.

Break the eggs into a large bowl and whisk until well blended; stir in the parsley.

Tip the vegetables from the pan into the eggs, and mix thoroughly until all the ingredients are well combined. Pre-heat the broiler.

Wipe out the omelette pan, then gently heat the margarine until it is beginning to foam but not burning.

Tip in the egg and vegetable mixture and smooth down. Cook over low to medium heat for about 8 minutes until the eggs have set and only the surface is runny.

Place the pan under the hot broiler and cook the top for about 3 minutes until golden and slightly risen.

Cut into 4 large wedges, and slide each onto a serving dish to serve.

VEGETARIAN	

PER SERVING	
Calories	270
% Calories from fat	45
Fat (g)	14
Saturated fat (g)	3.4
Cholesterol (mg)	318.7
Sodium (mg)	137
Protein (g)	12.2
Carbohydrate (g)	25.1
Calcium (mg)	65.9
EXCHANGES	
Milk	0.0
Vegetable	0.0
Fruit	0.0
Bread	2.0
Meat	1.0
Fat	2.0

There are two readily available varieties of sweet potato, one being bright orange inside when cooked, the other yellow with a chestnut flavor. Either sort would be suitable.

Sweet Potato and Chick Pea Cakes

Serves 4 (2 cakes per serving)

These crispy cakes are packed with flavor and goodness. They are ideal as a meal on their own or as a side dish. Serve hot with Tomato and Sweet Chili Relish (see page 122) and perhaps the Cucumber, Mint and Soy Yogurt Salad (see page 134).

1	large or 2 smaller sweet potatoes (about 1 lb)	1
1	medium onion, finely chopped	1
1	small leek, washed, finely chopped	1
3	cloves garlic, crushed	3
3 tbsps	vegetable oil	45 ml
1 tsp	vegan bouillon powder	1 tsp
1	green chili pepper, chopped finely, seeds discarded (optional)	1
1 1/2 tsps	ground cumin	1 1/2 tsps
1/2 tsp	ground cilantro	1/2 tsp
1/2 tsp	ground turmeric	1/2 tsp
1	14-oz can chick peas, drained (about 2 cups cooked from dried)	1
	salt and freshly ground pepper	
1 tbsp	all-purpose flour	1 tbsp
1 tbsp	sesame seeds	1 tbsp

Pre-heat the oven to 350F. Peel, cube and steam or boil sweet potato for 10–15 minutes until soft.

Drain well and, using a potato masher, mash until smooth.

Sauté the onion, leek and garlic in a frying pan in 1 tablespoon oil for about 15 minutes over medium heat, until soft.

Add the bouillon powder, chili and spices into the pan, stir well and continue cooking for 2 minutes.

In a large bowl, mash the chick peas, leaving them slightly chunky.

Add the onion mixture and sweet potatoes to the chick peas, combining well.

Season with salt and pepper, and leave to cool slightly.

On a large plate, mix the flour with the sesame seeds.

VEGAN

PER SERVING

Calories	386
% Calories from fat	30
Fat (g)	13.1
Saturated fat (g)	1.7
Cholesterol (mg)	0
Sodium (mg)	566
Protein (g)	8.6
Carbohydrate (g)	60
Calcium (mg)	112.8

EXCHANGES

Milk	0.0
Vegetable	0.0
Fruit	0.0
Bread	4.0
Meat	0.0
Fat	2.0

Divide the potato mixture into 8 and shape into round cakes about 1 inch thick. Roll each cake in the flour and sesame seeds.

In a large, clean frying pan, heat the remaining oil and fry the cakes for 4 minutes on each side over medium heat until golden.

Place on a baking sheet and finish off in the oven for 10 minutes until heated through.

Main Dishes—Fish, Meat and Vegetarian

Spicy Fillet of Beef Stroganoff

Rich Braised Beef

Seared Calves' Liver with Bacon and Wine Sauce

Chili Chicken with Basil and Coconut

Creole Chicken

Chicken Casseroled in Cider with Mushrooms and Mustard

Chicken and Mushroom Pie

Chicken Breasts with Mushroom, Bacon and Tarragon Sauce

Duck Breast with Orange and Red Wine Sauce

Roasted Leg of Duck with Ginger and Honey

Lamb Hot Pot with Pearl Barley

Marinated Lamb Kebabs

Lamb Tagine

Pork Steak with Hazelnut and Sage Crust

Fillet of Trout, East Indian Style

Grilled Fillet of Trout with Watercress Sauce

Fish, Shrimp and Leek Pie

Cajun Blackened Fish

Pan-Fried Tuna Steaks with Salsa Verde

Broiled Catfish with Soy, Honey and Horseradish Dressing

Crusted Fillet of Cod

Monkfish and Shrimp Brochettes

Crunchy Oat-Coated Mahi-Mahi Fillets

Potato-Crusted Haddock and Curried Tomato Bake

Smoked Fish Cakes

Smoked Trout Rarebit

Split Pea and Vegetable Pot Pie

Individual Mushroom and Walnut Strudels

This dish is also delicious made with pork fillet and more economical. If using pork fillet, cut in strips. They will need to be cooked slightly longer to ensure the pork is thoroughly cooked through, whereas beef fillet can be served slightly pink.

Spicy Fillet of Beef Stroganoff

Serves 4

This classic stroganoff is made with thin strips of beef fillet, which are cooked very quickly. I added cayenne to give it a bit of a kick! Serve this stroganoff with rice and some green vegetables.

1 lb	beef fillet mignon or tenderloin	450 g
1/2 lb	small button mushrooms, wiped	225 g
1 1/2 tbsp	vegan margarine	37 g
1	medium onion, halved and thinly sliced	1
1 1/4 tsp	cayenne pepper	1 1/4 tsp
1 cup	(scant) dry white wine or dry cider	240 ml
1 cup	(scant) good beef stock (chicken stock will also do)	240 ml
1/2 tbsp	vegetable oil	8 ml
3 tbsps	brandy	45 ml
3 tbsps	soy cream	45 ml
	salt and freshly ground black pepper	
	freshly ground nutmeg	
1 tbsp	chopped parsley	1 tbsp

Cut the beef fillet into thin strips 1/4 inch wide, 1/4 inch thick and 2 1/2 inches long. Trim the stalks and slice the mushrooms. Melt the margarine in a frying pan over medium heat, and cook the onion for about 5 minutes until soft.

Stir in the mushrooms and 1 teaspoon cayenne, increase the heat and cook for about 2 minutes.

Pour the wine over the mushrooms and allow to boil for a few seconds, then add the stock. Continue simmering until the liquid is about half the initial amount. Pour out into a bowl.

Heat the oil in a large, clean, heavy frying pan as hot as possible without burning. Drop in the beef strips.

Shake and toss over a fast heat to brown and seal the edges without overcooking in the middle. Take pan off the heat. Remove beef strips from pan.

Pour the brandy into the fairly hot pan. Set light to the brandy and when flames die down, pour in mushroom and stock mixture. Return the meat and allow to heat through for several minutes. Gently stir in 2 tablespoons of the soy cream, add salt and pepper and a good grating of fresh nutmeg. Serve in a warm serving dish.

Drizzle top with remaining soy cream and sprinkle the remaining 1/4 teaspoon of cayenne over the soy cream. Finely sprinkle the chopped parsley over the beef.

PER SERVING	
Calories	459
% Calories from fat	64
Fat (g)	30.1
Saturated fat (g)	10.4
Cholesterol (mg)	77.5
Sodium (mg)	608
Protein (g)	23.2
Carbohydrate (g)	6.8
Calcium (mg)	25.3

EXCHANGES	
Milk	0.0
Vegetable	1.0
Fruit	0.0
Bread	0.0
Meat	3.0
Fat	6.0

Rich Braised Beef

Serves 6

This is a wonderful way of cooking tougher cuts of meat and fairly easy to make. I quite often cook this for friends coming to supper, as it can be prepared well in advance and improves after a day or two. I have used round of beef, which is easy to prepare and has little wastage. Simply slice across in steak-like pieces, which looks much nicer than a casserole with small cubes of meat. Serve with baked or new potatoes, and the sauce from the pan will be enough to make them delicious without the need to add a butter substitute. This dish may be served with rice or potatoes and vegetables.

1½ lb	round of beef	675 g
8 oz	piece of lightly smoked bacon (buy whole from butcher)	225 g
1 tbsp	oil	15 ml
2	medium onions, sliced	2
3	cloves garlic, crushed	3
2	ribs celery, chopped	2
	seasoned flour (all-purpose flour with salt and pepper)	
1	bottle of red wine	750 ml
2 cups	good beef stock	480 ml
	a few sprigs of fresh thyme, stalks removed	
2	bay leaves	2
	salt and pepper	

Pre-heat the oven to 300F. Trim the meat and cut it into steak-like pieces (or ask butcher to do so) about 1 inch thick.

Next trim off the rind and excess fat from the bacon, and cut it into ¼-inch chunks.

Heat 1 teaspoon oil in a large frying pan. Fry the onions, garlic and celery for a few minutes, then tip them into a large, deep casserole dish.

Stir the bacon into the hot pan and fry for 1 minute; tip into the casserole dish with the onions.

Toss the meat in the seasoned flour. Heat remaining oil in the pan and brown the beef pieces very well, a few at a time. Place into the casserole dish when browned.

If the bottom of the pan becomes dark or too dry, remove the beef and pour in a little wine; scrape any sediment stuck on the

PER SERVING	
Calories	543
% Calories from fat	49
Fat (g)	25.4
Saturated fat (g)	8.2
Cholesterol (mg)	96.6
Sodium (mg)	1360
Protein (g)	38.9
Carbohydrate (g)	14.3
Calcium (mg)	37.2
EXCHANGES	
Milk	0.0
Vegetable	0.0
Fruit	0.0
Bread	1.0
Meat	6.0
Fat	3.0

bottom of the pan (this is called deglazing). Pour the pan liquid into the casserole dish. When all the meat is browned, deglaze the pan once more. Pour any remaining wine over the beef in the casserole dish, followed by the stock, thyme and bay leaves.

Cover the casserole dish with aluminum foil. Bake slowly for 3 hours or until meat is tender.

After this time, adjust the sauce by pouring all the liquid into a saucepan, leaving the meat in the casserole dish. Bring the liquid to a boil, and simmer until it has reduced by half and becomes slightly thicker and stronger tasting; season well with salt and pepper. (I sometimes add a dash of dark soy sauce instead of salt, which gives a good dark color to the sauce.) Pour sauce over the meat.

Return to the oven, uncovered, for about 10 minutes. Serve hot from the oven.

When buying calves' liver, it should be milky brown in color with a fine even texture.

Avoid pork liver, except for making pâtés and terrines.

Seared Calves' Liver with Bacon and Wine Sauce

Serves 4

The liver is best served slightly pink in the middle; if overcooked it becomes tougher and darker. Serve with potatoes and green vegetables.

1 tbsp	sunflower oil	15 ml
4	shallots, peeled and finely chopped	4
6	slices smoked back bacon, finely chopped	6
2 tsps	all-purpose flour	2 tsps
1¹/₂ tbsps	sherry vinegar	23 ml
¹/₂ cup	red wine	120 ml
1 cup	good beef stock	240 ml
1 tsp	chopped fresh sage	1 tsp
1 tsp	sugar	16 g
	salt and freshly ground pepper	
1 lb	calves' liver, ask butcher to slice into 4 slices each about ¹/₂ inch thick	450 g

PER SERVING	
Calories	294
% Calories from fat	47
Fat (g)	14.3
Saturated fat (g)	4.3
Cholesterol (mg)	360.6
Sodium (mg)	767
Protein (g)	24.9
Carbohydrate (g)	9.7
Calcium (mg)	27.3
EXCHANGES	
Milk	0.0
Vegetable	0.0
Fruit	0.0
Bread	0.5
Meat	3.0
Fat	2.0

	all-purpose flour for dusting	
	dash of oil for frying	
8	extra sage leaves for garnishing	8

Heat the oil in a small saucepan, and add the shallots and bacon. Cook slowly for 10 to 15 minutes until the shallots are soft and beginning to caramelize.

Sprinkle the flour over the shallots and stir well over medium heat for about half a minute; remove pan from the heat.

Pour in the vinegar and red wine and, stirring well, return to the heat.

Add the stock, sage and sugar and bring to a boil, then simmer for 5 minutes until the sauce thickens slightly. Season well.

To cook the calves' liver, heat a large, heavy frying pan, brushed with oil, to a high temperature.

Lightly dust the liver with some extra flour, and season with pepper.

Place the liver on the hot pan for about 2 minutes until the heat has cooked the liver through almost to the top.

Quickly flip over the liver, and cook briefly on the other side before serving browned underside up on warmed plates.

Reheat the sauce and carefully pour over the liver.

Garnish each portion with 2 fresh sage leaves and serve immediately.

An alternative to Chinese 5 spice powder is Thai 7 spice seasoning. It contains chili powder, garlic, cilantro powder, ground lemon peel, cinnamon, cumin, star anise, onion powder, jalapeño powder and cloves. If you cannot find it, use a combination of these spices from your cupboard.

For a vegan dish, omit the chicken and try using sautéed mushrooms, eggplant and chick peas. Be sure to use soy sauce and not fish sauce.

Chili Chicken with Basil and Coconut

Serves 4

This Thai-style chicken stir-fry is very quick and easy to prepare and makes a delicious meal served with Thai fragrant rice and salad.

Coconut milk, although fairly sweet, is a great addition to the lactose-free diet, as it not only contains some calcium but also gives dishes a lovely creamy taste. It is particularly good in Thai-style dishes, which have a hot and sweet taste.

4	chicken breast fillets (about 4 oz each)	4
2 tbsps	peanut oil	30 ml
1	onion, finely chopped	1
1	red chili pepper, de-seeded and finely sliced	1
1	red bell pepper, de-seeded and finely diced	1
2 tsps	Chinese 5 spice powder	2 tsps
2 tsps	chili sauce	2 tsps
2 tbsps	fish sauce or soy sauce	30 ml
1	large bunch fresh basil, shredded (save a few leaves for garnishing)	1
1	14-oz can coconut milk	1

Skin the chicken breasts and cut into 1/2-inch strips.

Heat a wok with the oil and quickly stir-fry the onion, chili and bell peppers for about 2 minutes, stirring constantly.

Stir in the chicken strips and 5 spice seasoning and sauté for about 3 minutes until chicken is tender.

Pour the chili sauce and fish sauce over the chicken and cook for a further minute.

Stir in the shredded basil leaves and the coconut milk, and simmer gently until well heated through.

Serve in a warmed dish.

PER SERVING	
Calories	462
% Calories from fat	64
Fat (g)	33.7
Saturated fat (g)	23.8
Cholesterol (mg)	65.7
Sodium (mg)	813
Protein (g)	30.2
Carbohydrate (g)	12.7
Calcium (mg)	60.6
EXCHANGES	
Milk	1.0
Vegetable	0.0
Fruit	0.0
Bread	0.0
Meat	3.0
Fat	5.0

Also delicious made with fillet of fish, shrimp or fillet of pork.

Creole Chicken

Serves 4

This Cajun-style dish has a rich and spicy flavor. The fiery heat of the dish is mellowed down by the addition of soy cream. Serve with the Spicy Potato Wedges on page 105 or with plain rice.

2 tbsps	all-purpose flour	2 tbsps
2 tbsps	sweet paprika	2 tbsps
2 tbsps	Cajun spice	2 tbsps
4	chicken breasts (about 4 oz each)	4
2 tbsps	olive oil	30 ml
1	large onion, chopped	1
2	cloves garlic, crushed	2
1	large red bell pepper (or 2 small), de-seeded, halved and sliced	1
1³/₄ cups	vegetable or chicken stock	420 ml
1 cup	(scant) soy cream	240 ml
¹/₂ tsp	dried basil	¹/₂ tsp

Mix the flour, paprika and Cajun spice on a large plate. Skin the chicken breasts and cut them into large chunks; roll them in the spiced flour mixture.

Heat a medium saucepan with 1 tablespoon oil. Sauté the onion, garlic and bell peppers for about 5 minutes over medium heat.

As soon as the onions are beginning to soften, tip the remaining spiced flour mixture into the pan. Cook gently for about a minute, stirring well.

Remove the pan from the heat and gradually add the stock. Return the sauce to the heat, bring to a boil, stirring constantly, and cook for about 1 minute until the sauce thickens.

Heat a large frying pan with the remaining oil. Sear the chicken pieces for several minutes on either side until golden.

Pour the sauce over the chicken and simmer for about 4 minutes.

Stir in the soy cream and basil and gently heat through. Serve the chicken on warm plates. Serve immediately.

PER SERVING	
Calories	297
% Calories from fat	40
Fat (g)	13.1
Saturated fat (g)	1.4
Cholesterol (mg)	65.7
Sodium (mg)	519
Protein (g)	28.6
Carbohydrate (g)	14.9
Calcium (mg)	32.6

EXCHANGES	
Milk	0.0
Vegetable	0.0
Fruit	0.0
Bread	1.0
Meat	3.0
Fat	1.0

Rather than cutting up a whole chicken, you may find it easier to use pre-cut chicken thighs and drumsticks. This also allows you to choose better quality chicken—the thighs and legs of organic or free-range chicken are often much cheaper than the breast. Allow for one whole thigh per person.

Chicken Casseroled in Cider with Mushrooms and Mustard

Serves 4–5

This delicious rich casserole could be served with a crisp jacket potato, steamed potatoes or brown rice. The addition of a mild variety of mustard blends with the stock and cider to give a rich, creamy sauce without the addition of a cream substitute. This casserole may be prepared a day or two in advance. It is also suitable for freezing so long as the chicken has not been previously frozen.

4 lb	roasting chicken, skin removed	1.8 kg
1 tbsp	all-purpose flour seasoned with salt and pepper	1 tbsp
2 tbsps	vegetable oil	30 ml
1	onion, finely chopped	1
1¼ cups	button mushrooms, halved (7 oz)	196 g
1¼ cups	dry cider (white wine could also be used)	300 ml
3 tbsps	Dijon mustard (mild variety)	3 tbsps
1¼ cups	chicken stock (preferably made earlier using chicken carcass)	300 ml
2	sprigs fresh thyme	2
1 tbsp	chopped parsley	1 tbsp

Pre-heat the oven to 375F. Cut-up the chicken into 8 pieces, and roll the pieces in the seasoned flour.

Heat a large frying pan with 1 tablespoon oil, and brown the pieces for approximately 4 minutes on either side. Remove the chicken pieces from the pan, and place in suitable oven casserole dish.

Heat the remaining oil and sauté the onion and mushrooms for about 4 minutes. Sprinkle over the remaining plain flour and stir well. Gradually pour in the cider and mustard, stirring well, and bring to a boil. Stir in the stock, mixing well, bring to a boil and allow to simmer for several minutes. Season with extra salt and freshly ground pepper if necessary, and add the thyme leaves pulled off their stalks. Pour this sauce over the browned chicken pieces.

Cover with foil and bake in the oven for about 1 hour until tender. Remove from the oven; the sauce should be the consistency of single cream. Garnish with chopped parsley before serving.

PER SERVING	
Calories	474
% Calories from fat	34
Fat (g)	16.8
Saturated fat (g)	3.4
Cholesterol (mg)	211
Sodium (mg)	588
Protein (g)	61.2
Carbohydrate (g)	7.7
Calcium (mg)	58.5

EXCHANGES	
Milk	0.0
Vegetable	0.0
Fruit	0.5
Bread	0.0
Meat	8.0
Fat	0.0

Chicken and Mushroom Pie

Serves 4

This traditional pie is perfect for a cold winter's day. It can be prepared in advance and kept chilled with the uncooked pastry top. Serve with some steamed Brussell's sprouts or spring greens.

2 tbsps	sunflower oil	30 ml
1	onion, finely chopped	1
2 tbsps	all-purpose flour	2 tbsps
1¼ cups	good strong chicken stock	300 ml
½ cup	soy milk	120 ml
1 tsp	chopped fresh tarragon or ½ teaspoon dried tarragon	1 tsp
1 tsp	Dijon mustard	1 tsp
	salt and freshly ground pepper	
¼ cup	soy cream	60 ml
3 lb	whole chicken, poached, skinned, boned and cut into large chunks	1.35 kg
1½ cups	button mushrooms, wiped and sliced (8 oz)	225 g
1 recipe	Shortcrust Pastry (see page 187)	1 recipe
	1 beaten egg mixed with pinch of salt and 1 teaspoon water (egg wash)	

Pre-heat the oven to 375F. Heat 1 tablespoon of oil in a large saucepan and sauté the onion for about 8 minutes until soft but not brown.

Remove the pan from heat, and stir in the flour. Return to a low heat and cook for 2 minutes until the flour is a pale golden brown.

Remove the pan from the heat, and gradually blend in the chicken stock.

Return once more to medium heat, and stir until you have a thick, shiny sauce.

Pour in the soy milk, stirring well, and gently bring the sauce to a boil.

Stir in the tarragon, mustard, seasoning and soy cream, and simmer for 2 minutes. Taste and add more seasoning if necessary. Allow to cool.

In a clean frying pan, heat up the remaining oil. When hot, quickly sauté the mushrooms for about 4 minutes until just cooked. Allow to cool slightly.

This same dish can be done with rabbit or pheasant instead of chicken.

Also you could just roast legs and thighs for this dish and save the breast, which would make it more economical.

Wait until the filling is cold before topping with pastry.

PER SERVING	
Calories	771
% Calories from fat	46
Fat (g)	38.1
Saturated fat (g)	9.2
Cholesterol (mg)	249.7
Sodium (mg)	450
Protein (g)	69.5
Carbohydrate (g)	33.3
Calcium (mg)	60.5
EXCHANGES	
Milk	0.0
Vegetable	0.0
Fruit	0.0
Bread	2.0
Meat	9.0
Fat	3.0

Roll the pastry on a floured board into a large ¼-inch-thick oval. Using an upturned oval pie dish, in which you will be baking the pie, cut around the pastry rim, making a lid for the pie.

Tip the mushrooms and the chicken into the sauce, mix well and then pour into the pie dish.

Wet the edge of the pastry and lift it, wet side down, onto the pie.

Use any leftover pastry to decorate the top of the pie if you wish.

Prick the top with a fork several times. Brush with beaten egg.

Bake for about 30 minutes, until the pastry top is golden and risen and the pie is well heated through.

This dish could be made with pheasant or guinea fowl breast.

Chicken Breasts with Mushroom, Bacon and Tarragon Sauce

Serves 4

This sauce makes a plain chicken breast into something rich and exotic. The peppercorns give an interesting spicy addition. Ideal served with rice or potatoes.

2 tbsps	olive oil	30 ml
4	chicken breasts, excess fat and skin removed	4
1	large onion, peeled, halved and sliced	1
2–3 slices	unsmoked bacon, finely chopped	2–3 slices
1½ cups	mushrooms, thinly sliced (8 oz)	225 g
½ cup	dry white wine	120 ml
2 tsps	chopped fresh tarragon	2 tsps
1 cup	(scant) vegetable or chicken stock	220 ml
1 cup	(scant) soy cream	220 ml
	salt and freshly ground pepper	

PER SERVING	
Calories	315
% Calories from fat	43
Fat (g)	14.4
Saturated fat (g)	2
Cholesterol (mg)	69.1
Sodium (mg)	271
Protein (g)	29
Carbohydrate (g)	9.5
Calcium (mg)	28.2
EXCHANGES	
Milk	0.0
Vegetable	1.0
Fruit	0.0
Bread	0.0
Meat	4.0
Fat	2.0

Pre-heat the oven to 350F. Heat a large non-stick frying pan with 1 tablespoon of the olive oil. When hot, add chicken breasts and sear for about 1 minute on each side until golden brown.

Place in an oven dish and bake for 15–20 minutes. Meanwhile, add the remaining olive oil to the frying pan and sauté the onion for about 5 minutes until just soft.

Add the bacon and mushrooms and, stirring well, continue cooking for a further 5 minutes.

Pour in the wine, tarragon and stock and bring to a boil; cook for about 4 minutes.

Lastly, add the soy cream, stir well and season, then warm over low heat.

Remove chicken from the oven and slice each breast in half on a diagonal. The meat should be white throughout; if any pinkness remains, cook the chicken longer.

When the chicken is done, arrange it on warm plates and spoon over the sauce.

Slashing the duck breast helps to cook it evenly and also releases more of the fat. Leaving the duck breast to rest for 5 minutes before carving will make the meat more tender.

Duck Breast with Orange and Red Wine Sauce

Serves 6

Duck breasts are increasingly easy to find nowadays and extremely popular with most people. They are best cooked at a higher temperature for a short time and served slightly pink in the middle.

This is a great dish when you want to serve something special. Make the sauce in advance and reheat to serve. Delicious served with the Potato and Celeriac Boulangère (see page 102), or try with the Stir-Fried Cabbage and Carrots with Caraway (see page 98).

1 tbsp	vegetable oil	15 ml
1	large onion, sliced	1
3	ribs of celery, chopped	3
2/3 cup	chopped mushroom stalks (4 oz)	112 g
1	carrot, sliced	1
1 1/4 cups	red wine	300 ml
2 1/2 cups	chicken stock	600 ml
	sprig of thyme	
2	bay leaves	2
1/2 cup	orange juice	120 ml
	zest of one orange	
4	duck breasts, trim excess fat (6 oz each)	4
	salt and freshly ground pepper	

Pre-heat the oven to 425F. In a large saucepan, heat the oil and cook the onion, celery, mushroom stalks and carrot for about 10 minutes until they begin to brown but not burn.

Pour in the red wine to deglaze the pan, and allow to boil for a few seconds.

Next, add the stock and herbs and simmer uncovered for about 30 minutes, until it has reduced by about two-thirds.

Pass everything through a fine sieve, and put back the gravy along with the orange juice and zest. Set aside until you begin to cook the duck.

PER SERVING	
Calories	563
% Calories from fat	41
Fat (g)	25.1
Saturated fat (g)	6.5
Cholesterol (mg)	313.1
Sodium (mg)	326
Protein (g)	65.1
Carbohydrate (g)	7.8
Calcium (mg)	45.2

EXCHANGES	
Milk	0.0
Vegetable	1.0
Fruit	0.0
Bread	0.0
Meat	9.0
Fat	1.0

Slash the skin of the duck diagonally about 4 times on each breast, and season with salt and pepper.

Heat a large pan (preferably one with oven-proof handles) until hot, and add duck breasts skin side up.

Cook for 2 minutes, then turn skin side down and cook for a further 2 minutes.

Pour off excess duck fat, and put duck breasts in the oven for a further 10 minutes. Remove from oven and allow to rest for 5 minutes.

Meanwhile, return the sauce to the stove, bring to a boil and simmer for about 5 minutes until it begins to thicken slightly.

Pour any excess juices (not the fat) from the duck breasts into the sauce.

Slice each duck breast into about 4 diagonal slices, and place slices on a warm plate. Pour over the hot sauce before serving.

Chicken legs could be used instead of duck.

Roasted Leg of Duck with Ginger and Honey

Serves 4

Duck legs are often the most affordable way of buying duck. As with chicken legs, duck legs benefit from a longer, slower roasting time, and as a result, they will be tender and well cooked. For this recipe I have slashed the duck legs prior to marinating, which allows the spices to infuse into the duck, and this, along with the ginger and honey, gives the duck a delicious oriental taste. The longer you can marinate the duck legs, the more the flavor will develop. Serve with Sesame Noodles on page 107 and some stir-fry vegetables.

4	duck legs, about 2½ oz each, skin removed	4
4 tsps	Chinese 5 spice powder	4 tsps
1 inch	fresh gingerroot, peeled and very finely chopped	2.5 cm
¼ cup	honey	¼ cup
4 tsps	dark soy sauce	20 ml
4 tsps	light soy sauce	20 ml

   Slash the duck legs with a sharp knife and rub them over with the Chinese 5 spice.
   Lay the duck legs in an oven-proof dish and allow to marinate in the fridge for 3 hours or overnight.
   Pre-heat the oven to 350F. Place the duck legs in the oven for 40 minutes until well cooked through. Remove from the oven, and drain off any surrounding fat.
   In a small bowl, mix together the ginger, honey and the light and dark soy sauces. Drizzle over duck legs and serve.

PER SERVING	
Calories	213
% Calories from fat	20
Fat (g)	4.6
Saturated fat (g)	1
Cholesterol (mg)	78.7
Sodium (mg)	619
Protein (g)	22.7
Carbohydrate (g)	19.7
Calcium (mg)	31.1
EXCHANGES	
Milk	0.0
Vegetable	0.0
Fruit	1.0
Bread	0.0
Meat	3.0
Fat	0.0

For variety, place a layer of thinly sliced peeled potato on the top 40 minutes before the end of the cooking time.

Lamb Hot Pot with Pearl Barley

Serves 8

This rustic dish contains almost all the ingredients for a complete meal, although perhaps a baked potato served alongside to mop up all the juice would make it more complete! I have used pearl barley, which provides a good source of calcium as well as an interesting nutty flavor to the dish. By cooking the meat on the bone, it remains more succulent and tender.

2½ lb	lean shoulder cut of lamb	1.125 kg
3½ cups	good stock (beef, lamb or chicken)	840 ml
1	large onion, sliced	1
3	ribs celery, cut into ½-inch chunks	3
5	carrots, cut into 1-inch chunks	5
3	bay leaves	3
1	sprig of fresh rosemary	1
3 tbsps	pearl barley	75 g
	salt and freshly ground pepper	

Pre-heat the oven to 350F. Cut the meat into chops, trimming away excess fat.

Heat a heavy pan without oil (as the lamb is naturally quite fatty), and sauté the lamb to brown all sides of it.

Place the browned lamb chops into a large casserole dish.

Deglaze the pan with a splash of the stock, scraping the bottom of the pan to remove all the sediment.

Place the onion, celery, carrot and herbs in the casserole dish with the lamb.

Pour over the stock and pearl barley. Season and cover with aluminum foil.

Place in oven and cook for 2 hours (remove foil after 1 hour, and continue cooking uncovered). The lamb should be tender and beginning to fall away from the bone. Check the sauce for seasoning.

Serve hot from the casserole dish.

PER SERVING	
Calories	379
% Calories from fat	61
Fat (g)	25.2
Saturated fat (g)	10.6
Cholesterol (mg)	98.7
Sodium (mg)	969
Protein (g)	26.2
Carbohydrate (g)	10.3
Calcium (mg)	45.8
EXCHANGES	
Milk	0.0
Vegetable	0.0
Fruit	0.0
Bread	1.0
Meat	3.0
Fat	3.0

Made into smaller kebabs, it could also be a little starter served with Tomato and Sweet Chili Relish (see page 122).

Don't forget to soak the wooden skewers before threading on the meat to prevent charring.

Marinated Lamb Kebabs

Serves 6

These Middle Eastern-style kebabs remind me of summer barbecues. It is one of my husband's favorite dishes, which I often cook served with Spiced Rice, see page 109, a Tomato and Mint Salsa, see page 120, and a Cucumber, Mint and Soy Yogurt Salad, see page 134, for a perfect combination. In this recipe I have broiled the kebabs; however, they are also perfect for barbecuing.

1½ lb	cubed lean leg of lamb	675 g
3 tbsps	olive oil	45 ml
2 tbsps	soy sauce	30 ml
1	large sprig of rosemary, leaves pulled off the stalk	1
4	cloves garlic, crushed	4
2	red or green bell peppers	2
2	onions	2
12	bay leaves	12
6	wooden or metal skewers	6
1	lemon to garnish	1

In a large bowl, mix the lamb pieces with the olive oil, soy sauce, rosemary and garlic.

Put in the fridge to marinate for 4 hours or more.

Cut peppers and onions into ¾-inch squares.

Thread the lamb pieces onto the skewers, alternating each piece of lamb with a square of onion, then pepper; thread 2 bay leaves on each skewer.

Place on high shelf under hot broiler for 4–6 minutes each side, until the outside is well browned and the inside is still slightly pink and juicy.

Serve with wedges of lemon.

PER SERVING	
Calories	315
% Calories from fat	62
Fat (g)	21.6
Saturated fat (g)	7.2
Cholesterol (mg)	75.3
Sodium (mg)	394
Protein (g)	22.3
Carbohydrate (g)	7.9
Calcium (mg)	35.7
EXCHANGES	
Milk	0.0
Vegetable	1.0
Fruit	0.0
Bread	0.0
Meat	3.0
Fat	3.0

Follow the recipe using chicken legs and thighs to make Chicken Tagine.

This dish is equally delicious made with dried apricots.

Lamb Tagine

Serves 8

This Moroccan meat stew derives its name from its traditional round dish with a conical lid resembling a pointed hat. The pieces of meat are slow cooked with spices and either prunes or apricots. The generous quantities of black pepper and spices provide a delicate balance with the sweetness of the fruit. I have used boned shoulder of lamb, although leg of lamb would be equally good. You could serve this dish with the traditional accompaniment of couscous and a crisp salad.

1 cup	pitted dried prunes (8 oz)	225 g
2 lb	boned shoulder of lamb	900 g
1 tbsp	all-purpose flour	1 tbsp
2 tsps	ground cumin	2 tsps
1 tsp	ground cinnamon	1 tsp
2 tsps	ground cilantro	2 tsps
1 tsp	ground black pepper	1 tsp
2 tbsps	vegetable oil	30 ml
1	large onion, finely chopped	1
2	cloves garlic, crushed	2
3 cups	good stock (beef, lamb or chicken)	720 ml
	salt	
1 tbsp	chopped fresh cilantro	1 tbsp

Put the prunes in a small bowl and pour over enough water to cover completely. Leave to soak overnight.

Pre-heat the oven to 325F.

Cut the lamb into large chunks about 2 x 2 inches and remove excess fat, skin and gristle.

On a large plate, mix the flour, cumin, cinnamon, cilantro and pepper. Roll the lamb pieces in the flour mixture, coating well.

Heat a large frying pan with half a tablespoon of oil, and brown half of the lamb pieces. Place lamb pieces in a large casserole dish or a tagine. Brown the rest of the lamb in another half a tablespoon of oil, and place in the dish.

Add remaining 1 tablespoon of oil to the pan with the onion and garlic, cook for about 2 minutes then tip in the remaining flour and spice mixture.

Stir for 1 minute, then gradually pour in half of the stock and mix well.

PER SERVING	
Calories	249
% Calories from fat	33
Fat (g)	9
Saturated fat (g)	2.3
Cholesterol (mg)	73
Sodium (mg)	809
Protein (g)	24.8
Carbohydrate (g)	17
Calcium (mg)	36.7
EXCHANGES	
Milk	0.0
Vegetable	0.0
Fruit	1.0
Bread	0.0
Meat	3.0
Fat	0.0

Pour this sauce and the remaining stock over the lamb, cover with foil and bake for 1½ hours until the meat is tender and beginning to fall apart.

Remove from oven and pour off the liquid into a medium saucepan. Stir the prunes and their soaking liquid into the saucepan. Bring to a boil over medium heat, and reduce until slightly thick; you should have about ¾ pint of liquid.

Season well with salt. Pour over the lamb and either leave to cool until required or reheat in the oven until piping hot, approximately 20 minutes. Sprinkle with fresh cilantro to serve.

This could be made with roast of pork, cut into medallions, or for a more economical dish use pork chops.

Pork Steak with Hazelnut and Sage Crust

Serves 4

In this recipe a simple pork steak is coated in a crisp hazelnut and sage crust, transforming it into something far more exotic. I recommend you make the Cider and Wholegrain Mustard Sauce (see page 115) to complement the pork steak perfectly.

2⅓ cups	hazelnuts (5 oz)	140 g
10	fresh sage leaves	10
4	lean leg of pork steaks, off the bone (4 oz each)	450 g
1 tbsp	all-purpose flour, seasoned with salt and pepper	1 tbsp
1	large egg, beaten	1
1 tbsp	soy milk	15 ml
1 tsp	vegetable oil	5 ml
	salt and pepper	

In a food processor, grind the hazelnuts with the sage leaves until quite fine but not completely powdery. Tip onto a large plate. Trim any excess fat off the pork, and roll in the seasoned flour. Next, coat the floured pork steaks evenly in the beaten egg mixed with the soy milk.

Lastly, roll the pork steaks in the hazelnut and sage mixture. Refrigerate until needed. Pre-heat the oven to 400F.

In a large frying pan, bring the oil to medium heat.

Place the pork in the hot fat, and cook for several minutes until golden brown. Turn over and repeat on other side.

Put the pork steaks in an oven-proof dish, and bake in oven for about 8 minutes.

PER SERVING	
Calories	694
% Calories from fat	71
Fat (g)	56.6
Saturated fat (g)	6.2
Cholesterol (mg)	121.9
Sodium (mg)	68
Protein (g)	37.6
Carbohydrate (g)	15.3
Calcium (mg)	128.5

EXCHANGES	
Milk	0.0
Vegetable	0.0
Fruit	0.0
Bread	1.0
Meat	3.0
Fat	10.0

This could also be done with whole trout. Slash the skin with 3 diagonal cuts on both sides and marinate. Cook under a hot broiler for about 4 minutes on either side so that the skin turns crispy brown.

Try this dish using other fish fillets such as salmon, cod or haddock.

Garam masala is a blend of spices you can find in Indian markets or ethnic food sections.

Fillet of Trout, East Indian Style

Serves 4

For anyone who may find plain fish bland, this dish is interesting in both color and flavor. Serve with Minted Yogurt Sauce on page 116, some brown rice and a salad.

2 tsps	grated fresh gingerroot	2 tsps
2	cloves garlic, crushed	2
1 tsp	salt	1 tsp
1 tsp	ground cumin	1 tsp
1/2 tsp	chili powder	1/2 tsp
1 tsp	ground turmeric	1 tsp
2 tsps	paprika	2 tsps
1 tbsp	sunflower oil	15 ml
2 tbsps	lemon juice	30 ml
2 tbsps	garam masala	2 tbsps
2	big or 4 small trout fillets (12 oz total)	2
1 tbsp	peanut oil	15 ml
1	lemon cut in wedges	1
	watercress to garnish	

Mix all the marinade ingredients together in a bowl.

Spread the marinade over the trout fillets, putting most of the marinade on the skinless side.

Leave in the fridge to marinate for up to 6 hours.

Heat a large non-stick pan with the peanut oil.

Fry the fillets 2–4 minutes on each side until golden and crisp (the time depends on thickness of fillet).

Serve on a warm plate garnished with lemon wedges and watercress.

PER SERVING	
Calories	214
% Calories from fat	54
Fat (g)	13.2
Saturated fat (g)	2
Cholesterol (mg)	49.3
Sodium (mg)	634
Protein (g)	18.9
Carbohydrate (g)	6.6
Calcium (mg)	84.6
EXCHANGES	
Milk	0.0
Vegetable	0.0
Fruit	0.0
Bread	0.0
Meat	3.0
Fat	1.0

Try this sauce with salmon, cod, trout fillet or smoked fish.

If watercress is unavailable, baby spinach leaves make a good alternative.

For a delicious vegetarian dish, serve the sauce with warm new potatoes and hard-boiled eggs.

Grilled Fillet of Trout with Watercress Sauce

Serves 4

This sauce has a lovely creaminess and color that complements grilled fillets of sea trout perfectly. Serve with new potatoes and steamed vegetables. Watercress is a valuable source of vitamins and minerals. It is rich in potassium, calcium and phosphorus, as well as having good quantities of iron, iodine, sodium and magnesium. For this sauce the watercress is hardly cooked at all, which helps retain the nutrients and the color.

1/2 tbsp	mild olive oil or sunflower oil	8 ml
4	trout fillets (about 6 oz each)	4
1 1/4 cups	good fish stock (could use chicken or vegetable bouillon)	300 ml
2 cups	watercress, washed	2 cups
1 cup	(scant) low-fat mayonnaise	1 cup
	salt and freshly ground pepper	
1 tbsp	freshly squeezed lemon juice	15 ml

Lightly oil the fish and lay the fillets on a baking sheet. Pre-heat the broiler.

In a small pan bring the stock to a boil.

Remove the stock from the heat and stir in the watercress. Pour into a processor and blend thoroughly until you have a smooth green liquid.

Pour the sauce back into the pan and gradually whisk in the mayonnaise; it should slightly thicken and have the consistency of cream. Season well with salt and pepper.

Place the fish fillets under hot broiler.

Cook for 4–5 minutes, turn, and cook for 2 minutes until the fish is just cooked through (the cooking time will vary slightly depending on the thickness of the fish fillets).

Arrange the fish fillets on warm serving plates.

Gently warm the sauce, whisking continuously, and gradually add the lemon juice.

Spoon the sauce over the fish fillets and serve.

PER SERVING	
Calories	373
% Calories from fat	41
Fat (g)	16.8
Saturated fat (g)	3
Cholesterol (mg)	110.1
Sodium (mg)	1115
Protein (g)	36.6
Carbohydrate (g)	17.4
Calcium (mg)	138.4

EXCHANGES	
Milk	0.0
Vegetable	0.0
Fruit	0.0
Bread	1.0
Meat	5.5
Fat	0.0

For an alternative, omit the shrimp and use 2 hard-boiled eggs instead.

Fish, Shrimp and Leek Pie

Serves 6

This dish can be prepared in advance and chilled prior to final cooking. It is an impressive and tasty supper for your friends. Serve with new or boiled potatoes and green vegetables.

12 oz	fish fillet (haddock, cod, salmon, etc.)	340 g
	salt and freshly ground pepper	
2 tbsps	vegan margarine	50 g
2	small leeks, finely sliced	2
1 tbsp	all-purpose flour	1 tbsp
2/3 cup	vegetable stock	150 ml
2/3 cup	soy milk	150 ml
2 tbsps	chopped parsley	2 tbsps
1 tsp	chopped dill or tarragon	1 tsp
1 tbsp	capers, drained (optional)	1 tbsp
1/2 tbsp	lemon juice	8 ml
1/2 lb	freshly peeled boiled shrimp or thawed frozen shrimp	225 g
1 lb	puff pastry	450 g
1	egg beaten for the glaze	1

Pre-heat the oven to 425F. Lay the fish in a greased baking dish, season well with salt and pepper, and dot with 1/2 oz of the margarine.

Cover with aluminum foil and bake for 15–20 minutes until the fish is just cooked; remove from the oven and allow to cool. Remove the skin and any bones from the fish, and flake into large pieces.

Melt remaining margarine in a saucepan, add the leeks and gently sauté for 10–15 minutes, stirring regularly, until the leeks are tender.

Stir the flour into the leeks and cook for about 2 minutes over medium heat until the flour is cooked but not browned.

Gradually stir the stock and soy milk into the flour, stirring continuously; simmer for about 5 minutes until the sauce becomes thick.

Season with herbs, capers, lemon juice, salt and pepper.

Carefully stir the fish into the sauce, then allow to cool completely. When cool, stir in the shrimp.

PER SERVING	
Calories	587
% Calories from fat	54
Fat (g)	34.9
Saturated fat (g)	8.5
Cholesterol (mg)	141.3
Sodium (mg)	432
Protein (g)	26.8
Carbohydrate (g)	40.9
Calcium (mg)	69.4
EXCHANGES	
Milk	0.0
Vegetable	0.0
Fruit	0.0
Bread	2.5
Meat	3.0
Fat	5.0

On a floured surface, roll the pastry into a 14-inch square.
Lift onto a large oiled baking sheet, and lightly glaze the edge of the pastry with the beaten egg.
Spoon the cold fish and shrimp filling into the center of the pastry.
Pull the opposite corners of the pastry to the center and pinch all the edges together firmly, so you have a square with the pinched edges in the shape of a cross.
Glaze pastry all over with beaten egg.
Bake for 25–30 minutes, until pastry is golden and risen. Serve immediately.

Choose fish fillets of an even thickness and preferably no more than 3/4 inch thick for best results. This allows the spices to be well absorbed into the fish.

Cajun Blackened Fish

Serves 4

This is a really interesting way of cooking any fish fillet such as haddock, cod or red fish. It is also delicious made with salmon fillet and served with a tangy salsa. Serve with plain basmati rice.

3 tbsps	Cajun spice mix (if you are unable to buy Cajun spice mix, follow the recipe on page 126)	3 tbsps
2 tsps	sweet paprika powder	2 tsps
4	fish fillets (about 7 oz each), skinned	4
1 tbsp	sunflower oil	15 ml
2 oz	vegan margarine	56 g

Mix 2 tablespoons of the Cajun spices with the paprika (remember to save 1 tablespoon of Cajun spice mix for later).
Coat the fish liberally in the spice mix and refrigerate for 6–8 hours. The longer the fish is left coated in the spice mix, the more flavor it will have.
Heat a large non-stick shallow pan over high heat with the oil. Place fillets in hot pan to cook 2 minutes on high heat.
Turn and cook a few minutes longer until it is just cooked through.
Each side of the fish should be well charred. Remove the fish from the pan and keep warm.
In the same pan, melt the margarine, gently so it does not separate, and mix in the remaining tablespoon of Cajun spice mix.
Serve fish on warm plates, and pour the spiced margarine over each fillet.

PER SERVING	
Calories	316
% Calories from fat	49
Fat (g)	17
Saturated fat (g)	2.9
Cholesterol (mg)	112.5
Sodium (mg)	270
Protein (g)	37.9
Carbohydrate (g)	1.4
Calcium (mg)	73.3
EXCHANGES	
Milk	0.0
Vegetable	0.0
Fruit	0.0
Bread	0.0
Meat	6.0
Fat	0.0

Tuna is readily available from most supermarkets and fish markets. Provided it is fresh (not previously frozen), it may be stored in your freezer.

Pan-Fried Tuna Steaks with Salsa Verde

Serves 4

This sauce is unusually tangy. It goes extremely well with fresh tuna or swordfish. You can store the salsa in the fridge for several days. Serve this dish with rice or new potatoes.

1 tbsp	olive oil	15 ml
¼ cup	drained cornichons or gherkins (2 oz)	56 g
2 tbsps	drained capers	2 tbsps
	juice from 1 lemon	
	bunch fresh parsley	
	bunch fresh dill	
	bunch fresh cilantro	
4	4-oz tuna steaks, about ¾ inch thick	4
	oil for brushing	
	salt and freshly ground pepper	

Place all the salsa ingredients in a food processor or blender, and blend until just smooth.

Lightly oil a non-stick fry pan, brush tuna with oil and sprinkle with salt and pepper.

When pan is very hot, fry the tuna steaks for about 1 minute. Turn the fish when it has changed to a white color. Cook on the other side for about 30 seconds.

Cook according to personal preference, but I personally like it to be slightly pink in the middle, which keeps the tuna tender.

Transfer to warm plates and spoon a dollop of salsa on each steak.

PER SERVING	
Calories	214
% Calories from fat	39
Fat (g)	9.1
Saturated fat (g)	1.9
Cholesterol (mg)	42.8
Sodium (mg)	280
Protein (g)	27.1
Carbohydrate (g)	5.3
Calcium (mg)	33.9
EXCHANGES	
Milk	0.0
Vegetable	1.0
Fruit	0.0
Bread	0.0
Meat	3.0
Fat	0.0

This dressing would also be suitable served with tilapia.

If preferred, substitute grated fresh ginger for the horseradish.

Broiled Catfish with Soy, Honey and Horseradish Dressing

Serves 4

The warm dressing adds an oriental touch to the dish. Delicious served with noodles or rice and stir-fry vegetables. Have your fish filleted at the fish market.

4	fillets of catfish, each about 4 oz	4
1 tbsp	olive oil	15 ml
Dressing		
4	green onions	4
2 tbsps	light soy sauce	30 ml
2 tbsps	peanut oil	30 ml
1 tsp	balsamic vinegar	5 ml
2 tsps	fresh grated horseradish	2 tsps
2 tsps	honey	2 tsps

Cut 2 of the green onions into thin julienne strips for garnish. Finely chop the remaining 2.

In a small saucepan, combine the chopped onions, soy sauce, peanut oil, balsamic, horseradish and honey and mix well.

Heat the broiler, place the fillets on a lightly oiled baking sheet, brush the fish with olive oil and season with salt and pepper.

Broil for about 4 minutes either side until the fish is cooked through and golden.

Arrange the fish on a warm platter. Warm the dressing up slightly and spoon over the catfish.

Garnish each fillet with strips of green onion.

PER SERVING	
Calories	264
% Calories from fat	64
Fat (g)	18.7
Saturated fat (g)	3.6
Cholesterol (mg)	52.9
Sodium (mg)	358
Protein (g)	18.4
Carbohydrate (g)	4.9
Calcium (mg)	27.6
EXCHANGES	
Milk	0.0
Vegetable	1.0
Fruit	0.0
Bread	0.0
Meat	2.0
Fat	3.0

Use any white fish fillets. The uncooked fish fillets topped with the crust may be prepared the day before and stored in the fridge.

Crusted Fillet of Cod

Serves 4

This is a great way to cook plain white fish. We have made this dish at our family restaurants with a herb and fresh Parmesan crust, so I was surprised at how tasty it was made with the soy cheese and mustard powder instead of Parmesan. Serve with the Aioli Sauce (see page 112), new potatoes and green vegetables.

4	cod fillets (about 7–8 oz each)	4
8–10 slices	white bread (about 6 oz)	170 g
1/2 cup	soy cheese	110 g
1 tsp	mustard powder	1 tsp
1	bunch of parsley	1
	sprig of fresh dill	
	sprig of fresh basil	
2 tbsps	olive oil	30 ml
	salt and freshly ground pepper	

Pre-heat the oven to 375F. Lay the fish fillets skin side down on a large greased baking sheet.

In a food processor, process the bread, soy cheese, mustard powder and herbs until well crumbed.

Stir in the olive oil and season well. Press the mixture on the top of the fish fillets so it lies evenly about 1/4 inch thick.

Roast in the oven for 15–20 minutes until the crust is golden and the fish is cooked through.

Serve on warm plates.

PER SERVING	
Calories	485
% Calories from fat	42
Fat (g)	22.4
Saturated fat (g)	3.8
Cholesterol (mg)	85.1
Sodium (mg)	551
Protein (g)	42.1
Carbohydrate (g)	27.2
Calcium (mg)	108.7
EXCHANGES	
Milk	0.0
Vegetable	0.0
Fruit	0.0
Bread	2.0
Meat	5.0
Fat	1.5

If using wooden skewers, soak them in hot water for several minutes before threading the food onto them. This helps prevent charring during cooking.
  The brochettes would be equally delicious made using salmon or swordfish.

Monkfish and Shrimp Brochettes

Serves 4

Monkfish is an ideal fish for brochettes, as it has a slightly meaty texture and holds its shape well. These would be perfect for a barbecue or a smart dinner party dish. They could be served with plain basmati rice, which looks quite stylish put into a ramekin and turned out onto each plate as a timbale shape.

1lb 4oz	fresh monkfish tail	560 g
16	large shrimp, uncooked, either in or out of shell	16
4	wooden or metal skewers	4
	Lime and Cilantro Dressing (see page 142)	

Prepare monkfish: skin, fillet and cut into 1-inch cubes (aim for 16–20 cubes in total).

Push alternate cubes of monkfish and shrimp onto the 4 skewers. Cover and leave in the fridge until required. Pre-heat the broiler. Place the kebabs on a suitable baking dish for broiling.

Brush the kebabs with the dressing. Cook under hot broiler 5–8 minutes. Turn and repeat until the fish becomes slightly golden in color. Baste occasionally with the dressing. Serve on warm plates.

Pour any juices from the oven dish over the brochettes.

Warm the remaining dressing in a small saucepan and spoon some of it over each brochette, ensuring that each person gets plenty of chili, ginger and cilantro mixture.

Garnish with chopped cilantro leaves.

PER SERVING	
Calories	336
% Calories from fat	61
Fat (g)	22.8
Saturated fat (g)	4
Cholesterol (mg)	77.1
Sodium (mg)	416
Protein (g)	26.8
Carbohydrate (g)	5.9
Calcium (mg)	32.2
EXCHANGES	
Milk	0.0
Vegetable	0.0
Fruit	0.0
Bread	0.0
Meat	4.0
Fat	2.5

Mahi-mahi should be bought very fresh. Make sure the fish you choose is bright, rigid and shiny, not dull and tired looking.

Crunchy Oat-Coated Mahi-Mahi Fillets

Serves 4

For this dish the fillets are cooked in crunchy oatmeal, making them more appealing to those who may not be fish lovers but who know the benefits of eating fresh fish.

4	mahi-mahi fillets, about 4–6 oz each	4
1/4 cup	soy milk	60 ml
1/4 cup	oatmeal, uncooked	1/4 cup
2 tbsps	olive oil	30 ml
1	large lemon, cut into wedges	1

Remove any small bones from the fillets.

Dip each fillet in the soy milk, then roll it liberally in the oatmeal.

Heat a large frying pan with the oil.

When hot, fry the fillets for 2–3 minutes on either side until crisp and golden and just cooked through.

Serve on a warm plate with wedges of lemon.

PER SERVING	
Calories	185
% Calories from fat	39
Fat (g)	8.2
Saturated fat (g)	1.2
Cholesterol (mg)	82.5
Sodium (mg)	103
Protein (g)	22.5
Carbohydrate (g)	6.6
Calcium (mg)	36.7

EXCHANGES	
Milk	0.0
Vegetable	0.0
Fruit	0.0
Bread	0.5
Meat	3.0
Fat	0.0

For a delicious vegan dish, try using parsnips instead of haddock and potatoes. Garam masala, an Indian blend of spices, may be found in ethnic sections or Indian grocery stores.

Potato-Crusted Haddock and Curried Tomato Bake

Serves 4

Serve as a complete meal, maybe with a few salad leaves or baby spinach. The bake can be made a day in advance and kept in the fridge before cooking. The addition of coconut milk gives the dish a delicious buttery flavor.

4–6	potatoes (about 1½ lb)	675 g
2 tbsps	olive oil	30 ml
1	medium onion, finely chopped	1
1 tbsp	chopped fresh gingerroot	1 tbsp
2	cloves garlic, crushed	2
1 tsp	garam masala	1 tsp
1 tsp	ground turmeric	1 tsp
2 tsps	ground cumin	2 tsps
1 tsp	ground cilantro	1 tsp
6	tomatoes (about 1 lb), chopped coarsely (or use one 14-oz can of chopped tomatoes)	6
1 tsp	vegan bouillon powder	1 tsp
2 tbsps	chopped fresh cilantro leaves	2 tbsps
4	small fillets or 2 large fillets fresh haddock, skinned, about 6–7 oz per person	4
²/₃ cup	reduced-fat coconut milk	150 ml
	salt and freshly ground pepper	

Pre-heat the oven to 375F. Peel and slice the potatoes about ¼ inch thick.

Boil or steam the potatoes for 8–10 minutes until half cooked; allow to cool.

Heat 1 tablespoon of the olive oil in a medium pan, and sauté the onion, ginger and garlic for about 5 minutes until soft.

Stir in the ground spices and cook, stirring well, for about 2 minutes.

Add the tomatoes and bouillon powder and stir over the heat for 5–10 minutes or until tomato is tender; stir in the fresh cilantro and season well.

Layer half the potatoes in a large, greased baking dish.

Cut the fish fillets into quarters and lay them over the potatoes. Spoon the tomato sauce over the fish, covering well.

PER SERVING	
Calories	433
% Calories from fat	23
Fat (g)	10.9
Saturated fat (g)	2.5
Cholesterol (mg)	96.4
Sodium (mg)	391
Protein (g)	39.7
Carbohydrate (g)	44.6
Calcium (mg)	116
EXCHANGES	
Milk	0.0
Vegetable	0.0
Fruit	0.0
Bread	3.0
Meat	4.0
Fat	0.0

Top with the remaining potatoes, pour over the coconut milk and drizzle with 1 tablespoon olive oil. Season with salt and freshly ground pepper.

Bake for about 25 minutes until cooked through.

Broil the top if necessary for a golden potato crust.

You could also use smoked herring fillets in this recipe. As they have many small pin bones, I suggest you process the herring in a food processor first. The dish would contain plenty of calcium, as the bones will have been ground up.

Smoked Fish Cakes

Serves 4 (2 cakes per serving)

These fish cakes make a pleasant change from the cod and salmon variety you can buy from supermarkets. I recommend that you serve them with the Tangy Mayonnaise on page 120 and a crisp salad.

6–8	potatoes (about 1 lb)	450 g
1 lb	mixed fish fillets (such as smoked haddock, smoked salmon, tilapia, white fish)	450 g
3	green onions, washed, cut into thin rings	3
1	large egg, beaten	1
2 tsps	capers, drained	2 tsps
2 tbsps	chopped parsley	2 tbsps
1 tbsp	lemon juice	15 ml
1 tsp	anchovy paste	1 tsp
	freshly ground pepper	

Coating

1½ tbsps	all-purpose flour seasoned with salt and pepper	1½ tbsps
1	egg, beaten	1
1 tbsp	soy milk	15 ml
⅔ cup	breadcrumbs	150 g
	vegetable oil for pan-frying the fish cakes	
	lemon wedges to garnish	

Pre-heat the oven to 350F. Peel and chop the potatoes. Boil until soft, then mash well.

Place the fish (except those smoked, which have already been cooked) on a greased baking sheet, cover with aluminum foil and

PER SERVING	
Calories	361
% Calories from fat	12
Fat (g)	5
Saturated fat (g)	1.2
Cholesterol (mg)	194
Sodium (mg)	1126
Protein (g)	38.7
Carbohydrate (g)	39.4
Calcium (mg)	142.9
EXCHANGES	
Milk	0.0
Vegetable	0.0
Fruit	0.0
Bread	2.5
Meat	4.0
Fat	0.0

bake for about 20 minutes, until the fish is just cooked. Allow to cool slightly.

Flake the fish into a large bowl, discarding any skin and bones.

In a large bowl, mix together the mashed potato, the flaked fish and all the remaining fish cake ingredients and seasonings; mix thoroughly.

Divide the mixture into 8 equal balls, flatten out and pat into a neat shape.

Dip each fish cake into the flour, then the beaten egg mixed with soy milk, then the breadcrumbs.

Pan-fry the fish cakes in a small amount of vegetable oil for about 3 minutes on either side over medium heat until golden brown.

Then transfer the fish cakes to the oven and cook for 10–15 minutes to ensure they're well heated throughout and crisp on the outside.

Serve with lemon wedges.

Smoked Trout Rarebit

Serves 4

Smoked fish goes very well with a tomatoes-and-cheese-style topping. For anyone missing the flavor of real cheese, this tastes quite convincingly cheesy! Delicious served with rice or potatoes.

4	smoked trout fillets (6–7 oz each), skinned and cut in half	4
4	large tomatoes	4
1	egg	1
1	egg yolk	1
2 tbsps	Dijon mustard	2 tbsps
3/8 cup	soy cheese	80 g
1 tsp	Worcestershire sauce	1 tsp
	salt, freshly ground pepper and a pinch of cayenne	
1 tbsp	freshly chopped parsley	1 tbsp
	watercress to garnish	

If you prefer, use smoked salmon fillet. Be sure to remove all the pin bones before covering with rarebit topping.

PER SERVING	
Calories	392
% Calories from fat	40
Fat (g)	17
Saturated fat (g)	3.5
Cholesterol (mg)	237.3
Sodium (mg)	1678
Protein (g)	48.6
Carbohydrate (g)	8.3
Calcium (mg)	118.8
EXCHANGES	
Milk	0.0
Vegetable	0.0
Fruit	0.0
Bread	0.0
Meat	7.0
Fat	0.0

Pre-heat the oven to 350F. Lay the fillets in a large greased baking dish, keeping them separate.

Cut each tomato into six discs. Cover the fillets with a layer of sliced tomatoes.

Beat together all the remaining ingredients. Spread over the tomatoes to form an even layer.

Bake for 20–25 minutes or until golden and slightly risen.

Place each fillet onto a warm plate garnished with sprigs of watercress.

This dish is equally nice with other types of beans or lentils. Instead of the split peas, aduki beans are particularly good.

The scones could be baked separately as savory "cheese-style" scones.

Split Pea and Vegetable Pot Pie

Serves 6

This pot pie is a vegetable bake with a savory scone topping. It is a hearty, filling meal and extremely economical. This version uses yellow split peas, giving an interesting texture. The addition of soy flour makes the scones more nutritious, and along with the yeast extract and mustard powder, gives them a savory cheese taste. Serve with some leafy vegetables. Any leftover is great reheated.

VEGAN

PER SERVING	
Calories	229
% Calories from fat	28
Fat (g)	7.4
Saturated fat (g)	1.2
Cholesterol (mg)	0
Sodium (mg)	530
Protein (g)	9.1
Carbohydrate (g)	33.2
Calcium (mg)	110
EXCHANGES	
Milk	0.0
Vegetable	0.0
Fruit	0.0
Bread	2.0
Meat	1.0
Fat	1.0

Split pea and vegetable base

1/2 cup	dry yellow split peas (3 1/2 oz), soaked in cold water for 10 minutes	98 g
1	large onion, finely chopped	1
1 tbsp	olive oil	15 ml
1	leek, finely chopped	1
2	ribs celery, finely chopped	2
3	cloves garlic, crushed	3
2	medium carrots, peeled and diced	2
1	14-oz can chopped tomatoes	1
2 tbsps	tomato purée	2 tbsps
3/4 cup	vegetable stock (or use vegan bouillon powder)	180 ml
1/2 cup	stringbeans, top and tailed and cut into quarters lengthways (4 oz)	112 g
1	large sprig fresh thyme	1
1 tbsp	freshly chopped parsley	1 tbsp
	salt and freshly ground pepper	

Scone topping

³/₄ cup	self-rising flour	³/₄ cup
2 tbsps	soy flour (use whole wheat flour if preferred)	2 tbsps
1 tsp	mustard powder	1 tsp
2 tbsps	vegan margarine	50 g
1 tsp	yeast extract (Marmite)	1 tsp
¹/₂ cup	cold water	120 ml
	soy milk for brushing	

Pre-heat the oven to 400F. Drain the yellow split peas, then tip into a small saucepan covered with cold water, bring to a boil and simmer for 20–25 minutes until just tender (not over-cooked, as they will be cooked further).

In a separate large saucepan, over medium heat sauté the onion in the olive oil.

After a couple of minutes, add the leek, celery, garlic and carrots, and continue cooking for about 8 minutes.

Add the chopped tomatoes, purée, stock and stringbeans. Continue cooking until the vegetables are just tender but still slightly crisp (5–10 minutes).

Mix in the split peas and herbs, and season well.

Pour into a large oven-proof dish (preferably shallow; if the dish is too deep the mixture will not heat through in time). Smooth down and set to one side while you make the scone topping.

Mix the flours and mustard powder, and rub in the margarine until it resembles breadcrumbs.

Stir the yeast extract into the water until dissolved.

Using a knife, pour the water into the flour mixture and blend until it forms dough. Knead lightly in extra flour.

Roll out to about ¹/₂ inch thick and, using a 1¹/₂- or 2-inch fluted or plain pastry cutter, cut out about 12 scones (allowing for 2 scones per serving).

Place the scones on top of the vegetable mixture, and brush with a little soy milk.

Bake in pre-heated oven for 15–20 minutes, until scones are golden and risen.

To serve, spoon onto individual plates with 2 scones arranged on top.

If you are unable to find all these mushrooms, don't worry. Ordinary mushrooms will be fine, although not as exotic.

Individual Mushroom and Walnut Strudels

Serves 4

These tasty strudels can be made in advance and cooked when required. Serve with a crisp dressed salad and perhaps Roasted Tomato Sauce (see page 119).

3–4 slices	stale bread (about 4 oz)	112 g
3	cloves garlic, peeled	3
	bunch of fresh parsley	
2 tbsps	olive oil	30 ml
1	onion, chopped	1
1	small leek, chopped	1
1/2 lb	mixed mushrooms, such as oyster shiitake, morel, flat and wild	225 g
2 tbsps	soy flour	2 tbsps
1 tbsp	soy sauce	15 ml
1 tsp	vegan vegetable bouillon powder	1 tsp
1 tsp	chopped fresh tarragon	1 tsp
2 tbsps	roughly chopped walnut pieces (2 oz)	56 g
	freshly ground pepper	
2 tbsps	vegan margarine	50 g
4	sheets of filo pastry, each measuring about 18 x 12 inches	4
	sesame seeds to sprinkle	

Pre-heat the oven to 400F. Place the bread, garlic and parsley in a food processor and process for about 30 seconds or until finely crumbed; tip this breadcrumb mixture into a bowl.

Heat the olive oil in a large pan and sauté the onion and leek over medium heat for about 5 minutes.

If using shiitake and morel mushrooms, chop finely; roughly chop flat, oyster or wild mushrooms.

Add the chopped mushrooms to the onions and cook for a further 5 minutes.

Mix in the soy flour, soy sauce, bouillon, tarragon and walnuts, and fry gently for a further minute. Season with pepper; you may not need to add salt. Allow to cool.

VEGAN

PER SERVING	
Calories	317
% Calories from fat	50
Fat (g)	17.8
Saturated fat (g)	2.8
Cholesterol (mg)	0.3
Sodium (mg)	824
Protein (g)	7
Carbohydrate (g)	33.5
Calcium (mg)	79.4
EXCHANGES	
Milk	0.0
Vegetable	0.0
Fruit	0.0
Bread	2.0
Meat	0.0
Fat	3.5

Melt the margarine in a small saucepan.

Lay out a single sheet of filo pastry on floured surface, shortest side at the front, and brush the sheet with the margarine.

Sprinkle with a handful of the breadcrumb mixture, covering the entire sheet.

Spoon one-quarter of the mushroom mixture at the front of the rectangle, leaving about 3 inches at either end.

Begin to roll up. After one rotation, brush the ends and fold them in 3 inches from either side; brush dry sides and roll up into sausage. The mixture should be completely contained in the filo pastry.

Repeat for the remaining strudels, and arrange all 4 on a greased baking sheet. Brush with margarine and sprinkle with sesame seeds.

Bake for 15–20 minutes or until pastry is crisp and golden.

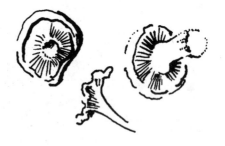

Vegetables

Cumin-Spiced Cauliflower

Stringbeans à la Greque

Stir-Fried Cabbage and Carrots with Caraway

Piquant Vegetables

Fava Beans with Smoked Bacon

Roasted Parsnips with Sesame and Honey

Potato and Celeriac Boulangère

Wholegrain Mustard Mashed Potatoes

Roasted Garlic Mashed Potatoes

Spicy Potato Wedges

Pan-Fried "Cheese" Polenta

Sesame Noodles

Sicilian Caponata

Spiced Rice

Yorkshire Puddings

Try this dish with broccoli instead.

Cumin-Spiced Cauliflower

Serves 6

This is an interesting way to cook cauliflower; delicious with rice and other Indian dishes or as a quick light supper with naan bread.

1	large cauliflower	1
1 tbsp	peanut oil	15 ml
1 tsp	cumin seeds	1 tsp
1 tsp	black mustard seeds	1 tsp
1 tsp	ground cumin	1 tsp
1 tsp	ground cilantro	1 tsp
1/2 tsp	ground turmeric	1/2 tsp
2/3 cup	vegetable stock	150 ml

Break cauliflower into florets, keeping as much stalk as possible. Cut the bigger florets if necessary.

Heat oil in a large wok or frying pan. When hot add cumin seeds and mustard seeds.

Cook for 1 minute stirring continuously, without burning.

Add ground cumin, cilantro and turmeric, and cook for 1 further minute.

Add cauliflower and toss the florets in the spices. Pour in the vegetable stock and mix thoroughly.

Cover and simmer for about 5 minutes over medium heat until the cauliflower is cooked but still firm.

Serve immediately.

PER SERVING	
Calories	56
% Calories from fat	43
Fat (g)	3
Saturated fat (g)	0.4
Cholesterol (mg)	0
Sodium (mg)	106
Protein (g)	3.7
Carbohydrate (g)	5.4
Calcium (mg)	44.1

EXCHANGES	
Milk	0.0
Vegetable	1.0
Fruit	0.0
Bread	0.0
Meat	0.0
Fat	0.5

You can also use okra for this dish, as it contains large amounts of calcium.

This dish is good to freeze, and it is also a great way of using up zucchini.

Stringbeans à la Greque

Serves 4–6

This has to be one of the nicest ways of cooking stringbeans. In the summer my parents are always giving me buckets full of home-grown beans. I usually cook a large batch of this recipe and eat them either hot with a baked potato or cold as part of a salad. This dish seems to improve when reheated the following day.

2 tbsps	olive oil	30 ml
2	cloves garlic, crushed	2
3–4 cups	stringbeans, tops and tails removed (12 oz)	340 g
1 cup	vegetable stock	240 ml
1/2 cup	tomato purée	1/2 cup
1 tsp	sugar	8 g
	salt and freshly ground pepper	

Heat olive oil in a medium saucepan. Add garlic and stringbeans and stir over medium heat for 2 minutes.

Add stock and tomato purée and stir well.

Simmer over low heat, stirring occasionally, for 15–20 minutes until sauce has reduced slightly and thickened and the beans are just cooked.

Season with sugar, salt and pepper before serving.

PER SERVING	
Calories	115
% Calories from fat	53
Fat (g)	7.3
Saturated fat (g)	0.9
Cholesterol (mg)	0
Sodium (mg)	179
Protein (g)	2.7
Carbohydrate (g)	11.8
Calcium (mg)	51.1
EXCHANGES	
Milk	0.0
Vegetable	2.0
Fruit	0.0
Bread	0.0
Meat	0.0
Fat	1.5

Use other vegetable combinations, such as zucchini, red cabbage, Chinese cabbage, etc.

You may omit the caraway seeds for children. If you don't like caraway, black mustard seeds are also a good combination with cabbage.

Stir-Fried Cabbage and Carrots with Caraway

Serves 4

This is an ideal way of cooking vegetables to retain the maximum amount of water-soluble vitamins, and the addition of stock gives the stir-fry more flavor. To make more of a meal, add chopped bacon to the vegetables and serve with Spicy Potato Wedges (see page 105).

1 lb	white cabbage	450 g
1–2	medium carrots (1/2 lb)	225 g
2 tbsps	olive oil, or walnut oil	30 ml
2/3 cup	vegetable or chicken stock	150 ml
1 tsp	caraway seeds	1 tsp
	salt and freshly ground pepper	

Shred the cabbage finely. Peel the carrots and either cut into thin julienne strips or use a vegetable peeler to make ribbons. Heat a large wok or frying pan, heat the oil until hot and throw in the cabbage and carrots.

Stir-fry for several minutes, then add the stock, caraway seeds and seasonings.

Continue frying for a further 3 or 4 minutes until the cabbage is cooked but still slightly crisp.

Serve in a warm dish.

PER SERVING	
Calories	108
% Calories from fat	57
Fat (g)	7.3
Saturated fat (g)	1
Cholesterol (mg)	0
Sodium (mg)	177
Protein (g)	2.7
Carbohydrate (g)	9.7
Calcium (mg)	141.3
EXCHANGES	
Milk	0.0
Vegetable	2.0
Fruit	0.0
Bread	0.0
Meat	0.0
Fat	1.5

Suitable for freezing. Otherwise it lasts well for several days in the fridge.

Piquant Vegetables

Serves 4

I discovered this dish while experimenting with Cajun cooking. It makes a delicious accompaniment to Cajun-style fish or chicken.

1	medium onion	1
1	medium green bell pepper	1
1	small red chili pepper	1
3	ribs celery	3
1 tsp	vegetable oil	5 ml
2	cloves garlic, crushed	2
1 tsp	paprika	1 tsp
1 tsp	Cajun spice mix (either bought or the homemade recipe on page 126)	1 tsp
1	14-oz can chopped tomatoes	1
1/4 tsp	Tabasco	1/4 tsp
1 cup	water	240 ml
1/2 tsp	dried oregano	1/2 tsp
1 tsp	sugar	8 g
	salt and freshly ground pepper	

Finely chop onion, peppers and celery.

Heat a large frying pan with the oil, and sauté the vegetables and garlic for about 5 minutes.

Stir in the spices and cook for 1 minute; then mix in the tomatoes, Tabasco, water, oregano and sugar and simmer uncovered for about 12 minutes.

Season with salt and pepper before serving.

PER SERVING	
Calories	67
% Calories from fat	21
Fat (g)	1.8
Saturated fat (g)	0.2
Cholesterol (mg)	0
Sodium (mg)	355
Protein (g)	2.7
Carbohydrate (g)	12.1
Calcium (mg)	39.9

EXCHANGES	
Milk	0.0
Vegetable	2.0
Fruit	0.0
Bread	0.0
Meat	0.0
Fat	0.0

The season for fava beans is fairly short, although you could use beans defrosted from frozen, which are available throughout the year. Also try with other beans such as cooked kidney, cannellini or butter beans.

Fava Beans with Smoked Bacon

Serves 4

Delicious as a vegetable accompaniment or as a quick supper dish with rice, pasta or potatoes.

2 lb	fava beans	900 g
2 tbsps	olive oil	30 ml
1	large red onion, cut in half and thinly sliced	1
6–8 slices	bacon (about 6 oz)	170 g
2	cloves garlic, crushed	2
½ tbsp	sherry vinegar	8 ml
1 tbsp	chopped parsley	1 tbsp
	salt and freshly ground pepper	

Remove the beans from the pods. Steam or boil for 5–8 minutes until just tender.

Remove the rind from the bacon and cut into strips.

Meanwhile, in large frying pan, heat 1 tablespoon olive oil, and sauté the onion for about 5 minutes.

Add the bacon and garlic and cook for a further 8–10 minutes over medium heat, until beginning to caramelize and turn golden at the edges. Toss in the sherry vinegar and cook for a further minute.

Tip the beans into the mixture and heat through for several minutes.

Remove from heat; add remaining olive oil, parsley, salt and pepper.

PER SERVING

Calories	511
% Calories from fat	48
Fat (g)	29.4
Saturated fat (g)	8.6
Cholesterol (mg)	36.1
Sodium (mg)	735
Protein (g)	30.8
Carbohydrate (g)	41.9
Calcium (mg)	96

EXCHANGES

Milk	0.0
Vegetable	0.0
Fruit	0.0
Bread	3.0
Meat	0.0
Fat	6.0

Try a combination of root vegetables such as carrots, beets, sweet potatoes, etc.

Roasted Parsnips with Sesame and Honey

Serves 4

This jazzes up your Sunday roast and might make parsnips more appealing to children.

4	medium parsnips (1 lb)	450 g
1 tbsp	vegetable oil	15 ml
	salt and freshly ground pepper	
1 tbsp	sesame oil	15 ml
1 1/2 tsps	honey	1 1/2 tsps
2 tsps	sesame seeds	2 tsps

Pre-heat the oven to 400F. Peel and cut parsnips into about 3-inch-long by 1-inch-thick sticks.

In a large baking dish, mix the parsnips with the vegetable oil, salt and pepper.

Roast for about 30 minutes, turning once or twice.

When the parsnips are cooked through, golden and slightly crisp, remove from oven.

Mix sesame oil and honey together.

Toss the parsnips with the oil and honey mixture until completely covered.

Sprinkle over sesame seeds. Return to oven and cook for a further 10 minutes.

Serve immediately.

PER SERVING

Calories	168
% Calories from fat	40
Fat (g)	7.9
Saturated fat (g)	1.1
Cholesterol (mg)	0
Sodium (mg)	12
Protein (g)	1.9
Carbohydrate (g)	24.4
Calcium (mg)	43.9

EXCHANGES

Milk	0.0
Vegetable	0.0
Fruit	0.0
Bread	1.5
Meat	0.0
Fat	1.5

Try with parsnips instead of the celeriac.

Potato and Celeriac Boulangère

Serves 4

This combination is a winner. It is a great low-fat vegetable accompaniment, with the stock preventing the dish from becoming dry.

5–6	small potatoes (about 7/8 lb)	400 g
5/8 lb	celeriac (10 oz)	280 g
1	onion, sliced	1
1 1/2 cups	chicken or vegetable stock	360 ml
1 tbsp	olive oil	15 ml
	salt and freshly ground pepper	

Pre-heat the oven to 350F. Peel potatoes and celeriac. Cut into thin slices. Lay alternating slices of celeriac and potato with the onion in a shallow, greased roasting pan, making sure the onion is not on the top.

Season the stock with salt and pepper. Pour the stock over the potatoes and celeriac, and brush the top with the olive oil, drizzling the remainder over.

Bake uncovered for about 1 hour until lightly browned on top. To test if the vegetables are cooked, push a metal skewer or sharp knife into the dish; it should feel soft.

If after about 40 minutes, the top is burning but it is not cooked, cover with foil and continue cooking. When done, serve immediately.

PER SERVING	
Calories	178
% Calories from fat	21
Fat (g)	4.4
Saturated fat (g)	0.5
Cholesterol (mg)	9.4
Sodium (mg)	165
Protein (g)	7.4
Carbohydrate (g)	28.7
Calcium (mg)	54.9
EXCHANGES	
Milk	0.0
Vegetable	0.0
Fruit	0.0
Bread	2.0
Meat	0.0
Fat	1.0

Wholegrain Mustard Mashed Potatoes

Serves 4

Delicious with pork or liver, or as a topping for savory pies such as the Smoked Ham and Lentil Pie (see page 42).

6–8	small potatoes (about 1½ lb)	675 g
1 tbsp	vegan margarine	25 g
2 tbsps	soy cream	30 ml
1 tbsp	wholegrain mustard	1 tbsp
	salt and freshly ground pepper	

Peel and cut potatoes into halves or quarters depending on size.

Steam or boil the potatoes until they are cooked through and fairly soft; drain.

In a large pan, gently melt margarine with soy cream, then remove from the heat.

Tip in the potatoes, and mash well until completely smooth.

Stir in mustard and seasonings. Serve hot.

PER SERVING	
Calories	191
% Calories from fat	17
Fat (g)	3.7
Saturated fat (g)	0.6
Cholesterol (mg)	0
Sodium (mg)	96
Protein (g)	5.8
Carbohydrate (g)	34.3
Calcium (mg)	33.3

EXCHANGES	
Milk	0.0
Vegetable	0.0
Fruit	0.0
Bread	2.5
Meat	0.0
Fat	0.5

Try using sweet potatoes or parsnips for a more exotic touch.

Roasted Garlic Mashed Potatoes

Serves 4–6

This is a great way of making mashed potatoes without butter and cream; it is also a lot more nutritious. Don't worry, once the garlic is roasted it is not as potent as a whole bulb of raw garlic might seem, and think how healthy it is. Delicious served with meats, fish or just about anything.

1	bulb of garlic, whole	1
6–8	small potatoes (about 1 1/2 lb)	675 g
3 tbsps	olive oil	45 ml
1 tsp	salt	1 tsp
	freshly ground pepper to taste	

Pre-heat the oven to 400F. Slice approximately 1/2 inch off the top stalk-end of the garlic so as to just reveal each clove.

Roast garlic in the oven for 20–25 minutes until soft and golden, not dark brown.

Meanwhile, peel the potatoes and either steam or boil them until cooked. Don't worry if they are slightly overcooked, as this makes for a wetter mashed potato.

When garlic is cool enough to handle, peel off skin and pop out the whole garlic cloves, which should be soft.

In a bowl, mash the garlic, olive oil and salt to form a paste.

Add the garlic paste to the mashed potatoes and more olive oil if they seem dry, then season with freshly ground pepper.

Heat through gently before serving.

PER SERVING	
Calories	257
% Calories from fat	35
Fat (g)	10.5
Saturated fat (g)	1.4
Cholesterol (mg)	0
Sodium (mg)	583
Protein (g)	6.3
Carbohydrate (g)	36.7
Calcium (mg)	48.9

EXCHANGES	
Milk	0.0
Vegetable	0.0
Fruit	0.0
Bread	2.5
Meat	0.0
Fat	2.0

A great way to use up any
leftover new potatoes.

Spicy Potato Wedges

Serves 4

Perfect as an accompaniment to pork and lamb dishes.
The addition of Cajun spices makes the potatoes rather special.
Even my children love these, despite the slightly spicy kick.

4–6	new potatoes (about 1 lb), washed but unpeeled	450 g
2 tsps	Cajun spice mix, bought (or see page 126)	2 tsps
1 tsp	paprika	1 tsp
1 tsp	salt	1 tsp
1	clove garlic, crushed	1
1 tbsp	olive oil	15 ml

Pre-heat the oven to 400F. Boil the potatoes until nearly
cooked.

Leaving skins on the potatoes, cut them into quarters
lengthways.

Place potatoes in a roasting dish and cover them evenly with
the spices, salt, crushed garlic and olive oil until well coated.

Bake in the oven for about 20 minutes until cooked through,
crisp and golden brown. Serve hot.

PER SERVING	
Calories	138
% Calories from fat	23
Fat (g)	3.7
Saturated fat (g)	0.5
Cholesterol (mg)	0
Sodium (mg)	815
Protein (g)	4
Carbohydrate (g)	23.7
Calcium (mg)	28.6

EXCHANGES	
Milk	0.0
Vegetable	0.0
Fruit	0.0
Bread	1.5
Meat	0.0
Fat	0.5

Suitable for a gluten-free diet. Make ahead and store for up to 2 days in the fridge.

Pan-Fried "Cheese" Polenta

Serves 4

Delicious served with Italian dishes such as Sicilian Caponata (see page 108). Usually this is made with strong cheddar, but with the addition of mustard, soy flour and yeast extract, a cheese flavor is achieved.

2½ cups	water	600 ml
½ cup	easy cook, fine polenta (4 oz)	112 g
2 tbsps	soy flour	2 tbsps
2 tsps	French mustard	2 tsps
1 tsp	yeast extract (Marmite)	1 tsp
	salt and freshly ground pepper	
1–2 tbsps	olive oil	15–30 ml

Bring the water to a boil in a medium-size pan. When the water is at a rolling boil, add the polenta, beating the mixture vigorously to stop lumps from forming.

Simmer for about 10 minutes, stirring occasionally.

Continue beating and add the soy flour, mustard, yeast extract and seasonings.

Continue cooking over medium heat for several minutes.

Pour into an 8-inch greased ceramic dish and smooth down flat.

Refrigerate for about 2 hours until set. When cool, cut into quarters.

Heat the olive oil in a large non-stick frying pan. Place the polenta slices in the frying pan.

Cook over medium heat for about 8 minutes each side.

The polenta is ready to serve when it is golden brown on either side.

PER SERVING	
Calories	104
% Calories from fat	36
Fat (g)	4.2
Saturated fat (g)	0.5
Cholesterol (mg)	0
Sodium (mg)	137
Protein (g)	2.8
Carbohydrate (g)	13.6
Calcium (mg)	6.7

EXCHANGES	
Milk	0.0
Vegetable	0.0
Fruit	0.0
Bread	1.0
Meat	0.0
Fat	1.0

For a complete meal, stir-fry vegetables and strips of chicken or pork and add this to the noodles.

Sesame Noodles

Serves 6

Suitable as an accompaniment to Chinese meat dishes and stir-fry vegetables.

1	12-oz pkg medium egg noodles	340 g
2 tbsps	sesame oil	30 ml
2 tbsps	sesame seeds	2 tbsps
5	green onions, finely chopped	5

Bring a large pan of water up to a rolling boil. Add the noodles and make sure they are fully covered in water.

Boil for about 4 minutes (or until just cooked). Strain the noodles.

Pour sesame oil into the pan, add sesame seeds and green onions, and stir over medium heat for several minutes to heat through.

Return the noodles to the pan and stir thoroughly. Serve immediately.

PER SERVING	
Calories	276
% Calories from fat	27
Fat (g)	8.4
Saturated fat (g)	1.4
Cholesterol (mg)	54
Sodium (mg)	9
Protein (g)	8.9
Carbohydrate (g)	41.6
Calcium (mg)	29.2

EXCHANGES	
Milk	0.0
Vegetable	0.0
Fruit	0.0
Bread	3.0
Meat	0.0
Fat	1.5

Sicilian Caponata

Serves 4

This is a sweet-and-sour type of ratatouille. It can be served hot, at room temperature or cold. Leaving it to stand allows the flavors to develop. Delicious with Italian bread such as the foccacia on page 173 for a light meal. Alternatively, serve with rice, polenta or pasta.

2 tbsps	olive oil	30 ml
1	red onion, chopped	1
3	cloves garlic, crushed	3
1	red chili pepper, de-seeded and finely chopped	1
1	red bell pepper, de-seeded and cut in long strips	1
1	yellow bell pepper, de-seeded and cut in long strips	1
1	large eggplant, cut in 1-inch strips	1
1	14-oz can chopped tomatoes	1
1 tbsp	tomato purée	1 tbsp
2/3 cup	vegetable stock	150 ml
1 tbsp	white wine vinegar	15 ml
1 tbsp	sugar	25 g
15	pitted olives, sliced	15
1 tbsp	drained capers	1 tbsp
	salt and freshly ground pepper	
2 tbsps	chopped fresh basil	2 tbsps

In large pan, heat 1 tablespoon of olive oil, and fry onion and garlic for about 2 minutes.

Add chili pepper, bell peppers and eggplant, and stir well for about 4 minutes.

Add canned tomatoes, purée, stock, vinegar and sugar, and simmer for about 25 minutes or until eggplant and peppers are tender.

Add olives and capers, and season well.

Just before serving, mix in fresh chopped basil and the remaining tablespoon of olive oil.

PER SERVING	
Calories	195
% Calories from fat	41
Fat (g)	9.6
Saturated fat (g)	1.2
Cholesterol (mg)	0
Sodium (mg)	513
Protein (g)	4.8
Carbohydrate (g)	26.4
Calcium (mg)	60.3

EXCHANGES	
Milk	0.0
Vegetable	5.0
Fruit	0.0
Bread	0.0
Meat	0.0
Fat	1.5

Take care not to overcook basmati rice, as it goes very mushy. Brown long-grain rice is also very good cooked this way.

The spiced rice reheats well at a later date either covered with plastic wrap and microwaved or covered with foil and baked in the oven.

Garam masala is an Indian spice that may be found in ethnic aisles or at Indian grocery stores.

Spiced Rice

Serves 4–6

This rice dish has been one of my family's favorites for a long time. After making the spiced onion mixture it will taste surprisingly strong before the rice is added, but don't be alarmed. Once the rice has been added the taste will be much more subtle. I often serve this dish with barbecues, with a tomato relish and lamb kebabs, accompanied by a cucumber and yogurt salad.

1 1/2 cups	basmati rice	330 g
2 tbsps	sunflower oil	30 ml
2	medium onions, very finely chopped	2
3 tsps	ground cumin	3 tsps
1 tsp	curry powder	1 tsp
2 tsps	garam masala	2 tsps
1/2 tsp	turmeric	1/2 tsp
1 tsp	salt	1 tsp

Put rice in a large pan of boiling salted water. Cook until just tender, drain well and set aside.

In a large frying pan, heat the oil and gently fry the onions for about 12 minutes until tender and just turning golden.

Turn the heat up and add spices and salt; stir well and cook for 1 further minute.

Tip the rice into the spiced onions and mix together well. Heat through to serve.

PER SERVING	
Calories	320
% Calories from fat	25
Fat (g)	8.9
Saturated fat (g)	0.7
Cholesterol (mg)	0
Sodium (mg)	588
Protein (g)	5.7
Carbohydrate (g)	55.7
Calcium (mg)	65.6
EXCHANGES	
Milk	0.0
Vegetable	0.0
Fruit	0.0
Bread	3.5
Meat	0.0
Fat	1.5

You can make a batch and freeze some for another time.

Yorkshire Puddings

Serves 4

I was surprised at how good these were, and how hard it was to tell that they were not made with cow's milk.

3 tbsps	all-purpose flour	3 tbsps
	pinch of salt	
1	egg	1
½ cup	soy milk	120 ml
	salt and freshly ground pepper	
2 tbsps	vegetable oil	30 ml
	sunflower oil or olive oil for the roasting pan	

You will need a Yorkshire pudding pan (or a cupcake/muffin pan) with about 12 individual holes or 8 larger ones.

Alternatively, make one large pudding in a roasting pan, which will need to be baked longer.

Pre-heat the oven to 425F. Make the batter: sift the flour and salt into a bowl. Make a well in the center of the flour and crack the egg into it. Beat the egg into the flour, then slowly beat in the soy milk until all the flour is incorporated. An electric whisk may be used.

Generously grease the pudding pan with oil in each section. Put the pan in the oven for about 5 minutes until very hot and sizzling. Pour batter into the molds.

Bake for about 15 minutes in the hot oven until well risen, crisp and golden. Serve as soon as possible.

PER SERVING	
Calories	110
% Calories from fat	70
Fat (g)	8.7
Saturated fat (g)	1.3
Cholesterol (mg)	53.1
Sodium (mg)	20
Protein (g)	3
Carbohydrate (g)	5.2
Calcium (mg)	8.2
EXCHANGES	
Milk	0.0
Vegetable	0.0
Fruit	0.0
Bread	0.0
Meat	0.0
Fat	2.0

Savory Sauces and Accompaniments

Aioli Sauce

Basil and Nut Pesto

Chili Bean Salsa

Cider and Wholegrain Mustard Sauce

Creamy Curried Coconut Sauce

Minted Yogurt Sauce

Peanut and Coconut Chili Sauce

Roasted Sweetcorn and Lime Salsa

Roasted Tomato Sauce

Tangy Mayonnaise

Tomato and Mint Salsa

Tomato and Pimiento Coulis

Tomato and Sweet Chili Relish

Velouté Sauce

Bread Sauce

Onion Marmalade

Spiced Walnuts

Cajun Spice Mix

Flour Tortillas (Tortillas de Harina)

If the sauce curdles, remove from the heat and try whisking in a little cold water.

You can now buy concentrated fish stock in liquid form from supermarkets. Vegetable bouillon could be used instead of fish stock.

Aioli Sauce

Serves 8 (2 tablespoons per serving)

This is a lovely creamy garlic sauce, which is very simple and perfect for the lactose-intolerant diner as it uses mayonnaise. It complements many types of fish such as white fish, haddock or salmon.

1³/₄ cups	fish stock	420 ml
2	cloves garlic, crushed	2
1 tsp	arrowroot or other thickener	1 tsp
6 tbsps	low-fat mayonnaise	6 tbsps
1 tbsp	finely chopped parsley	1 tbsp

Bring the stock and the crushed garlic to a boil.

Add the arrowroot and whisk until the mixture begins to thicken.

Remove from heat and allow the pan to cool several minutes before you whisk in the mayonnaise; if the sauce becomes too hot it will curdle.

When the mayonnaise is all whisked in, add the parsley and season.

Warm over very low heat. Spoon over the fish to serve. Makes about 2 cups.

PER SERVING	
Calories	45
% Calories from fat	77
Fat (g)	3.8
Saturated fat (g)	0.7
Cholesterol (mg)	4.2
Sodium (mg)	166
Protein (g)	1.3
Carbohydrate (g)	1.2
Calcium (mg)	4.3
EXCHANGES	
Milk	0.0
Vegetable	0.0
Fruit	0.0
Bread	0.0
Meat	0.0
Fat	1.0

Smoked Trout Chowder
(page 16)

Chive Cream Cheese Dip
(page 20)

Smoked Salmon and Spinach
Quiche (page 51)

Chili Chicken with Basil
and Coconut (page 66)

Celeriac, Walnut and
Apple Salad with Mint
Tofu Mayonnaise
(page 133)

Tangy Citrus Cheesecake
(page 163)

Chocolate Brownies
(page 162)

Blueberry Muffins and Banana Oat Shake
(pages 189 and 192)

Try different variations with different herbs, such as fresh cilantro, and different nuts.

Basil and Nut Pesto

Serves 16 (2 tablespoons per serving)

Most bought pesto contains cheese, usually in the form of Parmesan. I have included here a successful version of my own, which is equally if not more delicious with a fresher taste. It may be stored in the fridge for up to two weeks. Serve with a bowl of pasta for a delicious supper.

1 cup	(scant) extra-virgin olive oil	220 ml
2 tbsps	cashew nuts	2 tbsps
2 tbsps	Brazil nuts	2 tbsps
2	cloves garlic, peeled and roughly chopped	2
1 cup	mixed basil and flat leaf parsley, large stalks removed (3 oz)	85 g
1 tsp	salt	1 tsp
2 tbsps	cider vinegar	30 ml
1 tbsp	lemon juice	15 ml
	freshly ground pepper	

Place all the ingredients in a food processor and blend for 30 seconds; scrape around inside with spatula and process again for a further 30 seconds and taste for seasoning.

Scrape out and store in a screw-top jar.

Use as required. Makes approximately 2 cups.

PER SERVING	
Calories	154
% Calories from fat	91
Fat (g)	15.7
Saturated fat (g)	2.3
Cholesterol (mg)	0
Sodium (mg)	147
Protein (g)	1.2
Carbohydrate (g)	2.4
Calcium (mg)	10.1

EXCHANGES	
Milk	0.0
Vegetable	0.0
Fruit	0.0
Bread	0.0
Meat	0.0
Fat	3.0

This salsa makes a delicious meal with chunks of canned tuna.

Chili Bean Salsa

Serves 6 (¹/₂ cup per serving)

Salsa in Mexico means salad, yet we tend to think of it more as a sauce accompaniment. This version is also a lovely salad in its own right. Varying the types of beans or the peppers gives the salsa a more colorful look. Serve with the Spicy Chicken Quesadillas (see page 49).

1	14-oz can of kidney, butter or pinto beans, drained (2 cups)	1
1	green bell pepper, de-seeded and finely diced	1
1	red chili pepper, seeds removed, finely chopped	1
2	green onions, finely chopped	2
1 tbsp	fresh chopped cilantro	1 tbsp
1 tbsp	lemon juice	15 ml
2 tbsps	olive oil	30 ml
	salt and freshly ground pepper	

Mix all the ingredients together in a bowl and season well. Serve chilled. Makes about 3 cups.

PER SERVING	
Calories	123
% Calories from fat	34
Fat (g)	4.9
Saturated fat (g)	0.7
Cholesterol (mg)	0
Sodium (mg)	293
Protein (g)	4.9
Carbohydrate (g)	15.9
Calcium (mg)	27.4

EXCHANGES	
Milk	0.0
Vegetable	0.0
Fruit	0.0
Bread	1.0
Meat	0.0
Fat	1.0

This sauce would also go very well with chicken, pork and ham dishes.

Cider and Wholegrain Mustard Sauce

Serves 16 (2 tablespoons per serving)
This mouth-watering sauce is adapted from the sauce I make with sugar-baked ham. This version is slightly richer and creamier. Serve hot with the Pork Steak with Hazelnut and Sage Crust on page 78.

2 tsps	vegan margarine	16 g
2 tsps	all-purpose flour	2 tsps
1 cup	(scant) dry cider	220 ml
1/2 cup	chicken or vegetable stock	120 ml
2 tsps	honey	2 tsps
2 tsps	soy sauce	10 ml
1 tbsp	wholegrain mustard	1 tbsp
2/3 cup	soy cream	150 ml
	freshly ground pepper	

Melt the margarine in a large frying pan, add flour and cook several minutes until flour is cooked.

Gradually stir in cider and stock until smooth.

Bring to a boil, stirring well for 3 minutes until sauce thickens. Stir in the honey, soy sauce and mustard.

Finally, pour in soy cream, and season with freshly ground pepper. Gently warm to serve. Makes about 2 cups.

PER SERVING

Calories	26
% Calories from fat	43
Fat (g)	1.2
Saturated fat (g)	0.1
Cholesterol (mg)	0
Sodium (mg)	79
Protein (g)	0.2
Carbohydrate (g)	2.1
Calcium (mg)	3.3

EXCHANGES

Milk	0.0
Vegetable	0.0
Fruit	0.0
Bread	0.0
Meat	0.0
Fat	0.0

For a quick chicken curry, fry strips of chicken breast and add to this sauce.

Creamy Curried Coconut Sauce

Serves 24 (2 tablespoons per serving)

I originally made this to go with kedgeree. However, I now often serve it with salmon or smoked haddock fish cakes for a light supper.

1 tbsp	peanut oil	15 ml
1	medium onion, very finely chopped	1
2 tsps	curry powder	2 tsps
2 tsps	cumin powder	2 tsps
1 tsp	ground turmeric	1 tsp
1 tbsp	all-purpose flour	1 tbsp
1 cup	vegetable stock	240 ml
1	14-oz can reduced-fat coconut milk	1

In a medium-size pan, heat oil and slowly fry onion for about 8 minutes until soft.

Add curry powder, cumin and turmeric and cook for 1 minute, stirring continuously.

Add flour and stir well, slowly incorporating stock until smooth.

Bring to a boil, stirring well, and cook for about 1 minute. Add coconut milk, heat well and serve. Makes about 3 cups.

Serve warm with Kedgeree on page 191.

PER SERVING	
Calories	22
% Calories from fat	64
Fat (g)	1.6
Saturated fat (g)	0.7
Cholesterol (mg)	0
Sodium (mg)	28
Protein (g)	0.2
Carbohydrate (g)	1.7
Calcium (mg)	4.4
EXCHANGES	
Milk	0.0
Vegetable	0.0
Fruit	0.0
Bread	0.0
Meat	0.0
Fat	0.0

Minted Yogurt Sauce

Serves 8 (2 tablespoons per serving)

This is similar to the sauce found in Indian restaurants served with popadoms. It cools down any hot curry dishes and is ideal as a creamy accompaniment to dry spicy vegetable curries. I have served it with the trout recipe on page 79.

3 tbsps	plain soy yogurt	3 tbsps
3 tbsps	low-fat mayonnaise	3 tbsps
1	heaping teaspoon honey	1
2 tbsps	chopped fresh mint	2 tbsps
	salt and freshly ground pepper	

In a liquidizer or food processor, mix all the above ingredients. Process for about 1 minute until well blended; chill. Serve at room temperature. Makes about 1 cup.

PER SERVING	
Calories	16
% Calories from fat	24
Fat (g)	0.4
Saturated fat (g)	0.1
Cholesterol (mg)	1.1
Sodium (mg)	53
Protein (g)	0.2
Carbohydrate (g)	2.9
Calcium (mg)	21.2
EXCHANGES	
Milk	0.0
Vegetable	0.0
Fruit	0.0
Bread	0.0
Meat	0.0
Fat	0.0

If the sauce becomes too thick, thin it down with a drop of water and mix well. This sauce thickens on cooling, so it needs to be heated through thoroughly before serving.

Peanut and Coconut Chili Sauce

Serves 8 (¹/₄ cup per serving)

This is great for the lactose-intolerant person who feels he or she has been deprived of rich fattening sauces. It is really a satay-style sauce and goes well with chicken or pork kebabs. I have served it with the Marinated Lime and Sesame Chicken Sticks on page 31.

2 tsps	peanut oil	10 ml
1	medium onion, very finely chopped	1
1	clove garlic, peeled and crushed	1
1	red chili pepper, de-seeded and finely chopped	1
²/₃ cup	vegetable or chicken stock	150 ml
2 tbsps	crunchy peanut butter	2 tbsps
²/₃ cup	reduced-fat coconut milk	150 ml
1 tsp	soy sauce	5 ml
1 tbsp	chopped fresh mint or cilantro	1 tbsp
	freshly ground black pepper	

Heat the oil in a small pan, and sauté the onion, garlic and chili for about 5 minutes until soft.

Pour in the stock, and simmer for several minutes.

Next, stir in the peanut butter and mix well.

Pour in coconut milk. Simmer for a few minutes, during which time the sauce should become slightly thicker.

Stir in the soy sauce and mint, mix and season with pepper. Serve warm. Makes about 2 cups.

PER SERVING	
Calories	58
% Calories from fat	63
Fat (g)	4.2
Saturated fat (g)	1.3
Cholesterol (mg)	0
Sodium (mg)	10.8
Protein (g)	1.6
Carbohydrate (g)	4
Calcium (mg)	8.3

EXCHANGES	
Milk	0.0
Vegetable	0.0
Fruit	0.0
Bread	0.0
Meat	0.0
Fat	1.0

Roasted Sweetcorn and Lime Salsa

Serves 8 (¹/₄ cup per serving)

This is one of my favorite styles of salsa. Broiling the sweetcorn gives a more intense nutty sweetness. This makes a great salad or a delicious accompaniment to Mexican empañadas, enchiladas or tortilla crisps for a snack. It can also be served with barbecued burgers.

2	fresh cobs of corn	2
1	small red onion, finely chopped	1
4	small tomatoes, seeded, finely chopped	4
1	small red chili pepper, seeded, finely chopped	1
2 tbsps	fresh lime juice	30 ml
3 tbsps	olive oil	45 ml
2 tbsps	coarsely chopped fresh cilantro	2 tbsps
	salt and freshly ground pepper	

Pre-heat the broiler. Place the cobs under the heat and toast for about 10 minutes, turning occasionally, until the outside is brown.

When cool, scrape off all the kernels using a sharp knife.

Combine the kernels in a bowl with remaining ingredients, and leave in the fridge for about an hour to allow the flavors to develop.

Season with salt and freshly ground pepper. Serve chilled. Makes about 2 cups.

PER SERVING	
Calories	83
% Calories from fat	55
Fat (g)	5.6
Saturated fat (g)	0.8
Cholesterol (mg)	0
Sodium (mg)	10
Protein (g)	1.5
Carbohydrate (g)	8.6
Calcium (mg)	6.3

EXCHANGES	
Milk	0.0
Vegetable	0.0
Fruit	0.0
Bread	0.5
Meat	0.0
Fat	1.0

Add ham and leeks for a delicious pasta sauce.

Roasted Tomato Sauce

Serves 6 (¹/₂ cup per serving)

This is a rich tomato sauce that goes really well with Italian pasta dishes.

6	medium tomatoes, quartered	6
4	cloves garlic, peeled and left whole	4
1 tbsp	red wine vinegar	15 ml
1 tsp	brown sugar	8 g
1	medium onion, roughly chopped	1
2 tbsps	olive oil	30 ml

Pre-heat the oven to 375F. Mix all the ingredients in a baking dish.

Roast uncovered about 30 minutes until the onions are soft.

Blend or process tomato mixture until smooth; if necessary, thin down with dash of water or tomato juice.

Pass the sauce through a sieve. Warm gently to serve. Makes about 3 cups.

PER SERVING	
Calories	78
% Calories from fat	52
Fat (g)	4.9
Saturated fat (g)	0.7
Cholesterol (mg)	0
Sodium (mg)	12
Protein (g)	1.4
Carbohydrate (g)	8.7
Calcium (mg)	14.1

EXCHANGES	
Milk	0.0
Vegetable	1.0
Fruit	0.0
Bread	0.0
Meat	0.0
Fat	1.0

Liquidize for a smoother sauce.

PER SERVING	
Calories	52
% Calories from fat	68
Fat (g)	4.1
Saturated fat (g)	0.7
Cholesterol (mg)	5.1
Sodium (mg)	165
Protein (g)	0.1
Carbohydrate (g)	4.2
Calcium (mg)	0.8
EXCHANGES	
Milk	0.0
Vegetable	0.0
Fruit	0.0
Bread	0.0
Meat	0.0
Fat	1.0

This salsa lasts only up to a day in the fridge. Any longer and the tomatoes tend to lose some of their brightness, and the salsa goes watery.

PER SERVING	
Calories	110
% Calories from fat	56
Fat (g)	7.4
Saturated fat (g)	1
Cholesterol (mg)	0
Sodium (mg)	17
Protein (g)	1.9
Carbohydrate (g)	11.3
Calcium (mg)	18.9
EXCHANGES	
Milk	0.0
Vegetable	2.0
Fruit	0.0
Bread	0.0
Meat	0.0
Fat	1.5

Tangy Mayonnaise

Serves 12 (2 tablespoons per serving)

This is really similar to tartar sauce and is delicious with most fried fish dishes or fish cakes. Delicious served with the Smoked Fish Cakes on page 89.

2 tbsps	cornichons (small gherkins)	2 tbsps
2 tbsps	drained capers	2 tbsps
1 cup	(scant) low-fat mayonnaise	1 cup
1 tbsp	chopped fresh dill	1 tbsp
1 tbsp	lemon juice	5 ml
	freshly ground pepper	

Finely chop the cornichons and the capers. Combine all the ingredients together in a bowl.

Cover and refrigerate until required. Serve chilled. Makes 1 1/2 cups.

Tomato and Mint Salsa

Serves 6 (1/4 cup per serving)

Most salsas require fresh cilantro, but I have masses of lovely home-grown mint in the summer and often make this to accompany barbecued lamb dishes. Again, like most salsas, it can be a refreshing salad.

8	ripe tomatoes	8
1	large red onion	1
1–2	red chili peppers	1–2
3 tbsps	olive oil	45 ml
	juice from 1 lime	
1 tsp	sugar	8 g
	bunch of fresh mint	
	salt and pepper	

Finely dice tomatoes into medium bowl. Personally, I don't fuss about skinning and de-seeding the tomatoes, as those bits are the best. Makes 1 1/2 cups.

Finely chop the red onion, then de-seed and finely chop the chili. Add to the bowl.

Stir in the olive oil, lime juice, sugar and plenty of freshly chopped mint.

Season with salt and pepper. Refrigerate until required. Serve chilled.

If you prefer, use fresh red bell peppers. Remove the skins by broiling the peppers until charred all over. Then allow them to cool slightly before removing the skins and halving the peppers to remove the seeds.

Tomato and Pimiento Coulis

Serves 14 (¹/₄ cup per serving)

This sauce would be a suitable accompaniment to vegetarian roasts or stuffed vegetables. It is also delicious with meatballs, meat loafs and pasta dishes.

2 tbsps	olive oil	30 ml
2	medium onions, finely chopped	2
2	cloves garlic, crushed	2
1	14-oz can chopped tomatoes	1
1 tbsp	tomato purée	1 tbsp
1	12-oz (approx.) can red pimientos, drained (about 1 cup)	1
1 tsp	sugar	8 g
	salt and freshly ground pepper	
1 tbsp	chopped fresh basil	1 tbsp

Heat the olive oil in a saucepan, and cook onions and garlic for about 5 minutes until soft.

Add tomatoes, tomato purée, drained pimientos and sugar, and cook for a further 5 minutes.

Liquidize, season well and stir in the chopped fresh basil. Serve hot. Makes about 3¹/₂ cups.

PER SERVING	
Calories	38
% Calories from fat	48
Fat (g)	2.1
Saturated fat (g)	0.3
Cholesterol (mg)	0
Sodium (mg)	130
Protein (g)	1
Carbohydrate (g)	4
Calcium (mg)	14.8

EXCHANGES	
Milk	0.0
Vegetable	1.0
Fruit	0.0
Bread	0.0
Meat	0.0
Fat	0.5

Sweet chili sauce containing vinegar, chilies, sugar, garlic and salt is used in Thai cooking. I find it a useful ingredient to keep in the fridge.

PER SERVING	
Calories	35
% Calories from fat	45
Fat (g)	1.9
Saturated fat (g)	0.3
Cholesterol (mg)	0
Sodium (mg)	56
Protein (g)	0.7
Carbohydrate (g)	4.5
Calcium (mg)	5.3
EXCHANGES	
Milk	0.0
Vegetable	1.0
Fruit	0.0
Bread	0.0
Meat	0.0
Fat	0.0

Try this sauce with white fish on a bed of steamed spinach for a healthy, tasty meal.
   Add a tablespoon of soy cream to make the sauce slightly richer and creamier.

PER SERVING	
Calories	54
% Calories from fat	73
Fat (g)	4.5
Saturated fat (g)	1
Cholesterol (mg)	0.8
Sodium (mg)	171
Protein (g)	2.1
Carbohydrate (g)	1.5
Calcium (mg)	4.1
EXCHANGES	
Milk	0.0
Vegetable	0.0
Fruit	0.0
Bread	0.0
Meat	0.0
Fat	1.0

Tomato and Sweet Chili Relish

Serves 8 (¼ cup per serving)

A quick and easy sauce to serve cold with barbecued burgers or sausages. Also great with vegetarian burgers or the Sweet Potato and Chick Pea Cakes on page 59.

4	ripe tomatoes, finely diced	4
1	small red onion, finely chopped	1
1 tbsp	olive oil	15 ml
½ tbsp	lemon juice	8 ml
2 tbsps	sweet chili sauce	2 tbsps

   Mix all the ingredients together and taste; adjust seasoning if necessary.
   Serve cold. Makes about 2 cups.

Velouté Sauce

Serves 6 (¼ cup per serving)

This is a slightly lower fat sauce, as it uses stock where many sauces use milk and cream. It goes well with broiled or pan-fried fish such as sole, cod, haddock, etc.

2 cups	good quality fish stock	480 ml
2 tbsps	vegan margarine	50 g
1½ tbsps	all-purpose flour	1½ tbsps

   Bring the fish stock to a boil. Meanwhile, melt the margarine in another pan, add flour and cook gently for about 1 minute.
   Allow to cool slightly, then slowly add the hot stock, stirring well until smooth.
   Return to the heat and simmer for about 20 minutes, stirring occasionally to avoid sticking.
   Serve hot, adding chopped fresh tarragon, dill or chives for a varied flavor. Makes about 1½ cups.

Bread Sauce

Serves 8 (¹/₄ cup per serving)

This sauce was one that I thought I had better include as it is traditionally served with roast chicken and turkey. Made with soy milk, it is hard to tell it is not the real thing. I challenge anyone to tell the difference.

1 cup	soy milk	240 ml
1	onion, chopped in quarters	1
6	cloves, or ¹/₂ teaspoon powdered cloves	6
2	bay leaves	2
6	black peppercorns	6
	pinch of nutmeg	
	salt	
¹/₄ cup	fresh white breadcrumbs	55 g
1 tbsp	vegan margarine	25 g

Pour soy milk into a saucepan, and add the onion, cloves, bay leaves, peppercorns, nutmeg and salt.

Heat over low heat for about 10 minutes to infuse the flavors into the soy milk.

Bring mixture to a higher temperature, but not boiling; remove from heat and leave to stand for a further 5 minutes.

Strain the sauce onto the breadcrumbs and, mixing well, add the margarine; check for seasoning.

If it appears too thick, add a little more soy milk. Serve warm or cool. Makes about 2 cups.

PER SERVING	
Calories	36
% Calories from fat	51
Fat (g)	2.1
Saturated fat (g)	0.4
Cholesterol (mg)	0
Sodium (mg)	29
Protein (g)	1.3
Carbohydrate (g)	3.3
Calcium (mg)	11.5

EXCHANGES	
Milk	0.0
Vegetable	0.0
Fruit	0.0
Bread	0.5
Meat	0.0
Fat	0.0

A nice filling for baked potatoes or with smoked ham.
  Make with red onions for a bit more depth in color.

Onion Marmalade

Serves 18 (2 tablespoons per serving)

I sometimes make a batch of this marmalade, as it stores well in a jar in the fridge for several weeks. It is delicious served with the Smoked Duck Salad on page 32. It is also particularly good with cold meats or pâtés in light lunch. For anyone who can eat goat's and sheep's cheese, the marmalade makes a delicious combination with either cold or grilled cheese.

5	large onions, each weighing about 8 oz, halved and sliced in half rings	5
1 tbsp	sunflower oil	15 ml
$2/_3$ cup	red wine	150 ml
$2/_3$ cup	balsamic vinegar	150 ml
2 tbsps	light brown sugar	50 g
$1/_4$ cup	water	60 ml
$1/_2$ tsp	salt	$1/_2$ tsp

In a large frying pan or saucepan, heat the oil and add the onions.
  Sauté over gentle heat for about 10 minutes, stirring continuously until the onions are almost soft; make sure they do not burn.
  Reduce the heat, and add red wine, vinegar, sugar, water and salt.
  Stir well, cover pan and simmer for about 30 minutes, adding a few spoons of water if it dries out.
  Remove lid and, stirring occasionally, cook for a further 5 minutes.
  The marmalade should still be moist with a tiny bit of thick liquid.
  Fill a large jar with boiling water, let rest for a few minutes and empty.
  Fill jar with onion marmalade and close lid firmly.
  Allow to cool and then refrigerate. Makes about 2$1/_4$ cups.

PER SERVING	
Calories	36
% Calories from fat	20
Fat (g)	0.8
Saturated fat (g)	0.1
Cholesterol (mg)	0
Sodium (mg)	66
Protein (g)	0.4
Carbohydrate (g)	5.5
Calcium (mg)	8.1

EXCHANGES	
Milk	0.0
Vegetable	1.0
Fruit	0.0
Bread	0.0
Meat	0.0
Fat	0.0

Garam masala is an Indian spice that may be found in ethnic aisles or at Indian grocery stores.

Spiced Walnuts

Serves 16 (2 tablespoons per serving)

This recipe works equally well made with whole almonds or cashew nuts and served as a great little snack. Also try mixing lots of varieties of spiced nuts in a large bowl when friends come around for drinks. Serve with Smoked Duck Salad on page 32.

1 tbsp	olive oil	15 ml
1 tsp	Chinese 5 spice powder	1 tsp
1 tsp	garam masala	1 tsp
2 cups	walnut halves	2 cups
1½ tsp	superfine sugar	12 g
½ tsp	salt	½ tsp

Heat the oil in a large frying pan over medium heat.
Add the spices, stirring well, and cook for 30 seconds.
Stir in the walnuts, followed by the sugar and salt.
Shake the pan continuously and cook for 1 further minute over low heat. Allow to cool. Makes about 2 cups.

PER SERVING	
Calories	108
% Calories from fat	83
Fat (g)	10.6
Saturated fat (g)	1
Cholesterol (mg)	0
Sodium (mg)	73
Protein (g)	2.3
Carbohydrate (g)	2.6
Calcium (mg)	16.5
EXCHANGES	
Milk	0.0
Vegetable	0.0
Fruit	0.0
Bread	0.0
Meat	0.0
Fat	2.5

Delicious with chicken and
fish dishes.

Cajun Spice Mix

Serves 12 (1 tsp per serving)

Since I have included a few Cajun dishes in this book, I thought
I would include a recipe for Cajun Spice Mix. It can be bought
from most supermarkets, but this homemade version tastes
better and has no salt.

1 tbsp	garlic powder (if unavailable use 4 cloves fresh garlic, crushed)	1 tbsp
1 tbsp	onion powder	1 tbsp
2 tsps	cracked black pepper	2 tsps
1 tsp	dried cumin	1 tsp
1½ tsps	cayenne pepper	1½ tsps
½ tsp	allspice	½ tsp
1 tsp	dried oregano	1 tsp
1 tsp	dried thyme	1 tsp

Mix the spices together and store in a jar. If you use fresh
garlic, you will need about 4 cloves crushed to a paste, and the
spice mix will then become a paste rather than a powder, in
which case store it in the fridge.

Use as required in Cajun recipes. Makes about ¼ cup.

PER SERVING	
Calories	8
% Calories from fat	13
Fat (g)	0.1
Saturated fat (g)	0
Cholesterol (mg)	0
Sodium (mg)	1
Protein (g)	0.3
Carbohydrate (g)	1.6
Calcium (mg)	10.7
EXCHANGES	
Milk	0.0
Vegetable	0.0
Fruit	0.0
Bread	0.0
Meat	0.0
Fat	0.0

A friend of mine recently used tortillas as wraps. This was a great idea, as once smothered in a sauce, they resemble crepes with slightly more texture.

Flour Tortillas (Tortillas de Harina)

Makes 12 tortillas

I find that the tortillas in the supermarket contain many unnecessary ingredients. The homemade variety is not only healthier but also a lot cheaper and fun to make. The other types of tortillas are made with masa harina, which is corn flour specially treated for tortillas. To make them, use 5 oz masa harina, pinch salt and 4 fl oz warm water; make pliable dough, rest for 20 minutes then proceed as with flour tortillas.

1¼ cups	all-purpose white flour	1¼ cups
2 tsps	salt	2 tsps
½ cup	white lard, cut into small pieces	110 g
7 tbsps	warm water	105 ml

Sieve the flour and salt into a large bowl. Rub in the fat until the mixture resembles breadcrumbs.

Gradually add the warm water until you have pliable dough. Knead for 5 minutes.

Divide into 12 balls and cover them with a damp cloth.

On a floured surface, roll each ball into a circle approximately 9 inches in diameter. The dough should be very thin.

Heat a large, heavy frying pan over medium heat and cook each tortilla, turning once.

Count to about 40 as you cook each side. Tortillas should come out lightly spotted with brown.

Stack the cooked tortillas with waxed paper between each one. Warm as recipe instructs before using.

PER SERVING	
Calories	123
% Calories from fat	63
Fat (g)	8.5
Saturated fat (g)	3.3
Cholesterol (mg)	8
Sodium (mg)	388
Protein (g)	1.3
Carbohydrate (g)	9.9
Calcium (mg)	2.2

EXCHANGES	
Milk	0.0
Vegetable	0.0
Fruit	0.0
Bread	1.0
Meat	0.0
Fat	1.5

Salads and Dressings

Chicken, Avocado and Watercress Salad

Bulgur Wheat Salad

Carrot and Sesame Salad

Celeriac, Walnut and Apple Salad with Mint Tofu Mayonnaise

Crisp Chinese Salad

Cucumber, Mint and Soy Yogurt Salad

Red Cabbage and Pumpkin Seed Coleslaw

Roasted Fennel and Beet Salad

Roasted Vegetable and Tuna Rice Salad

Warm Sweet Potato and Artichoke Salad

Tarragon French Dressing

Creamy Lemon Dressing

Creamy Tahini Dressing

Harissa Dressing

Lime and Cilantro Dressing

Oriental Sesame Dressing

Sun-Dried Tomato, Basil and Garlic Dressing

Tofu Mayonnaise

Even better, if you can use smoked chicken, this would be delicious. For a vegetarian alternative, omit chicken and add a handful of walnuts.

Chicken, Avocado and Watercress Salad

Serves 4

This makes a quick and tasty lunch if you have any spare chicken in your fridge, but prepare it just before serving, as the avocado will start to discolor. Delicious served with brown rice or crunchy bread. Also try it as a filling for hot pita bread or on a baguette for a lunchtime sandwich. Baby spinach would be equally as tasty as watercress.

1 cup	diced skinless cooked chicken	220 g
2	green onions, thinly sliced	2
1/2	large ripe avocado	1/2
1/2 recipe	Creamy Tahini Dressing (see page 141)	1/2 recipe
	salt and freshly ground pepper	
3–4 cups	watercress	3–4 cups

Mix chicken, green onions and avocado, then stir in the dressing. Season with salt and pepper and serve on a bed of watercress.

PER SERVING	
Calories	236
% Calories from fat	75
Fat (g)	20.1
Saturated fat (g)	2.5
Cholesterol (mg)	27.9
Sodium (mg)	57
Protein (g)	11.6
Carbohydrate (g)	3.5
Calcium (mg)	45.6

EXCHANGES	
Milk	0.0
Vegetable	0.0
Fruit	0.0
Bread	0.0
Meat	1.0
Fat	4.0

Check the preparation
instructions on the packet of
bulgur wheat, as brands may
vary.

Bulgur Wheat Salad

Serves 6–8

This refreshing summer salad is a variation of the traditional
Middle Eastern salad, tabbouleh. It may seem that there is a lot
of mint and parsley in the recipe; this adds to the character of
the salad.

1 cup	bulgur wheat	220 g
1 tsp	salt	1 tsp
2 cups	boiling water	480 ml
1/4 cup	olive oil	60 ml
3 tbsps	lemon juice	45 ml
1/2	cucumber	1/2
3	firm tomatoes	3
1	red bell pepper, de-seeded	1
4	green onions	4
3 tbsps	chopped fresh mint	3 tbsps
1/4 cup	chopped fresh parsley	4 tbsps
	salt and pepper	

Mix the bulgur wheat with the salt and boiling water. Leave it
for about 20 minutes until the wheat is tender. Drain off any
excess water and allow to dry out.

Mix the bulgur wheat with the lemon and olive oil, and
refrigerate for several hours if possible at this point to allow the
wheat to soak up the flavors.

Just before serving, chop the cucumber, tomatoes and bell
pepper into small dice.

Finely chop the green onions and include the green parts.

Mix the chopped vegetables and herbs with the bulgur wheat.
Season with salt and pepper. Serve chilled.

PER SERVING	
Calories	188
% Calories from fat	43
Fat (g)	9.6
Saturated fat (g)	1.3
Cholesterol (mg)	0
Sodium (mg)	401
Protein (g)	4.1
Carbohydrate (g)	24.4
Calcium (mg)	30

EXCHANGES	
Milk	0.0
Vegetable	1.0
Fruit	0.0
Bread	1.0
Meat	0.0
Fat	2.0

Substitute 1 tablespoon of the oil for sesame oil to give a fuller-flavored dressing.

Any leftover salad could be used in a sandwich with hummus or in pita bread.

Carrot and Sesame Salad

Serves 4–6

A quick and easy salad to prepare. The carrots and sesame seeds mixed with a tahini dressing are a delightful combination. Serve as part of a buffet.

6–8	medium carrots (about 1 lb)	450 g
2	ribs celery, chopped	2
3	green onions, finely sliced	3
2 tbsps	lemon juice	30 ml
3 tbsps	peanut oil	45 ml
1 tsp	tahini	1 tsp
1/2 tsp	honey (optional)	1/2 tsp
2 tbsps	toasted sesame seeds	2 tbsps
	salt and freshly ground pepper	

Peel carrots and grate into a bowl. Mix with the celery and green onions.

In a separate bowl, combine the dressing ingredients with 1 tablespoon of the sesame seeds.

Season with salt and pepper. Add dressing to the mixed carrot, celery and green onion.

Mix well and serve chilled sprinkled with remaining sesame seeds.

PER SERVING	
Calories	178
% Calories from fat	63
Fat (g)	13.2
Saturated fat (g)	2.2
Cholesterol (mg)	0
Sodium (mg)	61
Protein (g)	2.8
Carbohydrate (g)	14.4
Calcium (mg)	54.3

EXCHANGES	
Milk	0.0
Vegetable	3.0
Fruit	0.0
Bread	0.0
Meat	0.0
Fat	2.5

This could also be made with egg-based mayonnaise.

Celeriac, Walnut and Apple Salad with Mint Tofu Mayonnaise

Serves 6

Celeriac gives the salad an interesting crunchiness. The salad should be made just before serving to prevent the apple and celeriac from discoloring. Serve with hot bread or new potatoes for a delicious, nutritious lunch.

¹/₂	celeriac, peeled and cut into small chunks	¹/₂
2–3	apples, cored and cut into small chunks	2–3
¹/₂ cup	roughly chopped walnuts	¹/₂ cup
1 tbsp	chopped fresh mint	1 tbsp
1 tbsp	chopped fresh parsley	1 tbsp
	salt and freshly ground pepper	
¹/₂ recipe	Tofu Mayonnaise (see page 144)	¹/₂ recipe

Mix all salad ingredients with tofu mayonnaise. Serve chilled.

PER SERVING	
Calories	167
% Calories from fat	70
Fat (g)	13.8
Saturated fat (g)	1.4
Cholesterol (mg)	0
Sodium (mg)	141
Protein (g)	3.2
Carbohydrate (g)	9.9
Calcium (mg)	28.9

EXCHANGES	
Milk	0.0
Vegetable	0.0
Fruit	0.5
Bread	0.0
Meat	0.0
Fat	3.0

Try using Chinese cabbage, regular cabbage, cauliflower or broccoli.

PER SERVING	
Calories	172
% Calories from fat	64
Fat (g)	12.6
Saturated fat (g)	2
Cholesterol (mg)	0
Sodium (mg)	546
Protein (g)	3
Carbohydrate (g)	13.2
Calcium (mg)	82
EXCHANGES	
Milk	0.0
Vegetable	2.0
Fruit	0.0
Bread	0.0
Meat	0.0
Fat	3.0

Crisp Chinese Salad

Serves 4

This is a very colorful salad that can be made with a variety of raw vegetables.

2	large carrots, peeled	2
1/2	cucumber	1/2
6	green onions	6
1	red bell pepper	1
2–3 cups	bean sprouts (about 8 oz)	225 g
1 recipe	Oriental Sesame Dressing (see page 143)	1 recipe

Cut the carrot and cucumber into thin julienne strips, similar in length to the bean sprouts.

Discard the outer leaves of the green onion, keeping as much of the green as possible, and shred into similar strips.

Cut the bell pepper in half and remove seeds; cut into thin strips.

Mix everything with the bean sprouts.

Chill and toss with the dressing just before serving.

Cucumber, Mint and Soy Yogurt Salad

Serves 2

This refreshing salad is based on Greek tzatziki. It is ideal as a salad or as an accompaniment to dishes such as Sweet Potato and Chick Pea Cakes (page 59) or served with spicy dishes and barbecues.

1 1/2 cups	soy yogurt	1 1/2 cups
1/2	cucumber, chopped into small cubes	1/2
2 tbsps	chopped fresh mint	2 tbsps
1/2 tsp	honey	1/2 tsp
	salt and freshly ground pepper	

Mix all the ingredients and season well.

Refrigerate before serving. Serves 2 as a salad or enough for 4 as an accompaniment.

PER SERVING	
Calories	129
% Calories from fat	19
Fat (g)	2.7
Saturated fat (g)	0
Cholesterol (mg)	0
Sodium (mg)	32
Protein (g)	4.3
Carbohydrate (g)	21.8
Calcium (mg)	539.5
EXCHANGES	
Milk	0.5
Vegetable	2.0
Fruit	0.0
Bread	0.0
Meat	0.0
Fat	0.5

Red Cabbage and Pumpkin Seed Coleslaw

Serves 4–6

A lovely crisp salad full of goodness.

¹/₄ head	red cabbage (about 8 oz)	225 g
1	fennel bulb (about 4 oz)	112 g
2–3	carrots, peeled (about 6 oz)	170 g
1	red apple	1
2 tbsps	pumpkin seeds (could use sunflower seeds)	2 tbsps
¹/₂ recipe	Tarragon French Dressing (page 139)	¹/₂ recipe
2 tbsps	soy yogurt	2 tbsps

Wash and prepare the cabbage; remove the tough outer leaves and central core if it is too tough, and shred finely.

Shred the fennel, discarding the tough outer leaves.

Grate the carrots and mix in a large bowl with the cabbage and fennel.

Wash and core the apple, and cut into small dice, leaving the skin on for color.

Add the pumpkin seeds to the bowl. Toss everything together with the dressing and the yogurt.

Chill and serve.

PER SERVING	
Calories	325
% Calories from fat	76
Fat (g)	28.1
Saturated fat (g)	2.9
Cholesterol (mg)	0
Sodium (mg)	283
Protein (g)	2.3
Carbohydrate (g)	18.1
Calcium (mg)	85.8

EXCHANGES	
Milk	0.0
Vegetable	1.0
Fruit	0.0
Bread	1.0
Meat	0.0
Fat	5.0

Roasted Fennel and Beet Salad

Serves 4

Roasting fennel and beets is one of the best ways to cook these vegetables. If you are not keen on either vegetable, you may be pleasantly surprised. The roasting juices from the tomatoes combined with the beet, olive oil and vinegar make a delicious red dressing. Serve warm with steamed couscous and nut burgers or tofu fritters. Alternatively, serve with hot bread.

2	large beets	2
1	large or 2 small fennel bulbs	1
2 tbsps	olive oil	30 ml
2	medium tomatoes, cut into 8 wedges	2
4	green onions, cut into 1/2-inch slices	4
1 tbsp	balsamic vinegar	15 ml
	salt and freshly ground pepper	
3	sprigs fresh thyme	3
1 tbsp	fresh parsley	1 tbsp

Pre-heat the oven to 400F. Peel the beets and cut into segments about 1/2 inch across.

Trim the fennel and cut into segments similar size to beets. Place the beets and fennel in a large baking dish, pour over olive oil and shake well in the oil to get a good coating.

Roast in the hot oven for about 25 minutes until the vegetables are beginning to brown at the edges.

Add tomato wedges, onions and balsamic, and mix well. Return to oven for about 15 minutes.

Season with salt and pepper and sprinkle over with thyme leaves and chopped parsley.

If required, drizzle extra olive oil over the salad. Serve warm or chilled.

PER SERVING	
Calories	118
% Calories from fat	51
Fat (g)	7.2
Saturated fat (g)	1
Cholesterol (mg)	0
Sodium (mg)	71
Protein (g)	2.3
Carbohydrate (g)	13.1
Calcium (mg)	57.7

EXCHANGES	
Milk	0.0
Vegetable	2.0
Fruit	0.0
Bread	0.0
Meat	0.0
Fat	1.5

Substitute pasta instead of rice for a delicious pasta salad.

Roasted Vegetable and Tuna Rice Salad

Serves 4

This is perfect for a tasty summer lunch eaten outdoors. The vegetables should all slightly caramelize, giving an added natural sweetness. Serve with some salad leaves or watercress and the Sun-Dried Tomato, Basil and Garlic Dressing.

1	large red bell pepper	1
1	medium red onion	1
1 tbsp	olive oil and extra to drizzle	15 ml
1	clove garlic, crushed	1
	salt and pepper	
½ cup	baby corn (about 4 oz)	110 g
4 cups	cooked brown short-grain rice	4 cups
1	can tuna, water packed, drained weight 5¼ oz	1
2 recipes	Sun-Dried Tomato, Basil and Garlic Dressing (see page 143)	2 recipes

Heat the broiler, and when it is hot, place the whole red pepper underneath and leave for about 4 minutes before turning. Repeat until completely blistered and black (about 4 turns). Place the pepper in a small plastic bag.

Peel when cool enough to handle, removing seeds and stalk, and cut into chunks; leave to one side.

Peel the red onion, cube and pull layers apart; mix with the olive oil, garlic, salt and pepper in an oven dish.

Leave a gap on one side and lay the baby corn out next to the onions; drizzle over a little more olive oil.

Broil for about 5 minutes, turning from time to time. Add the peppers and mix with the onions. Continue broiling for a further 5 minutes until the baby corn is golden brown and the onions are soft and beginning to caramelize at the edges.

Allow to cool.

In a large bowl, mix the rice with the peppers, onions, baby corn and tuna chunks, and season well with salt and freshly ground pepper.

Refrigerate until needed. To serve, toss with the dressing.

PER SERVING	
Calories	455
% Calories from fat	37
Fat (g)	19
Saturated fat (g)	2.7
Cholesterol (mg)	11.2
Sodium (mg)	308
Protein (g)	16
Carbohydrate (g)	55.2
Calcium (mg)	45
EXCHANGES	
Milk	0.0
Vegetable	2.0
Fruit	0.0
Bread	3.0
Meat	2.0
Fat	2.0

Marinated artichoke hearts are found in most supermarkets and have a wonderful rich flavor.

Warm Sweet Potato and Artichoke Salad

Serves 4

This is an unusual salad, which served with warm crusty bread makes a delicious light lunch. Alternatively, it could be served alongside grilled meat or fish.

3–4	sweet potatoes, peeled but left whole (about 1 lb)	450 g
1 tbsp	olive oil	15 ml
	salt and freshly ground pepper	
1 cup	artichoke hearts packed in oil, drained	1 cup
2–3 cups	watercress, washed and thick stalks removed	2–3 cups
2–3 cups	crisp romaine lettuce, broken up	2–3 cups
2 tbsps	pine nuts	2 tbsps
1½ tbsps	balsamic vinegar	23 ml

Boil or steam the sweet potatoes for about 10 minutes, until firm but almost tender.

Slice into ³/₄-inch-thick discs. Coat in the olive oil and season well.

Heat a skillet and fry the potato slices in batches for about 2 minutes either side, until charred.

Slice the artichoke hearts in quarters and quickly warm in the skillet.

Combine the watercress and romaine in a large salad bowl.

Toss the warm potatoes, artichoke hearts and pine nuts together and tip over the leaves.

Mix 4 tablespoons of the artichoke oil from the jar with the balsamic vinegar, season with salt and freshly ground pepper, whisk well and drizzle over salad before serving.

PER SERVING	
Calories	206
% Calories from fat	40
Fat (g)	9.9
Saturated fat (g)	0.9
Cholesterol (mg)	0
Sodium (mg)	182
Protein (g)	3.5
Carbohydrate (g)	29.9
Calcium (mg)	52

EXCHANGES	
Milk	0.0
Vegetable	2.0
Fruit	0.0
Bread	1.0
Meat	0.0
Fat	2.0

Add any other fresh herbs or garlic for a different flavor.

Tarragon French Dressing

Serves 12 (2 tablespoons per serving)

This produces a slightly white and creamy dressing, which should stay thick and not need shaking before serving. The dressing lasts for up to a week in the fridge. Serve with crisp mixed leaf salads.

2 tbsps	Dijon mustard	2 tbsps
2 tbsps	apple cider vinegar	30 ml
1/2 tsp	salt	1/2 tsp
1 cup	(scant) sunflower oil	220 ml
1–2 tbsps	water	15–30 ml
2 tbsps	chopped fresh tarragon	2 tbsps
	freshly ground pepper	

In a medium bowl, whisk the mustard, vinegar and salt together.

Gradually add the oil, beating well to form an emulsion as if making mayonnaise.

When all the oil has been added, the dressing will appear quite thick.

Stir in the water to thin the dressing down, followed by the tarragon and freshly ground pepper.

Store in a sealed jar in the fridge until required. Makes about 1 1/2 cups.

PER SERVING	
Calories	164
% Calories from fat	99
Fat (g)	18.1
Saturated fat (g)	1.9
Cholesterol (mg)	0
Sodium (mg)	154
Protein (g)	0
Carbohydrate (g)	0.2
Calcium (mg)	1.6

EXCHANGES	
Milk	0.0
Vegetable	0.0
Fruit	0.0
Bread	0.0
Meat	0.0
Fat	3.5

I have also made this with limes, which is great with fish dishes such as Thai fish cakes. Try using honey instead of sugar.

Creamy Lemon Dressing

Serves 12 (2 tbsps per serving)
This will have a milky white appearance and a delicious, slightly tangy flavor that adds a special touch to many fish dishes such as fish mousses, crab cakes or fresh crab and lobster.

2	large lemons	2
1 tbsp	sugar	25 g
1/2 tsp	salt	1/2 tsp
1 cup	oil such as sunflower or vegetable	240 ml
	freshly ground pepper	

Using a sharp knife, cut tops and bottoms off the lemons, then moving from top to bottom, cut the lemon skins off and cut out the individual segments, ensuring there are no seeds or pith remaining.

Process the lemon segments, sugar and salt in a blender until smooth and slightly white.

Slowly add the oil while machine is running.

Taste and season with pepper and add more oil if necessary (depends on size of lemons). Makes about 1 1/2 cups.

PER SERVING

Calories	168
% Calories from fat	93
Fat (g)	18.2
Saturated fat (g)	1.9
Cholesterol (mg)	0
Sodium (mg)	97
Protein (g)	0.2
Carbohydrate (g)	2.9
Calcium (mg)	2.8

EXCHANGES

Milk	0.0
Vegetable	0.0
Fruit	0.0
Bread	0.0
Meat	0.0
Fat	3.5

Creamy Tahini Dressing

Serves 8 (2 tablespoons per serving)

This dressing is quite similar to Tarragon French Dressing, but the addition of mayonnaise and tahini makes it suitable for rice, beans and pasta salads.

PER SERVING	
Calories	141
% Calories from fat	96
Fat (g)	15.4
Saturated fat (g)	1.7
Cholesterol (mg)	1
Sodium (mg)	21
Protein (g)	0.3
Carbohydrate (g)	1.2
Calcium (mg)	2.8
EXCHANGES	
Milk	0.0
Vegetable	0.0
Fruit	0.0
Bread	0.0
Meat	0.0
Fat	3.0

2 tbsps	low-fat mayonnaise	2 tbsps
1 tbsp	apple cider vinegar	15 ml
1 tbsp	tahini	1 tbsp
1/2 cup	sunflower oil	120 ml
1/4 cup	cold water (or more for a thinner dressing)	60 ml
	salt and freshly ground pepper	

Whisk mayonnaise in a bowl with vinegar and tahini.

Gradually add the sunflower oil, whisking well until thick and smooth.

Thin down with the water and season with salt and pepper. Chill to serve. Makes about 1 cup.

Harissa Dressing

Serves 4 (2 tablespoons per serving)

Harissa is a fiery North African paste made from a mixture of chilies, tomato and garlic with various spices. Here I have made it into a dressing using sun-dried tomato paste, which I think adds a richer flavor. The dressing is delicious with roasted vegetables and couscous. Also great served with the Moroccan Lamb Burgers on page 41 and Spiced Rice on page 109.

PER SERVING	
Calories	139
% Calories from fat	88
Fat (g)	13.9
Saturated fat (g)	1.8
Cholesterol (mg)	0
Sodium (mg)	47
Protein (g)	0.8
Carbohydrate (g)	3.6
Calcium (mg)	23.3
EXCHANGES	
Milk	0.0
Vegetable	0.0
Fruit	0.0
Bread	0.0
Meat	0.0
Fat	3.0

1 tbsp	tomato purée	1 tbsp
1 tbsp	sun-dried tomato paste	1 tbsp
1	clove garlic, crushed	1
1 tbsp	ground cumin powder	1 tbsp
1 tsp	ground cilantro powder	1 tsp
1/2 tsp	chili powder	1/2 tsp
2	limes, squeezed	2
1/4 cup	olive oil	60 ml

Mix all the above ingredients well before serving. Makes 1/2 cup.

Fish sauce is a Thai alternative to soy sauce or salt, made from anchovy extract; if you are unable to find it, substitute a light soy sauce.

Lime and Cilantro Dressing

Serves 4 (2 tablespoons per serving)

This is a delicate Thai-style dressing that goes very well with fish dishes. Serve with monkfish and shrimp kebabs or just plain broiled fish and salad. Prepare dressing up to three days in advance.

3	limes	3
	peanut oil	
	handful of fresh cilantro	
1 tbsp	fish sauce (nam pla)	15 ml
1 inch	fresh gingerroot, peeled and finely chopped	2.5 cm
1	red chili pepper, de-seeded and finely chopped	1
2 tsps	sugar	16 g

Using a vegetable peeler, remove about 6 strips of lime zest, cut these into thin strips, then chop finely.

Squeeze the juice from the limes and pour it into a bowl with an equal amount of peanut oil.

Remove leaves from the cilantro, cut the stalks finely and chop the leaves.

Mix all the ingredients, including the zest. Stir thoroughly, taste and adjust seasoning if necessary. Dressing should be quite tangy, with enough sugar to cut acidity.

Refrigerate until needed. Makes about 1/2 cup.

PER SERVING	
Calories	201
% Calories from fat	88
Fat (g)	20.3
Saturated fat (g)	3.4
Cholesterol (mg)	0
Sodium (mg)	349
Protein (g)	0.6
Carbohydrate (g)	5.6
Calcium (mg)	6.3
EXCHANGES	
Milk	0.0
Vegetable	1.0
Fruit	0.0
Bread	0.0
Meat	0.0
Fat	4.0

If you don't have rice vinegar, cider or white wine vinegar will be fine.

PER SERVING	
Calories	134
% Calories from fat	82
Fat (g)	12.4
Saturated fat (g)	1.9
Cholesterol (mg)	0
Sodium (mg)	515
Protein (g)	1.3
Carbohydrate (g)	4.9
Calcium (mg)	45.7
EXCHANGES	
Milk	0.0
Vegetable	0.0
Fruit	0.0
Bread	0.0
Meat	0.0
Fat	3.0

The dressing may appear to separate slightly from the oil; just mix well before serving.

For a super vegan starter, serve with crisp French bread croutons topped with griddled slithers of mixed vegetables, such as asparagus, peppers, courgettes and aubergine.

PER SERVING	
Calories	51
% Calories from fat	92
Fat (g)	5.4
Saturated fat (g)	0.7
Cholesterol (mg)	0
Sodium (mg)	26
Protein (g)	0.2
Carbohydrate (g)	0.9
Calcium (mg)	3.1
EXCHANGES	
Milk	0.0
Vegetable	0.0
Fruit	0.0
Bread	0.0
Meat	0.0
Fat	1.0

Oriental Sesame Dressing

Serves 4 (2 tablespoons per serving)

This is a delicious dressing that will jazz up any crisp vegetable salad. The addition of sesame seeds and honey adds a lovely nutty sweetness.

2 tsps	honey	2 tsps
2 tbsps	rice vinegar	30 ml
3 tsps	sesame oil	15 ml
2 tbsps	peanut oil	30 ml
2 tbsps	soy sauce	30 ml
2 tbsps	toasted sesame seeds	2 tbsps

Thin the honey down with the rice vinegar until smooth.
Add the oils and soy sauce and taste.
Before serving, mix in toasted sesame seeds. Makes about 1/2 cup.

Sun-Dried Tomato, Basil and Garlic Dressing

Serves 5 (1 tablespoon per serving)

Great served with roasted vegetables. It has a delightful Italian flavor. Serve with the Grilled Fresh Tuna on Potato Niçoise on page 50.

1 tbsp	sun-dried tomato paste	1 tbsp
1	clove garlic, crushed	1
1 tbsp	red wine vinegar	15 ml
2 tbsps	olive oil	30 ml
1 tbsp	fresh basil	1 tbsp
	salt and freshly ground pepper	

Mix sun-dried tomato paste, garlic and vinegar together.
Slowly beat in the oil, then taste and season with basil and salt and pepper. Add more oil if necessary, depending on taste. Makes about 1/3 cup.

This dressing will store in a sealed jar for several days in the fridge.

Tofu Mayonnaise

Serves 8 (2 tablespoons per serving)

Although egg mayonnaise is acceptable for the lactose-free diet, this tofu mayonnaise is more nutritious and slightly lower in fat—especially good for a vegetarian diet.

1	pack (8 3/4 oz) silken tofu	1
2 tsps	wholegrain or Dijon mustard	2 tsps
1	clove fresh garlic (optional)	1
1/2 tsp	salt	1/2 tsp
	freshly ground pepper	
1 tbsp	white wine vinegar or lemon juice	15 ml
6 tbsps	sunflower oil	90 ml

Blend tofu, mustard, garlic, salt, pepper and 1 teaspoon vinegar in a processor.

Gradually pour in the oil and continue blending until smooth and creamy.

Add remaining vinegar and mix thoroughly. Taste for seasoning and serve. Makes about 1 cup.

PER SERVING	
Calories	104
% Calories from fat	91
Fat (g)	10.5
Saturated fat (g)	1.1
Cholesterol (mg)	0
Sodium (mg)	191
Protein (g)	2
Carbohydrate (g)	0.4
Calcium (mg)	13.1

EXCHANGES	
Milk	0.0
Vegetable	0.0
Fruit	0.0
Bread	0.0
Meat	0.0
Fat	2.0

Desserts and Sweet Sauces

Apricot and Almond Fool

Apricot Tart Tatin

Baked Apple Charlotte

Baked Chocolate and Almond Torte

Baked Orange Semolina Puddings

Banana Fritters

Caramelized Apple Pie

Chocolate, Prune and Whiskey Bread Pudding

Coconut Crème Caramel

Coffee Zabaglione

Fresh Raspberry Tart

*Honey-Glazed Pineapple and
Fig Kebabs with Orange Sabayon*

Mixed Berry and Peach Coconut Crumble

Pear and Ginger Upside Down Cake

Raisin, Lemon and Almond Rice Pudding

Rhubarb and Almond Tart

Chocolate Brownies

Tangy Citrus Cheesecake

Chocolate Fudge Sauce

Pastry Cream

Custard Sauce

Fresh Raspberry Coulis

Rich Butterscotch Sauce

Mocha Chocolate Sauce

Oat and Honey Cream

Tofu and Almond Cream

You could make this using either different dried fruit or fresh fruit.

Apricot and Almond Fool

Serves 4

This is a quick and simple vegan pudding. It contains lots of goodness in the almonds and the apricots. Try it on the children to jazz up soy yogurt. Serve with crisp cookies or macaroons.

2 cups	dried apricots, two reserved and chopped (about ¹/₂ lb)	225 g
1 cup	boiling water	240 ml
1 cup	soy yogurt	1 cup
²/₃ cup	blanched almonds (3 oz)	85 g
1 tbsp	maple syrup	15 ml
¹/₂ tsp	vanilla extract	¹/₂ tsp

Cover the apricots with the boiling water and soak overnight, or, alternatively, simmer in the water until soft.

Purée the apricots in the soaking liquid until smooth and allow to cool. When cold, fold in the yogurt.

Grind the almonds finely in a food processor or grinder, add enough water to make a thick cream and continue grinding until smooth.

Sweeten with maple syrup and vanilla extract.

Add the apricot purée and blend until smooth.

Spoon into four small dishes. Decorate with chopped apricots. Refrigerate before serving.

PER SERVING	
Calories	385
% Calories from fat	29
Fat (g)	13.5
Saturated fat (g)	1
Cholesterol (mg)	0
Sodium (mg)	25
Protein (g)	9.5
Carbohydrate (g)	64
Calcium (mg)	267.2
EXCHANGES	
Milk	0.0
Vegetable	0.0
Fruit	4.0
Bread	0.0
Meat	0.0
Fat	3.0

I have made this pudding with a variety of different fruits: apples, quinces, bananas, fresh or canned pineapple and pears with crystallized ginger, which was scrumptious.

Apricot Tart Tatin

Serves 8

This is one of my favorites, as it can be prepared in advance and cooked before serving. The pastry is deliciously crisp. Serve it with soy ice cream or soy yogurt. For an even healthier option, serve it with the Oat and Honey Cream or the Tofu and Almond Cream (see pages 169, 170).

Pastry

3/8 cup	all-purpose flour	3/8 cup
1 tsp	ground cinnamon	1 tsp
3 tbsps	superfine sugar	75 g
	pinch salt	
3 tbsps	vegan margarine	75 g
1	large egg, beaten	1

Filling

2 tbsps	vegan margarine	50 g
1/2 cup	superfine sugar	110 g
1 2/3 cups	dried apricots (about 1/2 lb)	225 g

Soak the apricots overnight or boil for about 20 minutes until soft and then drain.

Pre-heat the oven to 375F. Grease a 10-inch-round pie pan or dish.

To make the pastry, sift the flour and cinnamon into a bowl, add the sugar and salt and mix well.

In a small pan, gently melt the margarine, stir it into the flour, mixing well, and then mix in the egg.

Press the pastry into a ball and cover in a bowl. Place in the fridge for one hour.

For the filling, melt the margarine with the sugar.

Pour into the bottom of the pie dish, covering the base.

Place the apricots over this mixture.

Roll the pastry out on a floured surface to just larger than the pie dish. Don't worry if it breaks, as you can patch it up.

Carefully lift the pastry to cover the apricots, folding over the sides if it is too big.

Pierce a couple of holes in the pastry. Cook for about 25 minutes until firm to the touch and golden.

Cool slightly, then carefully turn onto a serving plate.

PER SERVING	
Calories	295
% Calories from fat	24
Fat (g)	8.1
Saturated fat (g)	1.6
Cholesterol (mg)	26.6
Sodium (mg)	95
Protein (g)	4.3
Carbohydrate (g)	53.8
Calcium (mg)	27.8
EXCHANGES	
Milk	0.0
Vegetable	0.0
Fruit	2.0
Bread	1.5
Meat	0.0
Fat	1.5

Baked Apple Charlotte

Serves 4

The jam on the bread tends to stick slightly to the side of the dish but gives it a nice crunchy texture. The walnut oil also provides an unusual taste rather than the usual margarine.
The dish is itself quite creamy and does not really require any further cream, although my children enjoy a spoonful of soy ice cream with it.

4–5	medium cooking apples (1³/₄ lbs)		800 g
1¹/₂ tbsps	superfine sugar		37 g
5	slices stale white bread, crusts removed		5
¹/₂ cup	apricot jam		110 g
2 tbsps	walnut oil, plus extra for brushing		30 ml
1 tsp	dark brown sugar		8 g

Pre-heat the oven to 375F. Peel, core and slice the apples and put them into a heavy pan.

Add the sugar and cook, without water, until very soft. Then, using a potato masher, mash the apples until they are smooth and creamy.

Oil a 1-quart oven dish. Cut each slice of bread into 4 triangles.

Gently warm the jam with a dash of water and the walnut oil, stirring well.

Dip the pieces of bread into this jam mixture to coat each slice.

Arrange the triangles to fit the bottom and sides of the dish, saving 6 to 8 triangles for the top.

Mix any leftover jam mixture with the apple and pour into the bread-lined dish; cover with remaining bread.

Brush with extra walnut oil and sprinkle the top with dark brown sugar.

Bake for about 30 minutes until crisp and golden. Allow to cool slightly before serving.

PER SERVING	
Calories	394
% Calories from fat	19
Fat (g)	8.7
Saturated fat (g)	0.9
Cholesterol (mg)	0.3
Sodium (mg)	181
Protein (g)	3.1
Carbohydrate (g)	78.9
Calcium (mg)	56

EXCHANGES	
Milk	0.0
Vegetable	0.0
Fruit	4.5
Bread	1.0
Meat	0.0
Fat	1.5

If you do not want to use Amaretto liqueur, use a strong black espresso instead.

For anyone who wants a chocolate mousse cake, follow the recipe and stop before the final cooking stage. Pour the uncooked filling over the cookie base and refrigerate. However, this would be unsuitable for pregnant or elderly people, as the eggs would be uncooked. Delicious for anyone else.

Baked Chocolate and Almond Torte

Serves 6

This rich, slightly gooey torte turned out to be a big success with my family one cold, rainy Sunday lunch. Serve with soy cream, or be really naughty and have some soy ice cream with it.

Base

1 tbsp	sliced almonds	1 tbsp
½ cup	crushed dairy-free cookies	110 g
2 tbsps	vegan margarine	50 g

Filling

8 oz	dairy-free good quality dark chocolate	225 g
4	eggs, separated	4
2 tbsps	Amaretto (optional) or use dark black coffee	30 ml

Pre-heat the oven to 350F. Slightly crush the almonds and mix with the crushed cookies.

In a small pan, gently melt the margarine, pour into cookie crumbs and mix well.

Tip into a greased oven dish approximately 10 inches in diameter, and pat the mixture down flat.

Bake in the oven for about 10 minutes until firm. Allow to cool while you make the filling.

Break the chocolate into pieces and melt in a bowl over a pan of boiling water. When the chocolate is melted, remove the bowl from the pan.

In a separate bowl, beat the yolks, and while chocolate is still quite hot pour slowly over yolks, beating continuously.

Stir in the Amaretto and leave to cool.

In a large clean bowl, whisk the egg whites until they form a peak. Fold the whites into the chocolate mixture.

Pour over base, and turn oven down to 325F.

Bake for about 15 minutes, but don't overcook, as it may dry out.

The torte should be eaten when cool, and it will still be quite sticky in the middle.

PER SERVING	
Calories	348
% Calories from fat	53
Fat (g)	22.2
Saturated fat (g)	9.7
Cholesterol (mg)	146.2
Sodium (mg)	124
Protein (g)	6.6
Carbohydrate (g)	35.2
Calcium (mg)	40

EXCHANGES	
Milk	0.0
Vegetable	0.0
Fruit	0.0
Bread	2.5
Meat	0.0
Fat	4.0

Use lemons or limes for a
different flavor.

Baked Orange Semolina Puddings

Serves 6

These add a new dimension to semolina. The addition of eggs
makes it into a soufflé-style pudding, well worth a try. Take care
not too cook these too hot and long, as they may curdle.

2–3	large juicy oranges	2–3
1 tbsp	granulated sugar	25 g
1 tbsp	semolina	1 tbsp
3	eggs, separated	3
	confectioner's sugar for dusting	

Pre-heat the oven to 375F. Grate rind and squeeze juice from
2 oranges, to make about 1 cup of juice. Use another orange if
necessary.

Place orange juice, rind, sugar and semolina in a pan and
simmer until thickened, stirring continuously.

Cool slightly, then stir in egg yolks.

Whisk whites until they are stiff, and fold them into the
orange mixture.

Spoon into 6 lightly oiled ramekin dishes.

Bake in the oven for 15–20 minutes until risen and golden,
and then dust with confectioner's sugar. Serve immediately.

PER SERVING	
Calories	70
% Calories from fat	34
Fat (g)	2.6
Saturated fat (g)	0.8
Cholesterol (mg)	106.2
Sodium (mg)	32
Protein (g)	3.6
Carbohydrate (g)	7.9
Calcium (mg)	17

EXCHANGES	
Milk	0.0
Vegetable	0.0
Fruit	0.5
Bread	0.0
Meat	0.5
Fat	0.0

Make sure the bananas are not too overripe for this recipe. For an equally delicious dessert, use fresh pineapple or apple rings.

Banana Fritters

Serves 4

Delicious crisp fritters. The addition of coconut to the batter makes the dish more exotic. Serve with soy ice cream, soy yogurt or even tofu and almond cream.

2 tbsps	all-purpose flour	2 tbsps
	pinch salt	
1	large egg	1
³/₈ cup	low-fat coconut milk	90 ml
1 tbsp	superfine sugar	25 g
4	firm bananas	4
	oil for shallow frying	
1 tsp	confectioner's sugar mixed with 1 teaspoon of dried coconut	1 tsp

Sift flour with salt in a bowl. Make a well in the center. Drop in the egg and mix with a wooden spoon, gradually incorporating all the flour, then slowly add the coconut milk, stirring well. Add more coconut milk as needed to reach a thick cream consistency. Stir in the sugar and allow the batter to rest for 20 minutes.

Peel bananas, cut in half lengthways and dip into the batter.

Heat ¹/₄-inch-deep oil in a frying pan. When hot, fry the fritters for about 2 minutes on each side until golden brown.

Drain and dust with confectioner's sugar and coconut mix. Serve immediately while the fritters are still crisp.

PER SERVING

Calories	171
% Calories from fat	15
Fat (g)	3.1
Saturated fat (g)	1.5
Cholesterol (mg)	53.1
Sodium (mg)	25
Protein (g)	3.2
Carbohydrate (g)	35.3
Calcium (mg)	13.5

EXCHANGES

Milk	0.0
Vegetable	0.0
Fruit	2.5
Bread	0.0
Meat	0.0
Fat	0.5

This is also good with pears, bananas or fresh apricots.

Caramelized Apple Pie

Serves 8

This is based on the French "Tarte Tatin" recipe. I have included it as it is a super-fast recipe for anyone wanting to produce a quick dessert for their lactose-free guests. Serve with soy yogurt, soy ice cream or Tofu and Almond Cream (page 170).

2 tbsps	dark brown sugar	50 g
1 tbsp	walnut oil	15 ml
1 tsp	ground cinnamon	1 tsp
3–4	medium apples, peeled, cored and very thinly sliced (about 1 lb.)	450 g
1/2 lb	puff pastry, shop bought	225 g

Pre-heat the oven to 400F. Oil a 10-inch round oven dish, which is at least 3/4 inch high. Sprinkle sugar on the bottom of dish and drizzle over oil and cinnamon.

Lay apples in a neat circle over the sugar, ensuring that all the base is covered. If necessary, layer more apples on top.

Roll out pastry and cut into a circle about 3/4 inch larger than the round base. Cover the apples with the pastry, pressing it down gently; fold the edges back over.

Bake in the oven for 20–25 minutes until well risen, crisp and golden.

Turn out onto a warm plate to serve.

PER SERVING	
Calories	218
% Calories from fat	51
Fat (g)	12.7
Saturated fat (g)	2.9
Cholesterol (mg)	0
Sodium (mg)	72
Protein (g)	2.2
Carbohydrate (g)	25
Calcium (mg)	13.3

EXCHANGES	
Milk	0.0
Vegetable	0.0
Fruit	1.0
Bread	1.0
Meat	0.0
Fat	2.0

If you don't have whiskey, use a brandy or liqueur; otherwise soak the prunes in orange juice.
Try using coconut milk instead of soy cream for a more exotic pudding.

Chocolate, Prune and Whiskey Bread Pudding

Serves 6

This is a good dinner party dessert, and your friends will not believe it is lactose-free. It is also a great way of using up any excess bread. Prunes not only increase the nutritional value of the dish but also make a wonderful combination with chocolate. Serve with soy cream or soy ice cream.

1/3 cup	pitted prunes, cut into 4 pieces	1/3 cup
2 tbsps	whiskey	30 ml
6	slices of thick-sliced white bread	6
1 tbsp	vegan margarine	25 g
3 oz	dark dairy-free chocolate, cut into small pieces	85 g
1 tbsp	cocoa powder	1 tbsp
1 1/8 cups	soy milk	270 ml
3 tbsps	superfine sugar	75 g
3	eggs	3
6 tbsps	soy cream	90 ml
	sprinkling of crystallized sugar, optional	

Pre-heat the oven to 350F. You will need an oven-proof dish with a base measurement of about 8 x 6 inches, 1 1/2 inches deep, lightly greased.

About 2 hours before you start, pour whiskey over the prunes in a small bowl and leave to soak.

Remove the crusts from the bread and lightly spread the slices with margarine. Cut each slice of bread into 4 squares, and lay half over the bottom of the oven-proof dish.

Cover with the prunes, whiskey and chocolate chunks, then place the remaining bread over the top, overlapping slightly, margarine side up.

Sieve the cocoa in a medium mixing bowl and gradually add the soy milk, making sure cocoa is mixed in thoroughly. Beat in the eggs, sugar and soy cream.

Pour this cocoa mixture over the bread. Press the top gently with a fork to ensure all the bread is coated.

Sprinkle on a little crystallized sugar.

Bake for 30–40 minutes. The pudding will rise slightly, and the surface should be crisp and golden.

PER SERVING	
Calories	283
% Calories from fat	37
Fat (g)	12
Saturated fat (g)	4.2
Cholesterol (mg)	107.6
Sodium (mg)	199
Protein (g)	7.4
Carbohydrate (g)	35.6
Calcium (mg)	51.2

EXCHANGES	
Milk	0.0
Vegetable	0.0
Fruit	0.5
Bread	2.0
Meat	0.0
Fat	2.5

Coconut contains a high proportion of saturated fats. It is a good addition to the vegetarian dairy-free diet, although those with a meat-centered diet should limit their intake.

Coconut Crème Caramel

Serves 4

When I tried to make a crème caramel with soy milk, the result was very watery and not particularly successful. Made with coconut milk, however, the result was a creamy light custard with a delicate coconut flavor.

3/4 cup	superfine sugar	170 g
1	14-oz can reduced-fat coconut milk	1
3	medium eggs	3

Pre-heat the oven to 300F. Put half of the sugar in a heavy pan over low heat.

Stir and let the sugar caramelize. When melted and golden brown (not burnt), pour the caramel equally into 4 ramekins.

In a small pan, heat the coconut milk over low heat until warm.

In a bowl, beat the eggs with the remaining sugar until light and creamy.

Gradually add the coconut milk, beating as you do so.

Strain the custard and pour into ramekins. Put the ramekins in a baking pan, and pour enough hot water around them so it comes halfway up the cups.

Bake for 30–40 minutes, until the coconut caramels are set. When cool, refrigerate in the ramekins.

To serve, run a knife around the edges of the bowls and invert onto plates. Makes 4 individual custards.

PER SERVING	
Calories	259
% Calories from fat	31
Fat (g)	9.1
Saturated fat (g)	4.7
Cholesterol (mg)	159.4
Sodium (mg)	87
Protein (g)	4.7
Carbohydrate (g)	40
Calcium (mg)	18.7

EXCHANGES	
Milk	0.0
Vegetable	0.0
Fruit	0.0
Bread	2.5
Meat	0.0
Fat	2.0

Note that any liqueur can be used, such as Amaretto or a chocolate liqueur (as long as it contains no cream).

Coffee Zabaglione

Serves 4

This pudding is surprisingly creamy and light and is excellent served warm with a crisp cookie. This dish can also be frozen and served as zabaglione ice cream.

4	egg yolks	4
2 tbsps	superfine sugar	50 g
1/4 cup	strong black coffee	60 ml
2 tbsps	coffee liqueur (such as Tia Maria)	30 ml
	cocoa powder for decoration	

Combine egg yolks and sugar in a bowl. Whisk for several minutes with an electric beater until pale and frothy. Transfer to top of double boiler.

Over simmering water, gradually beat in half the coffee and half the liqueur.

Beat constantly for about 10 minutes over heat until thick and creamy.

Then whisk in the remaining coffee and liqueur. If the mixture adheres to side of pan, quickly remove from heat and beat vigorously with wooden spoon, especially around base.

Pour into individual dishes.

Sprinkle with cocoa powder before serving.

PER SERVING

Calories	112
% Calories from fat	41
Fat (g)	5.2
Saturated fat (g)	1.6
Cholesterol (mg)	212.6
Sodium (mg)	8
Protein (g)	2.8
Carbohydrate (g)	10.4
Calcium (mg)	23.2

EXCHANGES

Milk	0.0
Vegetable	0.0
Fruit	0.0
Bread	1.0
Meat	0.0
Fat	1.0

When making flans or tarts, metal pans are preferable, as they conduct heat better; the result will be a crisper pastry shell. The filling could also be made using any ripe seasonal fruit such as strawberries, black currants, blackberries, peaches or nectarines. Or why not try it with a mixture of berries?

Fresh Raspberry Tart

Serves 8

This is a lovely summer dessert. It can be finished an hour or so before serving and refrigerated. The sweet pastry base retains its crispiness well.

1 recipe	Crisp Sweet Pastry (page 186)	1 recipe
1 recipe	Pastry Cream (page 165)	1 recipe
3 cups	firm ripe raspberries (about 1 lb)	450 g
1 tbsp	red currant jelly (or any other fruit jelly) to glaze	1 tbsp

Pre-heat the oven to 400F. On a floured surface, roll out the pastry thinly and line a greased pie pan approximately 9 inches in diameter and 2 inches deep, with fluted edges. Trim the pastry to fit pan and prick the base.

Fill with waxed paper and dried beans and bake blind for about 10 minutes.

Remove beans and paper and reduce oven temperature to 350F. Return to oven for about 7 minutes to dry out.

Remove from the oven and allow to cool.

Fill the pastry case with cooled pastry cream, smoothing down well.

Arrange the raspberries on top to cover completely; it doesn't matter if they overlap slightly.

Mix the jelly with a fork to let it loosen slightly (if necessary, warm slightly) and brush over the tart to cover the raspberries completely.

Refrigerate before serving.

PER SERVING	
Calories	196
% Calories from fat	39
Fat (g)	8.7
Saturated fat (g)	1.9
Cholesterol (mg)	132.9
Sodium (mg)	60
Protein (g)	4.3
Carbohydrate (g)	25.7
Calcium (mg)	29.3

EXCHANGES	
Milk	0.0
Vegetable	0.0
Fruit	1.0
Bread	1.0
Meat	0.0
Fat	1.0

For the non-alcoholic version, substitute extra orange juice for the Amaretto.

Honey-Glazed Pineapple and Fig Kebabs with Orange Sabayon

Serves 4

This is a relatively healthy dessert that leaves you feeling like you've had something wicked! For those not so keen on a sabayon-style sauce, the kebabs would be great with soy ice cream or, if you feel very virtuous, Oat and Honey Cream (see page 169).

Kebabs

1/2	medium, ripe pineapple	1/2
3	ripe figs, quartered	3
2 tbsps	honey	2 tbsps
4	long skewers	4

Sabayon

3	egg yolks	3
1 tbsp	superfine sugar	25 g
1/4 cup	orange juice	60 ml
	zest of one orange	
2 tbsps	Amaretto (optional)	30 ml

Peel the pineapple and remove any brown bits. Remove core and cut into 16 equal-sized cubes.

Alternate pieces of pineapple and fig so you have 4 pieces of pineapple and 3 pieces of fig on each skewer. Spoon over and cover well with the runny honey, and place skewers in an oven-proof dish.

Pre-heat broiler. Broil for about 3 minutes, turn skewer and broil 3 minutes on the other side. Fruit should be beginning to caramelize.

For the Sabayon: put all the ingredients in a double-boiler and simmer. Whisk until light and fluffy, about 5 minutes.

Serve immediately with the grilled kebabs.

PER SERVING

Calories	155
% Calories from fat	23
Fat (g)	4.2
Saturated fat (g)	1.2
Cholesterol (mg)	159.5
Sodium (mg)	7
Protein (g)	2.8
Carbohydrate (g)	28.7
Calcium (mg)	41.5

EXCHANGES

Milk	0.0
Vegetable	0.0
Fruit	2.0
Bread	0.0
Meat	0.0
Fat	1.0

Vary the fruit in this crumble according to availability. For example, use black currants or blackberries.

Mixed Berry and Peach Coconut Crumble

Serves 4

Crumbles are simple to make and a wonderful way of using seasonal fresh fruit. The topping for this crumble has the unusual addition of coconut, oats and almonds, which complement the hot fruit perfectly. Serve with soy ice cream, soy yogurt or soy custard.

1/2 cup	blueberries	110 g
1/2 cup	raspberries	110 g
2	fresh peaches	2
3 1/2 fl oz	black currant cordial or black currant syrup	105 ml

Topping

2 tbsps	all-purpose flour	2 tbsps
2 tbsps	ground almonds	2 tbsps
2 tbsps	vegan margarine	50 g
2 tbsps	dried coconut	2 tbsps
1 tbsp	superfine sugar	25 g
1 tbsp	quick-cooking oats	25 g

Pre-heat the oven to 350F. You will need a 1-quart oven dish.

Remove the stones from the peaches and cut flesh into small chunks.

Arrange the berries and peaches in the oven dish. Pour over the cordial. Alternatively, you could use elderberry cordial.

For the topping, put the flour and almonds in a bowl and rub in the margarine until the mixture resembles breadcrumbs.

Stir in the coconut, sugar and oats. Spread evenly over the top of the fruit.

Bake in oven for about 30 minutes, until the top is golden.

PER SERVING

Calories	256
% Calories from fat	30
Fat (g)	8.9
Saturated fat (g)	2
Cholesterol (mg)	0
Sodium (mg)	71
Protein (g)	2.2
Carbohydrate (g)	32.7
Calcium (mg)	21

EXCHANGES

Milk	0.0
Vegetable	0.0
Fruit	1.0
Bread	1.0
Meat	0.0
Fat	2.5

Pears could be substituted for with pineapple or apples.

Pear and Ginger Upside Down Cake

Serves 6

This is a favorite dessert of mine that keeps well and may be easily reheated. It is also nice eaten cold. Serve hot with soy ice cream, soy cream or soy custard.

2 tbsps	vegan margarine	50 g
3 tbsps	superfine sugar	75 g
2–3	large, firm but ripe pears, peeled, cored and cut into eighths	2–3
2	eggs, beaten	2
2 tbsps	molasses	2 tbsps
3 tbsps	vegan margarine, melted	75 g
2/3 cup	superfine sugar	150 g
3 tbsps	crystallized ginger, roughly chopped	3 tbsps
3 1/2 fl oz	soy milk	105 ml
2 tsps	ground ginger	2 tsps
1/2 tsp	ground cinnamon	1/2 tsp
3/4 cup	self-rising flour	3/4 cup

Pre-heat the oven to 350F. Grease a circular 10-inch-diameter, 2-inch-deep oven dish.

To make the topping, cream together the margarine and sugar.

Smear this mixture over the base of the dish and lay the pears neatly in a circle, tips touching, in the center of the dish.

Beat together the eggs, molasses, melted margarine, sugar, crystallized ginger and soy milk.

Sift the spices and flour into the egg mixture and mix thoroughly.

Pour over the pears, smooth down and bake for about 40 minutes until cooked through.

Leave for a few minutes, then, using a knife, go around the edge of the dish. Turn out onto a warm plate. Serve hot.

PER SERVING

Calories	367
% Calories from fat	28
Fat (g)	11.9
Saturated fat (g)	2.5
Cholesterol (mg)	70.8
Sodium (mg)	338
Protein (g)	4.5
Carbohydrate (g)	62.8
Calcium (mg)	88.3

EXCHANGES

Milk	0.0
Vegetable	0.0
Fruit	0.0
Bread	4.0
Meat	0.0
Fat	2.0

Egg yolks were used to increase the protein content of the pudding. However, if you are cooking for a vegan omit the egg yolks and the pudding will still be delicious.

Raisin, Lemon and Almond Rice Pudding

Serves 4

This is a tasty, nursery-style pudding that kids will love. The raisins swell up and become really juicy, giving the pudding added natural sweetness. I added the almonds to provide a creamy texture as well as increase the calcium content.

2 cups	vanilla rice milk	480 ml
2 tbsps	ground rice powder	2 tbsps
2 tbsps	raisins	2 tbsps
1 tbsp	ground almonds	1 tbsp
1 tsp	vanilla extract	1 tsp
2 tsps	honey	2 tsps
1	large lemon, grated zest only	1
2	egg yolks	2

In a large saucepan, whisk the rice milk slowly into the ground rice powder until smooth.

Add the raisins and ground almonds.

Cook over medium heat until the mixture thickens. Reduce the heat and simmer for about 6 minutes, stirring occasionally.

Stir in the vanilla, honey and grated rind, and remove from heat. Allow to cool slightly (about 5 minutes).

Beat in the egg yolks, return to heat and cook gently for about 5 minutes, taking care not to boil and curdle the yolks.

Serve hot in individual bowls.

PER SERVING	
Calories	192
% Calories from fat	31
Fat (g)	6.9
Saturated fat (g)	1.3
Cholesterol (mg)	106.3
Sodium (mg)	205
Protein (g)	23
Carbohydrate (g)	31.4
Calcium (mg)	421.7
EXCHANGES	
Milk	0.0
Vegetable	0.0
Fruit	0.0
Bread	2.0
Meat	0.0
Fat	1.0

Also delicious with gooseberries, apples, plums or fresh apricots, whatever is in season.

Tip: metal pans help make the pastry crisp.

Rhubarb and Almond Tart

Serves 8

This is an easy tart to prepare, as the pastry does not require pre-cooking. The tart is filled with an almond mixture with the uncooked rhubarb laid on top. It may be left in the fridge at this stage and put in the oven an hour before serving. Serve warm with soy cream or soy ice cream.

1 recipe	Shortcrust Pastry (see page 187)	1 recipe
2 tbsps	raspberry jam	2 tbsps
1/2 cup	vegan margarine	110 g
1/2 cup	brown sugar	110 g
2	eggs, beaten	2
1	orange	1
1/2 cup	ground almonds	1/2 cup
1 tbsp	all-purpose flour	1 tbsp
1 bunch	rhubarb, cut into 1/2-inch pieces (about 3/4 lb)	337 g
	red currant jelly for glazing	

Pre-heat the oven to 350F. On a floured surface, roll the pastry out thinly and line a greased 9-inch pie pan.

Prick base with a fork and smear over the jam.

In a medium bowl, beat the margarine and sugar until light and creamy, then gradually add the eggs and beat well. Grate in the zest from the orange, and squeeze the juice of half. Stir in the almonds and flour.

When well blended, pour into the pie pan and smooth down.

Arrange the rhubarb neatly over the top, pushing down slightly into the almond mixture, but not completely submerging.

Bake in the oven for 40–50 minutes until firm to the touch and golden.

Glaze with jelly. Serve warm or chilled.

PER SERVING

Calories	360
% Calories from fat	56
Fat (g)	23
Saturated fat (g)	4.8
Cholesterol (mg)	56.1
Sodium (mg)	191
Protein (g)	5.6
Carbohydrate (g)	34.5
Calcium (mg)	88.6

EXCHANGES

Milk	0.0
Vegetable	0.0
Fruit	0.5
Bread	2.0
Meat	0.0
Fat	4.0

Cut into smaller squares and serve for a picnic or buffet.

Chocolate Brownies

Serves 16 (1 per serving)

Serve with chocolate sauce and vanilla soy ice cream for a very indulgent yummy pudding. Alternatively, serve cold as an anytime treat. Store in an airtight container for up to 6 days.

10 oz	dark dairy-free chocolate	280 g
1 cup	vegan margarine	220 g
1 1/8 cups	brown sugar	247 g
4	eggs, beaten	4
1 tsp	vanilla extract	1 tsp
1/2 cup	self-rising flour	1/2 cup
1/2 tsp	baking soda	1/2 tsp
	pinch salt	
1 tbsp	cocoa powder	1 tbsp
3/4 cup	chopped hazelnuts	3/4 cup

Pre-heat the oven to 325F. Line the base of a baking pan approximately 8 x 12 inches and 2 inches deep with waxed paper.

Put the chocolate in a double-boiler, and stir until melted.

Cream the margarine and sugar by hand or in a food processor until well blended.

Gradually add the eggs and vanilla extract, mixing well. Pour in the chocolate slowly, beating constantly.

Sieve together the flour, baking soda, salt and cocoa.

Fold the flour and chopped hazelnuts into the chocolate mixture until well combined.

Pour into the lined baking pan and smooth down. Bake on the center shelf for 35–40 minutes.

Brownies should be firm and slightly dry around the edges, and a toothpick should come out almost clean when put into the confection.

Cut into 16 squares and serve warm.

PER SERVING	
Calories	323
% Calories from fat	60
Fat (g)	22.5
Saturated fat (g)	6.4
Cholesterol (mg)	54.5
Sodium (mg)	244
Protein (g)	3.7
Carbohydrate (g)	30.4
Calcium (mg)	49.7

EXCHANGES	
Milk	0.0
Vegetable	0.0
Fruit	0.0
Bread	2.0
Meat	0.0
Fat	4.0

For a differently flavored cheesecake, try using other fruit purées such as raspberry or strawberry.

Tangy Citrus Cheesecake

Serves 8

This is an extremely successful dessert. The addition of tofu and cashew nuts not only makes it quite nutritious but contributes to the creamy cheesecake texture. Serve decorated with seasonal fresh berries or Fresh Raspberry Coulis (see page 166). For a vegan cheesecake, use Jello instead of gelatin, following the manufacturer's instructions.

Base

6 oz	vanilla wafers (check that they are lactose free)	170 g
3 tbsps	vegan margarine	75 g

Filling

1	lime	1
1	lemon	1
1–2	oranges	1–2
3 tbsps	cashew nuts	3 tbsps
1/2 cup	firm tofu (about 4 oz)	112 g
1/2 cup	soy milk	120 ml
2 tbsps	superfine sugar	50 g
1	envelope gelatin (1/4 oz)	1

To make the base: crush the cookies to fine crumbs. Melt margarine in small pan, taking care not to overheat.

Stir the melted margarine into the cookie crumbs, mixing well.

Press into a lightly oiled 8-inch springform cake pan. Refrigerate to harden.

For the filling: grate the zest from all the fruit.

Squeeze the lime, lemon and oranges until there is about 1 cup of juice altogether.

In a liquidizer or food processor, blend the cashew nuts, tofu, soy milk and sugar until it becomes smooth and silky.

Reserving 4 tablespoons of citrus juice to one side, pour remaining juice into the food processor and continue processing.

Soak the gelatin in a bowl of cold water until it becomes soft. Heat the reserved citrus juice until warm, add softened gelatin, and melt over warm heat until dissolved.

Pour the melted gelatin into the cheesecake mixture, stirring well. Pour the filling over the base and allow to set in the fridge. Serve chilled.

PER SERVING	
Calories	207
% Calories from fat	50
Fat (g)	11.6
Saturated fat (g)	2.6
Cholesterol (mg)	0
Sodium (mg)	137
Protein (g)	3.9
Carbohydrate (g)	22.6
Calcium (mg)	39.3

EXCHANGES	
Milk	0.0
Vegetable	0.0
Fruit	0.0
Bread	1.5
Meat	0.0
Fat	2.0

If the sauce solidifies when cold, reheat slowly to sauce consistency.

Chocolate Fudge Sauce

Serves 8 (2 tablespoons per serving)

This sauce is easy to do with a result that is as good as any chocolate fudge sauce made using butter. Perfect for serving warm or cold as an accompaniment to ice creams or sponge cakes.

2 oz	dark dairy-free chocolate	56 g
1/2 cup	dark brown sugar	110 g
1 tbsp	cocoa powder, sifted	1 tbsp
2 tsps	vanilla extract	2 tsps

Place all the ingredients in a saucepan, along with 1 cup cold water. Slowly bring to a boil, stirring occasionally.

Boil for 2–3 minutes, stirring constantly, and remove from heat. Serve hot. Makes about 1 cup.

PER SERVING	
Calories	93
% Calories from fat	22
Fat (g)	2.4
Saturated fat (g)	1.4
Cholesterol (mg)	0.5
Sodium (mg)	6
Protein (g)	0.4
Carbohydrate (g)	18.2
Calcium (mg)	14.1
EXCHANGES	
Milk	0.0
Vegetable	0.0
Fruit	0.0
Bread	1.0
Meat	0.0
Fat	0.5

This confection can also be flavored with cocoa to make a delicious chocolate filling.

Another idea is to mix this with fruit purées such as apple and blackberry and pour into individual parfait glasses as a tasty pudding. Try this for your children.

Pastry Cream

Serves 6 (about 2¹/₂ tablespoons per serving)

Crème Pâtissière, or Pastry Cream, is the delicious custard-like filling used in many French tarts. It can be used as a creamy filling for many desserts and is excellent served with stewed fruit. I use it to fill a Fresh Raspberry Tart (see page 156).

1 cup	soy milk	240 ml
2	large egg yolks	2
2 tbsps	superfine sugar	50 g
³/₄ tbsp	all-purpose flour	³/₄ tbsp
³/₄ tbsp	cornstarch	³/₄ tbsp
¹/₂ tsp	vanilla extract	¹/₂ tsp
2 tbsps	soy cream	30 ml

In a medium saucepan, heat the soy milk until fairly hot but not boiling.

In a medium bowl, cream the yolks and sugar until pale, then whisk in the sieved flour and cornstarch.

Gradually pour in the milk and stir well. Return the mixture to the milk pan.

Slowly bring up to a boil, stirring continuously. It will begin to go thick and lumpy, but just stir well until smooth.

Allow to cool slightly, then add the vanilla and soy cream.

Use chilled as required. Makes 1 cup.

PER SERVING

Calories	62
% Calories from fat	41
Fat (g)	2.8
Saturated fat (g)	0.6
Cholesterol (mg)	70.9
Sodium (mg)	9
Protein (g)	2.1
Carbohydrate (g)	6.9
Calcium (mg)	9.4

EXCHANGES

Milk	0.0
Vegetable	0.0
Fruit	0.0
Bread	0.5
Meat	0.0
Fat	0.5

Tip: If you are not serving the custard immediately, lay waxed paper over to cover the top, and this will prevent a skin from forming.

PER SERVING	
Calories	119
% Calories from fat	36
Fat (g)	4.9
Saturated fat (g)	1.1
Cholesterol (mg)	106.3
Sodium (mg)	18
Protein (g)	4.7
Carbohydrate (g)	14.4
Calcium (mg)	16.4
EXCHANGES	
Milk	0.0
Vegetable	0.0
Fruit	0.0
Bread	1.0
Meat	0.0
Fat	1.0

Custard Sauce

Serves 4 ($^1/_2$ cup per serving)

In my household, custard has to be the number one favorite, especially with hot puddings. The yolks give the custard a higher protein content and also add creaminess.

2 cups	soy milk	480 ml
2	egg yolks	2
1 tsp	vanilla extract or fresh vanilla pod	1 tsp
$^1/_4$ cup	sugar or to taste	55 g

Warm the soy milk over medium heat, taking care not to let it boil.

In a bowl, mix the egg yolks and vanilla essence. Next, pour the warm milk over the mixture, beating well.

Return to the pan and stir over low heat until it thickens, taking care not to cook too quickly and curdle the eggs.

Sweeten with sugar to taste. Serve hot. Makes just over 2 cups.

This can be made using fresh strawberries or black currants.

PER SERVING	
Calories	45
% Calories from fat	6
Fat (g)	0.3
Saturated fat (g)	0
Cholesterol (mg)	0
Sodium (mg)	0
Protein (g)	0.6
Carbohydrate (g)	10.8
Calcium (mg)	13.6
EXCHANGES	
Milk	0.0
Vegetable	0.0
Fruit	1.0
Bread	0.0
Meat	0.0
Fat	0.0

Fresh Raspberry Coulis

Serves 4–6 (about $^1/_2$ cup per serving)

Serve with soy ice creams, fresh fruit pies, cheesecakes or even fresh fruit salad.

2 cups	fresh raspberries or frozen (about 11 oz)	310 g
2–3 tbsps	confectioner's sugar	2–3 tbsps

Defrost the raspberries if frozen. Push the fruit through a sieve to remove seeds.

Sift in the confectioner's sugar and mix well.

Taste for sweetness and add more sugar if necessary.

If the coulis is too thick, dilute with water or apple juice. Makes about 2 cups.

Rich Butterscotch Sauce

Serves 8 (2 tablespoons per serving)

Butterscotch sauce would usually be made with condensed milk, but this version using coconut milk works very well and is almost as delicious. Serve with soy ice cream, bananas, meringues or sponge cake or even try it with pineapple, banana or apple fritters.

1 cup	(scant) water	220 ml
½ cup	dark brown sugar	110 g
1 cup	(scant) reduced-fat coconut milk	220 ml
½ tbsp	arrowroot	½ tbsp

Place the water and sugar in a small saucepan over low heat. Stir until dissolved, then bring to a boil and simmer for 15 minutes.

Remove from heat and leave for several minutes; add coconut milk and stir well.

Mix arrowroot with a tablespoon of water until smooth.

Pour the arrowroot into the sauce and stir over gentle heat to thicken slightly.

Serve hot or cold. Makes just over 1 cup.

PER SERVING	
Calories	70
% Calories from fat	19
Fat (g)	1.5
Saturated fat (g)	1
Cholesterol (mg)	0
Sodium (mg)	16
Protein (g)	0
Carbohydrate (g)	14.4
Calcium (mg)	11.7

EXCHANGES	
Milk	0.0
Vegetable	0.0
Fruit	0.0
Bread	1.0
Meat	0.0
Fat	0.0

Try making this sauce with coconut milk instead of the soy cream.

Mocha Chocolate Sauce

Serves 8 (2 tablespoons per serving)

This rich chocolate and coffee sauce is perfect served hot with chocolate brownies, soy ice cream and many puddings.

5 oz	dark dairy-free chocolate, broken into chunks	140 g
2/3 cup	strong hot espresso coffee	150 ml
2/3 cup	soy cream	150 ml

Put the chocolate chunks into the top of a double-boiler over boiling water.

Melt the chocolate and stir until smooth. When thoroughly melted, remove from the heat.

Slowly pour some of the hot coffee into the chocolate, stirring gently. Initially the chocolate will appear to go thick and solid. Do not worry, but just continue stirring and adding hot coffee slowly. Eventually it will become smooth and silky.

Finally, add the soy cream and mix well. The result should be a smooth-pouring chocolate sauce.

This can be allowed to cool and then reheated either in a microwave or over a pan of boiling water.

Serve hot. Makes about 1 cup.

PER SERVING	
Calories	109
% Calories from fat	56
Fat (g)	7.3
Saturated fat (g)	3.5
Cholesterol (mg)	1.4
Sodium (mg)	7
Protein (g)	0.7
Carbohydrate (g)	12.3
Calcium (mg)	6.1

EXCHANGES	
Milk	0.0
Vegetable	0.0
Fruit	0.0
Bread	1.0
Meat	0.0
Fat	1.0

For a better result, use fine oatmeal rather than large oats.

Oat and Honey Cream

Serves 6 (¹/₄ cup per serving)

This cream has a lovely consistency. However, the cream will have a slightly grainy taste because the oats have been broken down during the processing. This does make it very nutritious, as hardly any parts of the oats have been removed.

Serve as very low-fat cream with hot puddings. Delicious with stewed fruits such as pear and apple or even a warm apple pie. Use in the Banana Oat Shake on page 192.

3 tbsps	quick-cooking oats	75 g
1¹/₂ cups	(scant) cold water (use more water for a thinner cream)	340 ml
2 tbsps	honey	2 tbsps

Soak the oats in the water and honey for at least 2 hours. Blend in a food processor or liquidizer until smooth.

Sieve well and refrigerate until required.

This will keep well in the fridge for several days. Makes about 1¹/₂ cups.

PER SERVING

Calories	31
% Calories from fat	5
Fat (g)	0.2
Saturated fat (g)	0
Cholesterol (mg)	0
Sodium (mg)	0
Protein (g)	0.4
Carbohydrate (g)	7.5
Calcium (mg)	1.6

EXCHANGES

Milk	0.0
Vegetable	0.0
Fruit	0.0
Bread	0.5
Meat	0.0
Fat	0.0

To make an alternative to sour cream, omit the vanilla and honey, and squeeze in a dash of lemon juice. Cashew nuts can also be used to produce a cream equally as delicious.

Once you start experimenting with this, many variations are possible by adding more nuts and less tofu, etc.

Tofu and Almond Cream

Serves 4 (¹/₄ cup per serving)

This makes a useful sauce to serve in place of dairy products such as cream, yogurt and ice cream. Based on tofu and almonds, it is more nutritious and fairly low in fat compared to many creams.

2 tbsps	soy milk	30 ml
¹/₂ cup	firm tofu (about 4 oz)	112 g
2 tbsps	blanched almonds (sliced, ground or whole)	2 tbsps
1 inch	vanilla pod (or 1 teaspoon vanilla extract)	2.5 cm
1 tsp	honey (more depending on taste)	1 tsp

Use a blender or food processor to blend all the ingredients, except honey, until smooth and creamy.

Add honey to taste, and blend again to mix well.

Refrigerate until required. This cream will last several days in the fridge. Makes about 1 cup.

PER SERVING	
Calories	62
% Calories from fat	53
Fat (g)	3.8
Saturated fat (g)	0.3
Cholesterol (mg)	0
Sodium (mg)	2
Protein (g)	3.7
Carbohydrate (g)	3.2
Calcium (mg)	57
EXCHANGES	
Milk	0.0
Vegetable	0.0
Fruit	0.0
Bread	0.0
Meat	0.5
Fat	0.5

Baking, Breakfasts and Beverages

Bacon, Onion and Sage Scones

Onion, Tomato and Rosemary Focaccia

Seedy Muffins

Polenta Bread Rolls

Carrot and Raisin Cake with Lemon and Orange Frosting

Chocolate and Almond Pithiviers

Coconut and Chocolate Oat Cakes

Raisin and Peanut Cookies

Fresh Strawberry Cake Roll

Orange and Almond Shortbread

Spiced Apple and Walnut Cake

Wicked Chocolate Cake

Cornmeal Pastry

Crisp Sweet Pastry

Quick Flaky Pastry

Shortcrust Pastry

Whole Wheat Pastry

Blueberry Muffins

Corn Griddle Cakes

Kedgeree

French Toast

Banana Oat Shake

Summer Berry Fruit Crush

These can be made with ham or pastrami for a slightly different flavor. Vegetarians should omit the bacon.

Bacon, Onion and Sage Scones

Serves 12 (1 scone per serving)

If I have run out of bread, I often make scones, as they take so little time to prepare and bake. These scones are particularly good served hot from the oven with a steaming bowl of homemade soup. They are also delicious cold as a sandwich with soy cream cheese and watercress or baby spinach for a picnic or packed lunch.

1 tbsp	olive oil	15 m
1	medium onion, finely chopped	
5–6 slices	smoked bacon, finely chopped (4 oz)	112
1¼ cups	self-rising flour	1¼ cup
	pinch salt	
1 tbsp	vegan margarine	25
8	sage leaves, chopped	
1 cup	soy milk	240 m

Grease 2 large baking sheets. Pre-heat the oven to 425F.

In a frying pan, heat the oil and sauté the onions for 5 minutes. Add the bacon and continue cooking for several minutes until cooked through.

Sift the flour and salt into a large mixing bowl. Lightly rub in the margarine until the mixture resembles breadcrumbs.

Stir the onion and bacon mixture, sage and soy milk into the flour to form sticky dough.

Turn out onto floured surface.

Knead gently until smooth, then roll the dough out to 1 inch thick, and stamp into small rounds.

Place scones on the prepared baking sheets.

Bake in the oven for about 15 minutes or until well-risen and golden brown.

Leave to cool on a wire rack, or serve hot from the oven. Makes 12.

PER SERVING	
Calories	94
% Calories from fat	41
Fat (g)	4.3
Saturated fat (g)	1
Cholesterol (mg)	2.8
Sodium (mg)	232
Protein (g)	3
Carbohydrate (g)	10.9
Calcium (mg)	49.8

EXCHANGES	
Milk	0.0
Vegetable	0.0
Fruit	0.0
Bread	1.0
Meat	0.0
Fat	0.5

Try other versions using fresh chopped basil and black olives.

Active dry yeast makes baking quicker and simpler. Unlike some ordinary dried yeasts, it does not need sugar or pre-mixing with warm water. If you wish to use ordinary dried yeast or fresh yeast, you will need to follow the manufacturer's instructions.

Onion, Tomato and Rosemary Focaccia

Serves 6–8

The combination of the caramelized onions, sun-dried tomatoes and rosemary gives this bread a wonderful flavor, particularly when still fresh from the oven. Serve with hot homemade soup or as part of a barbecue or buffet. I also recommend you try serving it with Sicilian Caponata (see page 108) to make an unusual starter or light meal.

2	medium onions, halved and thinly sliced	2
4 tbsps	olive oil	60 ml
3⅓ cups	bread flour	3⅓ cups
2 tsp	fine salt	2 tsp
1	¼-oz packet active dry yeast	1
1¾ cups	lukewarm water	420 ml
½ cup	sun-dried tomatoes packed in oil, drained and chopped	½ cup
	large sprig of fresh rosemary, stalks removed and leaves chopped	
1 tsp	coarse salt	1 tsp

Grease a large baking sheet. Sauté the onions in 1 tablespoon of olive oil over medium heat for about 8 minutes until tender but not too soft.

Sieve the flour and fine salt into a bowl, then stir in the yeast. Next, pour in 2 tablespoons of the olive oil, and then gradually work in the water a little at a time until you have a manageable, soft dough that is not too sticky. You may not need all the water.

Tip the dough out onto a floured surface and knead for about 8 minutes until you have a silky dough.

Work in the chopped sun-dried tomatoes and chopped rosemary, and continue kneading until they are all well incorporated.

Work the dough into a large flat circle about 14 inches in diameter.

Lay the dough on the prepared baking sheet, then, using your fingers, poke lots of holes over the top, cover with onions and drizzle with remaining 1 tablespoon of olive oil and sprinkle over the rock salt.

Leave in a warm place to rise slowly for about 45 minutes, until doubled in size.

PER SERVING	
Calories	393
% Calories from fat	27
Fat (g)	11.7
Saturated fat (g)	1.6
Cholesterol (mg)	0
Sodium (mg)	1191
Protein (g)	10.5
Carbohydrate (g)	61.2
Calcium (mg)	29

EXCHANGES	
Milk	0.0
Vegetable	0.0
Fruit	0.0
Bread	4.0
Meat	0.0
Fat	2.0

While the dough is rising, pre-heat the oven to 425F.

Bake in the oven for 15 minutes; check and turn tray around if the focaccia is cooking unevenly. Bake for further 7–8 minutes, until risen and golden brown with crisp, darkening onions.

Lift the focaccia off the tray onto a cooling rack. Serve warm or at room temperature.

Store for several days in an airtight container. When using seeds, check that they are fresh, as the essential oils can quickly become rancid. For a fruity muffin, use raisins and chopped apple.

Seedy Muffins

Serves 9 (1 muffin per serving)

Seeds and malted wheat give an excellent texture and provide valuable vitamins and minerals. These muffins are fairly quick and easy to prepare and can be served either sweet with fruit jams or honey or savory with soy cream cheese and slices of ham, bacon, gravlax or smoked salmon.

3 tbsps	all-purpose flour	3 tbsps
1/2 cup	whole-wheat flour	1/2 cup
1 1/2 tsps	baking powder	1 1/2 tsps
2 tbsps	brown sugar	50 g
1/2 tsp	salt	1/2 tsp
1 tbsp	sunflower seeds	1 tbsp
1 tbsp	sesame seeds	1 tbsp
1 tbsp	pumpkin seeds	1 tbsp
2	eggs	2
1/2 cup	rice milk	120 ml
1 tbsp	sunflower oil	15 ml
1 tbsp	malt extract	1 tbsp

Pre-heat the oven to 400F. Grease a 9-hole muffin pan or place 9 paper muffin cup cases on a baking sheet.
In a large bowl, combine the flours and baking powder, brown sugar, salt and seeds, mixing well.

In a separate bowl, beat the eggs, then whisk in the rice milk, sunflower oil and malt extract until well blended.

Pour this liquid over the dry ingredients and stir thoroughly. The mixture should have the consistency of a thick batter. Add more rice milk if necessary. Spoon the batter into the muffin molds.

Bake for 20–25 minutes until risen, firm and golden.
If using a pan, transfer the muffins to a wire rack; if using paper muffin cases, leave them in the cases and transfer them to the rack. Serve warm. Makes 9.

PER SERVING	
Calories	102
% Calories from fat	36
Fat (g)	4.5
Saturated fat (g)	0.8
Cholesterol (mg)	47.2
Sodium (mg)	250
Protein (g)	3.2
Carbohydrate (g)	14.4
Calcium (mg)	111.8

EXCHANGES	
Milk	0.0
Vegetable	0.0
Fruit	0.0
Bread	1.0
Meat	0.0
Fat	1.0

Just before shaping the rolls, knead in other ingredients such as sesame or sunflower seeds or currants for a different variation. Store in an airtight container for 2 days. Alternatively, the rolls will freeze well when fresh.

Polenta Bread Rolls

Serves 16 (1 roll per serving)

Polenta flour gives these rolls an interesting, slightly coarse texture and a golden color. Serve with hot soups or as sandwiches with various fillings. They are also good halved when cold, spread with crushed garlic and chopped herbs and then drizzled with olive oil. Wrap the rolls in aluminum foil and heat through in a hot oven for about 8 minutes for garlicky polenta rolls.

4–5 cups	bread flour (about 1 lb)	450 g
1 cup	fine polenta	220 g
1	$1/4$-oz packet active dry yeast	1
2 tsps	salt	2 tsps
$1^3/_4$ cups	warm water	420 ml
2 tbsps	olive oil	30 ml

Grease a large baking sheet. In a large bowl, mix the flour, polenta and dry yeast together.

In a separate bowl, dissolve salt in warm water, then add the olive oil.

Pour this liquid into the flour, stirring well to form dough.

Tip the dough onto a floured work surface and knead for 5 minutes.

Shape into 16 equal-size balls and place them on the prepared baking sheet.

Sprinkle with a little extra polenta.

Leave to rise in warm place for about 40 minutes until doubled in size.

While the rolls are rising, pre-heat the oven to 425F.

Bake in the hot oven for about 15 minutes, but turn the oven down slightly halfway through the cooking.

The rolls should be risen and golden, and the underneath should sound hollow when tapped.

Transfer the rolls onto a rack to cool. Makes 16 rolls.

PER SERVING

Calories	147
% Calories from fat	14
Fat (g)	2.3
Saturated fat (g)	0.3
Cholesterol (mg)	0
Sodium (mg)	292
Protein (g)	4.1
Carbohydrate (g)	27
Calcium (mg)	5.3

EXCHANGES

Milk	0.0
Vegetable	0.0
Fruit	0.0
Bread	1.5
Meat	0.0
Fat	0.5

If you have a juicer, in this recipe you could use the leftover carrot pulp from making carrot juice.

Carrot and Raisin Cake with Lemon and Orange Frosting

Serves 9

This is a lovely nutritious cake, and the tangy frosting makes it a real treat. It would also be welcomed in packed lunch boxes or on picnics.

Cake

3/4 cup	sunflower oil	180 ml
3/4 cup	superfine sugar	170 g
3	large eggs, beaten	3
1/2 cup	raisins	1/2 cup
	grated zest from 1 lemon and 1 orange	
1–2	medium carrots, peeled and grated	1–2
3/4 cup	all-purpose flour	3/4 cup
2 tsps	ground cinnamon	2 tsps
	grating of nutmeg	
1 tsp	baking powder	1 tsp
1 tsp	baking soda	1 tsp

Frosting

1 tbsp	lemon juice	15 ml
1 tbsp	orange juice	15 ml
1 cup	(scant) confectioner's sugar, sifted	1 cup

PER SERVING	
Calories	373
% Calories from fat	47
Fat (g)	20
Saturated fat (g)	2.4
Cholesterol (mg)	70.8
Sodium (mg)	219
Protein (g)	3.6
Carbohydrate (g)	47.1
Calcium (mg)	59

EXCHANGES	
Milk	0.0
Vegetable	0.0
Fruit	0.0
Bread	3.0
Meat	0.0
Fat	3.5

Grease and line a 7-inch-square cake pan. Pre-heat the oven to 350F.

In a large bowl, beat the oil and sugar together. Gradually beat in the egg, raisins, zest and grated carrot.

Sift the flour, cinnamon, nutmeg and rising agents into the bowl and fold the cake mixture until well combined.

Tip the mixture into the cake pan, smoothing it out, and bake on the middle shelf of the oven for 35–40 minutes, until well risen and firm to the touch.

Allow to cool for about 10 minutes, then turn the cake out onto a rack and leave to cool completely.

To make the frosting: sift the sugar into a bowl and gradually beat in the lemon and orange juice until you have a smooth, glossy icing.

Place the cake on a serving plate and pour the icing over, allowing it to drizzle down the sides of the cake.

Once the icing has set, serve the cake cut into 9 squares.

Great for a messy children's treat, although make sure the filling has cooled properly.

Chocolate and Almond Pithiviers

Serves 6 (1 pithivier per serving)

This was inspired by a visit to the local pâtisserie while on vacation in France. It is a crisp pastry with a gooey chocolate and almond filling. Most French-style buns and cakes such as croissants, pain au chocolat and pain au raisin always contain butter, so it was a good reason to try these pithiviers.

1/2 cup	vegan margarine	110 g
1/2 cup	confectioner's sugar, sifted	1/2 cup
1/2 cup	chopped almonds	1/2 cup
1 tsp	vanilla extract	1 tsp
6 oz	dark, dairy-free chocolate, chopped	170 g
1/2 lb	puff pastry (dairy-free), shop bought	225 g
	egg for glazing	
1 tbsp	confectioner's sugar, sifted	1 tbsp
2 tbsps	sliced almonds, toasted	2 tbsps

Pre-heat the oven to 425F. In a medium bowl, beat the margarine with the sifted sugar until soft and smooth.

Stir in the almonds and vanilla and beat to a smooth paste, then tip in the chocolate and mix well.

On a floured surface, roll out the pastry to about 1/8 inch thick.

Cut out 12 rounds, using a small bowl about 41/2 inches in diameter.

Spoon one-sixth of the chocolate paste into the center of 6 of the circles, leaving at least 1/2 inch around the edge; then brush the edges very lightly with water.

Place the 6 remaining circles over the tops to cover evenly.

Using a fork, press along edges, and refrigerate for about 30 minutes to allow to set.

Glaze with beaten egg. Bake for 12–15 minutes until risen and golden.

Remove from the oven, and allow to cool for about 5 minutes.

For icing, mix 1 tablespoon of sieved sugar with 1 tablespoon water until smooth.

Top the pithiviers with the icing, followed by a sprinkling of flaked almonds. Makes 6.

PER SERVING	
Calories	624
% Calories from fat	65
Fat (g)	46.9
Saturated fat (g)	13.1
Cholesterol (mg)	37.6
Sodium (mg)	284
Protein (g)	8
Carbohydrate (g)	48.7
Calcium (mg)	56.2
EXCHANGES	
Milk	0.0
Vegetable	0.0
Fruit	0.0
Bread	3.0
Meat	0.0
Fat	9.0

As the oat cakes cool they will become firm—if you can wait! They will store in a sealed container for 2–3 days.

Coconut and Chocolate Oat Cakes

Serves 12 (1 oat cake per serving)

The coconut and chocolate together make a delicious combination; the chocolate should remain as chunks when you bite into the oat cake. These cakes are gluten free as well as dairy free.

³/₄ cup	vegan margarine	170 g
³/₄ cup	dark corn syrup	180 g
1 cup	oats, uncooked	220 g
4 tbsps	dried coconut	4 tbsps
4 oz	dark, dairy-free chocolate, cut into small chunks	112 g

Pre-heat the oven to 350F. Grease a shallow, oblong baking pan measuring about 8 x 10 inches.

Melt the margarine with the syrup, stirring well, in a heavy pan over medium heat until dissolved. Remove from heat.

Stir in the oats and coconut, allow this to cool, then stir in chocolate chunks.

Pour into the baking pan and smooth down flat.

Bake for about 30 minutes until golden.

Allow to cool slightly for 5 minutes, then cut into squares. The cakes should become firm on cooling.

Turn out onto wire rack to cool completely. Makes about 12.

PER SERVING	
Calories	263
% Calories from fat	52
Fat (g)	15.9
Saturated fat (g)	4.7
Cholesterol (mg)	0.7
Sodium (mg)	165
Protein (g)	2.7
Carbohydrate (g)	30.5
Calcium (mg)	18.1
EXCHANGES	
Milk	0.0
Vegetable	0.0
Fruit	0.0
Bread	2.0
Meat	0.0
Fat	3.0

Make sure you don't give these to anyone with a nut allergy. Try using dark chocolate or pitted, chopped dates for different variations.

Raisin and Peanut Cookies

Serves 15 (1 cookie per serving)

These would be ideal to take on a picnic or put in a lunch box.

½ cup	soft vegan margarine	110 g
½ cup	brown or superfine sugar	110 g
1	egg, beaten	1
²/₃ cup	self-rising flour	²/₃ cup
1 tsp	pumpkin pie spice	1 tsp
½ cup	raisins	½ cup
½ cup	peanuts in skins, chopped	½ cup

Pre-heat the oven to 375F. Beat together all the ingredients, except the raisins and nuts, until well blended.

Mix in raisins and nuts, then, using a teaspoon, spoon onto greased baking sheets. Flatten them out into circles.

Bake for 10–15 minutes until golden brown around edges.

Cool slightly before lifting onto wire rack to cool completely. Makes about 15.

PER SERVING

Calories	152
% Calories from fat	51
Fat (g)	8.9
Saturated fat (g)	1.7
Cholesterol (mg)	14.2
Sodium (mg)	150
Protein (g)	2.4
Carbohydrate (g)	16.8
Calcium (mg)	35

EXCHANGES

Milk	0.0
Vegetable	0.0
Fruit	0.0
Bread	1.0
Meat	0.0
Fat	2.0

This should be eaten soon after rolling, as it will not store too well. Try making it with fresh raspberries.

Fresh Strawberry Cake Roll

Serves 6

The soy cream cheese is used as a substitute for heavy cream, and it combines wonderfully with the sweetened strawberries. This may be served as a cake or as a pudding.

Sponge Cake

3	eggs	
3 tbsps	superfine sugar	75
1/2 tsp	vanilla extract	1/2 ts
3 tbsps	all-purpose flour	3 tbsp
	pinch of salt	

Filling

3/4 cup	soy cream cheese	165
1 tbsp	soy cream	15 m
1 tbsp	superfine sugar	25
1/2 tsp	vanilla extract	1/2 ts
1 1/4 cups	fresh strawberries, hulled and sliced	1 1/4 cup

Cake: Pre-heat the oven to 350F. Grease a flat rectangular pa about 12 x 8 inches and 1 inch deep.

Cut a piece of waxed paper, allowing for an extra 2 inches on each side, and line it into the pan. Grease well with oil, and dust with flour and sugar.

Place eggs, sugar and vanilla in a double-boiler over simmering water. Whisk the mixture until light, thick and fluffy.

Remove from the heat and continue whisking until cool.

Sift the flour and salt together, and, with a large metal spoon, gently fold it into the mixture, taking care not to beat out any of the air.

Carefully pour the mixture into the prepared pan, tipping it so the mixture fills all the corners. Bake in the middle of the oven for about 15 minutes.

The sponge is cooked if it has shrunk slightly and the edges look crinkled. When pressed gently it will feel firm but spongy.

Lift the waxed paper with the sponge in it and cover with a clean, slightly damp tea towel and leave to cool.

Filling: In a small bowl, mix the cream cheese with the soy cream, beating well until smooth. Add sugar to taste and the vanilla extract.

Spread this cream mixture over the cake and top with sliced strawberries, reserving about 20 slices to decorate.

PER SERVING	
Calories	176
% Calories from fat	55
Fat (g)	10.8
Saturated fat (g)	2.8
Cholesterol (mg)	106.2
Sodium (mg)	167.9
Protein (g)	4.7
Carbohydrate (g)	14.6
Calcium (mg)	17.2

EXCHANGES	
Milk	0.0
Vegetable	0.0
Fruit	0.0
Bread	1.0
Meat	0.0
Fat	2.0

Keeping longest edge nearest you, hold each front edge of the waxed paper and slowly roll up the cake, pulling away the waxed paper as you roll.

Alternatively, cut the cake into 2 equal squares, spread filling over one, and top it off with the other square.

Place on a serving plate and decorate with sieved confectioner's sugar and remaining strawberries.

Refrigerate before serving.

Wash the orange well, and if possible use an organic one.

Orange and Almond Shortbread

Serves 16 (1 shortbread per serving)

The orange zest gives these breads a delicious flavor. They would also be equally good using lemon zest and chopped hazelnuts.

3/4 cup	vegan margarine	170 g
3 tbsps	superfine sugar	75 g
1	large orange, zest only	1
	few drops of almond extract	
2 tbsps	ground almonds	2 tbsps
2 tbsps	ground rice	50 g
3/4 cup	all-purpose flour	3/4 cup

Pre-heat the oven to 375F. Beat the margarine with the sugar until soft and creamy.

Using a vegetable peeler, peel rind carefully off the orange, trying just to get outer zest and not the pith. Then cut the zest into little pieces.

Mix the orange peelings with the sugar mixture, adding the almond extract and finally the almonds, ground rice and flour.

Work it together to form a ball, leaving the bowl clean.

Lay the dough on a large, greased baking sheet and press into an 8 x 8-inch square about 1/2 inch thick.

Prick the shortbread all over with a fork and mark out into finger shapes; sprinkle with extra sugar.

Bake for about 20 minutes until a pale golden color.

Allow to cool and become firm before cutting and transferring to a serving plate. Makes 12–16.

PER SERVING	
Calories	119
% Calories from fat	68
Fat (g)	9.1
Saturated fat (g)	1.7
Cholesterol (mg)	0
Sodium (mg)	100
Protein (g)	1
Carbohydrate (g)	8.5
Calcium (mg)	9.4
EXCHANGES	
Milk	0.0
Vegetable	0.0
Fruit	0.0
Bread	0.5
Meat	0.0
Fat	2.0

If you don't like walnuts, hazelnuts or pecans are a suitable alternative. Use half whole wheat flour if preferred.

Spiced Apple and Walnut Cake

Serves 8

This cake is one of my favorites. Serve for snacks or as a hot pudding with soy yogurt. Or how about trying it with the Oat and Honey Cream recipe on page 169?

1/2 cup	vegan margarine	110 g
3/4 cup	brown sugar	165 g
2	eggs, beaten	2
1 cup	all-purpose flour	1 cup
1 tsp	pumpkin pie spice	1 tsp
1 tsp	ground cinnamon	1 tsp
	grated nutmeg	
2 tsps	baking powder	2 tsps
1 cup	peeled and finely chopped cooking apple	220 g
3 tbsps	walnuts, chopped	3 tbsps
3 tbsps	soy milk	45 ml

Pre-heat the oven to 350F. Grease and line a deep 7-inch-diameter round cake pan with waxed paper.

In a large bowl, cream the margarine and sugar until pale and fluffy.

Add the eggs a little at a time, beating well.

Sift the flour, spices and baking powder into the bowl and stir into the mixture.

Fold in the chopped apples, walnuts and soy milk to make soft, dropping consistency.

Pour the mixture into the prepared pan and bake for about 1 hour. Check after about 40 minutes, and if necessary turn down heat. When cooked, the cake should be well risen and firm to touch.

Turn out onto a rack to cool. Makes 8–10 slices.

PER SERVING	
Calories	285
% Calories from fat	46
Fat (g)	14.8
Saturated fat (g)	2.8
Cholesterol (mg)	53.1
Sodium (mg)	280
Protein (g)	3.9
Carbohydrate (g)	35.5
Calcium (mg)	106.7

EXCHANGES	
Milk	0.0
Vegetable	0.0
Fruit	0.0
Bread	2.0
Meat	0.0
Fat	3.0

For a lemon or orange layer cake, use this same sponge recipe without cocoa but with orange or lemon zest. Then fill with lemon butter icing (made with vegan margarine), and top with lemon icing.

Wicked Chocolate Cake

Serves 8

A fabulous birthday party cake that will not leave the children feeling they have missed out.

Decorate with shavings of dark chocolate, using a vegetable peeler.

Sponge Cake

½ cup	soft vegan margarine	110 g
½ cup	superfine sugar	110 g
2	eggs, beaten	2
½ cup	self-rising flour, sifted	½ cup
1 tbsp	cocoa (omit cocoa for a plain sponge)	1 tbsp

Icing

2 tbsps	vegan margarine	50 g
3 oz	dark, dairy-free chocolate, broken up	85 g
¾ cup	confectioner's sugar	¾ cup

Cake: Pre-heat the oven to 325F. Line the base of two 7-inch sponge cake pans with waxed paper and lightly oil.

Cream together the margarine and sugar until light and fluffy, then gradually beat in the eggs.

Fold in the sifted flour and cocoa.

Pour evenly into the prepared pans, and smooth the mixture down.

Bake for 25–30 minutes.

Remove from the oven, loosen the edges and turn out onto a rack to cool.

Meanwhile, make the icing.

Icing: Put the margarine and chocolate into a double-boiler over hot water until the chocolate and margarine melt; mix well.

Beat in the sifted sugar and allow the icing to cool slightly.

To assemble: Lay one sponge on a plate, spoon over one-third of the icing and smear over evenly.

Cover with the other half of cake and spoon over the remaining icing.

Using a knife, smooth icing evenly around the sides of the cake.

PER SERVING	
Calories	319
% Calories from fat	52
Fat (g)	19.2
Saturated fat (g)	5.3
Cholesterol (mg)	53.9
Sodium (mg)	282
Protein (g)	3
Carbohydrate (g)	36.2
Calcium (mg)	41.5

EXCHANGES	
Milk	0.0
Vegetable	0.0
Fruit	0.0
Bread	2.0
Meat	0.0
Fat	4.0

Cornmeal Pastry

The result is a crisp pastry that makes a pleasant change from ordinary pastry. I use this pastry to make the Mexican-style Avocado and Shrimp Empañadas (see page 22). Try all sorts of fillings with this pastry for a picnic or crisp snack.

1 cup	(scant) plain white flour	1 cup
2/3 cup	cornmeal	2/3 cup
1 tsp	salt	1 tsp
6 tbsps	olive or vegetable oil	90 ml
1	egg, beaten	1
	dash of cold water	

Combine the flour, cornmeal and salt in a bowl.

Stir in the oil and beaten egg and enough water to make ingredients cling together.

Knead dough on lightly floured surface until it forms a smooth ball.

Cover and chill until required. Makes about 14 oz, enough for one 8-inch pie crust.

PER RECIPE

Calories	1582
% Calories from fat	51
Fat (g)	88.7
Saturated fat (g)	12.9
Cholesterol (mg)	212.5
Sodium (mg)	2394
Protein (g)	27
Carbohydrate (g)	167.5
Calcium (mg)	49.3

EXCHANGES

Milk	0.0
Vegetable	0.0
Fruit	0.0
Bread	11.0
Meat	0.0
Fat	17.0

Crisp Sweet Pastry

Sweet pastry generally cannot be bought commercially without containing dairy products. This variation is a lovely crisp, biscuity pastry, which will match up to any others of its kind, making it ideal for fresh fruit pies.

3/4 cup	all-purpose flour	3/4 cup
	pinch of salt	
3 tbsps	vegan margarine	75 g
3	medium egg yolks	3
3 tbsps	superfine sugar	75 g
	few drops vanilla extract	

Sift the flour and salt into a large bowl.

Cut the margarine into small chunks and, using the tips of your fingers, rub the margarine into the flour until the mixture resembles breadcrumbs.

Make a well in the center of the flour and add the yolks, sugar and vanilla. Using a knife, work in all the surrounding flour, then gently knead until smooth.

Place in bag and chill for at least 30 minutes.

Use as instructed. Makes about 1 1/8 cups (14 oz), enough for one 8-inch pie crust.

PER RECIPE	
Calories	963
% Calories from fat	47
Fat (g)	50.3
Saturated fat (g)	11.6
Cholesterol (mg)	637.9
Sodium (mg)	423
Protein (g)	18.4
Carbohydrate (g)	108.8
Calcium (mg)	95.3

EXCHANGES	
Milk	0.0
Vegetable	0.0
Fruit	0.0
Bread	7.0
Meat	0.0
Fat	10.0

Quick Flaky Pastry

This is a fairly easy crispy light pastry that can be used as a substitute for puff pastry if you are unable to buy it.

³/₄ cup	vegan margarine	165 g
1 cup	all-purpose flour	1 cup
¹/₂ tsp	salt	¹/₂ tsp
	cold water to mix	

Put the margarine in the freezer for about 1 hour.
Sift the flour and salt into a bowl.
Dip the margarine in the flour and quickly grate into the bowl.
Using a knife, mix the margarine into the flour. Gradually add some cold water a little at a time and, using a knife, mix to form dough that leaves the bowl clean.
Quickly bring together to form a ball with your hands.
Chill in the fridge for half an hour.
Use as required. Makes about 12 oz, enough for one 9-inch pie crust.

PER RECIPE	
Calories	1671
% Calories from fat	73
Fat (g)	137.4
Saturated fat (g)	26.9
Cholesterol (mg)	0
Sodium (mg)	2761
Protein (g)	14.4
Carbohydrate (g)	96.9
Calcium (mg)	70.2
EXCHANGES	
Milk	0.0
Vegetable	0.0
Fruit	0.0
Bread	7.0
Meat	0.0
Fat	27.0

Shortcrust Pastry

2 tbsps	vegan margarine	50 g
2 tbsps	lard	50 g
1 cup	all-purpose flour, sifted	1 cup
2 tbsps	cold water	30 ml
	pinch salt	

Rub the fats into the sifted flour and salt until the mixture resembles breadcrumbs.
Using a knife, add the water and mix to form a firm dough.
Cover and refrigerate for at least 30 minutes before using.
Makes about 1¹/₂ cups (12 oz), enough for one 9-inch pie crust.

PER RECIPE	
Calories	885
% Calories from fat	50
Fat (g)	49.1
Saturated fat (g)	14.5
Cholesterol (mg)	23.9
Sodium (mg)	268
Protein (g)	13.2
Carbohydrate (g)	95.6
Calcium (mg)	27.2
EXCHANGES	
Milk	0.0
Vegetable	0.0
Fruit	0.0
Bread	6.0
Meat	0.0
Fat	10.0

Take care not to overcook as it will burn easily, giving the pastry a bitter taste.

Whole Wheat Pastry

For a more wholesome pastry, use this recipe. This pastry rolls out quite thinly and does not require as much pre-cooking as shortcrust. The baking powder gives it a lighter texture.

The pastry should be left to rest longer than ordinary short-crust for the flour to absorb the liquid.

1 cup	whole wheat flour	1 cup
2 tsps	baking powder	2 tsps
	pinch of salt	
2 tbsps	vegan margarine	50 g
2 tbsps	vegetable shortening	50 g
1 tsp	brown sugar	8 g
2 tbsps	vegetable oil	30 ml
6 tbsps	cold water	90 ml

In a large bowl, mix the flour, salt and baking powder. Lightly rub in the fats until the mixture resembles breadcrumbs.

Combine sugar, oil and water and pour into flour.

Using knife blade, mix to light dough consistency.

Cover and refrigerate for at least 1 hour before using.

Makes about 12 oz, enough for one 9-inch pie crust.

PER RECIPE	
Calories	1092
% Calories from fat	61
Fat (g)	76.1
Saturated fat (g)	14.3
Cholesterol (mg)	0
Sodium (mg)	1249
Protein (g)	16.7
Carbohydrate (g)	94.3
Calcium (mg)	613.7

EXCHANGES	
Milk	0.0
Vegetable	0.0
Fruit	0.0
Bread	6.0
Meat	0.0
Fat	15.0

Try chocolate muffins for a special treat by substituting dark chocolate chunks.

Blueberry Muffins

Serves 8 (1 muffin per serving)

These are very quick and simple to make and a favorite with my children for breakfast or lunch; I think it is because blueberries are not as sharp as some fruit such as black currants. However, you could use other fruits or even dried fruits instead of the blueberries.

1 1/4 cups	self-rising flour	1 1/4 cups
2/3 cup	brown sugar	150 g
1	egg, beaten	1
1 cup	(scant) soy milk	200 ml
3 1/2 tbsps	sunflower oil	53 ml
2/3 cup	blueberries, rinsed	2/3 cup

Pre-heat the oven to 350F. Use either large paper muffin shells or a pan with 1-cup-capacity holes, well greased.

Sift the flour with the sugar, add the egg, soy milk and oil and beat well.

Stir in the blueberries.

Spoon mixture into prepared pan or the paper shells.

Bake in the oven for 20–25 minutes until risen and golden.

Place on a wire rack, and serve warm. Makes about 8 big muffins.

PER SERVING

Calories	217
% Calories from fat	30
Fat (g)	7.4
Saturated fat (g)	0.9
Cholesterol (mg)	26.6
Sodium (mg)	267
Protein (g)	3.6
Carbohydrate (g)	34.7
Calcium (mg)	86.6

EXCHANGES

Milk	0.0
Vegetable	0.0
Fruit	0.0
Bread	2.0
Meat	0.0
Fat	1.5

Corn Griddle Cakes

Serves 4 (2 cakes per serving)

These are delicious served with crisp bacon and maple syrup for a lactose-free breakfast.

½ cup	all-purpose flour	½ cup
1 tsp	baking powder	1 tsp
½ tsp	paprika	½ tsp
½ tsp	salt	½ tsp
1	egg, beaten	1
⅔ cup	soy milk	150 mL
½ cup	sweetcorn—either fresh off cob and quickly boiled, frozen or canned and drained	110 g
1 tbsp	sunflower oil	15 mL
	extra oil for frying	

Sift the dry ingredients into a bowl. Beat in the egg and then gradually add the soy milk until you have a smooth batter.

Stir in the sweetcorn and a tablespoon of oil.

Heat a large griddle pan or heavy frying pan, and pour on about 1 teaspoon oil.

Spoon out about 1 large heaping tablespoon of batter for each griddle cake.

Cook until the bubbles show on the surface, then turn the cakes over and cook the other sides until golden brown (about 1 minute on either side).

Serve on warmed plates. Makes about 8 cakes.

PER SERVING	
Calories	137
% Calories from fat	37
Fat (g)	5.7
Saturated fat (g)	0.9
Cholesterol (mg)	53.1
Sodium (mg)	435
Protein (g)	4.9
Carbohydrate (g)	17.3
Calcium (mg)	79.1

EXCHANGES	
Milk	0.0
Vegetable	0.0
Fruit	0.0
Bread	1.0
Meat	0.0
Fat	1.0

Most smoked white fish such as trout would be suitable for this dish. Garam masala is an Indian spice that can be found in ethnic aisles and Indian grocery stores.

Kedgeree

Serves 4

Kedgeree makes a hearty breakfast, one that even the children should enjoy. We often have it as a light supper, and any leftover I heat up for a quick breakfast.

Alternatively, serve hot for lunch or a light supper with the Creamy Curried Coconut Sauce (see page 116). It would also be an impressive starter for 8 if reheated in ramekins and turned onto small plates with the sauce poured around the edge.

1 lb	smoked haddock fillet, or cooked fresh salmon if preferred	450 g
1 cup	basmati rice	1 cup
1	medium onion, finely chopped	1
1 tbsp	vegan margarine	25 g
1 tsp	garam masala	1 tsp
1 tsp	ground cumin	1 tsp
1/2 tsp	ground turmeric	1/2 tsp
4	hard-boiled eggs, cut into quarters	4
2 tbsps	freshly chopped parsley	2 tbsps
	juice of half a lemon	
	salt and freshly ground pepper	

Pre-heat the oven to 375F. Bring a pan half-filled with water to a boil, and simmer the haddock for about 10 minutes—do not overcook.

Drain the fish, saving the cooking water. Remove the skin and bones and flake the fish.

Add a little more water and cook the rice in the fish water until just tender. Drain and allow to dry out a little.

Gently sauté the onion in the margarine for about 8 minutes until softened, add the spices and cook for a further 3 minutes. Remove from heat.

In a large, warm baking dish, combine the rice with the spiced onion mixture, eggs, parsley, lemon juice and flaked fish. Season with freshly ground pepper and salt only if haddock is not too salty.

Cover with aluminum foil and heat through in the oven for 15–20 minutes until piping hot.

PER SERVING	
Calories	399
% Calories from fat	23
Fat (g)	10.2
Saturated fat (g)	2.3
Cholesterol (mg)	299.8
Sodium (mg)	965
Protein (g)	38.5
Carbohydrate (g)	37
Calcium (mg)	117.9

EXCHANGES	
Milk	0.0
Vegetable	0.0
Fruit	0.0
Bread	2.5
Meat	4.0
Fat	0.0

For a light supper, try adding chopped ham to the eggs before frying.

PER SERVING	
Calories	237
% Calories from fat	49
Fat (g)	13.6
Saturated fat (g)	1.9
Cholesterol (mg)	209.4
Sodium (mg)	288
Protein (g)	10.8
Carbohydrate (g)	20.5
Calcium (mg)	58.5
EXCHANGES	
Milk	0.0
Vegetable	0.0
Fruit	0.0
Bread	1.5
Meat	0.0
Fat	3.0

For an iced shake, try chopping up the banana and freezing it before blending. Try experimenting with other fruits such as strawberries, peaches, raspberries, etc.

PER SERVING	
Calories	200
% Calories from fat	5
Fat (g)	1.1
Saturated fat (g)	0.3
Cholesterol (mg)	0
Sodium (mg)	2
Protein (g)	2.3
Carbohydrate (g)	50.1
Calcium (mg)	11.9
EXCHANGES	
Milk	0.0
Vegetable	0.0
Fruit	1.0
Bread	2.0
Meat	0.0
Fat	0.0

French Toast

Serves 4

This is especially enjoyed in our house for breakfast or a quick lunch. Complement it with crispy bacon and maple syrup.

3	eggs, beaten	3
1 tbsp	soy milk	15 ml
	pinch of salt	
4	thick slices of white or brown bread	4
2 tbsps	sunflower oil for frying	30 ml

Heat a large frying pan with half the oil over medium heat. Mix the eggs with milk and salt.

Dip the bread slices in the egg, allowing them to soak up as much as possible.

Turn the bread over and soak the other side.

Lift bread out of egg mixture, allowing excess to fall back into bowl.

Place in a hot frying pan, cook for 1–2 minutes, turn and repeat.

The French toast should be golden and cooked through. Serve immediately.

Banana Oat Shake

Serves 2

This is a creamy alternative to a milkshake and a lot better for you! The shake would be good for babies or toddlers (omitting honey for very young babies).

2	large ripe bananas	2
1 1/2 cups	chilled Oat and Honey Cream (see page 169)	360 ml

Blend the two ingredients together in a blender or processor. Pour into two glasses and serve immediately.

Supermarkets stock frozen summer fruits that can be used all year round.

Summer Berry Fruit Crush

Serves 2

This is pleasantly cooling and refreshing on hot summer days. Experiment with all different fruits, depending on the season. Peaches, melons or any other soft fruit would also create a delicious fruit crush.

1/2 cup	strawberries	1/2 cup
1/2 cup	raspberries	1/2 cup
1 cup	apple juice	240 ml
4	ice cubes	4
	clear honey or sugar to taste	

Using a blender, mix all the ingredients, excluding the ice. Sieve the mixture to remove any seeds. Return to blender with the ice cubes to finish the crush.

Serve immediately.

PER SERVING

Calories	84
% Calories from fat	4
Fat (g)	0.4
Saturated fat (g)	0
Cholesterol (mg)	0
Sodium (mg)	4
Protein (g)	0.6
Carbohydrate (g)	20.6
Calcium (mg)	20.5

EXCHANGES

Milk	0.0
Vegetable	0.0
Fruit	1.5
Bread	0.0
Meat	0.0
Fat	0.0

Helpful Organizations

American Academy of Allergy, Asthma & Immunology
611 East Wells Street
Milwaukee, WI 53202
Phone: (414) 272-6071
Fax: (414) 272-6070
Email: info@aaaai.org
Internet: www.aaaai.org

American Dairy Goat Association
209 West Main Street
Spindale, NC 28160
Phone: (828) 286-3801
Fax: (828) 287-0476
Email: info@adga.org
Internet: www.adga.org

American Dietetic Association (ADA)
216 West Jackson Boulevard
Chicago, IL 60606-6995
Phone: (312) 899-0040
Fax: (312) 899-1979
Internet: www.eatright.org

American Gastroenterological Association
7910 Woodmont Avenue, Seventh Floor
Bethesda, MD 20814
Phone: (301) 654-2055
Fax: (301) 652-3890
Email: webinfo@gastro.org
Internet: www.gastro.org

Anaphylaxis Canada
416 Moore Avenue, Suite 306
Toronto, ON M4G 1C9
Phone: (416) 785-5666
Fax: (416) 785-0458
Email: info@anaphylaxis.ca
Internet: www.anaphylaxis.org

The College of Family Physicians of Canada
2630 Skymark Avenue
Mississauga, ON L4W 5A4
Phone: (905) 629-0900
Toll Free: (800) 387-6197
Fax: (905) 629-0893
Internet: www.cfpc.ca

Dietitians of Canada
480 University Avenue, Suite 604
Toronto, ON M5G 1V2
Phone: (416) 596-0857
Fax: (416) 596-0603
Internet: www.dietitians.ca

The Food Allergy & Anaphylaxis Network
10400 Eaton Place, Suite 107
Fairfax, VA 22030-2208
Phone: (800) 929-4040
Fax: (703) 691-2713
Email: faan@foodallergy.org
Internet: www.foodallergy.org

Foundation for Digestive Health and Nutrition
7910 Woodmont Avenue, Suite 610
Bethesda, MD 20814-3015
Phone: (301) 222-4002
Fax: (301) 222-4010
Email: info@fdhn.org
Internet: www.fdhn.org

International Food Information Council Foundation
1100 Connecticut Avenue N.W., Suite 430
Washington, DC 20036
Phone: (202) 296-6540
Fax: (202) 296-6547
Email: foodinfo@ific.org
Internet: www.ific.org

International Foundation for Functional Gastrointestinal Disorders (IFFGD)
P.O. Box 170864
Milwaukee, WI 53217
Phone: (888) 964-2001 or (414) 964-1799
Fax: (414) 964-7176
Email: iffgd@iffgd.org
Internet: www.iffgd.org

National Digestive Diseases Information Clearinghouse
2 Information Way
Bethesda, MD 20892-3570
Phone: (800) 891-5389
Fax: (301) 907-8906
Email: nddic@info.niddk.nih.gov
Internet: www.niddk.nih.gov

National Institute of Nutrition
302-265 Carling Avenue
Ottawa, ON K1S 2E1
Phone: (613) 235-3355
Fax: (613) 235-7032
Email: nin@nin.ca
Internet: www.nin.ca

Index

Student Support Book
with answers

Higher

MATHEMATICS
for AQA GCSE (Modular)

Tony Banks and David Alcorn

Causeway
Press

Pearson Education Limited
Edinburgh Gate
Harlow
Essex
CM20 2JE
England

ISBN-13: 978-1-4058-3497-1
ISBN-10: 1-4058-3497-8

Exam questions
Past exam questions, provided by the *Assessment and Qualifications Alliance*, are denoted by the
letters AQA. The answers to all questions are entirely the responsibility of the authors/publisher
and have neither been provided nor approved by AQA.

Every effort has been made to locate the copyright owners of material used in this book.
Any omissions brought to the notice of the publisher are regretted and will be credited in
subsequent printings.

Page design
Billy Johnson

Reader
Barbara Alcorn

Artwork
David Alcorn

Cover design
Raven Design

Typesetting by Billy Johnson, San Francisco, California, USA

Printed and bound by Scotprint, Haddington, Scotland

preface

This book provides detailed revision notes, worked examples and examination questions to support students in their preparation for the new two-tier GCSE Mathematics examinations for the AQA Modular Specification – Higher Tier.

The book has been designed so that it can be used in conjunction with the companion book *Higher Mathematics for AQA GCSE (Modular)* or as a stand-alone revision book for self study and provides full coverage of the new AQA Specifications for the Higher Tier of entry.

In preparing the text, full account has been made of the requirements for students to be able to use and apply mathematics in written examination papers and be able to solve problems in mathematics both with and without a calculator.

The detailed revision notes, worked examples and examination questions have been organised into 41 self-contained sections which meet the requirements of the National Curriculum and provide efficient coverage of the specifications for Modules 1, 3 and 5.

Module 1: Sections 1 - 6
Module 3: Sections 7 - 17
Module 5: Sections 18 - 41

At the end of Module 1 and Module 3 there is an examination questions section with a compilation of exam and exam-style questions, organised for non-calculator and calculator practice, in preparation for the exams.

In Module 5 a section review is provided at the end of Sections 18 - 29 (Algebra) and another at the end of Sections 30 - 41 (Shape, Space and Measures) to give further opportunities to consolidate skills. At the end of the module there is a further compilation of exam and exam-style questions, organised for non-calculator and calculator practice, in preparation for the exams.

Also available *Without Answers: (ISBN: 1-405834-96-X)*
The book has been designed so that it can be used in conjunction with the companion book
Higher Mathematics for AQA GCSE (Modular) (ISBN: 1-405831-42-1)

contents

Module 1
Sections 1 - 6

Module 3
Sections 7 - 17

Module 5

Section Review - Algebra

Section Review - Shape, Space and Measures

Collection and Organisation of Data

What you need to know

- **Primary data** is data collected by an individual or organisation to use for a particular purpose. Primary data is obtained from experiments, investigations, surveys and by using questionnaires.

- **Secondary data** is data which is already available or has been collected by someone else for a different purpose. Sources of secondary data include the Annual Abstract of Statistics, Social Trends and the Internet.

- **Qualitative** data – Data which can only be described in words.   E.g. Colour of cars.

- **Quantitative** data – Data that has a numerical value.
  Quantitative data is either **discrete** or **continuous**.
  Discrete data can only take certain values.   E.g. Numbers of cars in car parks.
  Continuous data has no exact value and is measurable.   E.g. Weights of cars.

- **Data Collection Sheets** – Used to record data during a survey.

- **Tally** – A way of recording each item of data on a data collection sheet.

- **Frequency Table** – A way of collating the information recorded on a data collection sheet.

- **Grouped Frequency Table** – Used for continuous data or for discrete data when a lot of data has to be recorded.

- **Database** – A collection of data.

- **Class Interval** – The width of the groups used in a grouped frequency distribution.

- **Questionnaire** – A set of questions used to collect data for a survey.
  Questionnaires should: (1) use simple language,
                              (2) ask short questions which can be answered precisely,
                              (3) provide tick boxes,
                              (4) avoid open-ended questions,
                              (5) avoid leading questions,
                              (6) ask questions in a logical order.

- **Hypothesis** – A hypothesis is a statement which may or may not be true.

- When information is required about a large group of people it is not always possible to survey everyone and only a **sample** may be asked.
  The sample chosen should be large enough to make the results meaningful and representative of the whole group (population) or the results may be **biased**.

- **Two-way Tables** – A way of illustrating two features of a survey.

- In a **simple random sample** everyone has an equal chance of being selected.

- In a **systematic random sample** people are selected according to some rule.

- In a **stratified random sample** the original group is divided up into separate categories or strata, such as male/female, age group, etc, before a random sample is taken. A simple random sample is then taken from each category in proportion to the size of the category.

Exercise 1

1. To find out how long students spend on homework each night, Pat asks a class of Year 7 students how much time they spent on their homework last night.
   Give two reasons why his results may not be typical of all students.

2 The two-way table shows the number of credit cards and the number of bank accounts held by each of 50 people.

Number of credit cards

		0	1	2	3
Number of bank accounts	0	1	1	0	0
	1	12	15	8	2
	2	5	3	2	1

(a) How many people have exactly one bank account and one credit card?
(b) How many people have more than one credit card?

AQA

3 Jamie is investigating the use made of his college library. Here is part of his questionnaire:

> **Library Questionnaire**
> 1. How old are you? ....

(a) (i) Give a reason why this question is unsuitable.
    (ii) Rewrite the question so that it could be included.
(b) Jamie asks the librarian to give the questionnaires to students when they borrow books.
    (i) Give reasons why this sample may be biased.
    (ii) Suggest a better way of giving out the questionnaires.

4 The table shows the results of a survey of 500 people.

	Can drive	Cannot drive
Men	180	20
Women	240	60

A newspaper headline states: **Survey shows that more women can drive than men.**
Do the results of the survey support this headline? Give a reason for your answer.

5 This sample was used to investigate the claim: **"Women do more exercise than men."**

	Age (years)			
	16 to 21	22 to 45	46 to 65	Over 65
Male	5	5	13	7
Female	25	35	0	0

Give three reasons why the sample is biased.

6 At Paul's school there are 200 pupils in each of Years 7 to 11.
There are approximately equal numbers of girls and boys.
Describe how Paul could select a 10% stratified sample which is representative of all the pupils at the school.

AQA

7 A company has 24 managers, 35 secretaries and 65 other staff in work on a particular day.
A stratified sample of 18 of these 124 employees is to be chosen.
How many employees of each type should be chosen?

AQA

8 The table shows the number of employees at each of two factories.

Factory	A	B
Number of employees	733	467

A stratified random sample of 200 employees is to be taken from these factories.
(a) Calculate the number of employees which should be sampled from each factory.

There were 300 male employees at factory A.
(b) Calculate how many female employees should be part of the sample from factory A.

AQA

What you need to know

- There are three types of **average**: the **mode**, the **median** and the **mean**.
  The **mode** is the most common value.
  The **median** is the middle value (or the mean of the two middle values) when the values are arranged in order of size.
  The **Mean** $= \dfrac{\text{Total of all values}}{\text{Number of values}}$

- The **range** is a measure of **spread**, and is the difference between the highest and lowest values.

  Eg 1 The number of text messages received by 7 students on Saturday is shown.

  $$2 \quad 4 \quad 3 \quad 4 \quad 4 \quad 3 \quad 2$$

  Find   (a) the mode,   (b) the median,   (c) the mean,   (d) the range.

  (a) The mode is 4.

  (b) 2   2   3   ③   4   4   4   The median is 3.

  (c) The mean $= \dfrac{2+4+3+4+4+3+2}{7} = \dfrac{22}{7} = 3.14\ldots = 3.1$, correct to 1 d.p.

  (d) The range $= 4 - 2 = 2$

- To find the mean of a **frequency distribution** use: Mean $= \dfrac{\text{Total of all values}}{\text{Number of values}} = \dfrac{\Sigma fx}{\Sigma f}$

  Eg 2 The table shows the number of stamps on some parcels.

Number of stamps	1	2	3	4
Number of parcels	5	6	9	4

  Find the mean number of stamps per parcel.

  $$\text{Mean} = \frac{\text{Total number of stamps}}{\text{Number of parcels}} = \frac{1 \times 5 + 2 \times 6 + 3 \times 9 + 4 \times 4}{5 + 6 + 9 + 4} = \frac{60}{24} = 2.5$$

- To find the mean of a **grouped frequency distribution**, first find the value of the midpoint of each class.
  Then use: Estimated mean $= \dfrac{\text{Total of all values}}{\text{Number of values}} = \dfrac{\Sigma fx}{\Sigma f}$

  Eg 3 The table shows the weights of some parcels.

Weight (w grams)	Frequency
$100 \leqslant w < 200$	7
$200 \leqslant w < 300$	11
$300 \leqslant w < 400$	19
$400 \leqslant w < 500$	3

  Calculate an estimate of the mean weight of these parcels.

  $$\text{Mean} = \frac{\Sigma fx}{\Sigma f} = \frac{150 \times 7 + 250 \times 11 + 350 \times 19 + 450 \times 3}{7 + 11 + 19 + 3} = \frac{11\,800}{40} = 295 \text{ grams}$$

- You should be able to choose the best average to use in different situations for different sets of data.

1 The prices paid for eight different meals at a restaurant are:

£10   £9   £9.50   £12   £20   £11.50   £11   £9

(a) Which price is the mode?
(b) Find the median price.
(c) Calculate the mean price.
(d) Which of these averages best describes the average price paid for a meal?
     Give a reason for your answer.

2 (a) Calculate the mean of   13.9,   15.3,   11.7   and   16.2.
(b) Using your result from part (a), explain how to find quickly the mean of
                        14.9,   16.3,   12.7   and   17.2
(c) Calculate the median of the numbers in part (a).
(d) If the number 16.2 in part (a) was changed to 27.2, explain, without doing a calculation,
     whether the mean or the median would be more affected.   AQA

3 The graph shows the distribution of goals scored by a football team in home and away matches.

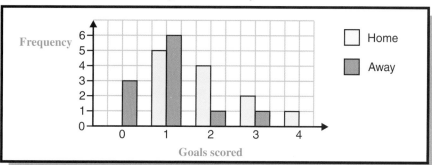

(a) What is the range of the number of goals scored at home matches?
(b) Calculate the mean number of goals per match for home matches.
(c) A supporter says,
             "The average number of goals per match is the same for
                both away matches and home matches."
     Which average is being used?   AQA

4 Four taxi drivers recorded how many passengers they carried on each journey during
one evening. The table shows the numbers of journeys they made with different numbers of
passengers.

		Number of passengers carried			
		1	2	3	4
Taxi	**A**	6	6	4	0
	B	7	7	3	1
	C	5	7	2	0
	D	4	4	3	1

(a) Which taxi completed the most journeys that evening?
(b) Calculate the total number of journeys in which exactly 3 passengers were carried.
(c) There were 60 journeys made altogether.
     Calculate the mean number of passengers per taxi journey.   AQA

5 Fred records the time taken by 30 pupils to complete a cross-country run.

Time (*t* minutes)	20 ≤ t < 25	25 ≤ t < 30	30 ≤ t < 35	35 ≤ t < 45
Number of pupils	9	8	5	8

(a) Calculate an estimate of the mean time taken to complete the run.
(b) Which time interval contains the median time taken to complete the run?   AQA

Presentation of Data 1

What you need to know

- **Bar chart**. Used for data which can be counted.
  Often used to compare quantities of data in a distribution.
  The length of each bar represents frequency.

  > Bars can be drawn horizontally or vertically.

- **Bar-line graph**. Instead of drawing bars, horizontal or vertical lines are drawn to show frequency.
- **Pie chart**. Used for data which can be counted.
  Often used to compare proportions of data, usually with the total.
  The whole circle represents all the data.
  The size of each sector represents the frequency of data in that sector.

  Eg 1 The results of asking a group of children which board game they liked best is shown.

Board game	Chess	Draughts	Ludo	Snakes & Ladders
Number of children	4	9	2	5

  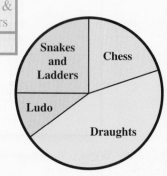

  Draw a pie chart to show this information.
  20 children were asked.
  Each child is represented by $\frac{360°}{20} = 18°$.

Chess:	$4 \times 18° = 72°$
Draughts:	$9 \times 18° = 162°$
Ludo:	$2 \times 18° = 36°$
Snakes & Ladders:	$5 \times 18° = 90°$

- **Stem and leaf diagrams**. Used to represent data in its original form.
  Data is split into two parts.
  The part with the higher place value is the stem.   E.g. 15 = stem 1, leaf 5.
  A key is given to show the value of the data.   E.g. 3|4 means 3.4, etc.
  The data is shown in numerical order on the diagram.   E.g. 2|3 5 9 represents 23, 25, 29.
  Back to back stem and leaf diagrams can be used to compare two sets of data.

  Eg 2 The times, in seconds, taken by 10 students to complete a puzzle are shown.

  9   23   17   20   12   11   24   12   10   26

  Construct a stem and leaf diagram to represent this information.

  ```
                          2 | 0  means 20 seconds
           0 | 9
           1 | 0   1   2   2   7
           2 | 0   3   4   6
  ```

- A **scatter graph** can be used to show the relationship between two sets of data.
- The relationship between two sets of data is referred to as **correlation**.
- You should be able to recognise **positive** and **negative** correlation.
  The correlation is stronger as points get closer to a straight line.
- When there is a relationship between two sets of data a **line of best fit** can be drawn on the scatter graph.
- **Perfect correlation** is when all the points lie on a straight line.
- The line of best fit can be used to **estimate** the value from one set of the data when the corresponding value of the other set is known.

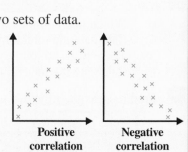

Positive correlation   Negative correlation

Eg 3 The table shows the weights and heights of 10 girls.

Weight (kg)	33	36	37	39	40	42	45	45	48	48
Height (cm)	133	134	137	140	146	146	145	150	152	156

(a) Draw a scatter graph for the data.
(b) What type of correlation is shown?
(c) Draw a line of best fit.
(d) A girl weighs 50 kg. Estimate her height.

> Mark a cross on the graph to show the weight and height of each girl.

(a)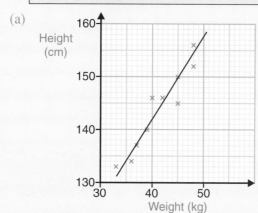

> **On a scatter graph:**
> The **slope** of the line of best fit shows the **trend** of the data.
> The line of best fit does not have to go through the origin of the graph.

(b) Positive correlation.
(c) The line of best fit has been drawn, by eye, on the graph.
(d) 158 cm. Read estimate where 50 kg meets line of best fit.

Exercise 3

1 Here are the highest November temperatures recorded in 12 European countries last year.

   13°C 9°C 14°C 17°C 14°C 20°C 7°C 14°C 18°C 21°C 10°C 22°C

(a) Construct a stem and leaf diagram to show this information.
(b) When the temperature in another European country is included in the data, the range increases by 2°C.
   What was the temperature recorded in that country? Explain your answer.

2 The table shows the results of asking a group of children which pet they prefer.

Pet	Dog	Cat	Rabbit	Guinea pig
Number of children	8	5	7	4

Draw a clearly labelled pie chart to represent this information.

AQA

3 The scatter graphs below show the results of a questionnaire given to pupils who have jobs.

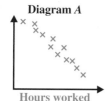

Diagram A
Hours worked

Diagram B
Hours worked

Diagram C
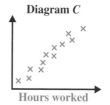
Hours worked

(a) Which scatter graph shows the number of hours worked plotted against:
   (i) the earnings of pupils,
   (ii) the time taken by pupils to travel to work?
(b) State which one of the graphs shows a negative correlation.

AQA

4 The bar chart shows information about the injuries of drivers involved in road accidents at a busy junction.

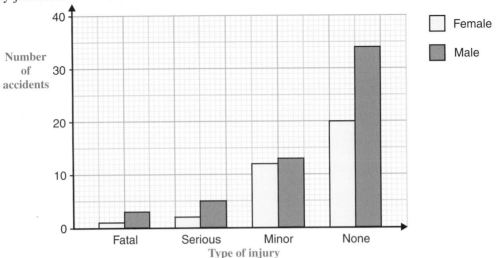

(a) What percentage of drivers had no injuries?
(b) What is the ratio of female to male drivers involved in these accidents?
Give your answer in its simplest form.
(c) Draw a pie chart to illustrate the proportion of drivers with each type of injury.

5 In a survey, parents were asked:

> **'Do you think the behaviour of children has improved in the last ten years?'**

The results of the survey are shown in the pie chart.

(a) Estimate the fraction of parents who think that the behaviour of children has got worse.
(b) 75 parents in the survey said, 'Don't know'.
This was 5% of all the parents.
Calculate the number of parents that took part in the survey.

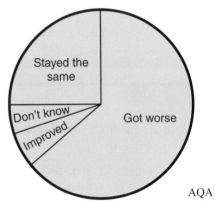

AQA

6 Twenty children were asked to estimate the length of a leaf.
Their estimates, in centimetres, are:

Boys									
4.5	5.0	4.0	3.5	4.0	4.5	5.0	4.5	3.5	4.5

Girls									
4.5	5.0	3.5	4.0	5.5	3.5	4.5	3.5	3.0	2.5

(a) Construct a back to back stem and leaf diagram to represent this information.
(b) Compare and comment on the estimates of these boys and girls.

7 The table shows the ages and heights of trees in a wood.

Age (years)	1	3	4	5	7	9	10
Height (m)	0.5	1.2	1.7	2.5	3.3	4.5	4.8

(a) Draw a scatter graph for the data.
(b) Draw a line of best fit.
(c) Use the graph to estimate the height of a tree which is
(i) 8 years old, (ii) 13 years old.
(d) Which of your answers in (c) is more likely to be reliable?
Give a reason for your answer.

AQA

Presentation of Data 2 ●●●●

What you need to know

- A **time series** is a set of readings taken at time intervals.

  Only the plotted points represent actual values. Points are joined by lines to show the **trend**.

- A **line graph** is used to show a time series.
- Variations in a time series which recur with the seasons of the year are called **seasonal variations**.
- **Moving averages** are used to smooth out variations in a time series so that the trend can be seen.

  Eg 1 The graph shows the amount of gas used by a householder each quarter over a period of 3 years.

  The blue crosses show the 4-quarterly moving average values.

  A line of best fit, drawn for the moving averages, shows the general **trend**.

  The trend shows a slight increase in the amount of gas used.

  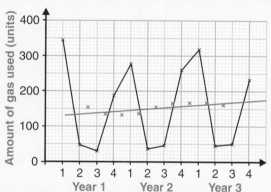

- **Frequency polygon**. Used to illustrate grouped frequency distributions. Often used to compare two or more distributions on the same diagram.

  Eg 2 The frequency distribution of the heights of some boys is shown.

Height (h cm)	$130 \leqslant h < 140$	$140 \leqslant h < 150$	$150 \leqslant h < 160$	$160 \leqslant h < 170$	$170 \leqslant h < 180$
Frequency	1	7	12	9	3

  Draw a frequency polygon to illustrate the data.

  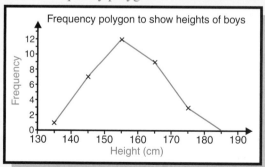

  Frequencies are plotted at the midpoints of the class intervals and joined with straight lines.

- **Histograms**. Used to illustrate grouped frequency distributions.
  The horizontal axis is a continuous scale.
  Bars are drawn between the lower and upper class boundaries for each class interval.
  When the classes have gaps between them the upper class boundary is halfway between the end of one class and the beginning of the next.
- Histograms can have equal or unequal class width intervals.
  With **equal** class width intervals: **frequency** is proportional to the **heights** of the bars.
  With **unequal** class width intervals: **frequency** is proportional to the **areas** of the bars.

  frequency = frequency density × class width interval

Eg 3 The times taken by 40 pupils to solve a puzzle are:

Time (t seconds)	$10 \leq t < 20$	$20 \leq t < 25$	$25 \leq t < 30$	$30 \leq t < 45$
Frequency	6	12	10	12

Draw a histogram to represent the data.

> **To find the height of each bar:**
> The height of each bar is given by the **frequency density** for each group, where:
> $$\text{frequency density} = \frac{\text{frequency}}{\text{class width interval}}$$
> E.g. For the group $10 \leq t < 20$: Frequency density $\frac{6}{10} = 0.6$
> Draw the bar to a height of 0.6

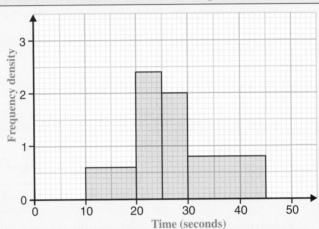

Exercise 4

1. The graph shows the age distribution of people in a nursing home.

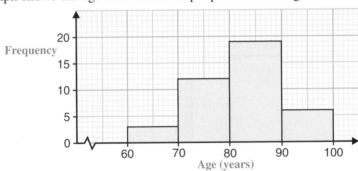

(a) Which age group is the modal class?
(b) How many people are in the nursing home?
(c) The table shows the age distribution of men in the home.

Age (a years)	$60 \leq a < 70$	$70 \leq a < 80$	$80 \leq a < 90$	$90 \leq a < 100$
Frequency	2	7	6	0

(i) Draw a frequency polygon to represent this information.
(ii) On the same diagram draw a frequency polygon to represent the age distribution of women in the home.
(iii) Compare and comment on the ages of men and women in the home.

2. Calculate the second average in a 3-point moving average for these values.

15   23   19   12   17   22   28   20   16

3 The table shows the number of units of electricity used each quarter by a householder over a period of 3 years.

Year	2003				2004				2005			
Quarter	1	2	3	4	1	2	3	4	1	2	3	4
Units used	680	810	470	740	640	850	420	750	970	880	490	760

(a) Plot these values on graph paper.
(b) Calculate a 4-point moving average.
(c) Plot the moving average values on your graph.
(d) Comment on the trend in the units of electricity used.

4 A London taxi driver keeps a record of the distance travelled for each of 50 journeys.

Distance travelled (d km)	Number of journeys
$0 < d \leqslant 2$	12
$2 < d \leqslant 3$	11
$3 < d \leqslant 4$	10
$4 < d \leqslant 6$	10
$6 < d \leqslant 10$	6
$10 < d \leqslant 15$	1

(a) (i) Draw a histogram to illustrate this data.
    (ii) Use your histogram to estimate the median distance.
(b) The mean distance is 3.7 km.
    Should the taxi driver use the mean or the median to represent the average distance for a journey?
    Give a reason for your answer.

AQA

5 The heights of a randomly selected group of 100 boys in a school are shown in this table.

Height (h cm)	$125 \leqslant h < 140$	$140 \leqslant h < 145$	$145 \leqslant h < 150$	$150 \leqslant h < 160$	$160 \leqslant h < 175$
Frequency	9	21	24	31	15

(a) Draw a histogram to show this information.

The heights of a randomly selected group of 100 girls in the school are shown in this histogram.

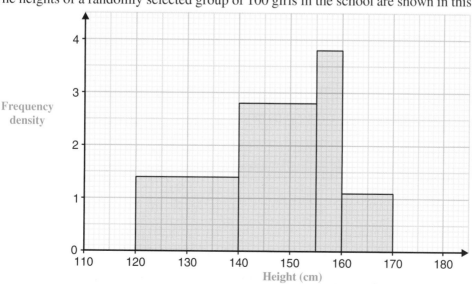

(b) Calculate an estimate of how many girls have a height of less than 145 cm.

AQA

Cumulative Frequency

What you need to know

- The information given in a frequency table can be used to make a **cumulative frequency table**.
- You should be able to **draw cumulative frequency graphs**.

To draw a cumulative frequency graph:
1. Draw and label: the variable on the horizontal axis, cumulative frequency on the vertical axis. 2. Plot the cumulative frequency against the upper class boundary of each class. 3. Join the points with a smooth curve.

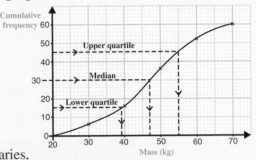

- If the question does not give the upper class boundaries,
  then the upper class boundary of each class is equal to the lower class boundary of the next class.
- When the classes have gaps between them then the upper class boundary is halfway between the end of one class and the beginning of the next.
- You should be able to **interpret cumulative frequency graphs**.

The **median** is the value of the middle number. The **lower quartile** is the value located at $\frac{1}{4}$ of the total frequency. The **upper quartile** is the value located at $\frac{3}{4}$ of the total frequency. The **interquartile range** measures the spread of the middle 50% of the data. Interquartile range = Upper Quartile − Lower Quartile

Eg 1 The times spent by students on the Internet one day are shown.

Time (t minutes)	$0 \leqslant t < 20$	$20 \leqslant t < 40$	$40 \leqslant t < 60$	$60 \leqslant t < 80$
Frequency	55	25	15	5

(a) Draw a cumulative frequency graph.
(b) Use your graph to find:
    (i) the median,
    (ii) the interquartile range.

(a) | Make a cumulative frequency table that can be used to draw the graph. |

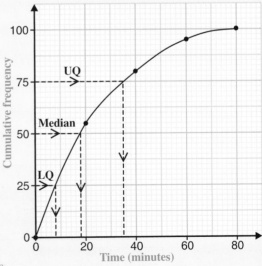

Time (mins) less than	0	20	40	60	80
Cumulative frequency	0	55	80	95	100

(b) Reading from the graph:
    (i) Median = 18 minutes
    (ii) Lower quartile (LQ) = 8 minutes
        Upper quartile (UQ) = 35 minutes
        Interquartile range = UQ − LQ = 35 − 8 = 27 minutes

● A **box plot** is used to represent the range, the median and the quartiles of a distribution.

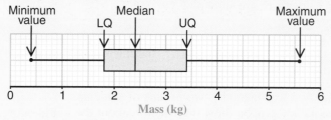

● The box plot shows how the data is spread out and how the middle 50% of data is clustered.

● Box plots can be used to compare two (or more) distributions.

● You should be able to draw and interpret box plots.

Eg 2 15 pupils were asked to estimate the size of an angle.
Their estimates, in degrees, are shown.

40 20 38 30 32 45 35 36 40 35 30 40 45 42 25

Draw a box plot to illustrate the data.

> Put the data in order and locate the median, lower quartile and upper quartile.
> Then use these values to draw the box plot.

20 25 30 ⟨30⟩ 32 35 35 ⟨36⟩ 38 40 40 ⟨40⟩ 42 45 45

LQ   Median   UQ

Size of angle (degrees)

Exercise 5

① As part of a lifesaving course a group of students were asked to swim as far as possible
wearing shoes and clothes.
The cumulative frequency graph shows the distances swum.

Cumulative
frequency

Distance (metres)

(a) Use the graph to find:
    (i) the median distance, 20 (ii) the interquartile range. 48
    82−41: 48
(b) Draw a box plot to illustrate the distances swum.

2 A group of children were asked to estimate the weight of a bucket of water.
Their estimates, in kilograms, are shown.

10	9	17.5	8	7.5	5	10	15	12.5	20	8	10	14	18	11

(a) Find (i) the median estimate, (ii) the interquartile range of these estimates.
(b) Draw a box plot to represent these estimates.

3 An English examination was taken by two groups of students.
The cumulative frequency graphs show information about the marks scored by each group.

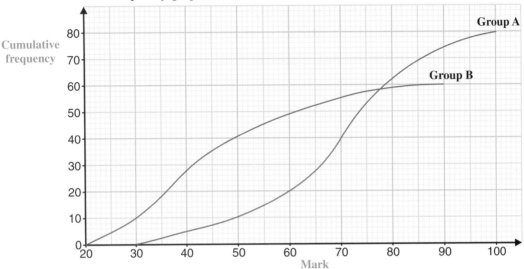

(a) Find the difference in the median marks of the two groups.
(b) (i) Which group had the larger interquartile range?
(ii) Find the interquartile range for this group.

AQA

4 The box plots illustrate the distribution of weights for a sample of eating apples and a sample of cooking apples.

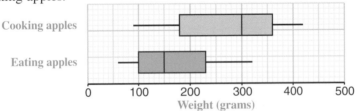

(a) What is the range in the weights of the eating apples?
(b) Which type of apple has the higher median weight?
(c) What is the interquartile range for cooking apples?
(d) Compare and comment on these distributions.

5 Laura and Joy played 80 games of golf together. The table below shows Laura's scores.

Scores x	$70 < x \leqslant 80$	$80 < x \leqslant 90$	$90 < x \leqslant 100$	$100 < x \leqslant 110$	$110 < x \leqslant 120$
Frequency	2	8	30	34	6

(a) Draw a cumulative frequency diagram to show Laura's scores.
(b) Use your graph to find:
(i) Laura's median score,
(ii) the interquartile range of her scores.
(c) Joy's median score was 103. The interquartile range of her scores was 6.
(i) Who was the more consistent player? Give a reason for your choice.
(ii) The winner of a game of golf is the one with the lowest score.
Who won most of these 80 games? Give a reason for your choice.

AQA

Probability

What you need to know

- **Probability** describes how likely or unlikely it is that an event will occur. Probabilities are written as **fractions**, **decimals** or **percentages**.

- How to work out probabilities using **equally likely outcomes**.

$$\text{The probability of an event} = \frac{\text{Number of outcomes in the event}}{\text{Total number of possible outcomes}}$$

Eg 1 A box contains 7 red pens and 4 blue pens. A pen is taken from the box at random. What is the probability that the pen is blue?

$$P(\text{blue}) = \frac{\text{Number of blue pens}}{\text{Total number of pens}} = \frac{4}{11}$$

> P(blue) stands for the probability that the pen is blue.

- How to estimate probabilities using **relative frequency**.

$$\text{Relative frequency} = \frac{\text{Number of times the event happens in an experiment (or in a survey)}}{\text{Total number of trials in the experiment (or observations in the survey)}}$$

Eg 2 A spinner is spun 20 times. The results are shown.

$$
\begin{array}{cccccccccc}
4 & 1 & 3 & 1 & 4 & 2 & 2 & 4 & 3 & 3 \\
4 & 1 & 4 & 4 & 3 & 2 & 2 & 1 & 3 & 2
\end{array}
$$

What is the relative frequency of getting a 4?

$$\text{Relative frequency} = \frac{\text{Number of 4's}}{\text{Number of spins}} = \frac{6}{20} = 0.3$$

> Relative frequency gives a better estimate of probability the larger the number of trials.

- How to use probabilities to **estimate** the number of times an event occurs in an **experiment** or **observation**.

$$\text{Estimate} = \text{total number of trials (or observations)} \times \text{probability of event}$$

Eg 3 1000 raffle tickets are sold. Alan buys some tickets.
The probability that Alan wins first prize is $\frac{1}{50}$.
How many tickets did Alan buy?   Number of tickets $= 1000 \times \frac{1}{50} = 20$

- **Mutually exclusive events** cannot occur at the same time.

$$\text{When A and B are mutually exclusive events:}\quad P(A \text{ or } B) = P(A) + P(B)$$

Eg 4 A box contains red, green, blue and yellow counters.
The table shows the probability of getting each colour.

Colour	Red	Green	Blue	Yellow
Probability	0.4	0.25	0.25	0.1

A counter is taken from the box at random.
What is the probability of getting a red or blue counter?

P(Red or Blue) = P(Red) + P(Blue) = 0.4 + 0.25 = 0.65

- $$\text{The probability of an event, A, } \textbf{not happening} \text{ is:}\quad P(\text{not } A) = 1 - P(A)$$

For example, the probability I will get a phone call today is 0.9.
So, the probability I will **not** get a phone call today is $1 - 0.9 = 0.1$.

- How to find all the possible outcomes when two events are combined.
  - By **listing** the outcomes systematically.
  - By using a **possibility space diagram**.
  - By using a **tree diagram**.

- The outcomes of **independent events** do not influence each other.

> When A and B are independent events: $P(A \text{ and } B) = P(A) \times P(B)$

Eg 5 Box A contains 3 white cubes (W) and 1 blue cube (B).
Box B contains 2 white cubes (W) and 3 blue cubes (B).
A cube is drawn from each box at random.
(a) Draw a tree diagram to show all the possible outcomes.
(b) Calculate the probability of getting two white cubes.

(a)

Box A	Box B	Outcome

```
            2/5
        W ------- W    WW
   3/4 /
      W
     /      3/5
    /    ------- B    WB
   /
   \        2/5
    \   ------- W    BW
   1/4 \
        B
            3/5
        ------- B    BB
```

(b)

> To calculate P(WW), multiply the probabilities along the branches of the tree diagram.

$$P(WW) = \frac{3}{4} \times \frac{2}{5}$$
$$= \frac{6}{20}$$
$$= \frac{3}{10}$$

- **Conditional probabilities** arise when the probabilities of particular events occurring are affected by other events.

Eg 6 In a drawer there are 4 black socks and 2 green socks. Two socks are taken at random. What is the probability that they are both the same colour?

> The probabilities for the second sock are **dependent** on the colour of the first sock.

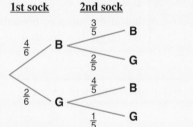

1st sock	2nd sock

$P(\text{same colour}) = P(BB) + P(GG)$

$$= \left(\frac{4}{6} \times \frac{3}{5}\right) + \left(\frac{2}{6} \times \frac{1}{5}\right)$$
$$= \frac{12}{30} + \frac{2}{30}$$
$$= \frac{14}{30} = \frac{7}{15}$$

$P(\text{same colour}) = \frac{7}{15}$

Exercise 6

1 The letters of the word   A   B   B   E   Y   are written on separate cards and placed in a box.
A card is taken from the box at random.
(a) What is the probability that it is the letter B?
(b) The probability that it is a vowel is 0.4.
What is the probability that it is not a vowel?

2 Petra has 5 numbered cards. She uses the cards to do this experiment:

> Shuffle the cards and then record the number on the top card.

She repeats the experiment 20 times and gets these results.

3	3	2	3	4	3	5	2	3	4
3	5	3	3	4	2	5	3	4	2

(a) What is the relative frequency of getting a 3?
(b) What numbers do you think are on the five cards? Give a reason for your answer.
(c) She repeats the experiment 500 times.
Estimate the number of times she will get a 5. Give a reason for your answer.

3 Jeff tosses a coin three times.
   (a)   List all the possible outcomes.
   (b)   What is the probability that he gets one head and two tails?

4 A box contains counters. The counters are numbered 1, 2, 3, 4 or 5.
A counter is taken from the box at random.
   (a)   Copy and complete the table to show the probability of each number being chosen.

Number on counter	1	2	3	4	5
Probability	0.20	0.30	0.15		0.10

   (b)   Is the number on the counter chosen more likely to be odd or even?
       You must show your working.

AQA

5 The table shows information about the colour and type of symbol printed on some cards.

Colour of symbol

		Red	Yellow	Blue
Type of	**O**	9	4	5
symbol	**X**	2	7	3

   (a)   A card is taken at random.
       (i)   What is the probability that it has a red symbol?
       (ii)   What is the probability that it has a blue symbol **or** an X?
   (b)   A yellow card is taken at random.
       What is the probability that it has the symbol X?

AQA

6 On Tuesday Jim has to catch a bus and a train to get to work.
The probability that the train is late is 0.4. The probability that the bus is late is 0.7.
   (a)   Copy and complete the tree diagram.

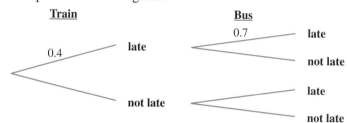

   (b)   What is the probability that both the bus and the train are late?
   (c)   What is the probability that either the train or the bus is late but not both?

7 (a)   A box contains 2 red (R) counters and 3 green (G) counters.

       Two counters are taken at random from the box.
       Calculate the probability that the two counters are a different colour.

   (b)   Box A and Box B contain the following counters.

       Box A   **Box B**

One counter is taken at random from Box A and put in Box B.
One counter is then taken at random from Box B and put in Box A.
What is the probability that Box A now contains counters of the same colour?

AQA

Do not use a calculator for this exercise.

1 Sylvester did a survey to find the most popular pantomime.
The results for children are shown in the table.

Pantomime	Aladdin	Cinderella	Jack and the Bean Stalk	Peter Pan
Number of children	45	35	25	15

Draw a clearly labelled pie chart to illustrate this information.

2 Winston has designed a data collection sheet to record the number of bottles that each person puts into a bottle bank.

Number of bottles	0 to 2	3 to 6	6 to 8
Tally			
Frequency			

(a) Give **three** criticisms of the class intervals that Winston has chosen.

Anna and Patrick watch people using the bottle bank.
Anna watches 60 people and calculates the mean to be 8.5 bottles per person.
Patrick watches 15 people and calculates the mean to be 9.2 bottles per person.
(b) Which of the two means would you expect to give the more reliable estimate of the mean number of bottles per person? Give a reason for your answer.

AQA

3 The lengths of 20 bolts, in centimetres, is shown.

| 7.4 | 5.8 | 4.5 | 5.0 | 6.5 | 6.6 | 7.0 | 5.4 | 4.8 | 6.4 |
| 5.4 | 6.2 | 7.2 | 5.5 | 4.8 | 6.5 | 5.0 | 6.0 | 6.5 | 6.8 |

(a) Draw a stem and leaf diagram to show this information.
(b) What is the range in the lengths of these bolts?

4 The table shows information about a group of students.

	Can speak French	Cannot speak French
Male	5	20
Female	12	38

(a) One of these students is chosen at random.
What is the probability that the student can speak French?
(b) Pru says, "If a female student is chosen at random she is more likely to be able to speak French than if a male student is chosen at random."
Is she correct? Explain your answer.

5 The table shows the rainfall (cm) and the number of hours of sunshine for various towns in August one year.

Rainfall (cm)	0.1	0.1	0.2	0.5	0.8	1	1	1.5	1.5	1.9
Sunshine (hours)	200	240	210	190	170	160	130	100	120	90

(a) Use this information to draw a scatter graph.
(b) Draw a line of best fit on your diagram.
(c) Use your line of best fit to estimate the number of hours of sunshine for a town that had:
    (i)   1.4 cm of rain in August that year,   (ii)   2.5 cm of rain in August that year.
(d) Which of the answers from part (c) would you expect to be the more reliable?
Give a reason for your answer.

AQA

6 After plans for a by-pass to a large town were announced, the local newspaper received twelve letters on the subject. Eleven were opposed to it.
The newspaper claimed:

> 'OVER 90% ARE AGAINST NEW BY-PASS'

(a) Give **two** reasons why the newspaper could be criticised for making this claim.
(b) The local council is to carry out a survey to find the true nature of local opinion.
Give **two** factors that should be taken into account when selecting the sample.　　AQA

7 The graph shows the distribution of the best height jumped by each girl in a high jump competition.

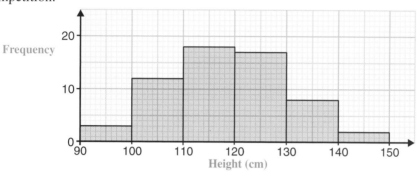

(a) Which class interval contains the median height?
(b) Calculate an estimate of the mean of these heights.

8 A sack contains a number of gold and silver discs.
An experiment consists of taking a disc from the sack at random, recording its colour and then replacing it.
The experiment is repeated 10, 50, 100, 150 and 200 times. The table shows the results.

Number of experiments	10	50	100	150	200
Number of gold discs	3	8	23	30	38

(a) Draw a graph to show how the relative frequency of a gold disc changes as the number of experiments increases.
(b) The sack contains 1000 discs. Estimate the number of gold discs in the sack.
Explain how you estimated your answer.　　AQA

9 Students in Year 11 were asked to write an essay on "Popstars".
(a) The table shows the distribution of the times taken by male students to complete the essay.

Time (t minutes)	$10 \leqslant t < 20$	$20 \leqslant t < 30$	$30 \leqslant t < 40$	$40 \leqslant t < 50$
Frequency	8	27	19	6

   (i) Draw a cumulative frequency graph for the data.
   (ii) Use your graph to estimate the median and the interquartile range.
(b) The box plot illustrates the distribution of the times taken by female students to complete the essay.

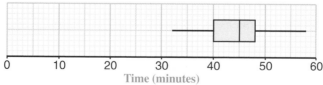

Estimate the median and the interquartile range.
(c) Compare and comment on the times taken by male students and the times taken by female students to complete the essay.

10 At a fete Jessie has one go on the hoopla and one go on the darts.
The probability she wins a prize on the hoopla is 0.3.
The probability she wins a prize on the darts is 0.4.
(a)   Copy and complete the tree diagram for these two events.

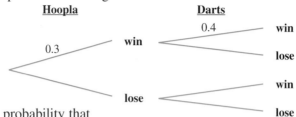

Hoopla   **Darts**

0.3   win   0.4   win
  lose
  lose   win
  lose

(b)   Calculate the probability that
(i)   she does not win a prize,   (ii)   she wins only one prize.

11 A leisure company runs two sports clubs, *A* and *B*.
The age distribution of the members of club *A* is shown in this table.

Age (y years)	$15 \leqslant y < 20$	$20 \leqslant y < 25$	$25 \leqslant y < 35$	$35 \leqslant y < 50$	$50 \leqslant y < 60$
Frequency	13	30	50	45	12

(a)   (i)   Show the distribution for club *A* on a histogram.
    (ii)   Estimate the number of members of club *A* in the age group $40 \leqslant y < 55$.
(b)   Club *B* has a total of 250 members.
The distribution of the ages of the male and female members are shown in this table.

Age (y years)	$y < 20$	$20 \leqslant y < 50$	$\geqslant 50$
Male	20	120	30
Female	5	60	15

A survey of the club *B* membership is carried out using a stratified random sample of size 100.
(i)   Find the number of male and female members of different ages included in the sample.
(ii)   Give a reason why a stratified random sample should be used rather than a simple random sample.

AQA

12 A survey was carried out to find the average length of a garden.
The histogram shows the results.

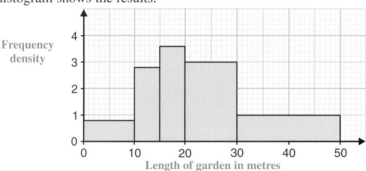

(a)   How many gardens were included in the survey?
(b)   Use the histogram to estimate:
(i)   the percentage of gardens less than 12 metres in length,
(ii)   the median length of a garden.

13 In a class of 25 students, 5 are left-handed and the rest are right-handed.
Two students are chosen at random, one at a time.
Calculate the probability that:
(a)   they are both left-handed,
(b)   one is left-handed and one is right-handed.

You may use a calculator for this exercise.

1 The mean weight of 7 netball players is 51.4 kg.
   (a)   Find the total weight of the players.

   The mean weight of the 7 players and the reserve is 52.3 kg.
   (b)   Calculate the weight of the reserve.

                AQA

2 Karina is playing a game with these cards.   X   Y   1   1   3

   One card is taken at random from the letters.
   One card is taken at random from the numbers.
   (a)   List all the possible outcomes.
   (b)   Explain why the probability of getting   X   1   is not $\frac{1}{4}$.

3 Corrin throws a dice 40 times. Her results are shown.

Score	1	2	3	4	5	6
Frequency	7	6	7	6	6	8

   (a)   Which score is the mode?
   (b)   Calculate the mean score.
   (c)   What is the median score?

4 One person is to be chosen at random from four men and two women.

    Jack   **Trevor**   **Eric**   **Jeff**   **Joan**   **Jill**

   Four events are defined as
   Event *J*: Someone with a name beginning with J is chosen.   **Event *M*:** A man is chosen.
   Event *N*: Someone reading a newspaper is chosen.   **Event *W*:** A woman is chosen.
   What is the probability that, if **one person** is chosen at random:
   (a)   both *J* and *M* are true,
   (b)   both *J* and *N* are true,
   (c)   either *N* or *W* is true?

                AQA

5 The table shows the weight distribution of the fish caught in a fishing competition.

Weight (*g* grams)	Frequency
$0 \leqslant g < 100$	0
$100 \leqslant g < 200$	16
$200 \leqslant g < 300$	36
$300 \leqslant g < 400$	20
$400 \leqslant g < 500$	8
$500 \leqslant g < 600$	0

   (a)   Calculate an estimate of the mean weight of a fish.
   (b)   Draw a frequency polygon to represent this distribution.

                AQA

6 A bag contains a number of counters.
Each counter is coloured red, white or blue. Each counter is numbered 1, 2 or 3.
The table shows the probability of colour and number for these counters.

Colour of counter

		Red	White	Blue
Number on counter	1	0.2	0.1	0
	2	0.1	0.3	0.1
	3	0.1	0	0.1

(a) A counter is taken from the bag at random.
    (i) What is the probability that the counter is red or white?
    (ii) What is the probability that the counter is white or numbered 2?
(b) There are 10 blue counters in the bag. How many counters are in the bag altogether?

A counter is taken from the bag at random.
The colour is noted and the counter is then **returned** to the bag.
Another counter is then taken from the bag at random.
(c) What is the probability that both counters are the same colour?
AQA

7 Here is a list of the last 8 quarterly gas bills for a householder.

Month	Jan.	Apr.	Jul.	Oct.	Jan.	Apr.	Jul.	Oct.
Amount	£67	£188	£27	£18	£139	£103	£23	£27

Calculate the first two 4-point moving averages for this data.

8 John is taking part in a spelling test. Words are chosen at random.
The probability that he spells a word correctly is $\frac{7}{10}$. John is given two words to spell.
(a) What is the probability that he spells both words correctly?
(b) What is the probability that he spells only one of the words correctly?
AQA

9 (a) The frequency distribution table gives information about the distances travelled to school by pupils at a primary school.

Distance (k kilometres)	Frequency
$0 \leqslant k < 1$	36
$1 \leqslant k < 2$	76
$2 \leqslant k < 3$	28
$3 \leqslant k < 4$	12
$4 \leqslant k < 5$	8

    (i) Draw a cumulative frequency graph to illustrate the data.
    (ii) Use your graph to find the median and the interquartile range.
(b) A survey of the distances travelled to school by pupils at a secondary school gave the following information.

    Shortest distance 0.2 km   Longest distance 9.6 km
    Median 2.8 km   Lower quartile 2.0 km   Upper quartile 3.4 km

    Draw a box plot to illustrate the data.
(c) Compare and comment on the distances travelled to school by pupils at these schools.

10 A pupil cycles to school. On her route, there is a set of traffic lights and a railway crossing.
She will be late for school if she has to stop at the traffic lights **and** at the railway crossing.
Otherwise she will be on time.
The probability that she does **not** have to stop at the traffic lights is 0.4.
The probability that she does **not** have to stop at the railway crossing is 0.9.
Calculate the probability that she is on time for school.
AQA

11 The table shows the distribution of the times, in minutes, that people had to wait for their meals at a restaurant.

Time (t minutes)	$0 \leqslant t < 10$	$10 \leqslant t < 15$	$15 \leqslant t < 25$	$25 \leqslant t < 40$
Frequency	25	21	24	9

(a) Draw a histogram to represent these waiting times.
(b) Estimate the median waiting time.
(c) Estimate how many people had to wait more than 30 minutes for their meal.

12 A bag contains 5 lemon, 4 orange and 3 cherry flavoured sweets.
Ivan eats three sweets at random. Calculate the probability that he has eaten
(a) one lemon and two orange flavoured sweets,
(b) at least one cherry flavoured sweet.

13 1000 people visit a museum one day. The table shows the number of each type of visitor.

	Child	Adult	Senior Citizen
Number of visitors	318	452	230

Peter wants to find out the views of the visitors.
He decides to take a stratified sample of 50 visitors.
Calculate the number of each type of visitor he should choose.

AQA

14 A bag contains two black discs and three white discs.
Three children play a game in which each draws a disc from the bag.
Parveen goes first, then Seema, and Jane is last.
Each time a disc is withdrawn it is not replaced.
The first child to draw a white disc wins the game.

(a) In a game, calculate the probability that
(i) Parveen wins, (ii) Seema wins.

They replace the discs and play the game a second time.
(b) Calculate the probability that
(i) Parveen wins neither the first nor the second game,
(ii) Jane wins both games.

AQA

15 The histogram shows the lengths of leaves of a certain species of plant.

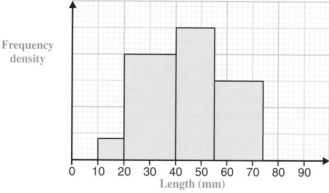

Forty-two leaves measured 25 mm or less.
How many leaves measured 60 mm or more?

AQA

16 Whether or not Jonathan gets up in time for school depends on whether he remembers to set his alarm clock the evening before.
For 85% of the time he remembers to set the clock; the other 15% of the time he forgets.
If the clock is set, he gets up in time for school on 90% of the occasions.
If the clock is not set, he does not get up in time for school on 60% of the occasions.
On what proportion of the occasions does he get up in time for school?

AQA

Whole Numbers ● ● ● ● ● ● ● ●

What you need to know

- You should be able to read and write numbers expressed in figures and words.
- Be able to recognise the place value of each digit in a number.

  Eg 1 In the number 5384 the digit 8 is worth 80, but in the number 4853 the digit 8 is worth 800.

- Know the Multiplication Tables up to 10×10.
- Use non-calculator methods for addition, subtraction, multiplication and division.
- Know the order of operations in a calculation.

First Brackets and Division line **Second** Divide and Multiply **Third** Addition and Subtraction	**Eg 2** $4 + 2 \times 6 = 4 + 12 = 16$
	Eg 3 $9 \times (7 - 2) + 3 = 9 \times 5 + 3 = 45 + 3 = 48$

- You should be able to add, subtract, multiply and divide with negative numbers.
- Be able to use these rules with negative numbers.

When adding or subtracting:	**When multiplying:**	**When dividing:**
$+ \; +$ can be replaced by $+$ $- \; -$ can be replaced by $+$ $+ \; -$ can be replaced by $-$ $- \; +$ can be replaced by $-$	$+ \times + = +$ $- \times - = +$ $+ \times - = -$ $- \times + = -$	$+ \div + = +$ $- \div - = +$ $+ \div - = -$ $- \div + = -$

Eg 4 Work out.

(a) $(-5) - (-8) = -5 + 8 = 3$

(b) $(-2) \times (-3) = 6$

(c) $\dfrac{(-8) \times (+2) + (-4)}{(-5) \times (-1)} = \dfrac{-16 - 4}{5} = \dfrac{-20}{5} = -4$

Exercise 7

Do not use a calculator for this exercise.

1 (a) Write one million five thousand and ten in figures.
(b) Given that $235 \times 640 = 150\,400,$ work out $1\,504\,000 \div 64$.

2 Work out. (a) $7096 + 2974$ (b) $8042 - 1357$ (c) 731×137 (d) $2002 \div 13$

3 (a) Using each of the digits 9, 2, 3 and 6 write down
(i) the largest odd number,   (ii) the smallest even number.
(b) What is the answer when the smallest even number is subtracted from the largest odd number?

4 Last year Mr Alderton had the following household bills.

Gas	£364	Electricity	£158	Telephone	£187
Water	£244	Insurance	£236	Council Tax	£983

He paid the bills by 12 equal monthly payments. How much was each monthly payment?

5 Naomi has collected £357 from her friends for concert tickets. The tickets cost £17 each. How many people have paid for tickets?

6 James packs teddy bears into boxes. He packs 283 teddy bears every hour.
James works 47 hours in one week.
How many teddy bears does James pack in this week? AQA

7 Mrs Preece is printing an examination for all Year 11 students.
Each examination uses 14 sheets of paper.
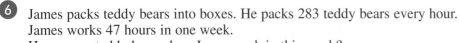
(a) There are 235 students in Year 11.
How many sheets of paper does she need?
(b) A ream contains 500 sheets of paper.
How many reams of paper does she need to print all the examinations? AQA

8 (a) A travel company takes a party of people to a hockey match at Wembley.
17 coaches are used. Each coach has seats for 46 passengers.
There are 12 empty seats altogether.
How many people are in the party?
(b) 998 football supporters use another travel company to go to a football match at Wembley.
Each coach has seats for 53 passengers.
   (i) How many coaches are needed?   (ii) How many empty seats are there? AQA

9 Work out.
(a) $12 - 6 + 2$
(b) $12 \div 6 \times 2$
(c) $(27 + 8) \times 3$
(d) $\dfrac{9 - 4 + 3 \times 5}{2 \times 3 + 4}$

10 Chris is 10 cm taller than Steven. Their heights add up to 310 cm. How tall is Steven? AQA

11 (a) Copy and complete this magic square, so that every row,
column and diagonal adds up to 3.
(b) Paul says, "If I multiply each number in the square by -6,
the new total for each row, column and diagonal will be -18."
Show **clearly** that this is true for the first row of numbers.

2	–3	4
3	1	
–2		0

AQA

12 Work out.
(a) $(-9) - (-5) + (-3)$
(b) $\dfrac{(-7) \times (-3) - (-6)}{(-9)}$
(c) $\dfrac{(-3) \times (-5) - (-7) \times (+3)}{(-4) + (-2)}$

13 A quiz consists of ten questions. Beth, John and Sue take part.
These are their results.

	Beth	John	Sue
Number of answers correct	4	6	5
Number of answers incorrect	4	3	1
Number of questions not attempted	2	1	4

A correct answer scores 3 points. An incorrect answer scores -2 points.
A question not attempted scores 0 points.
Who scores the most points? Show your working. AQA

14 The number of bacteria in a certain colony doubles every day.
At the start of an experiment there are 96 bacteria.
How many bacteria will there be 10 days later?

15 The prizes paid out in last Saturday's Lottery are shown in the table.

Number of winners	Value of each prize
1	£6 469 676
27	£73 728
708	£1 757
41 422	£66
812 558	£10

How much was paid out in prizes in last Saturday's Lottery?

SECTION **8**

Decimals and Fractions

What you need to know

- You should be able to use non-calculator methods for addition, subtraction, multiplication and division of decimals.

  Eg 1 Work out.

  (a) 5.1×0.43

  $$\begin{array}{r} 5.1 \quad (1\,\text{d.p.}) \\ \times \quad 0.43 \quad (2\,\text{d.p.}) \\ \hline 153 \leftarrow 51 \times 3 \\ + 2040 \leftarrow 51 \times 40 \\ \hline 2.193 \quad (3\,\text{d.p.}) \end{array}$$

  (b) $1.64 \div 0.2$

  $\frac{1.64}{0.2} = \frac{16.4}{2} = 8.2$

  > When a number is **multiplied** by a number between 0 and 1 the result will be **smaller** than the original number.
  > When a number is **divided** by a number between 0 and 1 the result will be **larger** than the original number.

- Be able to use decimals to solve problems involving money and other measures.

- The top number of a fraction is called the **numerator**, the bottom number is called the **denominator**.

- Fractions which are equal are called **equivalent fractions**. For example, $\frac{8}{20} = \frac{4}{10} = \frac{2}{5}$

  Eg 2 Write $\frac{20}{28}$ as a fraction in its simplest form.

  $\frac{20}{28} = \frac{20 \div 4}{28 \div 4} = \frac{5}{7}$

  > Divide the numerator and denominator by the largest number that divides into both.

- $2\frac{1}{2}$ is an example of a **mixed number**. It is a mixture of whole numbers and fractions.

- $\frac{5}{2}$ is an **improper** (or '**top heavy**') fraction.

- Fractions must have the **same denominator** before **adding** or **subtracting**.

  Eg 3 Work out.

  (a) $\frac{3}{4} + \frac{2}{3} = \frac{9}{12} + \frac{8}{12} = \frac{17}{12} = 1\frac{5}{12}$

  (b) $\frac{4}{5} - \frac{1}{2} = \frac{8}{10} - \frac{5}{10} = \frac{3}{10}$

  > Add (or subtract) the numerators only. When the answer is an improper fraction change it into a mixed number.

- Mixed numbers must be changed to **improper fractions** before **multiplying** or **dividing**.

  Eg 4 Work out.

  (a) $1\frac{1}{4} \times 2\frac{1}{5} = \frac{5}{4} \times \frac{11}{5} = \frac{11}{4} = 2\frac{3}{4}$

  > The working can be simplified by cancelling.

  (b) $1\frac{1}{3} \div 1\frac{3}{5} = \frac{4}{3} \div \frac{8}{5} = \frac{4}{3} \times \frac{5}{8} = \frac{5}{6}$

  > Dividing by $\frac{8}{5}$ is the same as multiplying by $\frac{5}{8}$.

- All fractions can be written as decimals.

  > To change a fraction to a decimal divide the **numerator** by the **denominator**.

  Eg 5 Change $\frac{4}{5}$ to a decimal.

  $\frac{4}{5} = 4 \div 5 = 0.8$

- Some decimals have **recurring digits**. These are shown by:

  a single dot above a single recurring digit,

  Eg 6 $\frac{2}{3} = 0.6666\ldots = 0.\dot{6}$

  a dot above the first and last digit of a set of recurring digits.

  Eg 7 $\frac{5}{11} = 0.454545\ldots = 0.\dot{4}\dot{5}$

1 (a) Lucy works out 0.2×0.4 . She gets the answer 0.8.
      Explain why her answer must be wrong.
   (b) Work out. (i) 0.3×0.4 (ii) 0.3×0.2

2 Paddy worked out that $\frac{30}{0.05} = 60$.
   His friend did a quick mental calculation and told him he had made a mistake.
   Show how Paddy's friend could have done this calculation mentally.

3 Work out. (a) $5 - 2.36$ (b) 4.8×2.5 (c) $0.294 \div 12$ (d) $\dfrac{54.4 \div 0.4}{0.2 \times 0.5}$

4 Two pieces of wood of length 0.75 m and 2.68 m are sawn from a plank 5 m long.
   What length of wood is left?

5 The following rule can be used to predict a child's height when it becomes an adult.

> **Step 1**: Add 12.5 cm to the mother's height.
> **Step 2**: Add this figure to the father's height and then divide by 2.

   The child's adult height will be within ± 8.5 cm of this value.

   (a) Salma's mother is 157.5 cm tall. Salma's father is 180.0 cm tall.
       Use the rule to find Salma's greatest height as an adult.
   (b) Bob is 180 cm tall as an adult. His father is 175 cm tall.
       Use the rule to find the least height his mother could have been.   AQA

6 Write these fractions in order of size, with the smallest first. $\frac{2}{3}$ $\frac{5}{8}$ $\frac{7}{12}$ $\frac{3}{4}$ AQA

7 (a) Write down a fraction that lies halfway between $\frac{1}{3}$ and $\frac{1}{2}$.
   (b) An examination is marked out of 48. Ashley scored 32 marks.
       What fraction of the total did he score?
       Give your answer in its simplest form.

8 Evaluate. (a) $3 - 1\frac{1}{5}$ (b) $4 \times 1\frac{1}{3}$ (c) $7\frac{1}{2} \div 1\frac{1}{2}$ AQA

9 Work out $\dfrac{81 \times \frac{1}{3}}{\frac{1}{16} \times 8}$.   AQA

10 (a) Change $\frac{1}{6}$ to a decimal. Give the answer correct to 3 d.p.
   (b) Write these numbers in order of size, starting with the largest.

   | 1.067 | 1.7 | 1.66 | $1\frac{1}{6}$ | 1.67 |

   (c) Change 0.65 to a fraction in its simplest form.

11 Work out. (a) $2\frac{2}{3} + 3\frac{3}{4}$ (b) $4\frac{3}{10} - 2\frac{1}{2}$ (c) $1\frac{3}{7} \times 2\frac{4}{5}$ (d) $2\frac{5}{6} \div 1\frac{2}{3}$

12 Three-fifths of the people at a party are boys.
   Three-quarters of the boys are wearing fancy dress.
   What fraction of the people at the party are boys wearing fancy dress?

13 In a sale the price of a microwave is reduced by $\frac{1}{5}$.
   The sale price is £96.
   What was the price of the microwave before the sale?

Sale Price
£96

14 David buys 0.6 kg of grapes and 0.5 kg of apples.
   He pays £1.36 altogether. The grapes cost £1.45 per kilogram.
   How much per kilogram are apples?   AQA

15 Work out $\dfrac{12.9 \times 7.3}{3.9 + 1.4}$. Write down your full calculator display.

SECTION **9**

Approximation and Estimation

What you need to know

- How to **round** to the nearest 10, 100, 1000.

- In real-life problems a rounding must be used which gives a sensible answer.

- How to approximate using **decimal places**.

> Write the number using one more decimal place than asked for.
> Look at the last decimal place and
> - if the figure is 5 or more round up,
> - if the figure is less than 5 round down.

Eg 1 Write the number 3.649 to
(a) 2 decimal places,
(b) 1 decimal place.

(a) 3.65,
(b) 3.6.

- How to approximate using **significant figures**.

> Start from the most significant figure and count the required number of figures.
> Look at the next figure to the right of this and
> - if the figure is 5 or more round up,
> - if the figure is less than 5 round down.
> Add noughts, as necessary, to preserve the place value.

Eg 2 Write each of these numbers correct to 2 significant figures.
(a) 365
(b) 0.0423

(a) 370
(b) 0.042

- You should be able to choose a suitable degree of accuracy.

> The result of a calculation involving measurement should not be given to a greater degree of accuracy than the measurements used in the calculation.

- Be able to use approximations to estimate that the actual answer to a calculation is of the right order of magnitude.

> Estimation is done by approximating every number in the calculation to one significant figure.
> The calculation is then done using the approximated values.

Eg 3 Use approximations to estimate $\dfrac{5.1 \times 57.2}{9.8}$.

$$\frac{5.1 \times 57.2}{9.8} = \frac{5 \times 60}{10} = 30$$

- Be able to use a calculator to check answers to calculations.

- Be able to recognise limitations on the accuracy of data and measurements.

Eg 4 Jamie said, "I have 60 friends at my party." This figure is correct to the nearest 10. What is the smallest and largest possible number of friends Jamie had at his party?

The smallest whole number that rounds to 60 is 55.
The largest whole number that rounds to 60 is 64.
So, smallest is 55 friends and largest is 64 friends.

Eg 5 A man weighs 57 kg, correct to the nearest kilogram.
What is the minimum weight of the man?
Minimum weight = 57 kg − 0.5 kg = 56.5 kg.

Eg 6 Calculate the upper bound of $\dfrac{a}{b}$ when:

$a = 7.6$, correct to 2 sig. figs.,   and $b = 50$, correct to 2 sig. figs.

Upper bound of $\dfrac{a}{b} = \dfrac{\text{upper bound of } a}{\text{lower bound of } b} = \dfrac{7.6 + 0.05}{50 - 0.5} = \dfrac{7.65}{49.5} = 0.154545\ldots$

Do not use a calculator for questions 1 to 7.   ⑨

1 Write the result shown on the calculator display
   (a)   to the nearest ten,
   (b)   correct to one decimal place,
   (c)   correct to one significant figure.

626.47

2 A newspaper's headline states: "20 000 people attend concert".
   The number in the newspaper is given to the nearest thousand.
   What is the smallest possible attendance?

3 A snack bar sells coffee at 48 pence per cup. In one day 838 cups are sold.
   By rounding each number to one significant figure, estimate the total amount received
   from the sale of coffee, giving your answer in pounds.   AQA

4 (a)   To estimate   97 × 49,   Charlie uses the approximations   100 × 50.
          Explain why his estimate will be larger than the actual answer.
   (b)   To estimate   1067 ÷ 48,   Patsy uses the approximations   1000 ÷ 50.
          Will her estimate be larger or smaller than the actual answer?
          Give a reason for your answer.

5 In 2005, Mr Symms drove 8873 kilometres.
   His car does 11 kilometres per litre. Petrol costs 89.9 pence per litre.
   (a)   By rounding each number to one significant figure, estimate the amount he spent
          on petrol.
   (b)   Without any further calculation, explain why this estimate will be larger than the
          actual amount.

6 A running track is 400 m correct to the nearest metre.
   (a)   What is the maximum length of the track?
   (b)   An athlete runs round the track four times.
          What is the minimum distance he has run?   AQA

7 Andrew says,
          "Answers given to two decimal places are more accurate
          than answers given to two significant figures."
   Is he right? Explain your answer.

8 Calculate the value of $\dfrac{45.6}{5.3 - 2.78}$.

   (a)   Write down your full calculator display.
   (b)   Give your answer correct to 3 significant figures.   AQA

9 Use your calculator to evaluate the following. $\dfrac{13.2 + 24.7}{21.3 - 17.2}$
   Give your answer correct to one decimal place.   AQA

10 (a)   Calculate $\dfrac{89.6 \times 10.3}{19.7 + 9.8}$.

   (b)   By using approximations show that your answer to (a) is about right.
          You **must** show all your working.   AQA

11 A school orders 20 copies of a book. Each book weighs 0.46 kg, correct to 2 decimal places.
   Calculate the lower bound and the upper bound of the total weight of the books.

12 p, q and r are three continuous measures.
   $p = 5.3$ to an accuracy of two significant figures.
   $q = 0.64$ and $r = 0.64$,   each to an accuracy of two decimal places.
   (a)   Calculate   (i)   the lower bound of $p - q$,   (ii)   the upper bound of $\dfrac{p + q}{r}$.
   (b) T is an integer where $T = 50$ to the nearest 5.
          Calculate the largest possible value of Tp.   AQA

Percentages and Money

What you need to know

- 10% is read as '10 percent'. 'Per cent' means out of 100. 10% means 10 out of 100.
- A percentage can be written as a fraction, 10% can be written as $\frac{10}{100}$.
- To change a decimal or a fraction to a percentage: **multiply by 100**.
- To change a percentage to a fraction or a decimal: **divide by 100**.
- How to express one quantity as a percentage of another.

  Eg 1 Write 30p as a percentage of £2.
  $$\frac{30}{200} \times 100 = 30 \times 100 \div 200 = 15\%$$

  > Write the numbers as a fraction, using the same units.
  > Change the fraction to a percentage.

- You should be able to use percentages to solve a variety of problems.
- Be able to find a percentage of a quantity.

  Eg 2 Find 20% of £64.
  £64 ÷ 100 = £0.64
  £0.64 × 20 = £12.80

  > 1. Divide by 100 to find 1%.
  > 2. Multiply by the percentage to be found.

- Be able to find a percentage increase (or decrease).

  $$\text{Percentage increase} = \frac{\text{actual increase}}{\text{initial value}} \times 100\%$$

  $$\text{Percentage decrease} = \frac{\text{actual decrease}}{\text{initial value}} \times 100\%$$

  Eg 3 Find the percentage loss on a micro-scooter bought for £25 and sold for £18.
  Percentage loss $= \frac{7}{25} \times 100 = 28\%$

- Be able to solve reverse percentage problems.

  Eg 4 Find the original price of a car which is sold at a loss of 20% for £1200.

  80% of original price = £1200
  1% of original price = £1200 ÷ 80 = £15
  Original price = £15 × 100 = £1500

  > First find 1% of the original value by dividing the selling price by (100 − % loss), then multiply by 100.

- **Hourly pay** is paid at a **basic rate** for a fixed number of hours.
  Overtime pay is usually paid at a higher rate such as time and a half, which means each hour's work is worth 1.5 times the basic rate.
- Everyone is allowed to earn some money which is not taxed. This is called a **tax allowance**.
- Tax is only paid on income earned in excess of the tax allowance. This is called **taxable income**.

  Eg 5 Tom earns £6080 per year.
  His tax allowance is £4895 per year and he pays tax at 10p in the £ on his taxable income.
  Find how much income tax Tom pays per year.

  Taxable income   = £6080 − £4895 = £1185
  Income tax payable = £1185 × 0.10   = £118.50

  > First find the taxable income, then multiply taxable income by rate in £.

- **Value added tax**, or **VAT**, is a tax on some goods and services and is added to the bill.
- When considering a **best buy**, compare quantities by using the same units.
  For example, find which product gives more grams per penny.

- Money invested in a savings account at a bank or building society earns **interest**.
- With **Simple Interest**, the interest is paid out each year and not added to your account.

$$\text{Simple Interest} = \frac{\text{Amount}}{\text{invested}} \times \frac{\text{Time in}}{\text{years}} \times \frac{\text{Rate of interest}}{\text{per year}}$$

Eg 6 Find the Simple Interest paid on £600 invested for 6 months at 8% per year.

Simple Interest $= 600 \times \frac{6}{12} \times \frac{8}{100} = 600 \times 0.5 \times 0.08 = £24$

- With **Compound Interest**, the interest earned each year is added to your account and also earns interest the following year.

Eg 7 Find the **Compound Interest** paid on £600 invested for 2 years at 6% per year.

1st year			**2nd year**		
Investment		$= £600$	Investment		$= £636$
Interest: $£600 \times 0.06$		$= £\ 36$	Interest: $£636 \times 0.06$		$= £\ 38.16$
Value after one year		$= £636$	Value after two years		$= £674.16$

Compound Interest $=$ Final value $-$ Original value $= £674.16 - £600 = £74.16$

This could be calculated as: $600 \times (1.06)^2 - 600 = £74.16$

Exercise 10

Do not use a calculator for questions 1 to 5.

1 What is 40 as a percentage of 500?

2 A test is marked out of 80. Colin scored 35% of the marks.
How many marks did Colin score?

3 A jacket normally costs £48. The price is reduced by 15% in a sale.
What is the price of the jacket in the sale?

4 Angela is paid £7.40 per hour for a basic 35-hour week. Overtime is paid at time and a half.
Last week Angela was paid £303.40.
How many hours did she work last week?

5 Mrs Tilsed wishes to buy a car priced at £2400.

> **Two options are available.**
> **Option 1** – A deposit of 20% of £2400 and 24 monthly payments of £95.
> **Option 2** – For a single payment the dealer offers a discount of 5% on £2400.

How much more does it cost to buy the car if option 1 is chosen rather than option 2?

6 Terry receives a bill for £284 for repairs to his car. VAT at $17\frac{1}{2}\%$ is then added to this amount.
Calculate the total amount which Terry pays. AQA

7 In a local election 3750 people could have voted. 2150 people actually voted.
What percentage of the people voted? AQA

8 Toffee is sold in bars of two sizes.
A large bar weighs 450 g and costs £1.69. A small bar weighs 275 g and costs 99p.
Which size of bar is better value for money? You must show all your working.

9 A pogo stick is bought for £12.50 and sold for £8. What is the percentage loss?

10 A farmer has 200 sheep. 90% of the sheep have lambs.
Of the sheep which have lambs 45% have two lambs.
How many of the sheep have two lambs?

11 Simon invests £360 at 6.4% per annum simple interest.
How much interest does he get at the end of 6 months?   AQA

12 Last year Sara had a tax allowance of £4895 and paid £3520 in tax.
The rates of tax were:

> 10p in the £ on the first £2090 of taxable income and
> 22p in the £ on all her remaining taxable income.

How much did Sara earn last year?   AQA

13 Nadia invests £400 in an account which pays 6.5% interest per year.
The interest is added to her investment at the end of each year.
Nadia does not withdraw any money.
Calculate the number of years Nadia must invest her money so that the total investment
has a value of more than £480. You must show all your working.   AQA

14

> ### 1st STOP Car Insurance
> **Typical insurance:**
> Vauxhall Corsa - £650 per year
> No Claims Discount Available

(a) Vanessa has a Vauxhall Corsa. She is given a no claims discount.
  After taking off her no claims discount she has to pay £390 to insure her car.
  Calculate her no claims discount as a percentage of £650.

(b) Cedric has a BMW car. He is given a 65% no claims discount.
  After the discount he has to pay £336 to insure his car.
  Calculate the price of the insurance before the discount.

15 This report appeared in a motoring magazine.

> In the first year of ownership a new car loses 20% of its value
> and in the second year it loses 15% of its one-year old value.

If this report is true, what is the percentage loss in the value of a new car in its first 2 years?

16 Questionnaires were sent to a number of people. 72 people replied.
This was only 18% of all the people that had been sent questionnaires.
How many people had been sent questionnaires?

17 A computer is advertised at £1116.25 including $17\frac{1}{2}$% VAT.
How much is the computer before VAT is added?

AQA

18 (a) Afzal invests £4000 at 7.5% per annum compound interest.
  Calculate the value of his investment at the end of 2 years.

(b) Leroy gets 5% per annum interest on his investment.
  After one year his investment has grown to £504.
  How much did he invest?   AQA

19 A garden centre buys plants and resells them at a profit of 28%.
How much was the original price of a rose bush which is sold for £4.80?   AQA

20 Jayne invests her money at 6% per annum compound interest.
What is the percentage increase in the value of her investment after 3 years?

SECTION 11

Working with Number

What you need to know

- **Multiples** of a number are found by multiplying the number by 1, 2, 3, 4, …

  Eg 1 The multiples of 8 are $1 \times 8 = 8$, $2 \times 8 = 16$, $3 \times 8 = 24$, $4 \times 8 = 32$, …

- **Factors** of a number are found by listing all the products that give the number.

  Eg 2 $1 \times 6 = 6$ and $2 \times 3 = 6$. So, the factors of 6 are: 1, 2, 3 and 6.

- The **common factors** of two numbers are the numbers which are factors of **both**.

- A **prime number** is a number with only two factors, 1 and the number itself.
  The first few prime numbers are: 2, 3, 5, 7, 11, 13, 17, 19, …
  The number 1 is not a prime number because it has only one factor.

- The **prime factors** of a number are those factors of the number which are prime numbers.

  Eg 3 The factors of 18 are: 1, 2, 3, 6, 9 and 18.
  The prime factors of 18 are: 2 and 3.

- The **Least Common Multiple** of two numbers is the smallest number that is a multiple of both.

  Eg 4 The Least Common Multiple of 4 and 5 is 20.

- The **Highest Common Factor** of two numbers is the largest number that is a factor of both.

  Eg 5 The Highest Common Factor of 8 and 12 is 4.

- An expression such as $3 \times 3 \times 3 \times 3 \times 3$ can be written in a shorthand way as 3^5.
  This is read as '3 to the power of 5'.
  The number 3 is the **base** of the expression. 5 is the **power**.

- Powers can be used to help write any number as the **product of its prime factors**.

  Eg 6 $72 = 2 \times 2 \times 2 \times 3 \times 3 = 2^3 \times 3^2$

- Numbers raised to the power of 2 are **squared**.

  Squares can be calculated using the $\boxed{x^2}$ button on a calculator.

  > **Square numbers** are whole numbers squared.
  > The first few square numbers are: 1, 4, 9, 16, 25, 36, …

  The opposite of squaring a number is called finding the **square root**.

  Square roots can be calculated using the $\boxed{\sqrt{}}$ button on a calculator.

  The square root of a number can be positive or negative.

  Eg 7 The square root of 9 can be written as $\sqrt{9}$ or $9^{\frac{1}{2}}$, and is equal to $+3$ or -3.

- Numbers raised to the power of 3 are **cubed**.

  > **Cube numbers** are whole numbers cubed.
  > The first few cube numbers are: 1, 8, 27, 64, 125, …

  The opposite of cubing a number is called finding the **cube root**.

  Cube roots can be calculated using the $\boxed{\sqrt[3]{}}$ button on a calculator.

  Eg 8 The cube root of 27 can be written as $\sqrt[3]{27}$ or $27^{\frac{1}{3}}$, and is equal to 3.

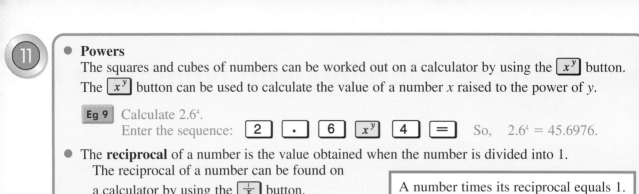

Powers

The squares and cubes of numbers can be worked out on a calculator by using the $\boxed{x^y}$ button.

The $\boxed{x^y}$ button can be used to calculate the value of a number x raised to the power of y.

Eg 9 Calculate 2.6^4.
Enter the sequence: $\boxed{2}$ $\boxed{\cdot}$ $\boxed{6}$ $\boxed{x^y}$ $\boxed{4}$ $\boxed{=}$ So, $2.6^4 = 45.6976$.

- The **reciprocal** of a number is the value obtained when the number is divided into 1.
  The reciprocal of a number can be found on
  a calculator by using the $\boxed{\frac{1}{x}}$ button.

> A number times its reciprocal equals 1.
> Zero has no reciprocal.
> The reciprocal of a number can be shown using an index of -1.

Eg 10 Find the reciprocal of 5.
The reciprocal of $5 = 5^{-1} = \frac{1}{5} = 0.2$

Using a calculator, press: $\boxed{5}$ $\boxed{\frac{1}{x}}$

- **Roots** can be calculated using the $\boxed{x^{1/y}}$ button.

Eg 11 Calculate $\sqrt[7]{128}$.
Enter the sequence: $\boxed{1}$ $\boxed{2}$ $\boxed{8}$ $\boxed{x^{1/y}}$ $\boxed{7}$ $\boxed{=}$ So, $\sqrt[7]{128} = 2$.

- **The rules of indices**

Multiplying powers with the same base	$a^m \times a^n = a^{m+n}$
Dividing powers with the same base	$a^m \div a^n = a^{m-n}$
Raising a power to a power	$(a^m)^n = a^{mn}$
Raising any number to the power zero	$a^0 = 1$ (also $a^1 = a$)
Negative powers and reciprocals	$a^{-m} = \dfrac{1}{a^m}$ a^{-m} is the reciprocal of a^m
Fractional powers and roots	$a^{\frac{1}{n}} = \sqrt[n]{a}$ and $a^{\frac{m}{n}} = \left(a^{\frac{1}{n}}\right)^m = \left(\sqrt[n]{a}\right)^m$

Eg 12 Simplify. Leave your answers in index form.
(a) $2^9 \times 2^4 = 2^{9+4} = 2^{13}$ (b) $2^9 \div 2^4 = 2^{9-4} = 2^5$ (c) $(4^9)^3 = 4^{9 \times 3} = 4^{27}$

- You should be able to use the function keys on a calculator to solve a variety of problems.

Exercise 11   Do not use a calculator for questions 1 to 17.

1   (a) Write down all the factors of 18.
     (b) Write down a multiple of 7 between 30 and 40.
     (c) Explain why 15 is not a prime number.

2   A number of counters can be grouped into 2's, 3's, 4's and 5's.
     Find the smallest possible number of counters.

3   (a) Work out the value of   (i) 5^3 (ii) $\sqrt{64}$
     (b) Between which two consecutive whole numbers does $\sqrt{30}$ lie?   AQA

4   Look at these numbers.

2	15	27	36	44	51	64

     (a) Which of these numbers is a prime number?
     (b) Which of these numbers is both a square number and a cube number?

5   (a) Write 36 as a product of its prime factors.
     (b) Write 45 as a product of its prime factors.
     (c) What is the highest common factor of 36 and 45?
     (d) What is the least common multiple of 36 and 45?

6 Jenny says that $2^2 + 3^2 = (2 + 3)^2$. Is she right? Show your working.

7 Use examples to show that the sum of the squares of two prime numbers can be odd or even.

8 (a) What is the cube root of 125?
(b) What is the reciprocal of 4?
(c) Which is smaller $\sqrt{225}$ or 2^4? Show your working.

9 A white light flashes every 10 seconds. A red light flashes every 6 seconds.
The two lights flash at the same time.
After how many seconds will the lights next flash at the same time?

10 In this question a and b represent **positive integers**. $a \neq b$.

(a) | $a\mathbf{H}b$ means the Highest Common Factor of a and b.

   Find (i) $15\mathbf{H}35$, (ii) $(15\mathbf{H}45)\mathbf{H}21$.

(b) | $a\mathbf{L}b$ means the Least Common Multiple of a and b.

   Find (i) $15\mathbf{L}25$, (ii) $(15\mathbf{L}45)\mathbf{L}60$.

(c) p is a prime number.
   (i) You are given $ap\mathbf{H}bp = p$. What can you say about the integers a and b?
   (ii) You are given $ap\mathbf{L}bp = bp$. What can you say about the integers a and b? AQA

11 Work out. (a) $2^3 \times 3^2$ (b) $\left(\sqrt{9} \times \sqrt{25}\right)^2$ (c) $2^3 \times \sqrt[3]{64}$

12 Work out the value of $2^1 - 2^0 + 2^{-1}$. AQA

13 Find the value of x in each of the following.
(a) $7^6 \times 7^3 = 7^x$ (b) $7^6 \div 7^3 = 7^x$ (c) $(7^6)^3 = 7^x$ (d) $7^0 = x$

14 Evaluate: (a) 2^{-2} (b) $32^{\frac{1}{5}}$ AQA

15 Evaluate: (a) $9^{\frac{1}{2}}$ (b) $64^{-\frac{1}{2}}$ (c) $25^{\frac{3}{2}}$ (d) $16^{-\frac{3}{4}}$

16 (a) Evaluate $49^{0.5} \times 3^{-2}$. Give your answer as a fraction.

(b) Work out $27^{\frac{2}{3}}$. AQA

17 Simplify, leaving your answers in fractional form.
(a) $64^{\frac{1}{2}} \times 125^{-\frac{1}{3}}$ (b) $27^{\frac{2}{3}} \times 3^{-4}$ (c) $\left(\frac{1}{2}\right)^{-3} \div \left(\frac{1}{5}\right)^{-2}$

18 Find the reciprocal of 7. Give your answer correct to two decimal places.

19 Calculate $\sqrt{\frac{3.9}{(0.6)^3}}$. AQA

20 (a) Use your calculator to find $3.5^3 + \sqrt{18.4}$. Give all the figures on your calculator.
(b) Write your answer to 3 significant figures. AQA

21 (a) Calculate the value of $\sqrt{3.1 + \frac{6}{3.1} - \frac{9}{3.1^2}}$.

(b) Show how to check that your answer is of the right order of magnitude. AQA

22 Calculate the value of $\sqrt{\frac{72.6}{8.3^2 - 8.89}}$. AQA

23 Calculate the value of:

(a) $5^{\frac{2}{5}}$ (b) $\frac{1}{(0.7)^5}$ (c) $\sqrt[3]{\frac{920\,000}{5^4}}$ (d) $\left(\frac{5.9}{\sqrt[5]{15}}\right)^{-3}$

Give your answers correct to two significant figures.

Standard Index Form

What you need to know

- **Standard index form**, or **standard form**, is a shorthand way of writing very large and very small numbers.

- In **standard form** a number is written as: **a number between 1 and 10 × a power of 10**. Large numbers (ten, or more) have a **positive** power of 10.

  Eg 1 Write 370 000 in standard form.
  $370\ 000 = 3.7 \times 100\ 000 = 3.7 \times 10^5$

  Eg 2 Write 5.6×10^7 as an ordinary number.
  $5.6 \times 10^7 = 5.6 \times 10\ 000\ 000 = 56\ 000\ 000$

  Small positive numbers (less than one) have a **negative** power of 10.

  Eg 3 Write 0.000 73 in standard form.
  $0.000\ 73 = 7.3 \times 0.000\ 1 = 7.3 \times 10^{-4}$

  Eg 4 Write 2.9×10^{-6} as an ordinary number.
  $2.9 \times 10^{-6} = 2.9 \times 0.000\ 001 = 0.000\ 002\ 9$

- You should be able to interpret the display on a calculator.

  Eg 5 The calculator display shows the answer to 0.007×0.09
  In standard form, the answer is 6.3×10^{-4}
  As an ordinary number, the answer is 0.000 63

6.3	−04

- You should be able to solve problems involving numbers given in standard form.

Exercise 12

Do not use a calculator for questions 1 to 7.

1 Write one million in standard form.

2 Look at these numbers.

$$2.6 \times 10^4 \qquad 6.2 \times 10^3 \qquad 9.8 \times 10^{-4} \qquad 8.9 \times 10^{-5}$$

(a) (i) Which number is the largest? (ii) Write your answer as an ordinary number.
(b) (i) Which number is the smallest? (ii) Write your answer as an ordinary number.

3 Write in standard index form. (a) 57 000 000 (b) 0.000 057

4 The table shows the average speed of planets that orbit the Sun.

Planet	Average speed of orbit (km/h)
Jupiter	4.7×10^4
Mercury	1.7×10^5
Neptune	1.2×10^4
Pluto	1.7×10^4
Saturn	3.5×10^4
Uranus	2.5×10^5

(a) Which planet is travelling the fastest?
(b) What is the difference between the average speeds of Neptune and Pluto?
Give your answer in standard form.

AQA

5 Work out.
  (a) $(6 \times 10^3) + (5 \times 10^4)$ (b) $(6 \times 10^3) \times (5 \times 10^4)$ (c) $(6 \times 10^3) \div (5 \times 10^4)$
  Give your answers in standard form.

6 (a) A company buys 2 340 000 packs of paper.
         Write this number in standard form.
   (b) A pack of paper has a thickness of 4.8 cm.
         There are 500 sheets of paper in each pack.
         Calculate the thickness of one sheet of paper in centimetres.
         Give your answer in standard form.   AQA

7 (a) Add 3.4×10^5 and 9.5×10^5.
   (b) Multiply 4×10^8 and 1.6×10^{-5}.
   Give your answers in standard form.   AQA

8 The population of Spain is 3.6×10^7 and there are 1.2×10^5 doctors in Spain.
   Calculate the average number of people per doctor.   AQA

9 (a) Calculate $\dfrac{7.2 \times 10^6}{0.0045}$.
         Give your answer in standard form.

   (b) Calculate $\dfrac{530}{6.7 \times 10^5}$.
         Give your answer as an ordinary number correct to two significant figures.

10 In England £1.012×10^{10} is spent on healthcare per year.
   There are 4.71×10^7 people in England.
   How much per person is spent on healthcare in England per year?   AQA

11 Very large distances in the Universe are measured in **parsecs** and **light-years**.
   One parsec is 3.0857×10^{13} kilometres.
   One parsec is 3.26 light-years.
   How many kilometres are in 1 light-year?
   Give your answer in standard form to an appropriate degree of accuracy.   AQA

12 Work out $\dfrac{3.5 \times 10^{-3}}{4.1 \times 10^2}$.
   Give your answer as an ordinary number correct to 2 significant figures.

13 Approximate figures for the amount of carbon dioxide entering the atmosphere from
   artificial sources are shown below.

Total amount (world wide)	7.4×10^9 tonnes
Amount from the United Kingdom	1.59×10^8 tonnes

   (a) What percentage of the total amount of carbon dioxide entering the
         atmosphere comes from the United Kingdom?
   (b) Approximately 19% of the amount of carbon dioxide from the
         United Kingdom comes from road transport.
         How many million tonnes of carbon dioxide is this?   AQA

14 In the United Kingdom:

4.53×10^{11} aluminium cans are used and 0.15% of them are recycled,
1.2×10^{10} steel cans are used and 11.7% of them are recycled.

   What percentage of the total number of cans used are recycled?   AQA

Standard Index Form

Ratio and Proportion

What you need to know

- The ratio 3 : 2 is read '3 to 2'.

- A ratio is used only to **compare** quantities.
  A ratio does not give information about the exact values of quantities being compared.

- In its **simplest form**, a ratio contains whole numbers which have no common factor other than 1.

  Eg 1 Write £2.40 : 40p in its simplest form.
  £2.40 : 40p = 240p : 40p
  $\quad\quad\quad\quad\quad = 240 : 40$
  $\quad\quad\quad\quad\quad = 6 : 1$

  > All quantities in a ratio must be in the **same units** before the ratio can be simplified.

- You should be able to solve a variety of problems involving ratio.

  Eg 2 The ratio of bats to balls in a box is 3 : 5.
  There are 12 bats in the box.
  How many balls are there?

  $12 \div 3 = 4$
  $3 \times 4 : 5 \times 4 = 12 : 20$
  There are 20 balls in the box.

  > For every 3 bats there are 5 balls.
  > To find an **equivalent ratio** to 3 : 5, in which the first number is 12, multiply each number in the ratio by 4.

  Eg 3 A wall costs £660 to build.
  The costs of materials to labour are in the ratio 4 : 7.
  What is the cost of labour?

  $4 + 7 = 11$
  $£660 \div 11 = £60$
  Cost of labour = £60 × 7 = £420

  > The numbers in the ratio add to 11.
  > For every £11 of the total cost, £4 pays for materials and £7 pays for labour.
  > So, **divide** by 11 and then **multiply** by 7.

- When two different quantities are always in the **same ratio** the two quantities are in **direct proportion**.

  Eg 4 20 litres of petrol cost £14.
  Find the cost of 25 litres of petrol.

  20 litres cost £14
  1 litre costs £14 ÷ 20 = £0.70
  25 litres cost £0.70 × 25 = £17.50

  > This is sometimes called the **unitary method**.
  > **Divide** by 20 to find the cost of 1 litre.
  > **Multiply** by 25 to find the cost of 25 litres.

- When as one quantity increases the other decreases, the quantities are in **inverse proportion**.

  Eg 5 3 people take 8 hours to deliver some leaflets.
  How long would it take 4 people?

  3 people take 8 hours.
  1 person takes 8 hours × 3 = 24 hours
  4 people take 24 hours ÷ 4 = 6 hours
  So, 4 people would take 6 hours.

  > This assumes that time is **inversely proportional** to the number of people.
  > **Multiply** by 3 to find how long 1 person would take.
  > **Divide** by 4 to find how long 4 people would take.

Exercise 13

Do not use a calculator for questions 1 to 6.

1. A toy box contains large bricks and small bricks in the ratio 1 : 4.
   The box contains 40 bricks. How many large bricks are in the box?

2 To make mortar a builder mixes sand and cement in the ratio 3 : 1.
The builder uses 2.5 kg of cement. How much sand does he use?

3 In a drama club the ratio of boys to girls is 2 : 3.
(a) What fraction of club members are girls?
(b) What percentage of club members are boys?

4 The ratio of men to women playing golf one day is 5 : 3.
There are 20 men playing. How many women are playing?

5 A gardener wants to make a display of red and yellow tulips.
He orders red and yellow tulip bulbs in the ratio of 3 : 5.
He orders a total of 2000 bulbs.
How many of each colour bulb will he get?   AQA

6 Dec shares a prize of £435 with Annabel in the ratio 3 : 2.
What is the difference in the amount of money they each receive?

7 A town has a population of 45 000 people. 1 in every 180 people are disabled.
How many disabled people are there in the town?   AQA

8 This is a list of ingredients to make 12 rock cakes.
You have plenty of margarine, sugar,
fruit and spice but only 500 g of flour.
What is the largest number of rock cakes
you can make?

Rock cakes (makes 12)
240 g flour   150 g fruit
75 g margarine $\frac{1}{4}$ teaspoon spice
125 g sugar
                                                                                     AQA

9 Two students are talking about their school outing.

My class went to Tower Bridge last week.
There are 30 people in my class.
The total cost was £345.

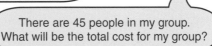

There are 45 people in my group.
What will be the total cost for my group?

10 A farmer estimates it will take 2 combine harvesters 6 days to harvest his crop.
Estimate how many days it will take 3 combine harvesters to harvest his crop.

11 When petrol is 80 pence a litre it costs £28.80 to fill the tank of my car with petrol.
How much will it cost to fill the tank of my car with petrol when petrol is 90 pence per litre?

12 On a map the distance between two towns is 5 cm.
The actual distance between the towns is 1 kilometre.
What is the scale of the map in the form of 1 : n?

13 A car is 2.86 m long. Two scale models are made of the car.

> Model A is made to a scale of 1 : 30.   Model B is 38 mm long.

What is the difference between the length of model A and the length of model B?
Give your answer to an appropriate degree of accuracy.   AQA

14 In a school, there are 750 pupils in total in years 9, 10 and 11.
The numbers of pupils in years 9, 10 and 11 are in the ratio 12 : 7 : 6.
How many pupils are there in each year?   AQA

15 At 80 km/h it takes 30 minutes to complete a journey.
How long would it take to complete the journey at 50 km/h?

Speed and Other Compound Measures

What you need to know

- **Speed** is a compound measure because it involves **two** other measures.

- **Speed** is a measurement of how fast something is travelling. It involves two other measures, **distance** and **time**. In situations where speed is not constant, **average speed** is used.

  $$\text{Speed} = \frac{\text{Distance}}{\text{Time}} \qquad \text{Average speed} = \frac{\text{Total distance travelled}}{\text{Total time taken}}$$

  > The formula linking speed, distance and time can be rearranged and remembered as:
  > $$S = D \div T$$
  > $$D = S \times T$$
  > $$T = D \div S$$

- You should be able to solve problems involving speed, distance and time.

  Eg 1 A greyhound takes 32 seconds to run 400 metres.
  Calculate its speed in metres per second.

  $$\text{Speed} = \frac{\text{Distance}}{\text{Time}} = \frac{400}{32} = 12.5 \text{ metres per second}$$

  Eg 2 Norrie says, "If I drive at an average speed of 60 km/h it will take me $2\frac{1}{2}$ hours to complete my journey." What distance is his journey?

  $$\text{Distance} = \text{Speed} \times \text{Time} = 60 \times 2\frac{1}{2} = 150 \text{ km}$$

  Eg 3 Ellen cycles 5 km at an average speed of 12 km/h.
  How many minutes does she take?

  $$\text{Time} = \frac{\text{Distance}}{\text{Speed}} = \frac{5}{12} \text{ hours} = \frac{5}{12} \times 60 = 25 \text{ minutes}$$

  > To change hours to minutes:
  > **multiply by 60**

- **Density** is a compound measure which involves the measures **mass** and **volume**.

  Eg 4 A block of metal has mass 500 g and volume 400 cm³.

  $$\text{Density} = \frac{\text{Mass}}{\text{Volume}} = \frac{500}{400} = 1.25 \text{ g/cm}^3$$

  > $$\text{Density} = \frac{\text{Mass}}{\text{Volume}}$$

- **Population density** is a measure of how populated an area is.

  Eg 5 The population of Cumbria is 489 700.
  The area of Cumbria is 6824 km².

  > $$\text{Population density} = \frac{\text{Population}}{\text{Area}}$$

  $$\text{Population density} = \frac{\text{Population}}{\text{Area}} = \frac{489\,700}{6824} = 71.8 \text{ people/km}^2.$$

Exercise 14

Do not use a calculator for questions 1 to 5.

1. Sean cycled 24 km at an average speed of 16 km/h.
   How long did he take to complete the journey?

2. Ahmed takes $2\frac{1}{2}$ hours to drive from New Milton to London.
   He averages 66 km/h.
   What distance does he drive?

3. A motorist travels a distance of 156 miles in $3\frac{1}{4}$ hours.
   Calculate the average speed of the motorist in miles per hour.

4. Kay walks 2.7 km in 45 minutes.
   Calculate her average walking speed in kilometres per hour.

5 The distance between Heysham and the Isle of Man is 80 km.
A hovercraft travels at 50 km per hour. How long does the journey take? AQA

6 Sheila lives 6 kilometres from the beach.
She jogs from her home to the beach at an average speed of 10 km/h.
She gets to the beach at 1000. Calculate the time when she left home. AQA

7 The diagram shows the distances, in miles, between some junctions on a motorway.

A coach is travelling west. At 1040 it passes junction 27 and at 1052 it passes junction 26.
(a) Calculate the average speed of the coach in miles per hour.

Between junctions 26 and 25 the coach travels at an average speed of 30 miles per hour.
(b) Calculate the time when the coach passes junction 25.

8 A train travels at an average speed of 80 miles per hour.
At 0940 the train is 65 miles from Glasgow. The train is due to arrive in Glasgow at 1030.
Will it arrive on time? Show your working.

9 A horse gallops at an average speed of 24 km/h for $4\frac{1}{2}$ minutes.
Calculate the distance it travels.

10 On Monday it took Helen 40 minutes to drive to work.
On Tuesday it took Helen 25 minutes to drive to work.
Her average speed on Monday was 18 miles per hour.
What was her average speed on Tuesday?

11 Henry completes a 200 m race in 25 seconds.
What is his average speed in kilometres per hour? AQA

12 A jet-ski travels 0.9 kilometres in 1.5 minutes.
Calculate the average speed of the jet-ski in metres per second.

13 The distance from the Earth to the Moon is 3.81×10^5 kilometres.
Light travels at a speed of 3×10^8 metres per second.
How long does it take light to travel from the Earth to the Moon?

14 (a) A goods train, 150 metres long, is travelling at 45 km/h.
How many seconds does it take to pass a signal?
(b) The goods train takes 5 seconds to pass a passenger train, 90 metres long, travelling in the opposite direction.
Calculate the speed of the passenger train in kilometres per hour.

15 A copper statue has a mass of 1080 g and a volume of 120 cm³.
Work out the density of copper.

16 A silver medal has a mass of 200 g. The density of silver is 10.5 g/cm³.
What is the volume of the medal?

17 The population of Jamaica is 2.8 million people. The area of Jamaica is 10 800 km².
What is the population density of Jamaica?

18 The population of France is 5.83×10^7 people.
The area of France is 5.47×10^5 square kilometres.

$$\text{Mean number of people} = \frac{\text{Population}}{\text{Area}}$$

Calculate the mean number of people per square kilometre in France.
Give your answer to a suitable degree of accuracy. AQA

Extending the Number System

What you need to know

- **Rational numbers** can be written in the form $\frac{a}{b}$, where a and b are integers ($b \neq 0$).

  Examples of rational numbers are: 2, -5, $\frac{2}{5}$, 0.6, 3.47, $1\frac{3}{4}$.

- All fractions can be written as decimals.

  For example, $\frac{1}{3} = 0.3333333\ldots = 0.\dot{3}$, $\frac{123}{999} = 0.123123123\ldots = 0.\dot{1}2\dot{3}$

- You should be able to convert a recurring decimal to a fraction.

  Eg 1 Find the fraction which is equal to $0.\dot{2}\dot{7}$, in its simplest form.

$x = 0.2727\ldots$ 2 digits recur, so, multiply by 100. $100x = 27.2727\ldots$ $99x = 27$ $x = \frac{27}{99} = \frac{3}{11}$ $0.\dot{2}\dot{7} = \frac{3}{11}$	Let x = the recurring decimal. Multiply both sides by a power of 10: • by $10^1 = 10$ if only 1 digit recurs, • by $10^2 = 100$ if 2 digits recur, and so on. Subtract the original equation from the new equation. Solve the resulting equation for x. If necessary, write the fraction in its simplest form.

- All **terminating** and **recurring decimals** are rational numbers.

- A **surd** is the root of a rational number which is not rational.
  A surd is an **irrational number**.

  These are examples of surds: $\sqrt{2}$ $\sqrt{0.37}$ $3 + \sqrt{2}$

  $\sqrt{9}$ is not a surd because $\sqrt{9} = 3$ which is rational.

  > $\sqrt{a}$ means the positive square root of a.

- Rules for manipulating and simplifying surds:

  > $\sqrt{ab} = \sqrt{a} \times \sqrt{b}$ $m\sqrt{a} + n\sqrt{a} = (m + n)\sqrt{a}$ $\sqrt{\dfrac{a}{b}} = \dfrac{\sqrt{a}}{\sqrt{b}}$

  Eg 2 Simplify the following leaving the answers in surd form.

  (a) $\sqrt{32} = \sqrt{16} \times \sqrt{2} = 4\sqrt{2}$ > Look for factors that are square numbers.

  (b) $\sqrt{8} + \sqrt{18} = \sqrt{4} \times \sqrt{2} + \sqrt{9} \times \sqrt{2} = 2\sqrt{2} + 3\sqrt{2} = 5\sqrt{2}$

  (c) $\sqrt{\dfrac{72}{20}} = \dfrac{\sqrt{72}}{\sqrt{20}} = \dfrac{\sqrt{36}\,\sqrt{2}}{\sqrt{4}\,\sqrt{5}} = \dfrac{6\sqrt{2}}{2\sqrt{5}} = \dfrac{3\sqrt{2}}{\sqrt{5}}$

- To **rationalise** the denominator of a fraction of the form $\dfrac{a}{\sqrt{b}}$ multiply both the numerator (top) and the denominator (bottom) of the fraction by $\sqrt{b}$.

  Eg 3 Rationalise the denominator and simplify where possible: $\dfrac{3\sqrt{2}}{6}$.

  $\dfrac{3\sqrt{2}}{\sqrt{6}} = \dfrac{3\sqrt{2}}{\sqrt{6}} \times \dfrac{\sqrt{6}}{\sqrt{6}} = \dfrac{3\sqrt{2}\,\sqrt{6}}{6} = \dfrac{3\sqrt{2}\,\sqrt{2}\,\sqrt{3}}{6} = \dfrac{6\sqrt{3}}{6} = \sqrt{3}$

- You should be able to use surds in calculations.

  > To keep an answer exact it is necessary to keep numbers like $\sqrt{3}$ in surd form.

Do not use a calculator for this exercise. (15)

1 (a) Change $\frac{5}{7}$ into a decimal.

(b) Find the fraction which is equal to $0.\dot{2}$.
Give your answer in its simplest terms.

2 Simplify. (a) $2\sqrt{5} + 3\sqrt{5}$ (b) $\sqrt{3} \times \sqrt{3}$ (c) $\sqrt{2} \times \sqrt{3} \times \sqrt{6}$ (d) $\sqrt{\frac{9}{16}}$

3 (a) Prove that $0.\dot{4}\dot{5} = \frac{5}{11}$.

(b) Write the number $0.\dot{6}\dot{3}$ as a fraction in its simplest form.

4 $x = 0.\dot{3}7\dot{8}$ (read as $x = 0.378378378...$)
(a) Write down the value of $1000x$.
(b) Hence, express x as a fraction in its simplest form.   AQA

5 Write $\sqrt{18}$ in the form of $a\sqrt{b}$ where a and b are prime numbers.

6 Simplify, leaving your answers where appropriate in surd form.

(a) $5\sqrt{3} - \sqrt{3}$ (b) $\sqrt{3} \times 3\sqrt{3}$ (c) $\frac{\sqrt{27}}{3}$ (d) $\sqrt{12} \times \sqrt{75}$

7 Simplify fully.

(a) $\sqrt{\frac{16}{25}}$ (b) $\sqrt{75}$ (c) $\sqrt{75} + \sqrt{12}$ (d) $\frac{6}{\sqrt{3}}$ AQA

8 The area of this rectangle is $30\,\text{cm}^2$.
Find the value of x, writing your answer in the form $a\sqrt{b}$,
where a and b are integers.

x cm

$3\sqrt{2}$ cm

AQA

9 (a) Express 20 as the product of its prime factors.
(b) a and b are prime numbers.

(i) $\sqrt{20}$ can be written in the form $a\sqrt{b}$. Calculate the values of a and b.

(ii) $\frac{1}{\sqrt{20}}$ can be written in the form $\frac{b^x}{a}$. Calculate the value of x.   AQA

10 Simplify the expression $\sqrt{24}(\sqrt{50} - \sqrt{8})$.

11 (a) Write $\sqrt{45}$ in the form $a\sqrt{b}$ where a and b are prime numbers.
(b) Find the value of $\left(\sqrt{45} - \sqrt{20}\right)^2$.   AQA

12 You are given that $u = \sqrt{3} + 1$ and $v = \sqrt{3} - 1$.

(a) $u + v = \sqrt{n}$. Find the value of n.

(b) Find the value of $\frac{uv}{u - v}$.   AQA

13 Rationalise the denominator of $\frac{2 + \sqrt{3}}{\sqrt{3}}$.
Simplify your answer fully.   AQA

14 (a) You are given that $2^x = 16^{-\frac{3}{4}} \times \sqrt{2}$.
Find the value of x.

(b) Express $\sqrt{8}(\sqrt{2} + 3)$ in the form $a + b\sqrt{c}$ where a and b are positive integers
and c is a prime number.   AQA

Linear and Quadratic Graphs

What you need to know

- **Coordinates** are used to describe the position of a point on a graph.
- The x axis is the line $y = 0$.   The y axis is the line $x = 0$.
- The graph of a linear function is a straight line.
  The general equation of a linear function is $y = mx + c$.
- You should be able to draw the graph of a **linear function**.

  Eg 1 Draw the graph of $y = x + 1$ for values of x from -2 to 2.

  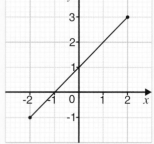

  > To draw a linear graph:
  > Find two corresponding values of x and y.
  > Plot the points.
  > Join the points with a straight line.

  When $x = -2$, $y = -2 + 1 = -1$. Plot $(-2, -1)$.
  When $x = 2$, $y = 2 + 1 = 3$. Plot $(2, 3)$.
  A straight line drawn through the points $(-2, -1)$ and $(2, 3)$ is the graph of $y = x + 1$.

- The graph of a **quadratic function** is a **smooth curve**.
  The general equation of a quadratic function is $y = ax^2 + bx + c$, where $a \neq 0$.
- You should be able to draw the graph of a **quadratic function**.

  Eg 2 (a) Draw the graph of $y = x^2 - x - 1$ for $-2 \leqslant x \leqslant 2$.
  (b) Hence, find the solutions of $x^2 - x - 1 = 0$.

  (a)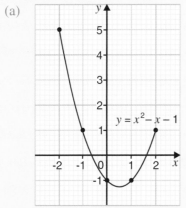

  > To draw a quadratic graph:
  > Make a table of values connecting x and y.
  > Plot the points.
  > Join the points with a smooth curve.

x	-2	-1	0	1	2
y	5	1	-1	-1	1

  (b) > To solve $x^2 - x - 1 = 0$, read the values
  > of x where the graph of $y = x^2 - x - 1$
  > crosses the x axis ($y = 0$).

  $x = -0.6$ and $x = 1.6$, correct to 1 d.p.

- Be able to use graphs of linear and quadratic functions to solve equations.

  Eg 3 You are given the graph of $y = 2x - x^2$.
  By drawing a suitable linear graph, on the same axes,
  find the solutions of $x^2 - 3x + 1 = 0$.
  To find the linear graph:
  Rearrange $x^2 - 3x + 1 = 0$ to give $1 - x = 2x - x^2$.
  Hence, the linear graph is $y = 1 - x$.
  Draw the graph of $y = 1 - x$ on the same diagram.

  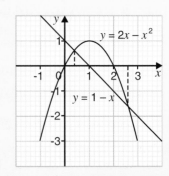

  > To solve $x^2 - 3x + 1 = 0$, read the values of x
  > where the two graphs intersect.

  So, $x = 0.4$ and $x = 2.6$, correct to 1 d.p.

1 (a) (i) Complete the table of values for $y = 2x + 1$.

x	-2	0	2	3
y				

      (ii) Draw the graph of $y = 2x + 1$.

    (b) On the same diagram, draw the graph of $y = 4 - x$ for values of x between -2 and 4.

    (c) Write down the value of x where the two graphs intersect.

2 (a) Complete the table of values for $y = x^2 - 2x$.

x	-2	-1	0	1	2	3
y	8		0	-1		

    (b) Draw the graph of $y = x^2 - 2x$ for values of x from -2 to 3.

3 (a) Complete the table of values for $y = x^2 - x - 5$.

x	-3	-2	-1	0	1	2	3	4
y	7	1			-5	-3		

    (b) Draw the graph $y = x^2 - x - 5$ for values of x between -3 and 4.

    (c) Write down the solutions of (i) $x^2 - x - 5 = 0$, (ii) $x^2 - x - 5 = 5$.

4 (a) Draw the graph of $y = x^2$ for values of x from -3 to 3.

    (b) On the same diagram, draw the graph of $y = x + 2$.

    (c) Explain how you can use your graphs to solve the equation $x^2 - x - 2 = 0$.
       Hence, write down the solutions of $x^2 - x - 2 = 0$.

5 The graph of $y = x^2 - 1$ is drawn.

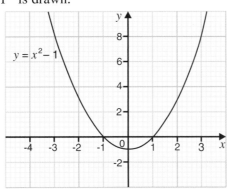

To solve the equation $x^2 = 2x + 2$ a line can be drawn on the graph.
What is the equation of the line?
AQA

6 (a) Draw the graph of $y = x^2 + x$ for values of x between -3 and 2.

    (b) By drawing a suitable linear graph find the solutions of $x^2 + 2x - 1 = 0$.

7 (a) Complete the table of values for $y = x^2 - 3x - 4$.

x	-3	-2	-1	0	1	2	3	4	5	6
y	14		0	-4	-6	-6		0	6	14

    (b) Draw the graph $y = x^2 - 3x - 4$ for values of x between -3 and 6.

    (c) Write down the solutions of $x^2 - 3x - 4 = 0$.

    (d) By drawing an appropriate linear graph, write down the solutions of $x^2 - 4x - 1 = 0$.
AQA

8 Draw the graph of $y = x^2 + 2x - 7$ for values of x between -5 and $+5$.
By drawing an appropriate linear graph on the same diagram,
write down the solutions of $x^2 - x - 11 = 0$.
AQA

Direct and Inverse Proportion

What you need to know

- **Direct proportion**

  If x and y are quantities such that $y : x^n$ is always constant, then y varies **directly** with x^n.

  This can be expressed:
  - in **words**: $\quad\quad y$ is **proportional** to x^n,
  - in **symbols**: $\quad\quad y \propto x^n \quad$ (where $\propto$ means "is proportional to"),
  - as an **equation**: $y = kx^n$ (where k is the **constant of proportionality**).

  Eg 1 The cost, £C, of tiling a floor is proportional to the area of the floor, $a\,\text{m}^2$.
  It costs £60 to tile a floor of area $2\,\text{m}^2$.
  (a) Find the formula connecting C and a.
  (b) A floor costs £150 to be tiled. What is the area of the floor?

  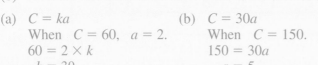

  (a) $\quad C = ka$ $\qquad\qquad$ (b) $\quad C = 30a$
  $\quad\quad$ When $C = 60, \quad a = 2$. $\qquad\quad$ When $C = 150$.
  $\quad\quad\quad 60 = 2 \times k$ $\qquad\qquad\qquad\quad 150 = 30a$
  $\quad\quad\quad\quad k = 30$ $\qquad\qquad\qquad\qquad\quad a = 5$
  $\quad\quad\quad\quad C = 30a$ $\qquad\qquad\qquad$ Area of floor $= 5\,\text{m}^2$

  > Constant of proportionality, k.
  > This can be calculated when corresponding values of C and a are known.

- **Inverse proportion**

  If x and y are quantities such that $y : \dfrac{1}{x^n}$ is always constant, then y varies **inversely** with x^n.

  This can be expressed:
  - in **words**: $\quad\quad y$ is **inversely proportional** to x^n,
  - in **symbols**: $\quad\quad y \propto \dfrac{1}{x^n}$,
  - as an **equation**: $y = \dfrac{k}{x^n} \quad$ or $\quad x^n y = k$.

  Eg 2 y is inversely proportional to x^2. When $x = 3, \quad y = 4$.
  (a) Find the equation connecting y and x. $\qquad$ (b) Find the value of y when $x = 2.4$.

  (a) $\quad y = \dfrac{k}{x^2}$ $\qquad\qquad\qquad\qquad$ (b) $\quad y = \dfrac{36}{x^2}$
  $\quad\quad$ When $x = 3, \quad y = 4$. $\qquad\qquad\qquad$ When $x = 2.4$.
  $\quad\quad 4 = \dfrac{k}{3^2}, \quad$ so, $\quad k = 36$ $\qquad\qquad\quad y = \dfrac{36}{(2.4)^2}$
  $\quad\quad y = \dfrac{36}{x^2}$ $\qquad\qquad\qquad\qquad\qquad\quad y = 6.25$

- The general form of a proportional relationship is $\quad y \propto x^n \quad$ or $\quad y = kx^n$.

  Direct proportion, $y = kx^n, \quad n > 0$ $\qquad\qquad$ **Inverse proportion, $y = kx^n, \quad n < 0$**

  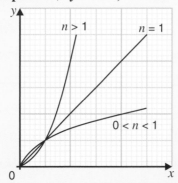 $\qquad\qquad$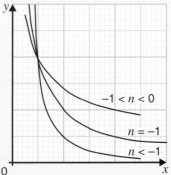

  When: $\qquad\qquad\qquad\qquad\qquad\qquad\qquad\qquad$ When:
  $\quad n = 1$: y increases at a constant rate. $\qquad\quad n = -1$: the graph is symmetrical about
  $0 < n < 1$: y increases at a rate that decreases. $\qquad\qquad\qquad$ the line $y = x$.
  $\quad n > 1$: y increases at a rate that increases.

1 The table shows values of m and n.

m	0.6	9	16.5
n	0.4	6	11

(a) Show that m is directly proportional to n.
(b) Find the value of   (i) m when $n = 1.8$,
                (ii) n when $m = 12.6$.

2 The table shows values of the variables x and y, where y is inversely proportional to x.

x	0.4	2.5	
y	5.0		0.02

(a) Find an equation expressing y in terms of x.
(b) Copy and complete the table.   AQA

3 y is proportional to x^3.
When $x = 3$, $y = 54$.
Find the value of x when $y = 250$.

4 R is inversely proportional to the square of P.
When $R = 36$, $P = 2$.
Find R when $P = 6$.   AQA

5 m is proportional to the square root of n.
$m = 6$ when $n = 81$.
(a) Find the equation connecting m and n.
(b) Calculate   (i)   the value of m when $n = 36$,
               (ii)   the value of n when $m = 10$.

6 An artist hand-paints circular plates of different sizes.
The price, $£C$, of a hand-painted plate is proportional to the square of the radius, r cm, of the plate.
The price of a plate of radius 6 cm is £9.
Calculate the price of a plate of radius 8 cm.

7 The wavelength, w metres, of radio waves is inversely proportional to the frequency, f kHz, of the waves.
(a) A radio wavelength of 1000 metres has a frequency of 300 kHz.
The frequency is doubled to 600 kHz.
What is the new wavelength?
(b) Calculate the frequency when the wavelength is 842 metres.
(c) Radio NEAB has a frequency in kHz which is numerically equal to its wavelength in metres.
Calculate the wavelength of Radio NEAB.   AQA

8 y is proportional to x^n.
Sketch a graph of y against x when $x \geqslant 0$ and   (a) $n = 2$,   (b) $n = -2$.

9 You are given that $y = 6x^n$ and that $y = 3$ when $x = 8$.
Find the value of n.

10 y is proportional to x^3.
(a) When $x = 4$, $y = 80$.   Find the value of y when $x = 8$.

Also, x is inversely proportional to the square root of z.
(b) When $y = 10$, $z = 16$.   Find the value of z when $x = 4$.   AQA

Module 3 — Exam Practice Non-calculator Paper

Do not use a calculator for this exercise.

1 Use these numbers to answer the following questions.

| 3 | 7 | 11 | 15 | 19 | 23 | 27 |

(a) Which number in the list is a factor of another number in the list?
(b) Which number is a cube number?
(c) (i) Which numbers are not prime numbers? Give a reason for your answer.
    (ii) The numbers are part of a sequence.
         What is the next number in the sequence which is not a prime number?

2 (a) Work out. (i) $5 - 0.26$ (ii) 0.2×0.4 (iii) $24 \div 0.3$
   (b) A turkey costs £3.60 per kilogram.
       What is the cost of a turkey which weighs 6.5 kilograms?

3 (a) Write these fractions in order, smallest first: $\frac{1}{2}$ $\frac{2}{3}$ $\frac{3}{5}$ $\frac{5}{8}$ $\frac{3}{4}$

   (b) Write down a fraction that lies halfway between $\frac{1}{5}$ and $\frac{1}{4}$.

   (c) Work out (i) $\frac{1}{4} + \frac{2}{5}$,   (ii) $\frac{2}{3} - \frac{1}{2}$,   (iii) $\frac{4}{5} \times \frac{2}{3}$.

4 A plane flies from Paris to Guadeloupe, a distance of 4200 miles.
   The plane has an average speed of 500 miles per hour.
   How long does the plane take for the journey?
   Give your answer in hours and minutes.   AQA

5 A teacher drives 19 miles to school each morning and the same distance home in the evening.
   He works 5 days each week. There are 39 weeks in a school year.
   (a) **Estimate** the number of miles the teacher drives to and from school each year.
   (b) The teacher drives approximately 12 000 miles each year altogether.
       (i) Approximately what percentage of his annual mileage is driving to and from school?
       (ii) The total cost of running his car is 42p a mile.
            Estimate the cost of his annual mileage.   AQA

6 Four cabbages cost £2.88.
   How much will five cabbages cost?   AQA

7 Two cucumbers and three lettuces cost £2.64.
   A cucumber costs 25% more than a lettuce.
   Find the cost of a lettuce.

8 (a) Which is smaller 3^5 or 5^3? Show all your working.
   (b) Work out. (i) $2^5 \times 3^2$ (ii) $30^3 \div 6^2$

9 A crowd of 54 000 people watch a carnival.
   $\frac{2}{3}$ of the crowd are children and $\frac{3}{5}$ of the children are girls.
   What percentage of the crowd are girls?

10 A youth club organises a skiing holiday for 45 children. The ratio of boys to girls is 5 : 4.
   40% of the boys have skied before.
   How many boys have skied before?

11 A train travels from Basingstoke to London in 40 minutes. The distance is 50 miles.
   Find the average speed of the train in miles per hour.   AQA

12 (a) Given that $59 \times 347 = 20\,473$, find the exact value of $\frac{20\,473}{590}$.

(b) Use approximations to estimate the value of $\frac{97.3 \times 3049}{0.49}$. Show all your working.

(c) Work out $\sqrt{0.25} \times 0.1^2$.

13 (a) 7 *Arctic* ice creams cost a total of £3.85.
How much will 12 *Arctic* ice creams cost?

(b) A large box of ice cream cones contains 750 cones to the nearest 10.
(i) What is the smallest possible number of cones in the box?
(ii) What is the largest possible number of cones in the box? AQA

14 (a) Write as a product of its prime factors. (i) 72 (ii) 96
(b) Hence, find (i) the least common multiple of 72 and 96,
(ii) the highest common factor of 72 and 96.

15 Trevor did a sponsored walk. The length of the walk, to the nearest kilometre, was 12 km.
Trevor's time was 110 minutes to the nearest minute.
(a) What was the longest length the walk could have been?
(b) What was Trevor's shortest possible time? AQA

16 Felix and Jan are in cars travelling in opposite directions along a motorway.
At 1015 they are 30 km apart and travelling towards each other.
Felix is travelling at an average speed of 70 km/h.
If they pass each other at 1027, what is Jan's average speed?

17 Here are the first four terms of a sequence of numbers written in standard form.

$$6 \times 10^{-1}, \quad 6 \times 10^{-3}, \quad 6 \times 10^{-5}, \quad 6 \times 10^{-7}, \quad \ldots$$

(a) Write down the 10th term of the sequence.
(b) (i) Write down the 1st term of the sequence as a decimal.
(ii) Write down the **sum** of the first four terms as a decimal. AQA

18 (a) Find an approximate value of $\frac{391 \times 3.08}{0.613}$.
You **must** show all your working.

(b) Write $0.000\,002\,4$ in standard form.

(c) Work out $64^{0.5} \times 3^{-2}$. Give your answer as a fraction. AQA

19 (a) Write these numbers in standard form. (i) 38 600 000 (ii) 0.000 054
(b) Calculate (i) 5×10^5 times 2×10^3, (ii) $(2 \times 10^3) \div (5 \times 10^5)$.
Give your answers in standard form.

20 The sale price of a pair of roller blades is £48.
What was the original price of the roller blades?

SALE
Sports Equipment
20% OFF

AQA

21 (a) Write 240 as the product of its prime factors.
(b) Hence, find the smallest whole number 240 must be multiplied by to give a perfect square.

22 Work out. (a) $1\frac{1}{4} + \frac{2}{3}$ (b) $1\frac{1}{4} \times 2\frac{2}{3}$ (c) $2\frac{1}{2} - 1\frac{2}{3}$ (d) $2\frac{1}{2} \div 1\frac{2}{3}$

23 Hugh buys a box of fireworks.
After lighting 40% of the fireworks he has 24 fireworks left.
How many fireworks did he buy?

24 The ratio of male to female passengers on a bus is 3 : 5.
At the next stop 5 females get off and 2 males get on.
The ratio of male to female passengers is now 4 : 5.
How many male passengers are now on the bus?

25 (a) Use approximations to estimate $\sqrt{\dfrac{40\,095}{(9.87^2)}}$.

(b) Work out $3 \times 10^5 \times 5 \times 10^{-2}$.
Give your answer in standard form.

(c) The value of a house has increased by 10% in one year.
It is now valued at £550 000.
What was the value of the house a year ago?

AQA

26 (a) What is the reciprocal of 2.5?

(b) Write these numbers in descending order.

$$5^{-1} \qquad \left(\tfrac{1}{4}\right)^{\frac{1}{2}} \qquad 2^{-3} \qquad 3^{-2} \qquad \left(\tfrac{1}{2}\right)^2$$

(c) Find the value of x when:

(i) $2^4 \times 2^3 = 2^x$,   (ii) $3^{-2} \div 3^{-4} = 3^x$,   (iii) $216^{\frac{1}{3}} = 6^x$.

(d) Work out $9^{-\frac{3}{2}}$. Give your answer as a fraction.

27 It takes 15 minutes to fill a paddling pool at the rate of 12 litres per minute.
How many minutes less would it take to fill the pool at the rate of 20 litres per minute?

28 Salt is sold in different sized blocks.
The weight of each block, B kilograms, is directly proportional to the cube of its
height, h metres. A block of weight $54\,\text{kg}$ has height $3\,\text{m}$.

(a) Find an equation connecting h and B.

(b) Find the weight of a block with a height of $1\,\text{m}$.

(c) Another block has a weight of $128\,\text{kg}$. Find its height.

AQA

29 Tim fits television aerials in houses. He buys 100 metres of television cable.
Each house needs 10 metres of television cable.
The length of cable which Tim buys is correct to the nearest metre.
The length of cable needed for each house is correct to the nearest half metre.
After working on nine houses, what is the minimum length of cable which Tim could
have left?

AQA

30 (a) Work out the exact value of $\left(\sqrt{3}\right)^4$.

(b) Write $\sqrt{32}$ in the form 2^p.

(c) Find the value of $(0.25)^{-1}$.

(d) Find the value of $81^{-\frac{3}{4}}$. Leave your answer as a fraction.

AQA

31 (a) Copy and complete the table of values for $y = 2x^2 + x - 10$.

x	-3	-2	-1	0	1	2	3
y		-4		-10	-7		11

(b) Draw the graph $2x^2 + x - 10 = 0$ for values of x from -3 to 3.

(c) By drawing an appropriate line on the same diagram, find the
solutions of $2x^2 - x - 9 = 0$.

32 T is directly proportional to the positive square root of M and $T = 32$, when $M = 16$.

(a) Calculate T when M is 100.

(b) Calculate M when T is 9.6.

AQA

33 (a) (i) Simplify the following expression, leaving your answer in surd form. $\sqrt{27} + \sqrt{75}$

(ii) **Hence**, simplify the expression $\dfrac{\sqrt{27} + \sqrt{75}}{\sqrt{12}}$.

(b) Calculate $64^{\frac{2}{3}}$.

(c) Calculate $27^{-\frac{1}{3}}$, giving your answer as a fraction.

(d) Write the number $0.\overset{\bullet}{2}\overset{\bullet}{1}$ as a fraction in its simplest form.

You may use a calculator for this exercise.

1 Jacob is 3.7 kg heavier than Isaac. The sum of their weights is 44.5 kg.
How heavy is Jacob?

2 A shop sells 4000 items in a week. 5% are returned.
$\frac{1}{4}$ of the returned items are faulty. How many items are faulty?   AQA

3 (a) (i) Calculate $\sqrt{3}$. Give your answer correct to two decimal places.
(ii) Calculate $(0.6)^3$.
(b) What is the value of m, if $47.6 \div m = 0.\dot{3}$?

4 Cheri is paid a basic rate of £6.40 per hour for a 35-hour week.
Overtime is paid at $1\frac{1}{2}$ times the basic rate. Last week she was paid £262.40.
How many hours did Cheri work last week?

5 The diagram shows the weights and prices of two packets
of gravy granules.
This week both packets are on special offer.
The smaller packet has one third off the normal price.
The larger packet has 30% off the normal price.
Which packet is better value this week? Show your working.

Gravy Granules 180 g
Normal price 54p

Gravy Granules 300 g
Normal price 90p

6 Kelly states that $a^2 + b^2$ is always an even number when a and b are prime numbers.
By means of an example, show that Kelly is **not** correct.   AQA

7 Harvey lives 3 kilometres from school. He walks to school at an average speed of 5 km/h.
The school day starts at 0900.
What is the latest time Harvey can leave home and still get to school on time?

8 (a) What is the reciprocal of 0.25?

(b) Work out $\dfrac{3.2^2}{\sqrt{0.04}}$.

9 A caravan is for sale at £7200. Stuart buys the caravan on credit.
The credit terms are:

| deposit 25% of sale price and 36 monthly payments of £175. |

FOR SALE £7200

Express the extra amount paid for credit, compared with the cash price,
as a percentage of the cash price.

10 Karina says,
"For some numbers the square root of the number is larger than the number itself."
For what numbers is this true?

11 A puppy weighed 1.50 kg when it was born.
(a) Its weight increased by 28% during the first month.
Calculate the puppy's weight at the end of the first month.
(b) In the second month the puppy's weight increased by 15% of its **new** weight.
Calculate its weight at the end of the second month.
(c) The puppy's weight continues to increase by 15% each month.
How many months old is the puppy when it has doubled its birth weight?
Show your working.   AQA

12 There are 52 cards in a pack.
A dealer shares the pack between two players in the ratio 5 : 8.
How many cards does each player receive?

AQA

13 At 20 miles per hour a bus journey takes 40 minutes.
A taxi does the same journey at 25 miles per hour.
How many minutes does the taxi take?

14 (a) Gerald invests £4000 at 4.5% per annum compound interest.
Calculate the interest on his investment at the end of 3 years.
(b) Steff invests her money at 5% per annum compound interest.
Calculate the percentage increase in the value of her investment after 3 years.

15 (a) Express as products of their prime factors. (i) 72   (ii) 80
(b) Two cars go round a race track.
The first car takes 1 minute 12 seconds to complete a circuit and the other car takes
1 minute 20 seconds.
They start together on the starting line.
Find the length of time, in minutes, before they are together again.

AQA

16 £1 can buy 1.54 euros.   £1 can buy 1.37 dollars.
How many dollars can be bought with 1000 euros?

17 Use your calculator to find the value of $\dfrac{29.7 + 17.3}{1.54 \times 68.5}$.

Give your answer to a suitable degree of accuracy **and** give a reason for your choice.

Hannah wishes to insure the contents of her house for £17 500.
She is quoted a premium of £1.30 for every £100 of contents.
(a) Find the premium which she is quoted.
(b) Hannah can receive a 20% discount for agreeing to pay the first £100 of any claim.
She then receives a further 8% discount because her house is in a neighbourhood
watch area.
Find the premium which Hannah actually pays.

AQA

19 $p = 3^2 \times 5 \times 7$ and $q = 2 \times 3 \times 5^2$. Find the least common multiple of p and q.

20 The population of China is 1.2×10^9.
The area of China is 9.5×10^6 square kilometres.
What is the population density of China?

21 (a) Place the following numbers in order, largest first: $\sqrt{6.9}$ 2.58 1.6^2 $2\frac{4}{7}$

(b) (i) Calculate $\dfrac{612 \times 29.6}{81.3 - 18.9}$.

(ii) Use approximations to show that your answer is about right. Show your working.

22 (a) You are given the formula $k = \frac{3}{4} m^2$.
Calculate the exact value of k, when $m = 4.8 \times 10^3$.
Give your answer in standard form.

(b) Calculate $\sqrt{\dfrac{5.2 \times 10^{-3}}{(0.039)^2}}$, correct to two decimal places.

23 **SALE "30% Off All Prices".**
A suitcase costs £44.66 in the sale.
How much was the suitcase before the sale?

24 Jennifer gets 6% per annum on her investment.
After one year the value of her investment is £1272.
How much did she invest?

25 Last year Alf had a tax allowance of £4895 and paid £4697 in tax. The rates of tax were:

> 10p in the £ on the first £2090 of taxable income and
> 22p in the £ on all the remaining taxable income.

How much did Alf earn last year?

26 The world harvest of garlic is 20 000 tonnes every day.
 (a) How much garlic is harvested in one year? Take a year to be 365 days.
    Give your answer in standard form.

France produces 5.29×10^4 tonnes of garlic in a year.
 (b) What percentage of the world total is produced by France? AQA

27 (a) Copy and complete the table of values for $y = 3x^2 - 2x + 1$.

x	-3	-2	-1	0	1	2	3	4
y	34	17	6	1	2		22	41

 (b) Draw the graph of $y = 3x^2 - 2x + 1$ for values of x between -3 and $+4$.
 (c) By drawing an appropriate linear graph, write down the solutions of $3x^2 - 6x + 2 = 0$. AQA

28 (a) What is the value of $2^0 + 2^{-3}$?
 (b) Work out $(6.5 \times 10^3) \div (9.2 \times 10^{-7})$.
    Give your answer in standard form correct to two significant figures.

29 (a) Simplify $\sqrt{18} + \sqrt{32}$
 (b) Rationalise $\dfrac{1}{\sqrt{6}}$ AQA

30 $p = 1.65 \times 10^7$ and $r = 6.17 \times 10^{-2}$.
The values of p and r are given correct to 3 significant figures.
Calculate the maximum possible value of $p \div r$.
Give your answer in standard form to an appropriate degree of accuracy. AQA

31 (a) Write $0.3\dot{4}$ as a fraction in its simplest form.
 (b) Write $0.6\dot{3}\dot{4}$ as a fraction in its simplest form. AQA

32 Charlie is building a house. She estimates the cost of concrete for the base.
When the lorry delivers the concrete, Charlie finds that she needs an extra 30% of concrete.
Because she has bought extra concrete, she is given a 15% discount on the full price of all
the concrete.
What is the percentage increase in the cost of the concrete which she has bought, compared
with her initial estimate? AQA

33 (a) Write $\sqrt{45}$ in the form $a\sqrt{b}$ where a and b are prime numbers.
 (b) Write $\dfrac{5}{\sqrt{10}}$ in the form $\dfrac{\sqrt{a}}{b}$ where a and b are whole numbers.

34 The electrical resistance, R, of a wire is inversely proportional to the square of its diameter, d.
When $R = 0.5$ ohms, $d = 6\,\text{mm}$.
 (a) Find an equation expressing R in terms of d.
 (b) (i) Calculate R when $d = 12\,\text{mm}$. (ii) Calculate d when $R = 12.5$ ohms. AQA

35 Calculate the value of $(5.8 \times 10^{-5})^{\frac{1}{3}}$.
Give your answer in standard form correct to 2 significant figures.

36 $V = ab - c^2$ $a = 1.7,$ measured to 2 significant figures.
         $b = 3.0,$ measured to 2 significant figures.
         $c = 1.32,$ measured to 3 significant figures.
Calculate the upper limit of V. AQA

Module 3: Calculator Paper

Introduction to Algebra

What you need to know

- You should be able to write **algebraic expressions**.

  Eg 1 An expression for the cost of 6 pens at n pence each is $6n$ pence.

  Eg 2 An expression for 2 pence more than n pence is $n + 2$ pence.

- Be able to **simplify expressions** by collecting **like terms** together.

  Eg 3 (a) $2d + 3d = 5d$ (b) $3x + 2 - x + 4 = 2x + 6$ (c) $x + 2x + x^2 = 3x + x^2$

- Be able to **multiply expressions** together.

  Eg 4 (a) $2a \times a = 2a^2$ (b) $y \times y \times y = y^3$ (c) $3m \times 2n = 6mn$

- Be able to recall and use these properties of powers:
  Powers of the same base are **added** when terms are **multiplied**.
  Powers of the same base are **subtracted** when terms are **divided**.
  Powers are **multiplied** when a power is raised to a power.

  $$a^m \times a^n = a^{m+n}$$
  $$a^m \div a^n = a^{m-n}$$
  $$(a^m)^n = a^{m \times n}$$

  Eg 5 (a) $x^3 \times x^2 = x^5$ (b) $a^5 \div a^2 = a^3$ (c) $6m^6 \div 2m^2 = 3m^4$ (d) $(2y^2)^3 = 8y^6$

- Be able to **multiply out brackets**.

  Eg 6 (a) $2(x - 5) = 2x - 10$ (b) $x(x - 5) = x^2 - 5x$ (c) $2m(m + 3) = 2m^2 + 6m$

- Be able to **factorise expressions**.

  Eg 7 (a) $3x - 6 = 3(x - 2)$ (b) $m^2 + 5m = m(m + 5)$ (c) $3a^2 - 6a = 3a(a - 2)$

Exercise 18

1 Godfrey is 5 years older than Mary.
Write expressions for the following
(a) Godfrey's age when Mary is t years old.
(b) Mary's age when Godfrey is x years old.

2 A cup of coffee costs x pence and a cup of tea costs y pence.
Write an expression for the cost of 3 cups of coffee and 2 cups of tea.

3 Simplify (a) $m + 2m + 3m$,   (b) $2m + 2 - m$,   (c) $m \times m \times m$.

4 Write an expression, in terms of x,
for the sum of the angles in this shape.

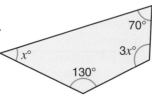

5 A muffin costs $d + 3$ pence.
Write an expression for the cost of 5 muffins.

6 Which of these algebraic expressions are equivalent?

$2y$	y^2	$2(y + 1)$	$y \times y$	$y + y$
$2y + 2$	$2y + y$	$2y^2$	$3y$	$2y + 1$

AQA

52

7 (a) Simplify   (i) $2x + 3 + x$,   (ii) $2x + y - x + y$.
     (b) Multiply out   (i) $2(x + 3)$,   (ii) $x(x - 1)$.
     (c) Multiply out and simplify   (i) $2(x - 1) - 3$,   (ii) $7 + 3(2 + x)$.
     (d) Factorise   (i) $2a - 6$,   (ii) $x^2 + 2x$.

8 (a) Ken works x hours a week for £y per hour.
         Write an expression for the amount he earns each week.
     (b) Sue works 5 hours less than Ken each week and earns £y per hour.
         Write an expression for the amount Sue earns each week.

9 Lorna buys some 1st class stamps and some 2nd class stamps.
She buys 12 stamps altogether.
     (a) She buys x 1st class stamps.
         Write an expression for the number of 2nd class stamps she buys.
     (b) 2nd class stamps cost d pence.
         A 1st class stamp costs 5 pence more than a 2nd class stamp.
         Write an expression for the cost of a 1st class stamp.
     (c) Write an expression, in terms of x and d, for the amount Lorna has to pay for
         her 12 stamps. Give your answer in its simplest form.

10 (a) Simplify $8a + ab - a + 2b + 3ab$.
      (b) Expand and simplify $5(x + 3) - x$.   AQA

11 Multiply out and simplify $3(4x - 1) + 2x - 6$.   AQA

12 Simplify.   (a) $y^3 \times y^2$ (b) $x^6 \div x^3$ (c) $\dfrac{z^4 \times z}{z^3}$ (d) $\dfrac{x^2 y}{xy^2}$

13 (a) Simplify   (i) $2a^5 \times 3a^2$,   (ii) $36a^6 \div 9a^2$.
      (b) Factorise completely $3x^2 - 9x$.   AQA

14 Simplify.   (a) $3a^5 \times 4a^2$ (b) $6a^4 \div 2a$ AQA

15 (a) Simplify $5 - 3(2n - 1)$.
      (b) Multiply out $(-3m) \times (-2m)$.
      (c) Factorise fully $8mn - 2m$.

16 Expand and simplify $3(2x + 3) - 2(5 + x)$.

17 (a) Simplify   (i) $2a^3 \times 3a$,   (ii) $6x^8 \div 3x^2$,   (iii) $\dfrac{3m^2 \times 4n^6}{6mn^2}$,   (iv) $4x^3 y \times 5x^2 y$.
      (b) Expand   (i) $(3m^3)^2$,   (ii) $(2a^2 b)^3$.

18 (a) Expand the brackets.   (i) $2x(x - 3y)$ (ii) $3a(3a + a^2)$
      (b) Factorise.   (i) $4xy - 2y^2$ (ii) $3m^2 - 12m$
      (c) Simplify. $2x^2 - x(1 + x)$

19 Simplify fully $\dfrac{2a^3 b^2 \times 6a^4 b^2}{4ab^3}$.   AQA

20 (a) Multiply out $2x(2y - xy)$.
      (b) Factorise $6pq - 3pq^2$.
      (c) Simplify $21m^6 \div 7m^3$.

21 Simplify.   (a) $\dfrac{6x^2 z \times 2x^2 y^2 z}{3x^3 y}$ (b) $\sqrt{\dfrac{1}{m^6}}$

22 Simplify $(3xy^2)^4$.   AQA

23 Simplify fully $\dfrac{3a^2}{bc} \times \dfrac{b^2}{6ac^2} \times \dfrac{2ac^2}{b}$.

- The solution of an equation is the value of the unknown letter that fits the equation.

- You should be able to solve simple equations by **inspection**.

- Be able to solve simple problems by **working backwards**.

  Eg 1 I think of a number, multiply it by 3 and add 4.   The answer is 19.

  x ⟶ | multiply by 3 | ⟶ | add 4 | ⟶ Answer 19

  5 ⟵ | divide by 3 | ⟵ 15 | subtract 4 | ⟵ 19

  The number I thought of is 5.

- Be able to use the **balance method** to solve equations.

  Eg 2 Solve these equations.

  (a) $d - 13 = -5$ (b) $-4a = 20$ (c) $5 - 4n = -1$

  $\quad d = -5 + 13$ $\quad a = \frac{20}{-4}$ $\quad -4n = -6$

  $\quad d = 8$ $\quad a = -5$ $\quad n = 1.5$

- Be able to solve equations with unknowns on both sides of the equals sign.

  Eg 3 Solve $3x + 1 = x + 7$.

  $\quad 3x = x + 6$

  $\quad 2x = 6$

  $\quad x = 3$

- Be able to solve equations which include brackets.

  Eg 4 Solve $4(3 + 2x) = 5(x + 2)$.

  $\quad 12 + 8x = 5x + 10$

  $\quad 8x = 5x - 2$

  $\quad 3x = -2$

  $\quad x = -\frac{2}{3}$

- Be able to solve equations which involve fractions.

  Eg 5 Solve $\frac{x}{2} + \frac{2x}{3} = 7$.

  $\quad 6 \times \frac{x}{2} + 6 \times \frac{2x}{3} = 6 \times 7$

  $\quad 3x + 4x = 42$

  $\quad 7x = 42$

  $\quad x = 6$

  Eg 6 Solve $\frac{x - 1}{3} = \frac{x + 1}{4}$.

  $\quad 4(x - 1) = 3(x + 1)$

  $\quad 4x - 4 = 3x + 3$

  $\quad 4x = 3x + 7$

  $\quad x = 7$

- You should be able to write, or form, equations using the information given in a problem.

Exercise 19

1   Solve these equations.   (a) $7 + x = 12$ (b) $5 - x = 3$ (c) $5x - 9 = 11$

2   (a)   I think of a number, add 3, and then multiply by 2.   The answer is 16.
       What is my number?
   (b)   I think of a number, double it and then subtract 3.   The answer is 5.
       What is my number?

3   Solve these equations.
   (a) $3x - 7 = 23$ (b) $5 + 7x = 47$ (c) $5(x - 2) = 20$ (d) $3x - 7 = x + 15$

4 The lengths of these rods are given, in centimetres, in terms of n.

 n 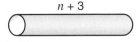 $n + 3$ 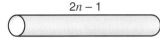 $2n - 1$

The total length of the rods is 30 cm.
By forming an equation, find the value of n.

5 Solve the equations.   (a) $4x + 7 = 13$ (b) $3x + 7 = 3 - x$ AQA

6 Solve the equation $5x - 7 = 3x + 5$.   AQA

7 Solve these equations.
(a) $7x + 4 = 60$ (b) $3x - 7 = -4$ (c) $2(x + 3) = -2$ (d) $3x - 4 = 1 + x$

8 Solve the equations   (a) $2x + 3 = 15$,   (b) $3(x - 1) = 6$,   (c) $x + 2 = 5 - x$.
   AQA

9 A small paving slab weighs x kilograms.
A large paving slab weighs $(2x + 3)$ kilograms.
(a) Write an expression, in terms of x, for the total weight of 16 small slabs and 4 large slabs.
Give your answer in its simplest form.

The total weight of the slabs is 132 kilograms.
(b) Write down an equation and find the value of x.   AQA

10 Solve these equations.
(a) $8x = 20$ (b) $3n - 7 = n + 5$ (c) $2m - 7 = -10$ (d) $3(2x + 3) = 2 - x$

11 Solve these equations.
(a) $\frac{x}{3} = -7$ (b) $2(x - 1) = 3$ (c) $5 - 2x = 3x + 2$ (d) $\frac{1}{4}x + 5 = 2$

12 Solve the equations   (a) $\frac{x - 7}{5} = 2$,   (b) $5x + 6 = 24 - 10x$.   AQA

13 Solve these equations.
(a) $\frac{x + 5}{2} = 3$ (b) $\frac{1 - 2x}{3} = 2$ (c) $\frac{3}{2} = \frac{3x}{5}$ (d) $\frac{x}{2} + \frac{x}{3} = 5$

14 The diagram shows a rectangle and a right-angled triangle.

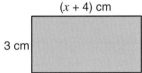
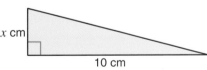

The area of the rectangle is equal to the area of the triangle.
By forming an equation work out the value of x.   AQA

15 Solve these equations.
(a) $2(x - 3) + 3(x + 1) = 2$
(b) $3(2 + 3a) = 5(a - 2)$
(c) $x - 3(x + 1) = 2(5 - 2x)$

16 Solve the equations   (a) $\frac{x - 3}{4} = 1 - x$,   (b) $\frac{x - 3}{2} = \frac{2x + 1}{3}$.

17 Solve the equation $\frac{1}{2}(3x + 1) = \frac{1}{4}(2x + 1)$.   AQA

18 Solve the equation $\frac{x - 1}{3} + \frac{x + 1}{2} = \frac{5}{6}$.

19 Solve the equation $\frac{3x - 1}{2} - \frac{2x - 1}{3} = 6$.   AQA

Formulae ●●●●●●●●●●●●

What you need to know

- An **expression** is just an answer using letters and numbers.
  A **formula** is an algebraic rule. It always has an equals sign.

- You should be able to **write simple formulae**.

  Eg 1 A packet of crisps weighs 25 grams.
  Write a formula for the total weight,
  W grams, of n packets of crisps.
  $$W = 25n$$

  Eg 2 Start with t, add 5 and then multiply
  by 3. The result is p.
  Write a formula for p in terms of t.
  $$p = 3(t + 5)$$

- Be able to **substitute** values into expressions and formulae.

  Eg 3 (a) $A = pq - r$
  Find the value of A
  when $p = 2$,
  $q = -2$ and $r = 3$.

  $A = pq - r$
  $A = 2 \times (-2) - 3$
  $A = -4 - 3$
  $A = -7$

  (b) $M = 2n^2$
  Find the value of M
  when $n = 3$.

  $M = 2n^2$
  $M = 2 \times 3^2$
  $M = 2 \times 9$
  $M = 18$

  (c) Find the value of $\dfrac{b^2c}{d}$
  when $b = \frac{1}{2}$, $c = 4.8$
  and $d = -3$.

  $\dfrac{b^2c}{d} = \dfrac{\left(\frac{1}{2}\right)^2 \times 4.8}{-3}$

  $\dfrac{b^2c}{d} = \dfrac{\frac{1}{4} \times 4.8}{-3}$

  $\dfrac{b^2c}{d} = \dfrac{1.2}{-3}$

  $\dfrac{b^2c}{d} = 0.4$

- Be able to **rearrange** a formula to make another letter (variable) the subject.

  Eg 4 $y = 2x + a$

  Make x the subject of the formula.

  $y = 2x + a$
  $y - a = 2x$
  $\dfrac{y - a}{2} = x$
  So, $x = \dfrac{y - a}{2}$

  Eg 5 $T = ab^2$

  Rearrange the formula to give b
  in terms of T and a.

  $T = ab^2$
  $\dfrac{T}{a} = b^2$
  $b = \pm \sqrt{\dfrac{T}{a}}$

Exercise **20**   Do not use a calculator for questions 1 to 12.

1 Given that $m = -3$ and $n = 5$, find the value of
   (a) $m + n$,   (b) $m - n$,   (c) $n - m$,   (d) mn.

2 If $p = 4$ and $q = -5$ find the value of   (a) $3pq$,   (b) $p^2 + 2q$.

3 $L = 5(p + q)$. Find the value of L when $p = 2$ and $q = -0.4$.

4 $A = b - cd$. Find the value of A when $b = -3$, $c = 2$ and $d = 4$.

5 What is the value of $10y^2$ when $y = 3$?

6 What is the value of $3x^3$ when $x = 2$?

7 $T = ab^2$. Find the value of T when $a = 4$ and $b = -5$.

8 $S = pq - 2r^2$. Find the value of S when $p = -5$, $q = -2$ and $r = -3$.

9 $T = \frac{uv}{w}$. Find the value of T when $u = 3$, $v = -2$ and $w = \frac{1}{2}$.

10 $M = \sqrt{\frac{a}{b}}$. Find the value of M when $a = 8$ and $b = \frac{1}{2}$.

11   Each year the High School has a disco for Year 7.
A teacher works out the number of cans of drink to buy,

using this rule: | 3 cans for every 2 tickets sold, plus 20 spare cans. |

(a)   This year, 160 tickets have been sold.
How many cans will he buy?
(b)   Using N for the number of cans and T for the number of tickets,
write down the teacher's formula for N in terms of T.
(c)   Last year, he bought 215 cans.
How many tickets were sold last year?   AQA

12   Given that $m = \frac{1}{2}$, $p = \frac{3}{4}$, $t = -2$, calculate   (a) $mp + t$ (b) $\frac{(m + p)}{t}$ AQA

13   A formula is given as $c = 3t - 5$. Rearrange the formula to give t in terms of c.

14   A formula for calculating distance is $d = \frac{(u + v)t}{2}$.

(a)   Find the value of d when $u = 9.4$, $v = 6.3$ and $t = 8$.
(b)   Make t the subject of the formula.
(c)   Find the value of t when $d = 60$, $u = 5.8$ and $v = 10.2$ AQA

15   You are given the formula $v = u + at$.
(a)   Find v when $u = 17$, $a = -8$ and $t = \frac{3}{5}$.
(b)   Rearrange the formula to give a in terms of v, u and t.

16   Make r the subject of the formula $p = \frac{gr}{s}$.

17   (a)   If $x = -4$, calculate the value of $3x^2$.
(b)   If $a = \frac{2}{3}$ and $b = \frac{2}{5}$, calculate the exact value of $a^2\left(1 - \frac{1}{b}\right)$.   AQA

18   Scientists use the formula $\frac{1}{f} = \frac{1}{u} + \frac{1}{v}$ to calculate the focal length, f, of a lens.

The lengths u, v and f are all measured in centimetres.
Calculate f when $u = 2.4$ and $v = -3.2$.   AQA

19   You are given the formula $V = \sqrt{PR}$.
Rearrange the formula to give P in terms of V and R.   AQA

20 s is given by the formula $s = ut + \frac{1}{2}at^2$.
Find the value of s when $u = 2.8$, $t = 2$ and $a = -1.7$.   AQA

21   You are given the formula $g = \frac{3}{5}h^2$.
(a)   Find the value of g when $h = 2.5 \times 10^3$.
(b)   Rearrange the formula to give h in terms of g.

22   Rearrange the formula $p = \frac{q}{5 - q}$ to make q the subject.

23   Make v the subject of the formula $w = \frac{uv}{u + v}$.

24 $n = \frac{3 + m}{m - 5}$. Rearrange the formula to give m in terms of n.

Sequences ●●●●●●●●●●●●

What you need to know

- A **sequence** is a list of numbers made according to some rule.
  The numbers in a sequence are called **terms**.

- You should be able to draw and continue number sequences represented by patterns of shapes.

- Be able to continue a sequence by following a given rule.

  Eg 1 The sequence 2, 7, 22, … is made using the rule:

  > Multiply the last number by 3, then add 1.

  The next term in the sequence = $(22 \times 3) + 1 = 66 + 1 = 67$

- Be able to find a rule, and then use it, to continue a sequence.

  > **To continue a sequence:**
  > 1. Work out the rule to get from one term to the next.
  > 2. Apply the same rule to find further terms in the sequence.

  Eg 2 Describe the rule used to make the following sequences.
  Then use the rule to find the next term of each sequence.

  (a) 5, 8, 11, 14, …   Rule: add 3 to last term.   Next term: 17.
  (b) 2, 4, 8, 16, …   Rule: multiply last term by 2. Next term: 32.
  (c) 1, 1, 2, 3, 5, 8, … Rule: add the last two terms. Next term: 13.

- Special sequences **Square numbers:**   1, 4, 9, 16, 25, …
  Triangular numbers: 1, 3, 6, 10, 15, …

- A number sequence which increases (or decreases) by the same amount from one term to the next is called a **linear sequence**.
  The sequence: 2, 8, 14, 20, 26, … has a **common difference** of 6.

- You should be able to find an expression for the nth term of a linear sequence.

  Eg 3 Find the nth term of the sequence: 3, 5, 7, 9, …
  The sequence is linear, common difference = 2.
  To find the nth term add one to the multiples of 2.
  So, the nth term is $2n + 1$.

- Be able to find an expression for the nth term of a **quadratic sequence**.

  Eg 4 Find the nth term of the sequence: 4, 7, 12, 19, …
  The sequence is not linear, because the differences between terms is increasing.
  Compare the sequence with the sequence of square numbers: 1, 4, 9, 16, …
  To find the nth term add 3 to the square numbers.
  So, the nth term is $n^2 + 3$.

Exercise 21

1 What is the next number in each of these sequences?

(a) 1, 2, 5, 10, …   (b) 1, 3, 9, 27, …   (c) 1, $\frac{1}{2}$, $\frac{1}{4}$, $\frac{1}{8}$, …

2 Ahmed writes down the first four numbers of a sequence: 10, 8, 4, −2, ...
   (a) What is the next number in this sequence?
   (b) Explain how you found your answer.   AQA

3 Look at this sequence of numbers. 2, 5, 8, 11, ...
   (a) What is the next number in the sequence?
   (b) Is 30 a number in this sequence? Give a reason for your answer.

4 The rule for a sequence is:

> Add the last two numbers and divide by 2.

Write down the next three terms when the sequence begins: 3, 7, ...

5 A sequence begins: 1, −2, ...
The next number in the sequence is found by using the rule:

> ADD THE PREVIOUS TWO NUMBERS AND MULTIPLY BY TWO

Use the rule to find the next **two** numbers in the sequence.   AQA

6 A sequence begins: 1, 6, 10, 8, ...
The rule to continue the sequence is: **double the difference between the last two numbers**.
Ravi says if you continue the sequence it will end in 0. Is he correct? Explain your answer.

7 The first three patterns in a sequence are shown.

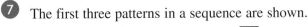

Pattern 1   **Pattern 2**   **Pattern 3**

   (a) How many squares are in pattern 20? Explain how you found your answer.
   (b) Write an expression for the number of squares in the nth pattern.

8 A sequence is given by 5, 12, 19, 26, 33, ...
   (a) What is the next term in this sequence? Explain how you got your answer.
   (b) Write down the nth term for the sequence.   AQA

9 Find the nth term of the following sequences.
   (a) 5, 7, 9, 11, ...   (b) 1, 5, 9, 13, ...

10 (a) Write down the first **three** terms of the sequence whose nth term is given by $n^2 + 4$.
      (b) Will the number 106 be in this sequence? Explain your answer.   AQA

11 Give the nth term of the following sequences.
   (a) 1, 4, 9, 16, 25, 36, ...   (b) 2, 5, 10, 17, 26, 37, ...   AQA

12 The nth term of a sequence is $\dfrac{5n}{4n + 5}$.
   (a) Write down the first two terms of this sequence.
   (b) Which term of the sequence has the value 1?   AQA

13 (a) Regular pentagons are used to form patterns, as shown.

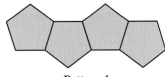

     Pattern 1   **Pattern 2**   **Pattern 3**   **Pattern 4**
     5 sides   **8 sides**   **11 sides**   **14 sides**

     Write, in terms of n, the number of sides in Pattern n.
    (b) A number pattern begins: 0, 3, 8, 15, 24, ...
     Write, in terms of n, the nth term in this pattern.   AQA

Straight Line Graphs

What you need to know

- The graph of a **linear function** is a **straight line**.

- The equation of the graph of a straight line is of the form $y = mx + c$, where m is the gradient and c is the y-intercept.

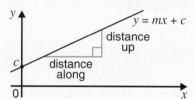

  The **gradient** of a line can be found by drawing a right-angled triangle.

  $$\text{Gradient} = \frac{\text{distance up}}{\text{distance along}}$$

  Gradients can be positive, zero or negative.

- You should be able to find the equation for a given line.

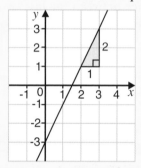

  Eg 1

  Find the equation of the line shown on this graph.

  $$\text{Gradient of line} = \frac{\text{distance up}}{\text{distance along}} = \frac{2}{1} = 2$$

  The graph crosses the y axis at the point $(0, -3)$, so, the y-intercept is -3.
  The equation of the line is $y = 2x - 3$.

- The points where a line crosses the axes can be found:
  by reading the coordinates from a graph,
  by substituting $x = 0$ and $y = 0$ into the equation of the line.

  Eg 2 The diagram shows a sketch of the line $2y = x + 3$.

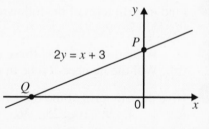

  Find the coordinates of the points P and Q.

  When $x = 0$, $2y = 0 + 3$, $2y = 3$, $y = 1\frac{1}{2}$.

  When $y = 0$, $0 = x + 3$, $x = -3$.

  The points are $P\left(0, 1\frac{1}{2}\right)$ and $Q(-3, 0)$.

- You should be able to find the gradient of a line which is perpendicular to a given line.

  If two lines are perpendicular to each other, the product of their gradients $= -1$.

  This can be written as: $m_{AB} \times m_{CD} = -1$

  where m_{AB} is the gradient of the line AB, and m_{CD} is the gradient of the line CD.

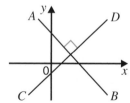

  $$m_{AB} = \frac{-1}{m_{CD}}$$

  Eg 3 Write down the gradient of the line which is perpendicular to the line with equation $y = -3x + 4$.
  The gradient of the line $y = -3x + 4$ is -3.
  The gradient of the line which is perpendicular to this line is $-1 \div (-3) = \frac{1}{3}$.

- Equations of the form $px + qy = r$ can be **rearranged** to the form $y = mx + c$.

Eg 4 The graph of a straight line is given by the equation $4y - 3x = 8$.
Write this equation in the form $y = mx + c$.

$4y - 3x = 8$
$4y = 3x + 8$
$y = \frac{3}{4}x + 2$

| The line has gradient $\frac{3}{4}$ and y-intercept 2. |

- You should be able to solve equations and problems involving straight line graphs.

Exercise 22

1 (a) Copy and complete the table of values for $y = 1 - 2x$.

x	−3	0	3
y		1	

(b) Draw the line $y = 1 - 2x$ for values of x from −3 to 3.
(c) Use your graph to find the value of y when $x = -1.5$.

2 (a) On the same axes, draw the graphs of $y = -2$, $y = x$ and $x + y = 5$.
(b) Which of these lines has a negative gradient?

3 The diagram shows a sketch of the line $2y = 6 - x$.

(a) Find the coordinates of the points P and Q.
(b) The line $2y = 6 - x$ goes through $R(-5, m)$.
What is the value of m?

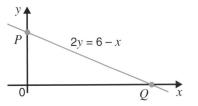

4

Points A, B and C are shown on the grid.

(a) Write down the equation of the line AB.
(b) (i) Use the grid to work out the gradient of the line CB.
(ii) Write down the equation of the line CB.

AQA

5 Match these equations to their graphs.

1 $y = 2x$

2 $y - x = 2$

3 $y + x = 2$

4 $2y = x$

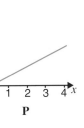
P

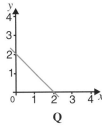
Q

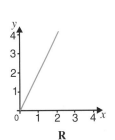
R

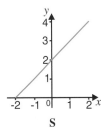
S

6 (a) Draw the graph of $2y = 3x - 6$ for values of x from −2 to 4.
(b) What is the gradient of the line $2y = 3x - 6$?
(c) Use your graph to find the value of x when $y = 1.5$.

7 The graph of a straight line is shown.
What is the equation of the line?

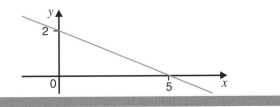

AQA

8 The table shows the largest quantity of salt, w grams, which can be dissolved in a beaker of water at temperature $t°C$.

$t°C$	10	20	25	30	40	50	60
w grams	54	58	60	62	66	70	74

(a) Draw a graph to illustrate this information.
(b) Use your graph to find
    (i) the lowest temperature at which 63 g of salt will dissolve in the water,
    (ii) the largest amount of salt that will dissolve in the water at 44°C.
(c) (i) The equation of the graph is of the form $w = at + b$.
        Use your graph to estimate the values of the constants a and b.
    (ii) Use the equation to calculate the largest amount of salt which will dissolve in the water at 95°C.

AQA

9 The total monthly bill for Ann's mobile phone is made up of two parts:
the fixed network charge and the cost of calls.

The graph shows the monthly bill, £B, for calls up to a total of 60 minutes.

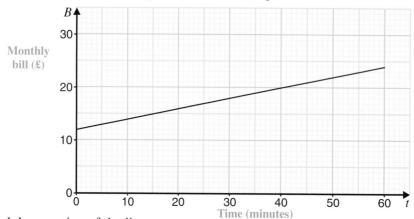

Find the equation of the line.

AQA

10 The equation of a line is $5y - 2x = 10$.
(a) Write this equation in the form $y = mx + c$.
(b) Write down the equation of the line, parallel to $5y - 2x = 10$, which passes through the point $(0, -1)$.

11 Show that the lines $5y = x + 4$ and $y = 6 - 5x$ are perpendicular to each other.

12 The diagram shows the graph of $2y = x + 4$.

Find the equation of the line through B which is perpendicular to the line $2y = x + 4$.

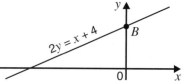

13 In the diagram, the lines AB and CD are perpendicular to each other and intersect at $(1, 3)$.
The line AB goes through $(0, 6)$.
The line CD goes through P.

Find the coordinates of P.

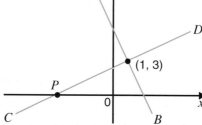

What you need to know

● A **gradient** measures the **rate of change** of one quantity with respect to another.
A **positive** gradient represents a **rate of increase**.
A **negative** gradient represents a **rate of decrease**.

● The gradient of a **distance-time graph** gives the speed.

> **Speed** is the rate of change of distance with respect to time.
> When the distance-time graph is **linear** the **speed is constant**.
> When the distance-time graph is **horizontal** the **speed is zero**.

Eg 1 The graph shows a car journey.

(a) Between what times does the car travel fastest?
Explain your answer.

(b) What is the speed of the car during this part
of the journey?

(a) 1200 to 1230. Steepest gradient.

(b) Speed $= \dfrac{\text{Distance}}{\text{Time}} = \dfrac{20\,\text{km}}{\frac{1}{2}\,\text{hour}} = 40\,\text{km/h}$

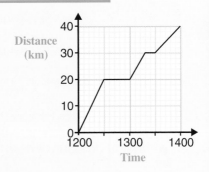

● The gradient of a **speed-time graph** gives the acceleration.

> **Acceleration** is the rate of change of speed with respect to time.
> When the speed-time graph is **linear** the **acceleration is constant**.
> When the speed-time graph is **horizontal** the **speed is constant** and the **acceleration is zero**.

● The **area** enclosed by the graph on a speed-time graph represents the **distance** travelled.

Eg 2 The graph shows the speed of a car against time between two roundabouts.

(a) Calculate the acceleration of the car.

(b) Calculate the distance travelled.

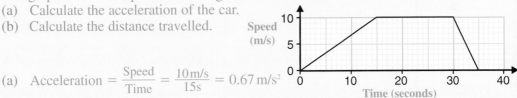

(a) Acceleration $= \dfrac{\text{Speed}}{\text{Time}} = \dfrac{10\,\text{m/s}}{15\,\text{s}} = 0.67\,\text{m/s}^2$

(b) Distance travelled $= \frac{1}{2}(15 + 35) \times 10 = 250$ metres

● You should be able to draw and interpret graphs which represent real-life situations.

Exercise 23

1 Water is poured into some containers at a constant rate.
Copy the axes given and sketch the graph of the depth of the water against time for each
container as it is filled.

(a)

(b)

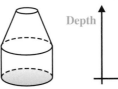

2 The distance-time graph shows a boat trip from Poole Quay to Wareham and back.

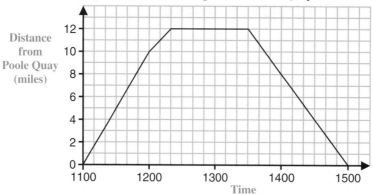

(a) Describe what happened to the speed of the boat at 1200 hours.
(b) How long did the boat stay in Wareham?
(c) What was the average speed of the boat on the return journey from Wareham to Poole Quay?

AQA

3 The graph shows the journey of a group of walkers.

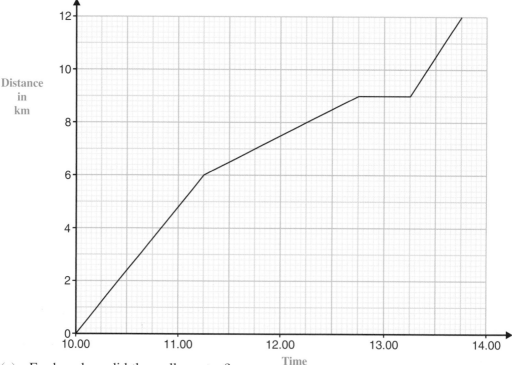

(a) For how long did the walkers stop?
(b) What was the speed for the first part of the journey?
(c) The slowest part of the journey was across boggy ground.
How far did they walk across the boggy ground?
(d) What was the average speed for the whole journey?

AQA

4 This diagram shows the speed-time graph of a local train on a journey between station *A* and station *B*.

(a) Calculate the acceleration of the train at the start of the journey.

(b) How far is it between station *A* and station *B*?

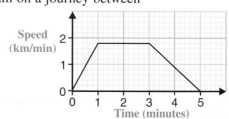

Inequalities

What you need to know

- **Inequalities** can be described using words or numbers and symbols.

Sign	Meaning
<	is less than
≤	is less than or equal to

Sign	Meaning
>	is greater than
≥	is greater than or equal to

- Inequalities can be shown on a **number line**.

  Eg 1 This diagram shows the inequality: $-2 < x \leq 3$

  -3 -2 -1 0 1 2 3 4

  The circle is: **filled** if the inequality is **included** (i.e. ≤ or ≥),
  not filled if the inequality is **not included** (i.e. < or >).

- **Solving inequalities** means finding the values of x which make the inequality true.

  The same rules for equations can be applied to inequalities, with one exception:
  When you **multiply** (or **divide**) both sides of an inequality by a negative number the inequality is reversed. For example, if $-3x < 6$ then $x > -2$.

  Eg 2 Solve these inequalities.

  (a) $7a \geq a + 9$
  $6a \geq 9$
  $a \geq 1.5$

  (b) $-3x < 6$
  $x > -2$

  Divide both sides by -3.
  Because we are dividing by a negative number the inequality is reversed.

  Eg 3 Find the integer values of n for which $-1 \leq 2n + 3 < 7$.
  $-1 \leq 2n + 3 < 7$
  $-4 \leq 2n < 4$
  $-2 \leq n < 2$

  Integer values which satisfy the inequality $-1 \leq 2n + 3 < 7$ are: $-2, -1, 0, 1$

- Inequalities can be shown on a graph. A line divides the graph into two **regions**.

  To show an inequality on a graph: Replace the inequality by '=' and draw the line.
  For > and < the line is **broken**. For ≥ and ≤ the line is **solid**.
  Test a point on each side of the line to see whether its coordinates satisfy the inequality.
  Label the required region.

Eg 4 Show the region which satisfies these inequalities:
$y < 3$, $1 < x < 4$ and $2y > x$.

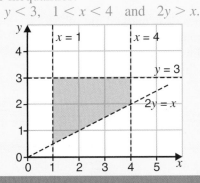

Eg 5 Use inequalities to describe the shaded region in this diagram.

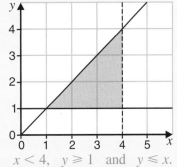

$x < 4$, $y \geq 1$ and $y \leq x$.

1 Solve these inequalities.
  (a) $5x > 15$
  (b) $x + 3 \geqslant 1$
  (c) $2x \leqslant 6 - x$
  (d) $3 - 2x > 7$

2 Draw number lines to show each of these inequalities.
  (a) $x \geqslant -2$
  (b) $\frac{x}{3} < -1$
  (c) $-1 < x \leqslant 3$
  (d) $x \leqslant -1$ **and** $x > 3$

3 List the values of n, where n is an integer such that:
  (a) $-2 \leqslant 2n < 6$
  (b) $-3 < n - 3 \leqslant -1$
  (c) $-5 \leqslant 2n - 3 < 1$

4 Solve the inequalities.
  (a) $2x - 5 > x + 2$
  (b) $-9 < 5x + 1 \leqslant 6$

5 Solve the inequality $x + 20 < 12 - 3x$.
  AQA

6 Solve the inequality $3(x - 2) < x + 7$.
  AQA

7 Match each of the inequalities to its **unshaded** region.
  1 $x + y < 2$
  2 $y > 2$
  3 $y > x$
  4 $x < 2$

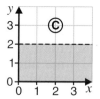 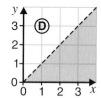

8 Draw and label axes for both x and y from 0 to 5.
  (a) On your diagram draw and label the lines $x = 1$ and $x + y = 4$.
  (b) Show clearly on the diagram the single region that is satisfied by all of these inequalities.
  $y \geqslant 0$ $x \geqslant 1$ $x + y \leqslant 4$.   Label this region R.
  AQA

9 (a) Draw and label axes for x from -1 to 6 and for y from -2 to 6.
      On your diagram draw and label the following lines. $y = 2x$ and $x + y = 5$
  (b) Show clearly the single region that is satisfied by **all** of these inequalities.
      $x + y \leqslant 5$ $y \geqslant 2x$ $x \geqslant 0$.   Label this region R.
  AQA

10 Write down three inequalities which describe the shaded region.

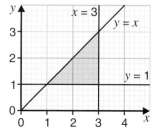

  AQA

11 (a) x is an integer such that $-4 \leqslant x < 2$.
      (i) Make a list of all the possible values of x.
      (ii) What is the largest possible value of x^2?
  (b) Every week Rucci has a test in Mathematics. It is marked out of 20.
      Rucci has always scored at least half the marks available.
      She has never quite managed to score full marks.
      Using x to represent Rucci's marks, write this information in the form of two inequalities.
  AQA

12 (a) Solve each of the following inequalities. (i) $5x - 4 \leqslant 2x + 8$ (ii) $2(2x - 1) > 6$
  (b) Write down the whole number values of x which satisfy both of the above inequalities simultaneously.
  AQA

13 Solve the following inequalities. (a) $2 > x - 4$ (b) $2(x + 3) > 3(2 - x)$ AQA

What you need to know

- The graph of a **quadratic function** is a smooth curve and is called a **parabola**.

- The general equation of a **quadratic function** is $y = ax^2 + bx + c$, where a cannot be zero. The graph of a quadratic function is symmetrical and has a **maximum** or **minimum** value. For example:

  $y = 5 - x^2$ has a **maximum value** and $y = x^2 + 2x - 3$ has a **minimum value**.

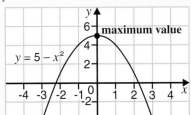
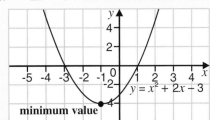

- The general form of a **cubic function** is $y = ax^3 + bx^2 + cx + d$, where a cannot be zero.

- The graph of the **reciprocal function** is of the form $y = \frac{a}{x}$, where x cannot be equal to zero.

- The graph of the **exponential function** is of the form $y = a^x$.

- The graph of a **circle**, centre $(0, 0)$, is of the form $x^2 + y^2 = r^2$, where r is the radius of the circle.

- You should be able to draw the graph of a function by plotting values.

- Be able to use the graphs of functions to solve equations.
  This may include drawing two graphs and looking for points of intersection.

  Eg 1 You are given the graph of $y = x^2 - 4$.
  Use the graph to solve the equations:

  (a) $x^2 - 4 = 0$,
  (b) $x^2 - 3x - 4 = 0$.

  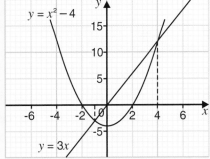

  (a) To solve $x^2 - 4 = 0$, read the values of x, at the points where the graph of $y = x^2 - 4$ crosses the x axis ($y = 0$).
  $x = -2$ and $x = 2$.

  (b) To solve $x^2 - 3x - 4 = 0$,
  rearrange $x^2 - 3x - 4 = 0$ to give $x^2 - 4 = 3x$.
  Draw the graph of $y = 3x$ on the same diagram.
  To solve $x^2 - 3x - 4 = 0$, read the values of x.
  Where the two graphs intersect.
  $x = -1$ and $x = 4$.

- You should be able to identify and sketch the graphs of functions. For example:

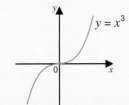
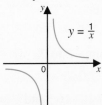
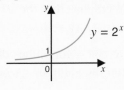
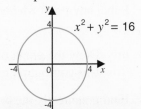

1 Match these equations to their graphs.

 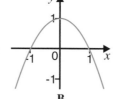 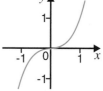 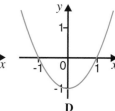

1 $y = 1 - x^2$

2 $y = x^3$

3 $y = x^2 - 1$

4 $y = 1 - 2x$

A   B   C   D

2 (a) Draw the graph of $y = x^2 - 2$ for values of x from -3 to 3.
   (b) Write down the values of x at the points where the line $y = 3$ crosses your graph.
   (c) Use your graph to solve the equation $x^2 - 2 = 0$.

3 A sky diver jumps from a plane. The table shows the distance he falls, d metres, in t seconds.

t (seconds)	0	0.5	1.5	2.5	3.5
d (metres)	0	1	11	31	61

   (a) Plot these points and join them with a smooth curve.
   (b) Use your graph to find how many seconds he takes to fall 50 m.
   (c) Use your graph to estimate how far he has fallen after 4 seconds.   AQA

4 (a) Copy and complete the table of values for $y = x^2 - 4x + 2$.

x	-1	0	1	2	3	4
y			-1		-1	2

   (b) Draw the graph of $y = x^2 - 4x + 2$ for values of x from -1 to 4.
   (c) Hence, solve the equation $x^2 - 4x + 2 = 0$.   AQA

5 (a) Draw the graph of $y = 5x - x^2$ for $-1 \le x \le 6$.
   (b) Use your graph to solve the equation   (i) $5x - x^2 = 0$,   (ii) $5x - x^2 = 3$.
   (c) Find, from your graph, the value of x for which y is a maximum.
        Hence, calculate the maximum value of y.

6 (a) Draw the graph of $y = 2x^2 - 3x + 2$ for values of x from -2 to 3.
   (b) Explain how the graph shows that there are no values of x for which $2x^2 - 3x + 2 = 0$.
   (c) State the minimum value of y.

7 (a) Using the same axes, draw the graphs with equations $y = 3x$ and $y = x^2 + 1$.
   (b) Explain how you can use these graphs to solve the equation $x^2 - 3x + 1 = 0$.
   (c) Hence, solve the equation $x^2 - 3x + 1 = 0$.

8 Draw the graph of $y = x^2 + x - 5$ for values of x between -4 and $+4$.
   By drawing an appropriate linear graph on the same diagram, write down the
   solutions of $x^2 - x - 8 = 0$.

9 (a) Draw the graph of $y = x^3 - x$ for $-3 \le x \le 3$.
   (b) Use your graph to find the value of x when $y = 10$.

10 On separate diagrams, sketch the graphs of these equations.
    Label any point where the graphs cross the x or y axes.
    (a) $y = -x^3$ (b) $xy = 4$ (c) $x^2 + y^2 = 9$

11 (a) Draw the graph of $y = 4^x$ for values of x from -2 to 2.
    (b) Use your graph to find the value of x when $y = 8$.

12 Find graphically the points of intersection of $x^2 + y^2 = 16$ and $2y = x - 1$.

Quadratic Equations

What you need to know

- Brackets, such as $(x + 2)(x + 3)$, can be multiplied out using the **diagram method**, or by **expanding**.

Eg 1 Multiply out $(x + 2)(x + 3)$.

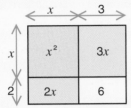

$$(x + 2)(x + 3) = x^2 + 3x + 2x + 6$$
$$= x^2 + 5x + 6$$

Eg 2 Expand $(x - 3)(2x + 1)$.

1. $x \times 2x = 2x^2$
2. $x \times 1 = x$
3. $-3 \times 2x = -6x$
4. $-3 \times 1 = -3$

$$(x - 3)(2x + 1) = 2x^2 + x - 6x - 3$$
$$= 2x^2 - 5x - 3$$

- **Factorising** is the opposite operation to removing brackets.

Eg 3 Factorise the following.

(a) $x^2 + 3x = x(x + 3)$

(b) $2x^2 - 8 = 2(x^2 - 4)$
$$= 2(x - 2)(x + 2)$$

(c) $x^2 + 2x - 15 = (x + 5)(x - 3)$

> When factorising, work logically.
> 1. Does the expression have a **common factor**?
> 2. Is the expression a **difference of two squares**?
> $$a^2 - b^2 = (a - b)(a + b)$$
> 3. Will the expression factorise into **two brackets**?

- Some **quadratic equations** can be solved by factorising.

Eg 4 Solve these equations.

(a) $x^2 - 5x = 0$
$x(x - 5) = 0$
$x = 0$ or $x = 5$

(b) $m^2 + m - 6 = 0$
$(m - 2)(m + 3) = 0$
$m = 2$ or $m = -3$

(c) $2a^2 - 5a - 3 = 0$
$(2a + 1)(a - 3) = 0$
$a = -\frac{1}{2}$ or $a = 3$

- The general form for a **quadratic equation** is $ax^2 + bx + c = 0$ where a cannot be zero.

- The solutions to a quadratic equation can be found using the **quadratic formula**.

> If $ax^2 + bx + c = 0$ and $a \neq 0$ then $x = \dfrac{-b \pm \sqrt{b^2 - 4ac}}{2a}$

Eg 5 Solve $x^2 - 3x - 2 = 0$.

$$x = \frac{-(-3) \pm \sqrt{(-3)^2 - 4(1)(-2)}}{2(1)}$$

$$x = \frac{3 \pm \sqrt{17}}{2}$$

$x = -0.56$ or $x = 3.56$, correct to two decimal places.

> Substitute: $a = 1$, $b = -3$ and $c = -2$,
> into $x = \dfrac{-b \pm \sqrt{b^2 - 4ac}}{2a}$

- Quadratic expressions, such as $x^2 + 8x + 20$, can be written in the form $(x + a)^2 + b$, where a and b are integers.

> In **completed square form**, $(x + a)^2 + b$:
> the value of a is half the coefficient of x, the
> value of b is found by subtracting the value of a^2
> from the constant term of the original expression.

Eg 6 $x^2 + 8x + 20 = (x + a)^2 + b$

$a = \frac{1}{2}(8) = 4$

$b = 20 - 4^2 = 4$

$x^2 + 8x + 20 = (x + 4)^2 + 4$

- Quadratic equations can be solved by **completing the square**.

Eg 7 Solve $x^2 + 4x = 5$.

$(x + 2)^2 - 4 = 5$

$(x + 2)^2 = 9$

$x + 2 = \pm 3$

$x + 2 = 3$ or $x + 2 = -3$

$x = 1$ or $x = -5$

> Write the left-hand side (LHS) of the equation in the form $(x + a)^2 + b$ by completing the square.
> $x^2 + 4x = (x + 2)^2 - 4$

- You should be able to form and solve quadratic equations.

Exercise 26

1 Multiply out and simplify.
 (a) $x(x - 7)$ (b) $(x - 2)(x + 5)$ (c) $(2x - 1)(x + 3)$ (d) $(3x + 2y)^2$

2 Factorise.
 (a) $x^2 - 6x$ (b) $x^2 + 2x - 15$ (c) $x^2 - 4x + 3$ (d) $x^2 - 9$

3 Solve these equations.
 (a) $x(x + 5) = 0$ (b) $(x - 3)(x + 2) = 0$ (c) $(2x + 3)(x - 1) = 0$

4 (a) Factorise $x^2 - x - 12$.
 (b) Hence, solve the equation $x^2 - x - 12 = 0$.   AQA

5 Solve these equations.
 (a) $x^2 - 3x = 0$ (b) $x^2 - 3x + 2 = 0$ (c) $x^2 + x - 6 = 0$

6 Solve, by factorisation, $x^2 - 2x - 3 = 0$.   AQA

7 Solve the equation $x^2 - 11x + 28 = 0$.

8 Factorise. (a) $2x^2 - 7x - 15$ (b) $x^2 - 25y^2$ AQA

9 (a) Factorise $2x^2 - 5x - 3 = 0$.
 (b) Hence, solve the equation $2x^2 - 5x - 3 = 0$.

10 Solve the equation $3x^2 - x - 2 = 0$.

11 The expression $x^2 + 6x - 5$ can be written in the form $(x + p)^2 + q$.
 Calculate the values of p and q.

12 (a) Write $x^2 - 4x - 8$ in the form $(x + a)^2 + b$.
 (b) Hence, solve the equation $x^2 - 4x - 8 = 0$, correct to 2 decimal places.

13 Solve the equation $x^2 + 3x - 5 = 0$.

14 Solve the equation $x^2 = 5x + 7$, giving your answers correct to 3 significant figures.   AQA

15 Solve the equation $2x^2 - 4x - 3 = 0$.
 Give your answers correct to 2 decimal places.   AQA

16 The area of a rectangle, with dimensions x cm by $(x + 2)$ cm, is 18 cm^2.
 Calculate the value of x, correct to one decimal place.

17 A number, x, is equal to its reciprocal plus $\frac{1}{2}$.
 (a) Show that $2x^2 - x - 2 = 0$.
 (b) Solve the equation $2x^2 - x - 2 = 0$.
 Give your answers to an accuracy of **two** decimal places.   AQA

Simultaneous Equations

What you need to know

- A pair of **simultaneous equations** has the same unknown letters in each equation.

- To solve a pair of simultaneous equations find values for the unknown letters that fit **both** equations.

- Simultaneous equations can be solved either **graphically** or **algebraically**.

- Solving simultaneous equations **graphically** involves:
  drawing the graphs of both equations,
  finding the point(s) where the graphs cross.
  When the graphs of both equations are parallel, the equations have no solution.

  Eg 1 Solve the simultaneous equations $x + 2y = 5$ and $x - 2y = 1$ graphically.

  Draw the graph of $x + 2y = 5$.
  Draw the graph of $x - 2y = 1$.

  The lines cross at the point (3, 1).
  This gives the solution $x = 3$ and $y = 1$.

  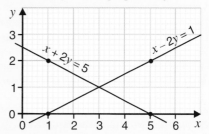

- Solving simultaneous equations **algebraically** involves using either:
  the **elimination** method, or the **substitution** method.

  Eg 2 Solve the simultaneous equations $5x + 2y = 11$ and $3x - 4y = 4$ algebraically.

  $$5x + 2y = 11 \quad \text{A}$$
  $$3x - 4y = 4 \quad \text{B}$$

  A × 2 gives $10x + 4y = 22 \quad$ C
  $ 3x - 4y = 4 \quad$ D

  | To make the number of y's the same we can multiply equation A by 2. |

  C + D gives $13x = 26 \quad$
  $ x = 2$

  | The number of y's is the **same** but the **signs** are **different**. To eliminate the y's the equations must be **added**. |

  Substitute $x = 2$ into. $5x + 2y = 11$.
  $$10 + 2y = 11$$
  $$2y = 1$$
  $$y = 0.5$$

  | You can check the solution by substituting $x = 2$ and $y = 0.5$ into $3x - 4y = 4$. |

  The solution is $x = 2$ and $y = 0.5$.

- You should be able to solve simultaneous equations in which one equation is linear and one is quadratic.

  Eg 3 Solve the simultaneous equations $y = x - 2$ and $x^2 + 3y = 12$.

  Substitute $y = x - 2$ into $x^2 + 3y = 12$.   Using $y = x - 2$.
  $x^2 + 3(x - 2) = 12$ When $x = -6$. When $x = 3$.
  $x^2 + 3x - 18 = 0$ $y = -6 - 2$ $y = 3 - 2$
  $(x + 6)(x - 3) = 0$ $y = -8$ $y = 1$
  $x = -6$ or $x = 3$

  This gives the solution: $x = -6$, $y = -8$ **and** $x = 3$, $y = 1$.

1 The graph of the equation $3y = x + 1$ is drawn on the grid. Copy the diagram.

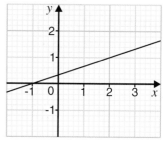

(a) On your diagram, draw the graph of the equation $y = 1 - x$.

(b) Use your graphs to solve the simultaneous equations $y = 1 - x$ and $3y = x + 1$.

AQA

2 (a) On the same axes, draw the graphs of $y + x = 4$ and $y - 3x = 2$ for values of x from -2 to 2.

(b) Hence, solve the simultaneous equations $y + x = 4$ and $y - 3x = 2$.

3 Solve graphically the simultaneous equations $y = 3 - x$ and $y = x - 2$.

4 The sketch shows the graph of $y = 2x - 1$. Copy the diagram.

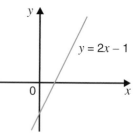

(a) On your diagram, sketch the graph of $y = 2x + 1$.

(b) Explain why the equations $y = 2x - 1$ and $y = 2x + 1$ cannot be solved simultaneously.

5 Solve these simultaneous equations. $6x + y = 15$
$$8x - y = 6$$

AQA

6 Solve the simultaneous equations $x + 3y = 13$ and $4x + 2y = 2$.

7 Solve the simultaneous equations. $2x + y = 2$
$$4x - 3y = 9$$

AQA

8 Heather sold 40 boxes of cards to raise money for charity.
She sold x small boxes at £4 each and y large boxes at £7 each.
She raised £184 altogether.
(a) Write down two equations connecting x and y.
(b) Solve these simultaneous equations to find how many of each size of box she sold.

9 Micro-scooters costs £x each and pogo sticks cost £y each.
2 micro-scooters and 4 pogo sticks cost £65.
1 micro-scooter and 3 pogo sticks cost £40.
(a) Write down two equations connecting x and y.
(b) Solve these simultaneous equations to find the cost of a micro-scooter and a pogo stick.

10 Solve these simultaneous equations. $4x - 3y = 17$ and $6x - 4y = 23$
AQA

11 Solve the simultaneous equations. $4x - 3y = 11$ and $6x + 2y = 10$
AQA

12 Use a graphical method to solve each of these pairs of simultaneous equations.
(a) $y = 4 - 2x$ (b) $y - x = 4$ (c) $y = 2x$
     $y = x^2 - 4$ $y = 6x - x^2$ $x^2 + y^2 = 25$

13 Use an algebraic method to solve the simultaneous equations
$$5y = 2x - 7 \quad \text{and} \quad xy = 6.$$

14 Solve the simultaneous equations.
(a) $y - x = -11$ (b) $y = 3 - x$ (c) $2x + y = 3$
     $x^2 = y + 13$ $x^2 + y^2 = 17$ $y = \dfrac{1}{x}$

Algebraic Methods

What you need to know

- An **identity** is true for all values of x. It is the same expression written in another form.
  For example: $(2x + 3)^2 + (2x + 9)(2x + 5) = 2(4x^2 + 20x + 27)$.

  > To show that an identity is true, either:
  >   start with the LHS and show that it is equal to the RHS, or
  >   start with the RHS and show that it is equal to the LHS.

- **Algebraic fractions** have a numerator and a denominator.

  > To write an algebraic fraction in its **simplest form**:
  >   factorise the numerator and denominator of the fraction, divide
  >   the numerator and denominator by their highest common factor.

  Eg 1 Simplify.

  (a) $\dfrac{2x - 4}{x^2 - 2x} = \dfrac{2(x - 2)}{x(x - 2)} = \dfrac{2}{x}$

  > The same methods used for adding, subtracting, multiplying and dividing numeric fractions can be applied to algebraic fractions.

  (b) $\dfrac{x^2 - 9}{x^2 + 2x - 3} = \dfrac{(x + 3)(x - 3)}{(x + 3)(x - 1)} = \dfrac{(x - 3)}{(x - 1)}$

  (c) $\dfrac{2}{x - 3} - \dfrac{1}{x} = \dfrac{2x - (x - 3)}{x(x - 3)} = \dfrac{x + 3}{x(x - 3)}$

- You should be able to solve equations involving algebraic fractions.

- The solutions to a variety of equations can be found using a process called **iteration**.

  > The process of iteration has three stages.
  > 1. Rearranging an equation to form an **iterative formula**.
  > 2. Choosing a **starting value**, x_1.
  > 3. **Substituting** the starting value, and then values of x_n into the iterative formula. Continuing the process until the required degree of accuracy is obtained.

  Eg 2 Find a solution to the equation $x^2 - 4x - 3 = 0$, correct to 2 decimal places, using iteration.

  Use the iterative formula $x_{n+1} = \sqrt{4x_n + 3}$.

  $$x_1 = 4$$
  $$x_2 = \sqrt{4 \times 4 + 3} = 4.3588\ldots$$
  $$x_3 = \sqrt{4 \times 4.3588\ldots + 3} = 4.5205\ldots$$
  $$x_4 = \sqrt{4 \times 4.5205\ldots + 3} = 4.5915\ldots$$
  $$x_5 = \sqrt{4 \times 4.5915\ldots + 3} = 4.6223\ldots$$
  $$x_6 = \sqrt{4 \times 4.6223\ldots + 3} = 4.6356\ldots$$
  $$x_7 = \sqrt{4 \times 4.6356\ldots + 3} = 4.6414\ldots$$
  $$x_8 = \sqrt{4 \times 4.6414\ldots + 3} = 4.6438\ldots$$
  $$x = 4.64, \text{ correct to 2 d.p.}$$

Trial and improvement is a method used to solve equations. The accuracy of the value of the unknown letter is improved until the required degree of accuracy is obtained.

Eg 3 Use a trial and improvement method to find a solution to the equation $x^3 + x = 40$, correct to one decimal place.

x	$x^3 + x$	Comment
3	$27 + 3 = 30$	Too small
4	$64 + 4 = 68$	Too big
3.5	$42.8... + 3.5 = 46.3...$	Too big
3.3	$35.9... + 3.3 = 39.2...$	Too small
3.35	$37.5... + 3.35 = 40.9...$	Too big

For accuracy to 1 d.p.
check the second decimal place.
The solution lies between
3.3 and 3.35.

$x = 3.3$, correct to 1 d.p.

Exercise 28

1 Expand and simplify $(x + 3)^2 - (x - 3)^2$.

2 Show that $2x(x + y) - (x + y)^2 = x^2 - y^2$.

3 (a) Show that $(3x + 4)^2 - (3x + 2)^2 = 12x + 12$.
   (b) Hence, solve the equation $(3x + 4)^2 - (3x + 2)^2 = (x + 1)(4x - 1)$.   AQA

4 Simplify. (a) $\dfrac{x^2 - 3x}{x}$ (b) $\dfrac{2x^2 - 6x}{4x - 12}$ (c) $\dfrac{x^2 + 2x + 1}{x^2 - 2x - 3}$ (d) $\dfrac{x^2 + x}{x^2 - 1}$

5 Simplify fully the expression $\dfrac{2x - 8}{2x^2 - 7x - 4}$.   AQA

6 Simplify. (a) $\dfrac{1}{x} + \dfrac{1}{2x}$ (b) $\dfrac{2x}{x + 1} + \dfrac{1}{2}$ (c) $\dfrac{1}{x + 2} + \dfrac{2}{2x - 5}$

7 Solve the equation $\dfrac{x}{2} - \dfrac{3}{x + 5} = 1$ correct to 2 decimal places.

8 Solve the equation $\dfrac{2}{2x - 1} - 1 = \dfrac{2}{x + 1}$.

9 Solve the equation $\dfrac{1}{1 - x} - \dfrac{1}{1 + x} = 2$.   AQA

10 (a) (i) Factorise $3p^2 + 16p + 5$.
      (ii) Hence, or otherwise, simplify $\dfrac{p^2 - 25}{3p^2 + 16p + 5}$.

   (b) Solve the equation $\dfrac{2}{x - 8} - \dfrac{1}{x - 3} = \dfrac{1}{x + 2}$.   AQA

11 (a) Expand and simplify $\left(x + \dfrac{1}{x}\right)\left(x + \dfrac{1}{x}\right)$. Write your answer in the form $x^2 + a + \dfrac{b}{x^2}$.

   (b) (i) Factorise $x^2 - 2 + \dfrac{1}{x^2}$.
      (ii) Hence, or otherwise, solve the equation $x^2 - 2 + \dfrac{1}{x^2} = 0$.   AQA

12 The iterative formula $x_{n+1} = \dfrac{3x_n + 10}{2x_n}$ can be used to solve a quadratic equation.

   (a) Write down the quadratic equation in the form $ax^2 + bx + c = 0$.
   (b) Use the iterative formula with $x_1 = 2$ to find the positive solution of the equation.
      Give your answer to an accuracy of one decimal place. You **must** show your iterations.
           AQA

13 Use a trial and improvement method to solve the equation $x^3 + x^2 = 300$.
Show all your trials. Give your answer correct to one decimal place.

Transforming Graphs

What you need to know

- **Function notation** is a way of expressing a relationship between two variables.
  For example

  Input, x → | function, f
e.g. *cube* | → Output, $f(x)$

  This notation gives $f(x) = x^3$

  $f(x)$ means 'a function of x'.
  In the example above, $f(x) = x^3$ is equivalent to the equation $y = x^3$ where $y = f(x)$.

- **Transformations**, such as **translations** and **stretches**, can be used to change the position and size of a graph.
  The equation of the transformed (new) graph is related to the equation of the original graph.

  In general

Original	New graph	Transformation	Note
$y = f(x)$	$y = f(x) + a$	**translation**, vector $\begin{pmatrix} 0 \\ a \end{pmatrix}$.	If a is **positive**, curve moves a units **up**. If a is **negative**, curve moves a units **down**.
$y = f(x)$	$y = f(x + a)$	**translation**, vector $\begin{pmatrix} -a \\ 0 \end{pmatrix}$.	If a is **positive**, curve moves a units **left**. If a is **negative**, curve moves a units **right**.
$y = f(x)$	$y = af(x)$	**stretch**, from the x axis, parallel to the y axis, scale factor a.	The y coordinates on the graph of $y = f(x)$ are **multiplied** by a.
$y = f(x)$	$y = f(ax)$	**stretch**, from the y axis, parallel to the x axis, scale factor $\frac{1}{a}$.	The x coordinates on the graph of $y = f(x)$ are **divided** by a.
$y = f(x)$	$y = -f(x)$	**reflection** in the x axis.	The y coordinates on the graph of $y = f(x)$ **change signs**.
$y = f(x)$	$y = f(-x)$	**reflection** in the y axis.	The x coordinates on the graph of $y = f(x)$ **change signs**.

Eg 1 The diagram shows the graph of $y = f(x)$.
Draw the graphs of $y = f(x - 2)$ and $y = f(x) - 2$.

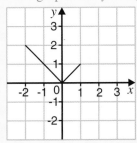 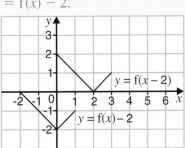

- You should be able to draw a suitable graph to find the relationship between a given set of variables.
  Linear functions have straight line graphs, such as $y = ax + b$.
  From the graph of y **against** x, the gradient $= a$ and the y-intercept $= b$.
  Non-linear functions, such as $y = ax^n + b$, can be written as the linear function $y = az + b$ by substituting $z = x^n$.
  From the graph of y **against** x^n, the gradient $= a$ and the y-intercept $= b$.

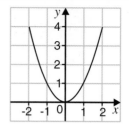

1 The graph of $y = f(x)$ for $-2 \leqslant x \leqslant 2$ is shown.
On separate diagrams draw the graphs of $y = f(x)$ and:

(a) $y = f(x + 2)$,   (b) $y = f(x) + 2$,

(c) $y = 2f(x)$,   (d) $y = -f(x)$.

2 The diagram shows a sketch of the graph of $y = f(x)$ for $-2 \leqslant x \leqslant 2$.
Each of the graphs below is a transformation of this graph.
Write down the equation of each graph.

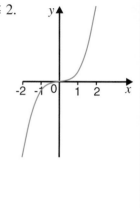

(a) 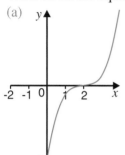   (b) 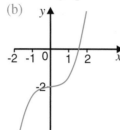   (c)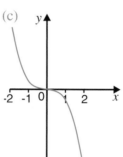

3 This is the graph of $y = \cos x$.

Below are shown three transformations
of the graph $y = \cos x$.
Give the equation of each graph.

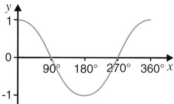

(a) 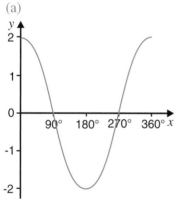   (b) 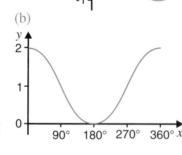   (c)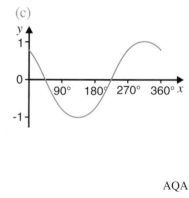

AQA

4 The table shows the results of an experiment.

x	5	12	20	24
y	5.5	6.9	8.5	9.3

(a) Draw a graph to show these results.

(b) The results are connected by the equation $y = ax + b$.
Find this equation and hence find the value of x when $y = 20$.

5 James has the following set of experimental results for values of x and y.

x	1	2.5	3	4	6	10
y	11.5	7.0	6.5	6.0	5.2	4.75

(a) Calculate the values of $\frac{1}{x}$ and plot the graph of y against $\frac{1}{x}$.

He knows that x and y are connected by the formula $y = \frac{a}{x} + b$, where a and b are constants.

(b) **Use your graph** to estimate the values of a and b.

AQA

Algebra
Non-calculator Paper

Do not use a calculator for this exercise.

1   Simplify   (a) $7x - 5x + 3x$,   (b) $a - 3b + 2a - b$,   (c) $3 \times m \times m$.

2   (a)   On graph paper, plot the points $A(-3, -2)$ and $B(1, 4)$.
      (b)   What are the coordinates of the midpoint of the line segment AB?

3   (a)   What is the next term in this sequence?   2,   9,   16,   23,   …
      (b)   Will the 50th term in the sequence be an odd number or an even number?
           Give a reason for your answer.

4   Here is a flow diagram.

      (a)   What is the output when the input is 3?
      (b)   What is the input when the output is -21?   AQA

5   Find the value of $3x + y^3$ when $x = -1$ and $y = -2$.

6   Hannah is x years old.
      (a)   Her sister Louisa is 3 years younger than Hannah.
           Write an expression, in terms of x, for Louisa's age.
      (b)   Their mother is four times as old as Hannah.
           Write an expression, in terms of x, for their mother's age.
      (c)   The total of their ages is 45 years.
           By forming an equation in x, find their ages.

7   Given that $s = 2t^3$,   find the value of t when $s = 250$.

8 $y = \frac{4}{5}(9 - x)$.   Find the value of x when $y = 6$.

9   (a)   Factorise   (i) $3a - 6$,   (ii) $k^2 - 2k$.
      (b)   Multiply out   (i) $m(m - 4)$,   (ii) $3x(x + 5)$.

      (c)   Solve   (i) $\frac{3x + 5}{2} = 7$,   (ii) $3 - 4x = x + 8$,   (iii) $3(2x + 1) = 6$.

10   (a)   On the same diagram draw the graphs $2y = x + 4$ and $y = \frac{1}{2}x + 1$.
      (b)   What do you notice about the two lines you have drawn?

11   (a)   Solve $4x - 8 < 12$ and show the solution on a number line.
      (b)   List all the values of n, where n is an integer, such that $-3 < 2x + 1 \leqslant 3$.
      (c)   Solve the simultaneous equations $5x - y = 7$ and $3x + y = 1$.

12   (a)   A sequence begins: -2,   1,   4,   7,   10,   …
           Write, in terms of n, the nth term of the sequence.
      (b)   Make x the subject of the formula $y = 2x - 5$.

13   (a)   Copy and complete the table of values for $y = x^2 - 2x + 1$.

x	-1	0	1	2	3
y		1	0		4

      (b)   Draw the graph of $y = x^2 - 2x + 1$ for values of x from -1 to 3.
      (c)   Use your graph to solve the equations
           (i) $x^2 - 2x + 1 = 0$,   (ii) $x^2 - 2x + 1 = 2$.

14 (a) Work out the value of $x^2 - 5x + 6$ when $x = -2$.
  (b) (i) Factorise $x^2 - 5x + 6$.
    (ii) Hence, solve the equation $x^2 - 5x + 6 = 0$.

15 (a) Find the gradients of these lines.

(i) 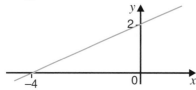   (ii)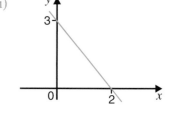

  (b) The equation of a different line is $4y - 3x = 8$.
    What is the gradient of this line?

16 (a) Simplify, giving your answer in index form. (i) $\dfrac{a^8}{a^4}$ (ii) $(a^2)^3$
  (b) Make q the subject of the formula $p = q^2 + r$.

AQA

17 (a) Solve the inequality $3x - 5 \leqslant 16$
  (b) Multiply out and simplify $(y - 7)^2$.
  (c) Simplify $2x^4 \times 3x^3$.
  (d) Factorise $p^2 + p - 12$.

AQA

18 Simplify. (a) $(3x^2y)^3$ (b) $\dfrac{3a^2b^3 \times 4a^5b}{6a^3b^2}$

19 Factorise the following. (a) $3x^2 - 75$ (b) $3x^2 - 8x + 5$

20 On separate diagrams, sketch the graphs of:
  (a) $x^2 + y^2 = 9$,   (b) $y = 2^x$, for $-3 \leqslant x \leqslant 3$.

21 The length of a rectangle is x centimetres.
  The perimeter of the rectangle is 38 cm and its area is 78 cm².
  Use this information to form an equation in x and solve it to find the length of the rectangle.

AQA

22 (a) Show that $(2x + 3)^2 - (2x + 1)^2 = 8(x + 1)$.
  (b) Hence, solve the equation $(2x + 3)^2 - (2x + 1)^2 = x^2 - 1$.

23 (a) Simplify the expression $\dfrac{2x^2 - 8}{x + 2}$.
  (b) You are given the equation $a - c = ac$.
    Rearrange this equation to give a formula for a in terms of c.
  (c) You are given that $(3x - b)^2 = ax^2 - 12x + c$, for all values of x.
    Find the values of a, b and c.

AQA

24 Rearrange the equation $x = \dfrac{y - 5}{3 - y}$ to make y the subject.

25 Find the equation of the line which is perpendicular to $2y + x = 6$ and goes through the point $(4, 1)$.

26 The sketch shows the graph $y = x^3$.
  Sketch the graphs indicated.

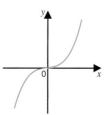

  p is a positive integer greater than 1.

  (a) $y = x^3 - p$ (b) $y = (x + p)^3$ (c) $y = \dfrac{x^3}{p}$

AQA

27 Solve the simultaneous equations $y = 2x + 1$ and $xy = 3$.

28 You are given that $\dfrac{1}{x + 1} - \dfrac{3}{2x - 1} = 2$.
  Show that $4x^2 + 3x + 2 = 0$.

You may use a calculator for this exercise.

1 The graph shows the journey of a cyclist from Halton to Kendal.
The distance from Halton to Kendal is 30 miles.

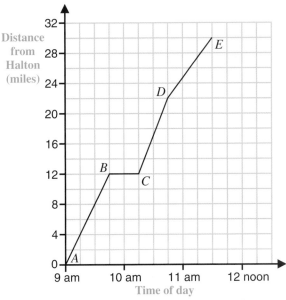

(a) For how long did the cyclist stop during the journey?

(b) What was the average speed for the part of the journey from A to B?

(c) On which part of the journey was the cyclist travelling at his fastest speed?
Explain clearly how you got your answer.

(d) The cyclist stayed in Kendal for 2 hours.
He then returned to Halton, without stopping, at an average speed of 12 miles per hour.
Calculate the time he arrived back in Halton.   AQA

2 (a) This rule is used to produce a sequence of numbers.

> MULTIPLY THE LAST NUMBER BY 3 AND SUBTRACT 1.

The second number in the sequence is 20. What is the first number?

(b) Another sequence begins   2,   5,   8,   11,   …

(i) One number in the sequence is x.
Write, in terms of x, the next number in the sequence.

(ii) Write, in terms of n, the n th term of the sequence.   AQA

3 A glass of milk costs x pence.
A milk shake costs 45 pence more than a glass of milk.

(a) Write an expression for the cost of a milk shake.

(b) Lou has to pay £4.55 for 3 milk shakes and a glass of milk.
By forming an equation, find the price of a glass of milk.

4 Use trial and improvement to find a solution to the equation $x^3 - 3x = 9$.
Give your answer correct to 1 decimal place.

5 (a) Solve.   (i) $5t + 3 = -1 + t$ (ii) $3 - x = 4(x + 1)$

(b) Multiply out and simplify   (i) $2(5x - 3) - 3(x - 1)$,   (ii) $(y + 4)(y - 5)$.

(c) Simplify   (i) $m^8 \div m^2$,   (ii) $n^2 \times n^3$.

6 (a) Write down the equations of the lines labelled **A**, **B** and **C** in the diagram.

(b) Write down three inequalities to describe the shaded region.

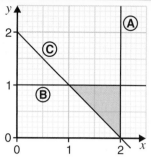

7 (a) List all the values of n, where n is an integer, such that $-2 \leqslant n - 3 < 1$.

(b) Solve the simultaneous equations $x + 4y = 15$ and $3x - 2y = 10$.

(c) Factorise $xy - y^2$.

(d) Solve the equation $x^2 - 7x + 10 = 0$.

AQA

8 You are given the formula $y = \sqrt{\dfrac{2x}{5}}$.

(a) Find the value of y when $x = 3.6 \times 10^{-4}$.

(b) Rearrange the formula to give x in terms of y.

9 Solve the equation $\dfrac{5x - 3}{3} - \dfrac{1 + 2x}{2} = 3$.

10 x is a number such that $x(x + 1)(x - 1) = 20$.

(a) Find the two consecutive whole numbers between which x must lie.

(b) Use the method of trial and improvement to find the solution correct to 3 significant figures.

AQA

11 Solve the equation $x^2 + 2x - 5 = 0$.

Give your answers correct to two decimal places.

12 The volumes of these cuboids are the same.

(a) Show that $3x^2 + 2x - 12 = 0$.

(b) By solving the equation $3x^2 + 2x - 12 = 0$, find the value of x.

Give your answer correct to one decimal place.

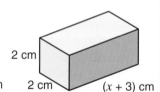

13 (a) Draw the graph of $y = 3 - 2x^2$ for values of x between -2 and 2.

(b) Use your graph to solve these equations. (i) $3 - 2x^2 = 0$ (ii) $3 - 2x^2 = x$

(c) A student wants to use the graph to solve the equation $2x^2 - x - 2 = 0$.

What is the equation of the line that needs to be drawn?

14 Solve the equation $2x^2 = 5x - 1$.

15 You are given that $y = 16x^n$ and that $y = 2$ when $x = 16$. Find the value of n. AQA

16 (a) Simplify fully the expression $\dfrac{2x^2 - 18}{2x^2 - 4x - 6}$.

(b) You are given the equation $xy = x + y$.

Rearrange the equation to give a formula for y in terms of x.

(c) You are given that $(2x - b)^2 - 5 = ax^2 - 4x + c$ for all values of x.

Find the values of a, b and c.

17 Solve the simultaneous equations $x + y = 4$ and $y = x^2 + 2x$.

18 (a) You are given that $(x + p)^2 + q = x^2 - 4x + 7$.

Find the values of p and q.

(b) Rearrange the equation $y(x - 3) = 1 + 2x$ to give a formula for x in terms of y.

19 Solve the equation $\dfrac{2}{x - 1} - \dfrac{1}{x + 1} = 1$.

What you need to know

- Types and names of angles.

Acute angle	Right angle	Obtuse angle	Reflex angle
$0° < a < 90°$	$a = 90°$	$90° < a < 180°$	$180° < a < 360°$

- Angle properties.

Angles at a point	Complementary angles	Supplementary angles	Vertically opposite angles
		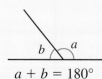	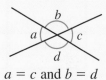
$a + b + c = 360°$	$x + y = 90°$	$a + b = 180°$	$a = c$ and $b = d$

- A straight line joining two points is called a **line segment**.

- Lines which meet at right angles are **perpendicular** to each other.

- Lines which never meet and are always the same distance apart are **parallel**.

- When two parallel lines are crossed by a **transversal** the following pairs of angles are formed.

Corresponding angles	Alternate angles	Allied angles
$a = c$	$b = c$	$b + d = 180°$

Arrowheads are used to show that lines are **parallel**.

- A **triangle** is a shape made by three straight sides.

- Triangles can be: **acute-angled** (all angles less than 90°),
  obtuse-angled (one angle greater than 90°),
  right-angled (one angle equal to 90°).

- The sum of the angles in a triangle is 180°.
  $a + b + c = 180°$

- The exterior angle is equal to the sum of the two opposite interior angles. $a + b = d$

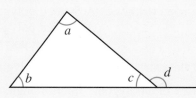

- Types of triangle:

Scalene	Isosceles	Equilateral

A **sketch** is used when an accurate drawing is not required. Dashes across lines show sides that are equal in length. Equal angles are marked using arcs.

- A two-dimensional shape has **line symmetry** if the line divides the shape so that one side fits exactly over the other.

- A two-dimensional shape has **rotational symmetry** if it fits into a copy of its outline as it is rotated through 360°.

- A shape is only described as having rotational symmetry if the order of rotational symmetry is 2 or more.

Order of rotational symmetry 5

- The number of times a shape fits into its outline in a single turn is the **order of rotational symmetry**.

- A **quadrilateral** is a shape made by four straight lines.

- The sum of the angles in a quadrilateral is 360°.

- Facts about these special quadrilaterals:

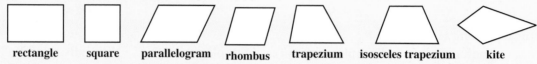

rectangle   square   parallelogram   rhombus   trapezium   isosceles trapezium   kite

Quadrilateral	Sides	Angles	Diagonals	Line symmetry	Order of rotational symmetry
Rectangle	Opposite sides equal and parallel	All 90°	Bisect each other	2	2
Square	4 equal sides, opposite sides parallel	All 90°	Bisect each other at 90°	4	4
Parallelogram	Opposite sides equal and parallel	Opposite angles equal	Bisect each other	0	2
Rhombus	4 equal sides, opposite sides parallel	Opposite angles equal	Bisect each other at 90°	2	2
Trapezium	1 pair of parallel sides				
Isosceles trapezium	1 pair of parallel sides, non-parallel sides equal	2 pairs of equal angles	Equal in length	1	1*
Kite	2 pairs of adjacent sides equal	1 pair of opposite angles equal	One bisects the other at 90°	1	1*

*A shape is only described as having rotational symmetry if the order of rotational symmetry is 2 or more.

- A **polygon** is a many-sided shape made by straight lines.

- A polygon with all sides equal and all angles equal is called a **regular polygon**.

- Shapes you need to know: A 5-sided polygon is called a **pentagon**.
                                              A 6-sided polygon is called a **hexagon**.
                                              An 8-sided polygon is called an **octagon**.

- The sum of the exterior angles of any polygon is 360°.

- At each vertex of a polygon: interior angle + exterior angle = 180°

- The sum of the interior angles of an n-sided polygon is given by:
    $(n - 2) \times 180°$

- For a regular n-sided polygon: exterior angle $= \dfrac{360°}{n}$

- A shape will **tessellate** if it covers a surface without overlapping and leaves no gaps.

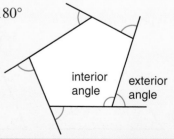

interior angle   exterior angle

1 Find the size of the lettered angles. Give a reason for each answer.

(a)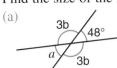

(b)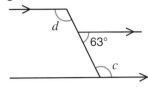

(c)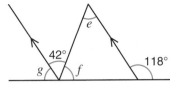

2 Find the size of the lettered angles.

(a)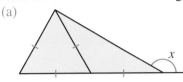

(b)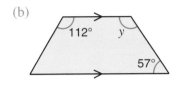

(c)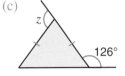

3 (a) Copy the diagram.
Shade two more squares so that the final diagram has line symmetry only.
(b) Make another copy of the diagram.
Shade two more squares so that the final diagram
has rotational symmetry only.

4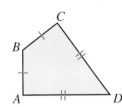

The diagram shows a quadrilateral *ABCD*.
$AB = BC$ and $CD = DA$.

Angle $ADC = 36°$ and   angle $BCD = 105°$.
Work out the size of angle *ABC*.

5 In the figure,
$AB = AD$ and $BD = BC$.
AB is parallel to *DC*   and   angle $DBC = 62°$.

Explain why *BC* is not parallel to *AD*.

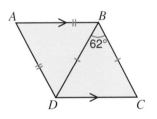

AQA

6 (a) A regular polygon has 9 sides.
Find the size of an interior angle.
(b) A regular polygon has an exterior angle of 20°.
Show that the sum of the interior angles is 2880°.

7 (a) In the diagram the lines *PQ*, *XR* and *TS* are parallel.
Angle $QRS = 65°$ and   angle $RST = 156°$.

Work out the size of angle *PQR*.

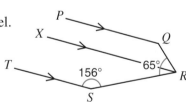

(b)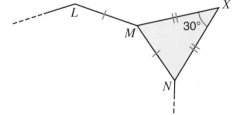

LM and *MN* are two sides of a regular
10-sided polygon.
MNX is an isosceles triangle with $MX = XN$.
Angle $MXN = 30°$.

Work out the size of the obtuse angle *LMX*.

AQA

8 *ABC* is an equilateral triangle.
AC and *CD* are two sides of a regular polygon
and *BC* and *CD* are two sides of an identical polygon.
How many sides has each of these polygons?

Circle Properties

What you need to know

- A **circle** is the shape drawn by keeping a pencil the same distance from a fixed point on a piece of paper.

- You should know the meaning of the words shown on the diagrams below.

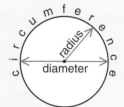 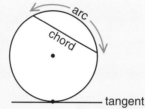 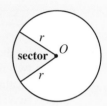

- The vertices of a **cyclic quadrilateral** lie on the circumference of a circle.

- **Circle properties**

 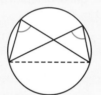 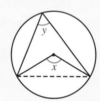

The angle in a semi-circle is a right angle.

Angles in the same segment are equal.

$x = 2y$
The angle at the centre is twice the angle at the circumference.

$p + r = 180°$ and $q + s = 180°$
Opposite angles of a cyclic quadrilateral are supplementary.

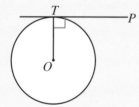 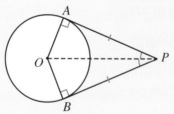 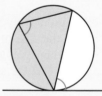

A tangent is perpendicular to the radius at the point of contact.

Tangents drawn to a circle from the same point are equal.

The angle between a tangent and a chord is equal to any angle in the alternate (opposite) segment.

- You should be able to use circle properties to solve problems.

O is the centre of the circle. Find the marked angles.
$a = 43°$ (angles in the same segment)
$b = 2 \times 43°$ ($\angle$ at centre = twice $\angle$ at circum.)
$b = 86°$
$c = 180° - 43°$ (opp. $\angle$'s of a cyclic quad)
$c = 137°$

You should be able to prove that:

- the angle at the centre is twice the angle at the circumference,
- the angle in a semi-circle is a right angle,
- angles in the same segment are equal,
- opposite angles of a cyclic quadrilateral are supplementary,
- the angle between a tangent and a chord is equal to any angle in the alternate segment.

① *O* is the centre of the circle.
Work out the size of the lettered angles. Give a reason for each of your answers.

(a)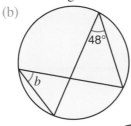
(b)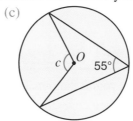
(c)
(d)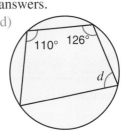

② *O* is the centre of the circle.
Work out the size of angle *x*.

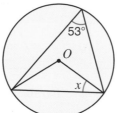

③ (a) *AB* is a tangent to the circle, centre *O*. Angle *OAB* = 28°.
Find the size of angle *BCO*.

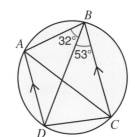

(b)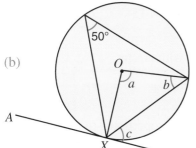

AXB is a tangent to the circle, centre *O*.
Find the size of the angles marked *a*, *b* and *c*.

④ *ABCD* is a cyclic quadrilateral. *AD* is parallel to *BC*.
∠*ABD* = 32° and ∠*CBD* = 53°.
Find   (a) angle *ADB*,   (b) angle *ACD*,
         (c) angle *ADC*,   (d) angle *BAD*.

⑤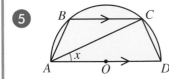

The diagram shows a semi-circle, centre *O*.
Angle *CAD* = *x*° and *BC* is parallel to *AD*.
Find, in terms of *x*, angle *ABC*.

⑥ *A*, *B* and *C* are points on the circumference of a circle, centre *O*.
D is a point on *BC* such that *AOD* is a straight line.
PA is a tangent to the circle at *A*. Calculate angles *x*, *y* and *z*.

AQA

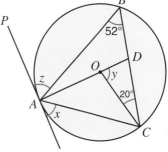

⑦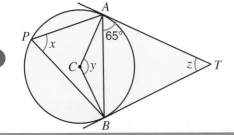

AT and *BT* are tangents to the circle, centre *C*.
P is a point on the circumference, as shown.
Angle *BAT* = 65°.

Calculate the size of   (a) *x*,   (b) *y*,   (c) *z*.   AQA

Perimeters and Areas

What you need to know

- **Perimeter** is the distance round the outside of a shape.
- **Area** is the amount of surface covered by a shape.
- You should be able to use these formulae to find areas.

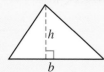 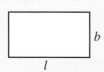 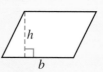 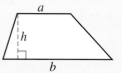

Triangle: $A = \frac{1}{2} \times b \times h$ **Rectangle:** $A = lb$ **Parallelogram:** $A = bh$ **Trapezium:** $A = \frac{1}{2}(a + b)h$

Eg 1 Calculate the area of this triangle.

$A = \frac{1}{2} \times b \times h$

$A = \frac{1}{2} \times 6 \times 4 \, cm^2$

$A = 12 \, cm^2$

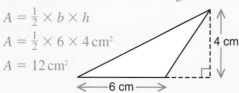

4 cm

6 cm

Eg 2 Find the area of this trapezium.

$A = \frac{1}{2}(a + b)h$

$A = \frac{1}{2}(6 + 9)5$

$A = \frac{1}{2} \times 15 \times 5$

$A = 37.5 \, cm^2$

6 cm

5 cm

9 cm

- You should be able to calculate **lengths** and **areas** associated with **circles**.

Circumference of a circle is given by: $C = \pi d$ or $C = 2\pi r$
Area of a circle is given by: $A = \pi r^2$

The **lengths of arcs** and the **areas of sectors** are proportional to the angle at the centre of the circle.

For a sector with angle $a°$

Length of arc $= \frac{a}{360} \times \pi d$

Area of sector $= \frac{a}{360} \times \pi r^2$

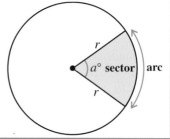

r

$a°$ **sector** arc

r

Take π to be 3.14 or use the π key on your calculator.

Eg 3 Find the circumference of a circle with radius 9 cm.
Give your answer to 1 d.p.

$C = 2 \times \pi \times r$
$C = 2 \times \pi \times 9$
$C = 56.548...$
$C = 56.5 \, cm$, correct to 1 d.p.

Eg 4 Find the area of a circle with radius 6 cm.
Give your answer to 3 sig. figs.

$A = \pi \times r^2$
$A = \pi \times 6 \times 6$
$A = 113.097...$
$A = 113 \, cm^2$, correct to 3 sig. figs.

Eg 5 A circle has a circumference of 25.2 cm. Find the diameter of the circle.

$C = \pi d$, so, $d = \frac{C}{\pi}$

$d = \frac{25.2}{\pi}$

$d = 8.021...$
$d = 8.0 \, cm$, correct to 1 d.p.

Eg 6 A circle has an area of 154 cm². Find the radius of the circle.

$A = \pi r^2$, so, $r^2 = \frac{A}{\pi}$

$r^2 = \frac{154}{\pi} = 49.019...$

$r = \sqrt{49.019...} = 7.001...$
$r = 7 \, cm$, to the nearest cm.

Eg 7 *OAB* is a sector of a circle of radius 7.2 cm.   Angle *AOB* = 50°.
Calculate   (a)   the length of arc *AB*,
(b)   the area of sector *AOB*.

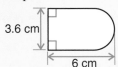

(a)   Length of arc $= \frac{a}{360} \times \pi d = \frac{50}{360} \times \pi \times 14.4$

$= 6.2831... = 6.28$ cm, correct to 3 s.f.

(b)   Area of sector $= \frac{a}{360} \times \pi r^2 = \frac{50}{360} \times \pi \times 7.2^2$

$= 22.619... = 22.6$ cm², correct to 3 s.f.

● Shapes formed by joining different shapes together are called **compound shapes**.
To find the area of a compound shape we must first divide the shape up into rectangles,
triangles, circles, etc., and find the area of each part.

Eg 8 Find the area of this metal plate.

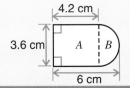

The plate can be divided into a rectangle, *A*, and a semi-circle, *B*.
Area *A* = 3.6 × 4.2 = 15.12 cm²
Area *B* = $\frac{1}{2} \times \pi \times 1.8^2$ = 5.089... cm²
Total area = 15.12 + 5.089... = 20.2 cm², correct to 3 s.f.

Exercise 32

Take π to be 3.14 or use the π key on your calculator.

1 Calculate the area of this shape.

1.5 cm
3 cm
2.5 cm
6.5 cm

2 Two triangles are joined together to form a rhombus, as shown.
The perimeter of the rhombus is 36 cm.
The perimeter of each triangle is 24 cm.
Find the value of *b*.

a   *a*
b
a   *a*   AQA

3 Calculate the area of triangle *PQR*.

Q
6 cm
P ← 9 cm → *R*

4 In the rectangle a triangular region has been shaded.
What percentage of the rectangle is shaded?
Give your answer to an appropriate degree of accuracy.

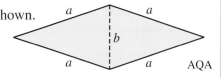

5 cm
7 cm
2 cm
3 cm   AQA

5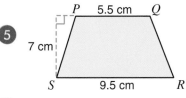

The diagram shows a trapezium, *PQRS*.
Calculate the area of the trapezium.

P 5.5 cm *Q*
7 cm
S 9.5 cm *R*

6 A rectangular carpet is twice as long as it is wide. The carpet covers an area of 24.5 m².
Calculate the length of the carpet.

7 (a) Calculate the circumference of a circle of diameter 26 cm.
 (b) Calculate the area of a circle of radius 2.5 cm.

8 Triangle *XYZ* has an area of 12 cm².
XZ = 5 cm.
Calculate *YP*.

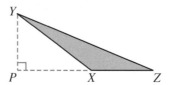

9 Tranter has completed three-fifths of a circular jigsaw puzzle.
The puzzle has a radius of 20 cm.
What area of the puzzle is complete?

10 The diagram shows the plan of a swimming pool.
The arc *QR* is a semi-circle.
PS = 12 m   and   *PQ* = *RS* = 20 m.
Calculate the area of the surface of the pool.

11 (a) Jayne has a circular hoop of radius 35 cm.
  Calculate the circumference of her hoop.
 (b) Rashida has a hoop with a circumference of 300 cm.
  Calculate the radius of Rashida's hoop.

12 Three circles overlap, as shown.
The largest circle has a diameter of 12 cm.
The ratio of the diameters *x* : *y* is 1 : 2.
Calculate the shaded area.
Give your answer in terms of π.

13 A circle has a circumference of 100 cm.
Calculate the area of the circle. Give your answer correct to three significant figures.

14 Alfie says, "A semi-circle with a radius of 10 cm has a larger area than a whole circle with half the radius." Is he correct?
You **must** show working to justify your answer.

15 The diagram shows a sector of a circle of radius 9 cm.
Find the perimeter of the sector.
Give your answer in terms of π.

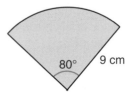

16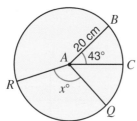

BAC is a sector of a circle, radius 20 cm, whose centre is at *A*.
Angle *BAC* = 43°.
 (a) Calculate the area of the sector *BAC*.
 (b) The area of sector *QAR* is 450 cm². Angle *QAR* is *x*°.
  Calculate the value of *x*.

17 *OAB* is a minor sector of a circle of radius 6 cm.
Angle *AOB* = 120°.
 (a) Calculate the area of the minor sector *OAB*.
  Give your answer in terms of π.
 (b) Calculate the perimeter of the minor sector *OAB*.
  Give your answer in terms of π.
 (c) The triangle *OAB* is reflected in the chord *AB* to form the quadrilateral *OAPB*.
  Does point *P* lie inside the circle, outside the circle, or on the arc *AB*?
  Explain your reasoning clearly.

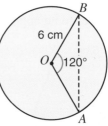

Maps, Loci and Constructions

What you need to know

- **Compass points** and **three-figure bearings** are used to describe direction.
- A **bearing** is an angle measured from the North line in a clockwise direction.
- A bearing can be any angle from 0° to 360° and is written as a three-figure number.
- To find a bearing: measure angle *a* to find the bearing of *Y* from *X*,
  measure angle *b* to find the bearing of *X* from *Y*.

- **Scales**
  The distances between points on a map are all drawn to the same scale.
  There are two ways to describe a scale.
  1. A scale of 1 cm to 10 km means that a distance of 1 cm on the map represents an actual distance of 10 km.
  2. A scale of 1 : 10 000 means that all distances measured on the map have to be multiplied by 10 000 to find the real distance.
- The path of a point which moves according to a rule is called a **locus**.
- The word **loci** is used when we talk about more than one locus.
- You should be able to draw the locus of a point which moves according to a given rule.

  Eg 1 A ball is rolled along this zig-zag.
  Draw the locus of *P*, the centre of the ball,
  as it is rolled along.

Using a ruler and compasses you should be able to:
- Construct the **perpendicular from a point to a line**.
- Construct the **perpendicular from a point on a line**.
- Construct the **perpendicular bisector of a line**.
- Construct the **bisector of an angle**.

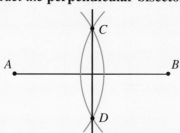

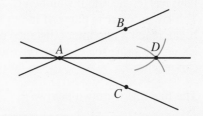

Points on the line *CD* are **equidistant** from the points *A* and *B*.

Points on the line *AD* are **equidistant** from the lines *AB* and *AC*.

- You should be able to solve loci problems which involve using these constructions.

  Eg 2 *P* is a point inside triangle *ABC* such that:
  (i)   *P* is equidistant from points *A* and *B*,
  (ii) *P* is equidistant from lines *AB* and *BC*.
  Find the position of *P*.

  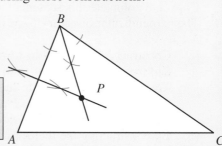

  To find point *P*:
  (i) construct the perpendicular bisector of line *AB*,
  (ii) construct the bisector of angle *ABC*.

  P is at the point where these lines intersect.

1 The diagram shows a sketch of the course to be used for a running event.

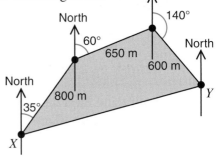

(a) Draw an accurate plan of the course, using a scale of 1 cm to represent 100 m.

(b) Use your plan to find
    (i) the bearing of X from Y,
    (ii) the distance XY in metres.

2 The ball is rolled along the zig-zag.
Copy the diagram and draw the locus of the centre of the ball as it is rolled from X to Y.

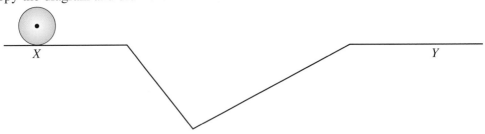

3 The diagram shows a plan of Paul's garden.
Draw the diagram using a scale of 1 cm to 1 m.

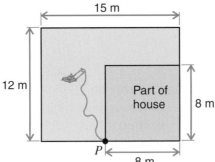

Paul has an electric lawnmower.
The lawnmower is plugged in at point P.
It can reach a maximum distance of 12 metres from P.
Using the same scale, show on your diagram the area of the garden which the lawnmower can reach.
    AQA

4 The line LM is drawn below.

        L ——————————————————————— M

Copy LM.
Use ruler and compasses to construct the perpendicular bisector of LM.
You **must** show clearly all your construction arcs.

Copy and complete this sentence.
The perpendicular bisector of LM is the locus of points which are ....
    AQA

5 (a) Construct a kite $PQRS$ in which $PQ = PS = 7$ cm, $QR = RS = 5$ cm and the diagonal $QS = 6$ cm.
    X is a point inside the kite such that:
    (i) X is equidistant from P and Q,
    (ii) X is equidistant from sides PQ and PS.
(b) By constructing the loci for (i) and (ii) find the position of X.
(c) Measure the distance PX.

- The movement of a shape from one position to another is called a **transformation**.

- **Single transformations** can be described in terms of a reflection, a rotation, a translation or an enlargement.

- **Reflection**: The image of the shape is the same distance from the mirror line as the original.

- **Rotation**: All points are turned through the same angle about the same point, called a centre of rotation.

- **Translation**: All points are moved the same distance in the same direction without turning.

- **Enlargement**: All lengths are multiplied by a scale factor.

  Scale factor = $\dfrac{\text{new length}}{\text{original length}}$ | New length = scale factor × original length |

  The size of the original shape is:

  increased by using a scale factor greater than 1,
  reduced by using a scale factor which is a fraction, i.e. between 0 and 1.
  When a shape is enlarged using a **negative scale factor** the image is **inverted**.

- You should be able to draw the transformation of a shape.

  Eg 1 Draw the image of triangle P after it has been translated with vector $\begin{pmatrix} -3 \\ 2 \end{pmatrix}$.

  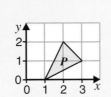

- You should be able to fully describe transformations.

Transformation	Image same shape and size?	Details needed to describe the transformation
Reflection	Yes	Mirror line, sometimes given as an equation.
Rotation	Yes	Centre of rotation, amount of turn, direction of turn.
Translation	Yes	Horizontal movement and vertical movement. Vector: top number = horizontal movement, bottom number = vertical movement.
Enlargement	No	Centre of enlargement, scale factor.

Eg 2 Describe the single transformation which maps
  (a) A onto B,
  (b) A onto C,
  (c) A onto D,
  (d) D onto E,
  (e) E onto F.

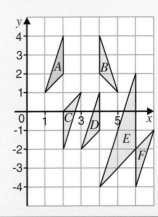

  (a) **Reflection** in the line $x = 3$.
  (b) **Rotation** of $180°$ about $(2, 1)$.
  (c) **Translation** with vector $\begin{pmatrix} 2 \\ -3 \end{pmatrix}$.
  (d) **Enlargement** scale factor 2, centre $(2, 0)$.
  (e) **Enlargement** scale factor $-\frac{1}{2}$, centre $(6, -2)$.

1 The diagram shows the positions of kites *P*, *Q*, *R* and *S*.

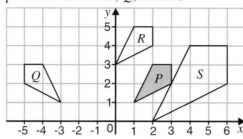

(a) (i) *P* is mapped onto *Q* by a reflection.
What is the equation of the line of reflection?
(ii) *P* is mapped onto *R* by a translation.
What is the vector of the translation?
(iii) *P* is mapped onto *S* by an enlargement.
What is the centre and scale factor of the enlargement?
(b) *P* is mapped onto *T* by a rotation through 90° clockwise about (1, −2).
On squared paper, copy *P* and draw the position of *T*.

2 In each diagram, *A* is mapped onto *B* by a single transformation. Describe each transformation.

(a)

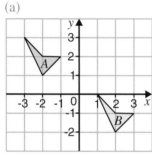

(b)

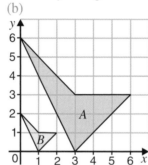

(c)

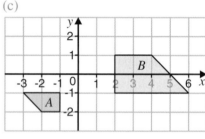

3 Triangle *X* has vertices (1, 2), (0, 3), (−1, 1).
Triangle *Y* has vertices (2, 1), (3, 0), (1, −1).
Describe the single transformation which maps *X* onto *Y*.

4 The diagram shows the position of *P*.
P has coordinates (3, 1).
(a) *P* is mapped onto *Q* by a reflection in the line $y = x$.
What are the coordinates of *Q*?

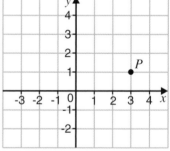

The translation $\begin{pmatrix} -2 \\ 1 \end{pmatrix}$ maps *P* onto *R*.

The translation $\begin{pmatrix} 3 \\ -4 \end{pmatrix}$ maps *R* onto *S*.

(b) (i) What are the coordinates of *S*?
(ii) What is the translation which maps *S* onto *P*?
(c) *T* has coordinates (−1, 1).
P is mapped onto *T* by a rotation through 90° anticlockwise about centre *X*.
What are the coordinates of *X*?

AQA

5 Triangle *PQR* has vertices *P*(2, −3), *Q*(−2, −5), *R*(−4, −3).
On squared paper, draw and label triangle *PQR*.

(a) Enlarge triangle *PQR* by scale factor $\frac{1}{2}$ from the centre of enlargement (4, −1).
Label the image *A*.
(b) Rotate triangle *PQR* through 180° about the point (−2, −1).
Label the image *B*.
(c) Describe fully the single transformation which maps triangle *A* onto triangle *B*.

Pythagoras' Theorem ●●●●●●

What you need to know

- The longest side in a right-angled triangle is called the **hypotenuse**.

- The **Theorem of Pythagoras** states:
    "In any right-angled triangle the square on the hypotenuse is equal to the sum of the squares on the other two sides."
    $$a^2 = b^2 + c^2$$

- When we know the lengths of two sides of a right-angled triangle, we can use the Theorem of Pythagoras to find the length of the third side.

$$a^2 = b^2 + c^2$$
Rearranging gives: $b^2 = a^2 - c^2$
$$c^2 = a^2 - b^2$$

Eg 1 Calculate the length of side a.

Eg 2 Calculate the length of side b.

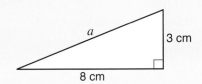

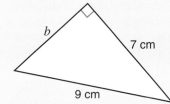

$a^2 = b^2 + c^2$
$a^2 = 8^2 + 3^2$
$a^2 = 64 + 9 = 73$
$a = \sqrt{73} = 8.544...$
$a = 8.5\,\text{cm}$, correct to 1 d.p.

$b^2 = a^2 - c^2$
$b^2 = 9^2 - 7^2$
$b^2 = 81 - 49 = 32$
$b = \sqrt{32} = 5.656...$
$b = 5.7\,\text{cm}$, correct to 1 d.p.

Exercise 35

Do not use a calculator for questions 1 and 2.

1 ABC is a right-angled triangle.
$AB = 5\,\text{cm}$ and $AC = 12\,\text{cm}$.
Calculate the length of BC.

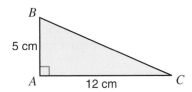

2 The positions of three villages, Oldacre (O), Adchester (A) and Byetoft (B), are shown on the diagram.
Angle $OAB = 90°$.
The distance from Oldacre to Adchester is 8 km.
The distance from Oldacre to Byetoft is 10 km.
Calculate the distance from Adchester to Byetoft.

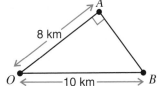

AQA

3

 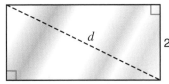

The diagram shows a rectangular sheet of paper.
The paper is 20 cm wide and the diagonal, d, is 35 cm.
Calculate the length of the sheet of paper.

4 Calculate the length of the line joining the points $A(-3, 2)$ and $B(6, -2)$.

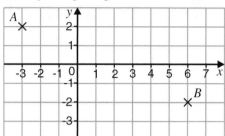

AQA

5

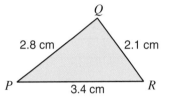

Is PQR: an acute-angled triangle,
an obtuse-angled triangle,
or a right-angled triangle?

Show your calculations and state your conclusions.

6 An oil rig is 15 km East and 12 km North from Kirrin.

(a) Calculate the direct distance from Kirrin to the oil rig.
(b) An engineer flew 14 km from Faxtown to the oil rig.
The oil rig is 10 km West of Faxtown.
Calculate how far South the oil rig is from Faxtown.

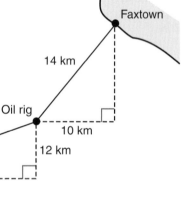

AQA

7

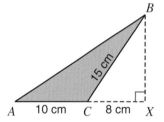

The diagram shows a triangle ABC.
Angle $BXA = 90°$, $BC = 15$ cm,
$CX = 8$ cm and $AC = 10$ cm.

Calculate the area of triangle ABC.
Give your answer correct to 3 significant figures.

AQA

8 A cuboid has dimensions 20 cm by 10 cm by 5 cm.

Calculate the length of the diagonal AB.
Give your answer to a suitable degree of accuracy.

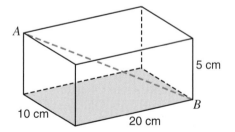

9

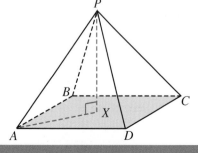

The diagram shows a square-based pyramid.
The edges $PA = PB = PC = PD = 9$ cm.
X is at the centre of the base $ABCD$.
$PX = 8$ cm.

Calculate the area of the base, $ABCD$.

- **Trigonometry** is used to find the lengths of sides and the sizes of angles in right-angled triangles.

- You must learn the **sine**, **cosine** and **tangent** ratios.

$$\sin a = \frac{\text{opposite}}{\text{hypotenuse}} \qquad \cos a = \frac{\text{adjacent}}{\text{hypotenuse}} \qquad \tan a = \frac{\text{opposite}}{\text{adjacent}}$$

- Each ratio links the size of an angle with the lengths of two sides. If we are given the values for two of these we can find the value of the third.

- When we look **up** from the horizontal the angle we turn through is called the **angle of elevation**.

- When we look **down** from the horizontal the angle we turn through is called the **angle of depression**.

- Bearings are used to describe the direction in which you must travel to get from one place to another. They are measured from the North line in a clockwise direction. A bearing can be any angle from 0° to 360° and is written as a three-figure number.

- You should be able to use trigonometry to find the lengths of sides and the sizes of angles when solving problems involving right-angled triangles.

Eg 1 Find the length, d.

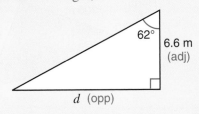

$\tan a = \dfrac{\text{opp}}{\text{adj}}$

$\tan 62° = \dfrac{d}{6.6}$

$d = 6.6 \times \tan 62°$

$d = 12.412\ldots$

$d = 12.4 \text{ m}$, correct to 3 s.f.

Eg 2 Find the size of angle a.

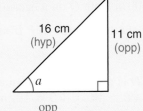

$\sin a = \dfrac{\text{opp}}{\text{hyp}}$

$\sin a° = \dfrac{11}{16}$

$a = \sin^{-1}\dfrac{11}{16}$

$a = 43.432\ldots$

$a = 43.4°$, correct to 1 d.p.

- When working in three dimensions the first task is to identify the length, or angle, that you are trying to find.
  The length, or angle, will always form part of a triangle together with either:
  two other sides of known length, or
  one side of known length and an angle of known size.
  Sometimes, more than one triangle is needed to solve a problem.

- A straight line meets a plane at a **point**.
  The angle XPT is the **angle between the line and the plane**.
  The line XT is perpendicular to the plane.

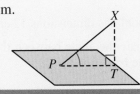

Do not use a calculator for question 1.

1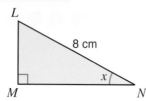

LMN is a right-angled triangle.   *LN* = 8 cm.
sin *x* = 0.6,   cos *x* = 0.8   and   tan *x* = 0.75.

Calculate the length of *MN*.

AQA

2   (a)   Calculate angle *x* in triangle *ABC*.

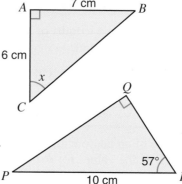

(b)   Calculate length *QR* in triangle *PQR*.

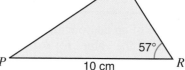

AQA

3   The diagram shows the side view of a wheelchair ramp.
The ramp makes an angle of 4° with the horizontal.

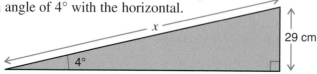

Calculate the length, marked *x*, of the ramp.
Give your answer in metres to a sensible degree of accuracy.

AQA

4   The diagram shows the path of a jet-ski from *P* to *Q* to *R*.

Q is 700 m from *P* on a bearing of 070°.
R is 500 m from *Q* on a bearing of 160°.

Calculate the bearing of *P* from *R*.

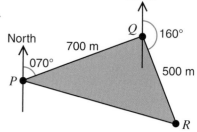

5   *VABCD* is a pyramid on a square base of side 10 cm.
VA = *VB* = *VC* = *VD* = 12 cm.

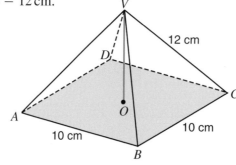

(a)   Calculate *VO*, the perpendicular height of the pyramid.
(b)   Find the angle between *VC* and the base.

AQA

6   A cuboid has dimensions 12 cm by 9 cm by 5 cm.

Calculate the angle between the diagonal *XA*
and the base *ABCD*.

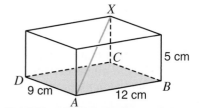

3-D Shapes ●●●●●●●●●●●●

What you need to know

- **You should be able to:**
- find the number of **faces**, **edges** and **vertices** of a 3-D shape,
- draw the **net** of a 3-D shape,
- use **isometric** paper to make a 2-D drawing of a 3-D shape.

- A **plane of symmetry** slices through a 3-D shape so that one half is the mirror image of the other half.

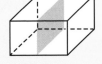

- Three-dimensional shapes can have **axes of symmetry**.

- **Plans and Elevations**
  The view of a 3-D shape looking from above is called a **plan**.
  The view of a 3-D shape from the front or sides is called an **elevation**.

  Eg 1 Draw diagrams to show the plan and elevation from **X**, for this 3-dimensional shape.

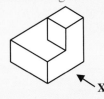

  X   plan   elevation X

  > Dotted lines are used to show hidden edges.

- **Volume** is the amount of space occupied by a 3-D shape.

- The formula for the volume of a **cuboid** is:
  Volume = length × breadth × height
  $V = l \times b \times h$

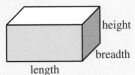

  height
  breadth
  length

- Volume of a **cube** is: $V = l^3$

- To find the **surface area** of a cuboid, find the areas of the 6 rectangular faces and add the answers together.

- **Prisms**
  If you make a cut at right angles to the length of a prism you will always get the same cross-section.

Triangular prism

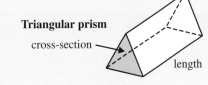

cross-section

length

- Volume of a prism = area of cross-section × length

  Eg 2 Calculate the volume of this prism.
  The cross-section of this prism is a trapezium.

  Area of cross-section = $\frac{1}{2}(5 + 3) \times 2.5$
  $= 4 \times 2.5$
  $= 10\,cm^2$
  Volume of prism = area of cross-section × length
  $= 10 \times 12$
  $= 120\,cm^3$

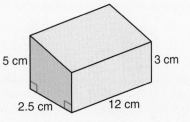

  5 cm   3 cm
  2.5 cm   12 cm

- A **cylinder** is a prism.
  Volume of a cylinder is: Volume = $\pi \times r^2 \times h$
  Surface area of a cylinder is: Surface area = $2\pi r^2 + 2\pi rh$

r
h

Eg 3 A cylinder has a radius of 4 cm and a height of 6 cm.
Calculate (a) the volume and (b) the surface area of the cylinder.

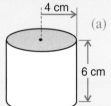

(a) $V = \pi r^2 h$
$= \pi \times 4 \times 4 \times 6$
$= 301.592...$
$= 302 \text{ cm}^3,$
   correct to 3 s.f.

(b) Surface area $= 2\pi r^2 + 2\pi rh$
$= 2 \times \pi \times 4 \times 4 + 2 \times \pi \times 4 \times 6$
$= 100.53... + 150.796...$
$= 251 \text{ cm}^2,$
   correct to 3 s.f.

● These formulae are used in calculations involving **cones**, **pyramids** and **spheres**.

Cone

$V = \frac{1}{3} \times \text{base area} \times \text{height}$
$V = \frac{1}{3} \pi r^2 h$
Curved surface area $= \pi r l$

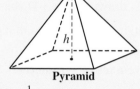

Pyramid

$V = \frac{1}{3} \times \text{base area} \times \text{height}$

Sphere

Volume $= \frac{4}{3} \pi r^3$
Surface area $= 4\pi r^2$

Eg 4 A cone is 6.4 cm high and has a radius of 4.8 cm.
Calculate the curved surface area of the cone.

Slant height, $l = \sqrt{6.4^2 + 4.8^2}$
$= \sqrt{64} = 8 \text{ cm}$

Curved surface area is given by:
$\pi r l = \pi \times 4.8 \times 8 = 120.637...$
$= 120.6 \text{ cm}^2,$ correct to 1 d.p.

Eg 5 A steel ball has a radius of 4 cm.
Calculate (a) the volume,
        (b) the surface area of the ball.

(a) Volume $= \frac{4}{3} \pi r^3 = \frac{4}{3} \times \pi \times 4^3$
$= 268.082...$
$= 268 \text{ cm}^3,$ correct to 3 s.f.

(b) Surface area $= 4\pi r^2 = 4 \times \pi \times 4^2$
$= 201.061...$
$= 201 \text{ cm}^2,$ correct to 3 s.f.

● A **frustum of a cone** is formed by removing the top of a cone with a cut parallel to its circular base.

Exercise 37

Do not use a calculator for questions 1 to 5.

1 The diagram shows a square-based pyramid.
(a) How many planes of symmetry has the pyramid?
(b) How many axes of symmetry has the pyramid?

2

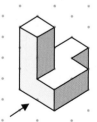

The diagram shows a solid drawn on isometric paper.
(a) Draw the plan of the solid.
(b) Draw the elevation of the solid from the direction shown by the arrow.

3
(a) Which of these cuboids has the larger volume?
Show all your working.
(b) Which cuboid has the larger surface area?

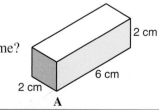

2 cm

6 cm

2 cm

A

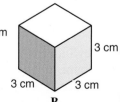

3 cm

3 cm

3 cm

B

4 A cuboid has a volume of 100 cm³. The cuboid is 8 cm long and 5 cm wide.
Calculate the surface area of the cuboid.

5 A cylinder has a radius of 6 cm and a height of 5 cm.
Calculate the volume of the cylinder.
Give your answer in terms of π.

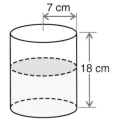

6 A cylinder of radius 7 cm and height 18 cm is half full of water.
One litre of water is added.
Will the water overflow? You must show all your working.

AQA

7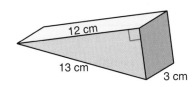
Calculate the volume of this wedge.

8 The cross-section of a prism is a sector of a circle, as shown.
Calculate the volume of the prism.
Give your answer in terms of π.

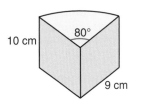

AQA

9
A cylindrical water tank has radius 40 cm and height 90 cm.
(a) Calculate the total surface area of the tank.

A full tank of water is used to fill a paddling pool.
(b) The paddling pool is a cylinder with diameter 2.4 metres.
Calculate the depth of water in the pool.

10 A container consists of a cylinder on top of a cone. The container is full of oil.
The diameter of the cylinder and cone is 200 cm.
The height of the cone is 90 cm and the height of the cylinder is 120 cm.
(a) Calculate the volume of oil in the container.

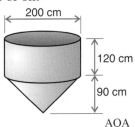

Oil flows from the container until it reaches a level 45 cm from the
bottom of the container.
(b) What volume of oil has flowed from the container?

AQA

11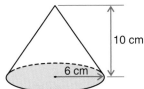
A cone is 10 cm high and has a base radius of 6 cm.
(a) Calculate the curved surface area of the cone.

The top of the cone is cut off to leave a frustum 8 cm high.
(b) Calculate the volume of the frustum.

12 Rachel buys a ball in a box. The ball touches each side of the box.
The box is a cube with sides of length 20 cm.
(a) Calculate the difference between the volume of the box and
the volume of the ball.
(b) Calculate the difference between the surface area of the box
and the surface area of the ball.

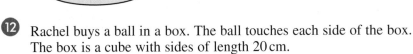

13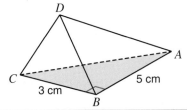
The diagram shows a triangular pyramid.
Angle $ABC = 90°$, $AB = 5$ cm and $BC = 3$ cm.
The volume of the pyramid is 28 cm³.
Calculate the height of the pyramid.

Understanding and Using Measures

What you need to know

- The common units — both **metric** and **imperial** — used to measure **length**, **mass** and **capacity**.

- How to convert from one unit to another. This includes knowing the connection between one metric unit and another and the approximate equivalents between metric and imperial units.

Metric Units	Imperial Units	Conversions
Length 1 kilometre (km) = 1000 metres (m) 1 m = 100 centimetres (cm) 1 cm = 10 millimetres (mm) **Mass** 1 tonne (t) = 1000 kilograms (kg) 1 kg = 1000 grams (g) **Capacity and volume** 1 litre = 1000 millilitres (ml) 1 cm³ = 1 ml	**Length** 1 foot = 12 inches 1 yard = 3 feet **Mass** 1 pound = 16 ounces 14 pounds = 1 stone **Capacity and volume** 1 gallon = 8 pints	**Length** 5 miles is about 8 km 1 inch is about 2.5 cm 1 foot is about 30 cm **Mass** 1 kg is about 2.2 pounds **Capacity and volume** 1 litre is about 1.75 pints 1 gallon is about 4.5 litres

- How to change between units of area.   For example $1\,m^2 = 10\,000\,cm^2$.

- How to change between units of volume.   For example $1\,m^3 = 1\,000\,000\,cm^3$.

- You should be able to recognise limitations on the accuracy of measurements.
A **discrete measure** can only take a particular value and a **continuous measure** lies within a range of possible values which depends upon the degree of accuracy of the measurement.

> If a **continuous measure**, c, is recorded to the nearest x, then the limits of the possible values of c can be written as $c \pm \frac{1}{2}x$.

Eg 1   A log is 12 m in length. The length is correct to the nearest metre.
What is the minimum length of the log?   Minimum length = 12 − 0.5 = 11.5 m

Eg 2   A road is 400 m long, to the nearest 10 m.
Between what lengths is the actual length of the road?
Actual length = 400 m ± 5 m   395 m ⩽ actual length < 405 m

Eg 3   A punnet of strawberries weighs 2.4 kg, correct to the nearest 100 g.
Between what limits must the weight of the strawberries lie?
Actual weight = 2.4 kg ± 0.05 kg
Lower limit   = 2.35 kg
Upper limit   = 2.45 kg
So,   2.35 kg ⩽ actual weight < 2.45 kg.

- By analysing the **dimensions** of a formula it is possible to decide whether a given formula represents a **length** (dimension 1), an **area** (dimension 2) or a **volume** (dimension 3).

Eg 4 p, q, r and s represent lengths.
By using dimensions, decide whether the expression $pq + qr + rs$
could represent a perimeter, an area or a volume.
Writing $pq + qr + rs$ using dimensions:
$$L \times L + L \times L + L \times L = L^2 + L^2 + L^2 = 3L^2$$
So, $pq + qr + rs$ has dimension 2 and could represent an area.

1 On a map the distance between two hospitals is 14.5 cm.
The map has been drawn to a scale of 1 to 250 000.
Calculate the actual distance between the hospitals in kilometres.

2 Debbie is 5 feet 4 inches tall and weighs 9 stone 2 lb. Joyce is 155 cm tall and weighs 60 kg.
Who is taller? Who is heavier? You must show your working.

3 Last year Felicity drove 2760 miles on business.
Her car does 38 miles per gallon.
Petrol costs 89 pence per litre.
She is given a car allowance of 25 pence per kilometre.
How much of her car allowance is left after paying for her petrol?
Give your answer to the nearest £.

4 (a) A towel measures 150 cm by 90 cm. Calculate the area of the towel in square metres.
(b) Change 0.2 m³ to cm³.

5 Vicky measures her handspan and writes down the result as:

> **18 cm, correct to the nearest centimetre.**

(a) Write down the greatest length her handspan could be.

Chris has measured his handspan as 17.5 cm, correct to the nearest half centimetre.
(b) Write down the smallest length his handspan could be.

Paul says that Chris should write his answer down as 17.50 cm.
(c) Give a reason why this is not appropriate. *AQA*

6 Bags of potatoes each weigh 25 kg correct to the nearest kg.
What is the minimum weight of 9 bags of potatoes? *AQA*

7 The dimensions of a triangular prism are shown.
The following formulae represent certain quantities
connected with the prism.

$$d(a + b + c) \quad \frac{abd}{2} \quad \sqrt{(a^2 + b^2)} \quad cd \quad \tfrac{1}{2}\,ab$$

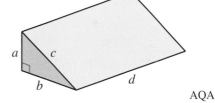

(a) Which of these formulae represents a length?
(b) Which of these formulae represents a volume? *AQA*

8 The measurements of a rectangular ticket are given as 5 cm by 3 cm,
correct to the nearest centimetre.
(a) Between what limits must the width of the ticket lie?
(b) Between what limits must the area of the ticket lie?
(c) The area of the ticket is given as $(15 \pm x)\,\text{cm}^2$.
    Suggest a suitable value for x.

9 The volume of a rectangular metal plate is calculated from the following measurements:

> **length 15.2 cm,   width 8.1 cm   and thickness 0.6 cm.**

Determine the minimum possible volume, in cm³, of the plate. *AQA*

10 Michael rides his bicycle to work.
The diameter of each wheel is 65 cm, correct to the nearest centimetre.
The distance he cycles to work is 2.4 km, correct to one decimal place.
Calculate the least number of turns each wheel makes when Michael cycles to work.

11 The volume of a cylinder is given as 880 ml, correct to 2 significant figures.
John measures its height as 11.2 cm (to the nearest mm).
Between what limits must the radius of the cylinder lie? *AQA*

Congruent Triangles and Similar Figures

What you need to know

- When two shapes are the same shape and size they are said to be **congruent**.

- There are four ways to show that a pair of triangles are congruent.

SSS	3 corresponding sides.	**ASA**	2 angles and a corresponding side.
SAS	2 sides and the included angle.	**RHS**	Right angle, hypotenuse and one other side.

Eg 1 Show that triangles *ABC* and *XYZ* are congruent.

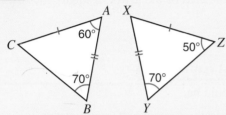

$AC = XZ$ (given)
$AB = XY$ (given)
$\angle BAC = \angle YXZ = 60°$ (sum of angles in $\Delta = 180°$)

So, triangles *ABC* and *XYZ* are congruent (SAS).

- When two figures are **similar**:
  their **shapes** are the same, their **angles** are the same,
  corresponding **lengths** are in the same ratio,
  this ratio is the **scale factor** of the enlargement.

$$\text{Scale factor} = \frac{\text{new length}}{\text{original length}}$$

- For **similar triangles**:
  corresponding lengths are opposite equal angles,
  the scale factor is the ratio of the
  corresponding sides.

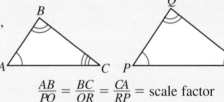

$$\frac{AB}{PQ} = \frac{BC}{QR} = \frac{CA}{RP} = \text{scale factor}$$

- You should be able to find corresponding lengths in similar triangles.

Eg 2 These two triangles are similar.
Find the lengths of the sides marked *x* and *y*.

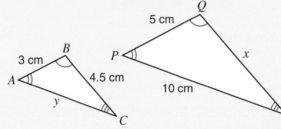

AB and *PQ* are corresponding sides.
$$\text{Scale factor} = \frac{PQ}{AB} = \frac{5}{3}$$

$x = 4.5 \times \frac{5}{3} = 7.5\,\text{cm}$

$y = 10 \div \frac{5}{3} = 6\,\text{cm}$

- You should be able to find corresponding lengths, areas and volumes in similar figures.

When the **length** scale factor $= k$, the **area** scale factor $= k^2$, the **volume** scale factor $= k^3$.

Eg 3 Two fish tanks are similar. The smaller tank is 12 cm high and holds 4 litres of water. The larger tank is 18 cm high. How many litres of water does it hold?

Ratio of heights is $\quad 12 : 18 = 2 : 3$.
Ratio of volumes is $\quad 2^3 : 3^3 = 8 : 27$.

To find the ratio of volumes, cube the ratio of lengths.

Water in larger tank $= 4 \times \frac{27}{8} = 13.5$ litres

1 The diagram shows rectangles **A**, **B** and **C**.

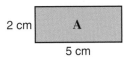 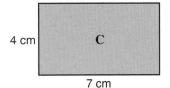

2 cm **A**   3 cm **B**   4 cm **C**

5 cm   7 cm

   (a) Explain why rectangles **A** and **C** are **not** similar.
   (b) Rectangles **A** and **B** are similar.
       Work out the length of rectangle **B**.

2 These triangles are similar.
   (a) Work out the length of the side *XY*.
   (b) Work out the length of the side *AC*.

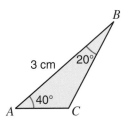 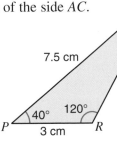 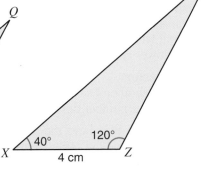

3 Which two of these triangles are congruent to each other?
   Give a reason for your answer.

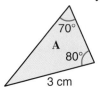 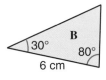 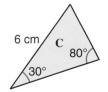 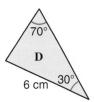

4 The diagram shows two regular hexagons.
   (a) Name a triangle which is similar but
       not congruent to triangle *BCD*.

   (b) *AB* : *PQ* is 2 : 3.
      (i) Angle *AEF* = 30°.
         What is the size of angle *PTU*?
      (ii) *AF* = 2.4 cm.
         Calculate the perimeter of the
         hexagon *PQRSTU*.

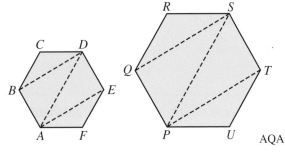

AQA

5 (a) Two bottles of perfume are similar to each other.
       The heights of the bottles are 4 cm and 6 cm.
       The smaller bottle has a volume of 24 cm³.
       Calculate the volume of the larger bottle.
   (b) Two bottles of aftershave are similar to each other.
       The areas of the bases of these bottles are 4.8 cm² and 10.8 cm².
       The height of the smaller bottle is 3 cm.
       Calculate the height of the larger bottle.

AQA

6 *A* and *B* are two similar cylinders.
   The height of cylinder *A* is 10 cm and its volume is 625 cm³.
   The volume of cylinder *B* is 5000 cm³.
   Calculate the height of cylinder *B*.

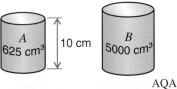

AQA

Congruent Triangles and Similar Figures

What you need to know

- Quantities which have both **size** and **direction** are called **vectors**.
  For example: **Displacement** – A combination of distance and direction.

- **Vector notation**
  Vectors can be represented by **column vectors** or by **directed line segments**.
  Vectors can be labelled using:
      capital letters to indicate the start and finish of a vector,
      bold lower case letters.

  In a **column vector**:
      The top number describes the **horizontal** part of the movement.
      The bottom number describes the **vertical** part of the movement.

  $$\overrightarrow{AB} = \mathbf{a} = \begin{pmatrix} 3 \\ 2 \end{pmatrix}$$

- Vectors are **equal** if they have the same length **and** they are in the same direction.
  Vectors **a** and −**a** have the same length **but** are in **opposite directions**.
  The vector $n\mathbf{a}$ is parallel to the vector **a**.
  The length of vector $n\mathbf{a} = n \times$ the length of vector **a**.

- **Vector addition**
  The combination of the displacement from A to B followed by the displacement from B to C is equivalent to a total displacement from A to C.

  This can be written using vectors as $\overrightarrow{AB} + \overrightarrow{BC} = \overrightarrow{AC}$. $\overrightarrow{AC}$ is called the **resultant vector**.

- Combinations of vectors can be shown on **vector diagrams**.

  Eg 1   **a** and **b** are shown. Draw vectors to represent   **a** + **b**   and   **a** − **b**.

  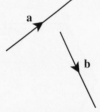

  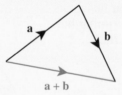
  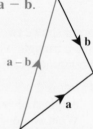

- You should be able to use **vector geometry** to solve simple geometrical problems, which can often involve parallel lines.

  Eg 2   *OAXB* is a quadrilateral.

  $\overrightarrow{OA} = \mathbf{a}$, $\overrightarrow{OB} = \mathbf{b}$ and $\overrightarrow{AX} = 2\overrightarrow{OB}$.

  (a)   Find, in terms of **a** and **b**,

      (i) $\overrightarrow{AX}$,   (ii) $\overrightarrow{BX}$.

  (b)   *M* and *N* are the midpoints of *OA* and *BX* respectively.

      (i)   Find $\overrightarrow{MN}$, in terms of **a** and **b**.
      (ii)   What can you say about the lines *OB* and *MN*?
      (iii)   What type of quadrilateral is *OMNB*?

  (a)   (i) $\overrightarrow{AX} = 2\mathbf{b}$ (ii) $\overrightarrow{BX} = \mathbf{a} + \mathbf{b}$

  (b)   (i) $\overrightarrow{MN} = 1\tfrac{1}{2}\,\mathbf{b}$ (ii) $2\overrightarrow{MN} = 3\overrightarrow{OB}$ (iii)   Trapezium
                                      MN is parallel to *OB*.

The diagrams in this exercise have not been drawn accurately.

1 In the diagram, $\overrightarrow{OX} = \mathbf{x}$ and $\overrightarrow{OY} = \mathbf{y}$.

  (a) Write, in terms of $\mathbf{x}$ and $\mathbf{y}$, the vector $\overrightarrow{XY}$.

  (b) P and Q are the midpoints of OX and OY respectively.

      Find, in terms of $\mathbf{x}$ and $\mathbf{y}$, the vector $\overrightarrow{QP}$.

2 A is the point $(-3, 5)$ and B is the point $(3, 1)$.

  (a) Find $\overrightarrow{AB}$ as a column vector.

  C and D are points such that $\overrightarrow{CB} = \begin{pmatrix} -2 \\ -3 \end{pmatrix}$, and $ABCD$ is a trapezium with $\overrightarrow{AB} = 2\overrightarrow{DC}$.

  (b) Find the coordinates of D.

3 The vectors $\mathbf{a}$ and $\mathbf{b}$ and the points P and Q are shown.

  (a) Write $\overrightarrow{PQ}$ in terms of $\mathbf{a}$ and $\mathbf{b}$.

  Copy P and Q onto squared paper.

  (b) $\overrightarrow{QR} = 4\mathbf{a} - 2\mathbf{b}$.

    (i) Show the position of R on your diagram.

    (ii) Write $\overrightarrow{RP}$ in terms of $\mathbf{a}$ and $\mathbf{b}$.

  (c) $\overrightarrow{RS} = -\overrightarrow{PQ}$

    (i) What can you say about the lines QR and PS?

    (ii) What type of quadrilateral is $PQRS$?

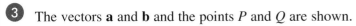

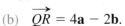

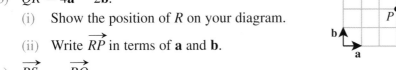

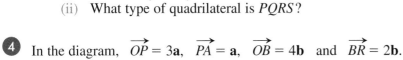

4 In the diagram, $\overrightarrow{OP} = 3\mathbf{a}$, $\overrightarrow{PA} = \mathbf{a}$, $\overrightarrow{OB} = 4\mathbf{b}$ and $\overrightarrow{BR} = 2\mathbf{b}$.
Q is the midpoint of AB.

  (a) Find, in terms of $\mathbf{a}$ and $\mathbf{b}$, the vectors

    (i) $\overrightarrow{AB}$,   (ii) $\overrightarrow{PQ}$.

  (b) Explain clearly why the points PQR lie on a straight line.

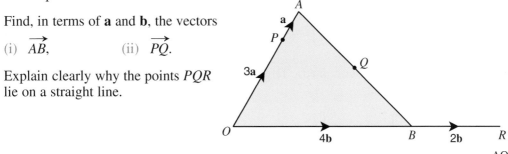

AQA

5 $OPQR$ is a parallelogram.
A and B are points on OP and OR respectively.

$\overrightarrow{OA} = \mathbf{a}$ and $\overrightarrow{OB} = \mathbf{b}$.

$\overrightarrow{OP} = 4\overrightarrow{OA}$ and $\overrightarrow{OR} = 3\overrightarrow{OB}$.

  (a) Find, in terms of $\mathbf{a}$ and $\mathbf{b}$,

    (i) $\overrightarrow{AB}$,   (ii) $\overrightarrow{RA}$,   (iii) $\overrightarrow{BQ}$.

  (b) S is a point on PQ such that BQ is parallel to AS.

    Find $\overrightarrow{AS}$ in terms of $\mathbf{a}$ and $\mathbf{b}$.

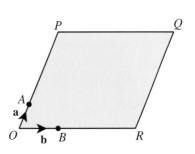

AQA

What you need to know

- The graphs of the trigonometric functions.

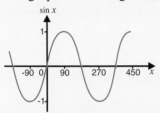

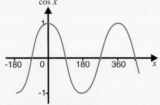

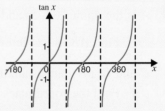

The **sine function** is a periodic function with period 360°.
$-1 \leqslant \sin x \leqslant 1$

The **cosine function** is a periodic function with period 360°.
$-1 \leqslant \cos x \leqslant 1$

The **tangent function** is a periodic function with period 180°.
Tan x is undefined at 90°, 270°, ...

- For every angle $x°$, the signs of $\sin x°$, $\cos x°$ and $\tan x°$ can be shown on a diagram.

  Positive angles are measured **anticlockwise**.
  Negative angles are measured **clockwise**.

  For angles greater than 360°: subtract 360°, or multiples of 360°, to get the equivalent angle between 0° and 360°.

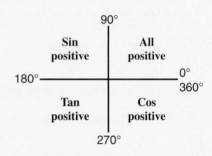

Eg 1 Sin 53.1° = 0.8, correct to 1 d.p.
  (a) Write down the other value of x for which $\sin x = 0.8$ for $0° \leqslant x \leqslant 360°$.
  (b) Solve the equation $\sin x = -0.8$ for $0° \leqslant x \leqslant 360°$.

(a) | Always work from 0° or 180° or 360°. When $\sin x$ is positive: $\sin x = \sin (180° - x)$ |

(b) | Sin x is negative, so values of x lie between 180° and 360° |

$x = 180° - 53.1° = 126.9°$

$x = 180° + 53.1° = 233.1°$
$x = 360° - 53.1° = 306.9°$
So, $x = 233.1°$ or $306.9°$

- The **exact values** of the trigonometric ratios for the angles 30°, 45° and 60° can be found from the triangles below.

	30°	45°	60°
sin	$\frac{1}{2}$	$\frac{1}{\sqrt{2}}$	$\frac{\sqrt{3}}{2}$
cos	$\frac{\sqrt{3}}{2}$	$\frac{1}{\sqrt{2}}$	$\frac{1}{2}$
tan	$\frac{1}{\sqrt{3}}$	1	$\sqrt{3}$

- You should be able to use the **sine rule** and the **cosine rule** to solve problems involving triangles which are not right-angled.

- **The Sine Rule**

$$\frac{a}{\sin A} = \frac{b}{\sin B} = \frac{c}{\sin C}$$

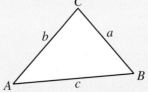

This can also be written as: $\dfrac{\sin A}{a} = \dfrac{\sin B}{b} = \dfrac{\sin C}{c}$

Eg 2 Calculate the length of side a.

$$\frac{a}{\sin 53°} = \frac{6}{\sin 47°}$$

$$a = \frac{6 \times \sin 53°}{\sin 47°}$$

$$a = 6.551\ldots$$

$$a = 6.6 \text{ cm, to 1 d.p.}$$

To find a **side** you need:
two angles of known size, **and** the length of a side which is opposite one of the known angles.

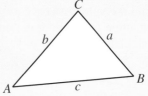

Eg 3 Calculate the size of angle P.

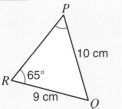

$$\frac{\sin P}{9} = \frac{\sin 65°}{10}$$

$$\sin P = \frac{9 \times \sin 65°}{10}$$

$$\sin P = 0.8156\ldots$$

$$P = 54.7°, \text{ to 1 d.p.}$$

To find an **angle** you need:
the length of the side opposite the angle you are trying to find, **and** the length of a side opposite an angle of known size.

- **The Cosine Rule**

$$a^2 = b^2 + c^2 - 2bc \cos A$$

When using the Cosine Rule to find the size of an angle it is sometimes easier to rearrange the above formula as:

$$\cos A = \frac{b^2 + c^2 - a^2}{2bc}$$

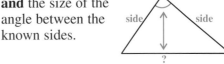

Eg 4 Calculate the length of side x.

$$x^2 = 6^2 + 7^2 - 2 \times 6 \times 7 \times \cos 73°$$

$$x^2 = 36 + 49 - 24.55\ldots$$

$$x^2 = 60.44\ldots$$

$$x = 7.8 \text{ cm, to 1 d.p.}$$

To find a **side** you need:
two sides of known length, **and** the size of the angle between the known sides.

Eg 5 Calculate the size of angle A.

$$\cos A = \frac{6^2 + 8^2 - 7^2}{2 \times 6 \times 8}$$

$$\cos A = 0.53125$$

$$A = 57.9°, \text{ to 1 d.p.}$$

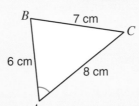

To find an **angle** you need:
three sides of known length.

- You should be able to find the area of a triangle which is not right-angled.

Eg 6 Calculate the area of triangle PQR.

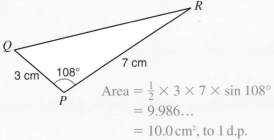

$$\text{Area} = \tfrac{1}{2} \times 3 \times 7 \times \sin 108°$$

$$= 9.986\ldots$$

$$= 10.0 \text{ cm}^2, \text{ to 1 d.p.}$$

To find the **area of a triangle** you need:
two sides of known length, **and** the size of the angle between the known sides.

$$\text{Area} = \tfrac{1}{2} ab \sin C.$$

- You should be able to solve problems involving triangles.

For **right-angled triangles** use:
the **trigonometric ratios** (sin, cos and tan), **Pythagoras' Theorem**.

For **triangles which are not right-angled** use:
the **Sine Rule** or the **Cosine Rule**.

Do not use a calculator for questions 1 and 2.

1 (a) Cos 60° = 0.5

    (i) Write down the other value of x for which $\cos x = 0.5$ for $0° \leqslant x \leqslant 360°$.

    (ii) Solve the equation $\cos x = -0.5$ for $0° \leqslant x \leqslant 360°$.

  (b) (i) On the same diagram, sketch the graphs of $y = \cos x$ and $y = \sin x$ for $0° \leqslant x \leqslant 360°$.

    (ii) Hence, solve the equation $\cos x = \sin x$ for $0° \leqslant x \leqslant 360°$.

2 (a) Draw a sketch of the graph of $y = \sin x$ for $-180° \leqslant x \leqslant 180°$.

  (b) One solution of the equation $\sin x = 0.9$ is $64°$, to the nearest degree.
Find the other solution of the equation $\sin x = 0.9$ for $-180° \leqslant x \leqslant 180°$.

  (c) Find all the solutions of the equation $\sin x = -0.9$ for $-180° \leqslant x \leqslant 180°$.　　AQA

3 In the triangle, $\sin x = \frac{2}{3}$.

  (a) Copy the diagram and mark the possible values of the lengths of the sides of the triangle.

  (b) Find the value of $\cos x$.

  (c) An angle y is such that $\sin y = \sin x$, and $0° < y < 360°$, and y is not equal to x.
Calculate the size of y.　　AQA

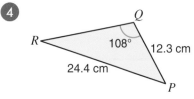

4

In the triangle PQR, angle $PQR = 108°$.
$PQ = 12.3$ cm and $PR = 24.4$ cm.

  (a) Calculate angle QRP.

  (b) Calculate the area of triangle PQR.

5 A gardener pegs out a rope, 19 metres long, to form a flower bed.
Calculate:

  (a) the size of the angle BAC,

  (b) the area of the triangular flower bed.

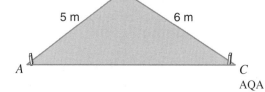

AQA

6 A, B and C are three points which lie in a straight line on horizontal ground.
BT is a vertical tower.
The angle of elevation of T from A is $21.5°$.
The angle of elevation of T from C is $13.3°$.
$AC = 1200$ m.

Calculate the height of the tower.

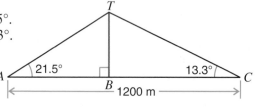

AQA

7

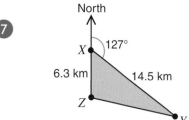

The diagram shows the positions of ships X, Y and Z.
X is 6.3 km due North of Z.
Y is 14.5 km from X on a bearing of $127°$.

Calculate the distance and bearing of Z from Y.

8 In the triangle ABC, $AB = 6$ cm and $AC = 9$ cm.
The area of triangle ABC is 24 cm².

  (a) Calculate the two possible values of angle BAC.

  (b) Calculate the length of BC, when angle BAC is obtuse.

Shape, Space and Measures
Non-calculator Paper

Do not use a calculator for this exercise.

1 Find the size of the angles marked a, b, c and d.

(a)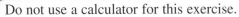

110°
116°
80°
a

(b)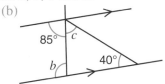

85° c
b
40°

(c)

75°
95°
d

2 The diagram shows a cuboid.
By rounding each of the measurements to one significant figure,
estimate the volume of the cuboid.
You must show all your working.

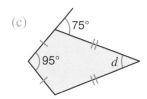

29.7 cm   20.3 cm
9.89 cm

AQA

3

North

A
B
C

The sketch shows the positions of
three footpaths which meet at A, B and C.
A is due north of C.
Triangle ABC is equilateral.

(a) Write down the three-figure bearing of B from C.
(b) Write down the three-figure bearing of A from B.

AQA

4 Mr Jones weighs his case on his bathroom scales which weigh to the nearest kilogram.
He finds that his case weighs 20 kg.
(a) What are the greatest and least weights of the case?
(b) On the way to the airport he removes a sweater from this case. At the airport the scales
give the weight of his case as 19.4 kg to the nearest tenth of a kilogram.
What is the heaviest weight that the sweater could be?

AQA

5 Copy the diagram onto squared paper.
(a) P is mapped onto Q by an enlargement, scale factor 2,
centre $(-1, 3)$. Draw and label Q.
(b) P is mapped onto R by a translation with vector $\begin{pmatrix} -3 \\ 2 \end{pmatrix}$.
Draw and label R.
(c) Describe the single transformation which maps Q onto R.

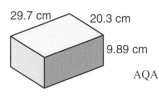

6 (a) Construct triangle ABC, in which
$AB = 9.5$ cm, $BC = 8$ cm and $CA = 6$ cm.
(b) Using ruler and compasses only,
(i) bisect angle BAC,
(ii) draw the locus of points that are equidistant from A and C.
(c) Shade the region inside the triangle where all the points are less than 7.5 cm from B,
nearer to A than to C and nearer to AC than to AB.

7 (a) Calculate the sum of the interior angles of a regular 10-sided polygon.
(b) The diagram shows a square and a regular hexagon which meet at M.
LM and MN are two sides of another regular polygon.
How many sides has this polygon?

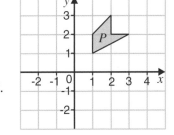

N
M
L

8 A circle has an area of $49\,\pi\,\text{cm}^2$.
Calculate the circumference of the circle in terms of π.

9 The following formulae represent certain quantities connected with containers, where a, b and c are dimensions.

$$\pi a \qquad abc \qquad \sqrt{a^2 - c^2} \qquad \pi a^2 b \qquad 2(a + b + c)$$

(a) Explain why abc represents a volume.

(b) Which of these formulae represent lengths?

10 (a) The diagram shows a right-angled triangle, ABC.
Angle $C = 90°$ and $AB = 10$ cm.
Given that $\cos B = 0.8$, $\sin B = 0.6$ and $\tan B = 0.75$, calculate the length of AC.

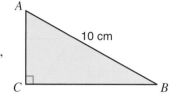

(b) Triangle PQR is similar to triangle ABC.

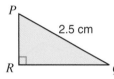

Given that angle P = angle A, angle Q = angle B and $PQ = 2.5$ cm, calculate the length of PR.

AQA

11 $\overrightarrow{OP} = -2\mathbf{a} + 4\mathbf{b}$ and $\overrightarrow{OQ} = 4\mathbf{a} - 2\mathbf{b}$.

(a) Express $\overrightarrow{PQ}$ in terms of $\mathbf{a}$ and $\mathbf{b}$.

R is the midpoint of PQ.

(b) Express $\overrightarrow{OR}$ in terms of $\mathbf{a}$ and $\mathbf{b}$.

$\overrightarrow{PS} = 7\mathbf{a} + \mathbf{b}$.

(c) Express $\overrightarrow{OS}$ in terms of $\mathbf{a}$ and $\mathbf{b}$.

(d) What **two** facts do $\overrightarrow{OR}$ and $\overrightarrow{OS}$ indicate about the points O, R and S?

AQA

12

The diagram shows a circle, centre O.
A, B, C and D are points on the circumference of the circle. AT is a tangent to the circle.

(a) What is the size of the angle marked w?
Give a reason for your answer.

(b) (i) What is the size of the angle marked x?
(ii) What is the size of the angle marked y?
Give a reason for your answer.

(c) What is the size of the angle marked z?

AQA

13 (a) Sketch the graph of $y = \cos x$ for $0° \leqslant x \leqslant 360°$.

(b) You are given that $\cos 27° = 0.891$.

(i) Solve the equation $\cos x = 0.891$ for $180° \leqslant x \leqslant 360°$.

(ii) Solve the equation $\cos x = -0.891$ for $0° \leqslant x \leqslant 360°$.

(iii) State a solution of the equation $\cos (x - 90°) = 0.891$ for $0° \leqslant x \leqslant 360°$.

(iv) State a solution of the equation $\sin x = 0.891$ for $0° \leqslant x \leqslant 360°$.

AQA

14 The diagram shows a triangle, ABC.
$AB = 6$ cm, $BC = 5$ cm and angle $B = 75°$.
You are given that $\sin 75° = 0.966$ to 3 significant figures.

Calculate the area of the triangle.
Give your answer to a suitable degree of accuracy.

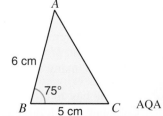

AQA

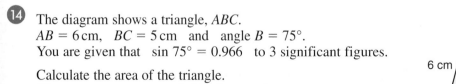

Shape, Space and Measures
Calculator Paper

● ● ● ● ● ●

You may use a calculator for this exercise.

1 Colin is 5 feet 10 inches tall and weighs 11 stones.
On a medical form he is asked to give his height in centimetres and his weight in kilograms.
What values should he give?

2 The area of the trapezium is 20 m^2.
The parallel sides a and b are different lengths.
The perpendicular height, h, is 4 m.
Find a possible pair of values for a and b.

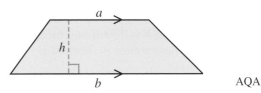

AQA

3

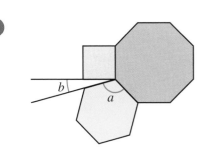

(a) The diagram shows the angle formed when
three regular polygons are placed together, as shown.
  (i)   Explain why angle a is $120°$.
  (ii)   Work out the size of the angle marked b.

(b) Do all regular polygons tessellate?
Give a reason for your answer.

4 The diagram shows the points $P(0, -4)$ and $Q(5, 2)$.
Find the coordinates of the midpoint of the line segment PQ.

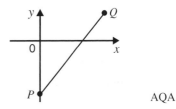

AQA

5 Three oil rigs, X, Y and Z, are supplied by boats from port P.
X is 15 km from P on a bearing of $050°$.
Y is 20 km from P on a bearing of $110°$.
Z is equidistant from X and Y and 30 km from P.
(a) By using a scale of 1 cm to represent 5 km, draw an accurate diagram to show the
positions of P, X, Y and Z.
(b) Use your diagram to find
  (i)   the bearing of Y from Z,
  (ii)   the distance, in kilometres, of Y from Z.

6 The diagram shows a kite $ABCD$.
(a) Calculate the area of the kite $ABCD$.
(b) Calculate the length of AC.

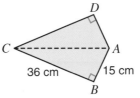

AQA

7

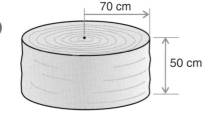

The diagram shows a bale of straw.
The bale is a cylinder with radius 70 cm and height 50 cm.
Calculate the volume of the bale.

AQA

8 A letter Z is drawn in a rectangle measuring 7 cm by 9 cm, as shown.
Calculate the size of the angle marked x.

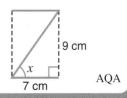

AQA

9 The diagram shows Fay's house, *H*, and her school, *S*.

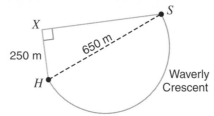

To get to school Fay has a choice of two routes.
She can either walk along Waverly Crescent or along the footpaths *HX* and *XS*.
Waverly Crescent is a semi-circle with diameter 650 m.
The footpath *HX* is 250 m and meets the footpath *XS* at right-angles.
Which of these routes is shorter? By how much?

10 Triangle *ABC* is similar to triangle *APQ*.

AB = 4.5 cm,   *BC* = 3 cm,   *PQ* = 5 cm   and   *CQ* = 1.6 cm.

(a)   Calculate the length of *AP*.

(b)   Calculate the length of *AC*.

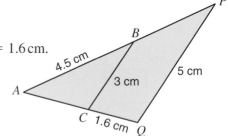

11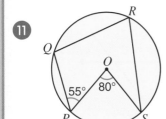

O is the centre of a circle through *P*, *Q*, *R* and *S*.

(a)   Work out the size of angle *QRS*.

(b)   *X* is a point on the minor arc *PS*.
Explain why angle *PXS* = 140°.

12 A sports field is bounded by three straight roads, *PQ*, *QR* and *RP*, as shown.

Angle *PRQ* = 63°   and   angle *PQR* = 90°.
The length of *QR* is 4.7 km.
Calculate the area of the sports field.

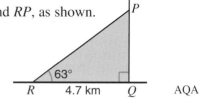

AQA

13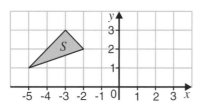

Copy the diagram.

(a)   Enlarge shape *S*, centre (−1, 2), scale factor −2.
Label the image *T*.

(b)   Describe the single transformation which
maps *T* onto *S*.

14 The diagram shows the roof of a building.
The base *ABCD* is a horizontal rectangle 10 m by 5 m.
The ends are equilateral triangles.
EFCB is an isosceles trapezium.
The length of the ridge of the roof, *EF*, is 7 m.
M is the midpoint of *AB*.
N is the midpoint of *CD*.

(a)   Find the perpendicular distance between
EF and *CB*, and hence find the area of *EFCB*.

(b)   Find the size of the angle *EMN*.

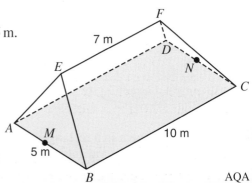

AQA

15 The diagram shows two concentric circles with centre O.
$\angle XOY = 118°$. $OX = 8.5$ cm.

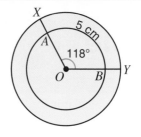

(a) Calculate the area of the sector XOY.

(b) The arc $AB = 5$ cm.
Calculate OA.

16

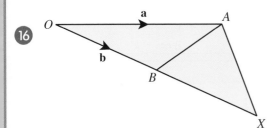

In the diagram $\overrightarrow{OA} = \mathbf{a}$ and $\overrightarrow{OB} = \mathbf{b}$.
B is the midpoint of OX.

(a) Find, in terms of $\mathbf{a}$ and $\mathbf{b}$, the vectors $\overrightarrow{OX}$ and $\overrightarrow{AX}$.

(b) M is the midpoint of AX.
Prove that BM is parallel to OA.

17 Find the two values of x between $0°$ and $360°$ which satisfy the equation $4 \sin x = -1$. AQA

18 The diagram shows a rectangular garden, $ABCD$.

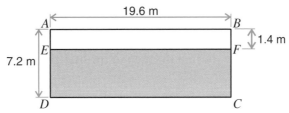

A lawn, $CDEF$, is shaded.
The unshaded area, $ABFE$, is a rectangular flower bed.
$AB = 19.6$ m, $AD = 7.2$ m and $BF = 1.4$ m, all correct to 1 decimal place.
Calculate the upper bound of the area of the lawn. AQA

19 (a) Calculate the area of triangle ABD.

(b) Calculate the length of BD.

(c) Calculate the size of angle BCD.

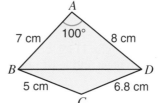

AQA

20

The stand on which the dog is sitting is the frustum of a cone.
The top of the stand has a radius of 0.5 m.
The bottom of the stand has a radius of 1 m.
The height of the stand is 0.6 m.

(a) Calculate the volume of the stand.
(b) The height of a similar stand is 0.4 m.
Calculate the volume of this stand.

21 The diagram shows a triangular piece of card.
Angle BAC is obtuse, $AB = 5.8$ cm and $AC = 7.4$ cm.
The area of the card is 20 cm².
Calculate the length of BC.
Give your answer to a suitable degree of accuracy.

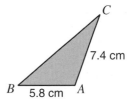

22 The volume of a cylinder is given as 680 cm³, correct to two significant figures.
The height is 9.6 cm to the nearest millimetre.
Calculate the upper and lower bounds of the radius.

Do not use a calculator for this exercise.

1 (a) Multiply out $5(x + 3)$.
(b) Solve the equations (i) $2(2x + 5) = 34$, (ii) $5x = 6 + x$.

2 Three-tenths of the area of this shape is shaded.

Calculate the shaded area.

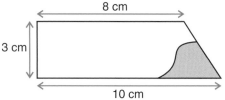

AQA

3 A jam doughnut costs t pence.
A cream doughnut costs 5 pence more than a jam doughnut.
Write an expression for the cost of 3 jam doughnuts and 2 cream doughnuts.

4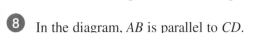

The diagram shows a sketch of a triangle.

By making an accurate drawing of the triangle, find the area of the triangle.

5 The numbers on these cards are coded. The sum of the numbers on these 3 cards is 41.

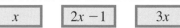

(a) Form an equation in x.
(b) By solving your equation, find the numbers on the cards.

6 A farmer has a crop circle in his field. The circle has a circumference of 12π metres.
Calculate, in terms of π, the area of the circle.

7 A concrete block weighs 11 kg, correct to the nearest kilogram.
Write down the greatest and least possible weight of the block.

8 In the diagram, AB is parallel to CD.

(a) State the value of x. Give a reason for your answer.
(b) Find the value of y.

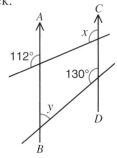

AQA

9 A sequence begins: -1, 2, 5, 8, 11, …
Write, in terms of n, the nth term of the sequence.

10 (a) Factorise. (i) $5a - 10$ (ii) $x^2 - 6x$
(b) Expand and simplify. (i) $3(a + 4) - 5(2 - a)$ (ii) $(x - 2)(x - 4)$
(c) Make t the subject of the formula. $S = 3t - 1$
(d) Simplify. $m^2 \times m^3$

11 $ABCD$ is part of a regular 12-sided polygon.
O is the centre of the polygon.

(a) Calculate the size of angle p.
(b) Hence, calculate the size of angle d.

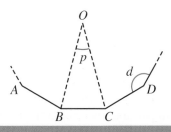

AQA

12 Copy shape A onto squared paper.

(a) A is mapped onto B by a translation with vector $\begin{pmatrix} 0 \\ -4 \end{pmatrix}$.
Draw the position of B on your diagram.

(b) A is mapped onto C by a rotation through $180°$ about $(3, 1)$.
Draw the position of C on your diagram.

(c) Describe the single transformation which maps B onto C.

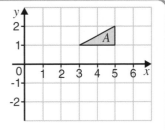

13 Cocoa is sold in cylindrical tins.
The height of a tin is $7.9\,\text{cm}$. The radius of a tin is $4.1\,\text{cm}$.
Use approximations to estimate the volume of a tin. Show all your working.

14 (a) Copy and complete the table of values for $y = x^2 - 3x + 1$.

x	-1	0	1	2	3	4
y		1	-1			5

(b) Draw the graph of $y = x^2 - 3x + 1$ for values of x from -1 to 4.
(c) Use your graph to find the value of y when $x = 1.5$.
(d) Use your graph to solve the equation $x^2 - 3x + 1 = 0$.

15 These formulae represent quantities connected with containers, where a, b and c are dimensions.
$$2(ab + bc + cd) \qquad abc \qquad \sqrt{a^2 + b^2} \qquad 4(a + b + c)$$
Which of these formulae represent lengths? Explain how you know.

16 (a) List the values of n, where n is an integer, such that $3 \leqslant 3n < 18$.
(b) Solve the simultaneous equations $2x + y = 9$ and $x - 2y = 7$.
(c) Factorise the expression $n^2 - n$.
(d) Simplify $3a^2b \times 2a^3b$.

AQA

17 The diagram shows a quadrilateral $ABCD$.
$AB = 9\,\text{cm}$ and $AC = 15\,\text{cm}$.

(a) Calculate the length of BC.
(b) Given that $\cos x = 0.7$, calculate the length of CD.

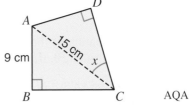

AQA

18 In these diagrams O is the centre of the circle.
Find the size of the angles a, b, c and x. Give a reason for each of your answers.

(a)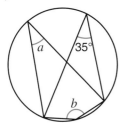

(b)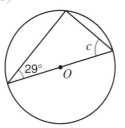

(c)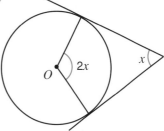

19 (a) Factorise completely. $3x^2 - 6x$

(b) Expand and simplify. $(3x + 2)(x - 4)$

(c) Make t the subject of the formula. $W = \dfrac{5t + 3}{4}$

AQA

20 These kites are similar.

(a) Work out the size of angle PQR.
(b) Calculate the length of BC.
(c) Express the area of $ABCD$ to the area of $PQRS$ as a ratio in the form $1 : n$.

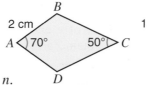

Not drawn accurately

21 The sketches show the graphs of four equations. Write down the equation for each graph.

(a)

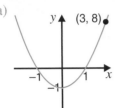

(b)

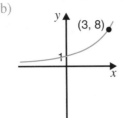

(c)

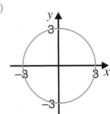

(d)

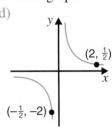

22 (a) Show that $(n - 3)^2 - 2(n - 3) = (n - 3)(n - 5)$.

(b) Solve the equation $x^2 + 3x - 10 = 0$.

23 Alex does a triple jump, i.e. a hop, step and jump.
The step is 5.14 metres and the jump is 6.75 metres. The total triple jump is 15.74 metres.
All these measurements are to the nearest centimetre.
What is the maximum length of Alex's hop?

AQA

24 (a) Simplify $(3a^3)^2$.

(b) Solve $\dfrac{2}{x + 1} + \dfrac{1}{x - 1} = 1$.

(c) Rearrange the formula $m = \dfrac{3(n + 1)}{2 - n}$ to make n the subject.

25 $OABC$ is a trapezium.

$\overrightarrow{OA} = 2\mathbf{a}$, $\overrightarrow{OC} = 8\mathbf{b}$ and $\overrightarrow{AB} = \frac{1}{4}\overrightarrow{OC}$.

Find, in terms of $\mathbf{a}$ and $\mathbf{b}$, (a) $\overrightarrow{BA}$, (b) $\overrightarrow{BC}$.

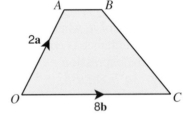

AQA

26 Find the equation of the line which is perpendicular to $5y + 2x = 10$ and goes through $(0, 0)$.

27 (a) Find the values of a and b such that $x^2 + 6x - 3 = (x + a)^2 + b$.

(b) Hence, solve the equation $x^2 + 6x - 3 = 0$, giving your answers in surd form. AQA

28 A sketch of $y = f(x)$ for $0° \leqslant x \leqslant 360°$ is shown.
Draw sketches to show each of these
transformations of $y = f(x)$.

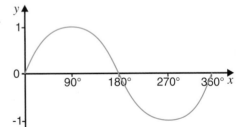

(a) $y = f(x) + 2$

(b) $y = 2f(x)$

(c) $y = f(2x)$

29 Draw the graphs of $y = \cos x°$ and $y = \sin 2x°$ for $0 \leqslant x \leqslant 360$.
Use the graph to find all the solutions of the equation $\cos x° = \sin 2x°$ for $0 \leqslant x \leqslant 360$.

AQA

30 Zarig took part in a 26-mile road race.
He ran the first 15 miles at an average speed of x mph.
He ran the last 11 miles at an average speed of $(x - 2)$ mph.
He took 4 hours to complete the race.
(a) Form an equation, in terms of x, and show that it can be written as $2x^2 - 17x + 15 = 0$.
(b) Solve this equation and obtain Zarig's average speed over the first 15 miles of the race.

AQA

31 Simplify the expression $\dfrac{2x^2 - 8x}{x^2 - 16}$.

AQA

You may use a calculator for this exercise.

1   (a)   Find the value of $3x + 5y$ when $x = -2$ and $y = 4$.

       (b)   Find the value of $3a^2 + 5$ when $a = 4$.   AQA

2   The graph shows the journey of a cyclist from Cordy to Dalton and back.

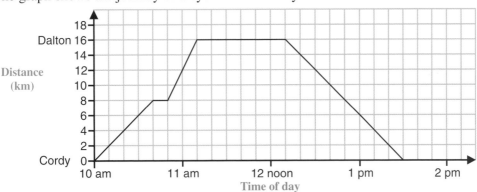

   (a)   During which part of the journey did the cyclist travel the fastest? Explain your answer.

   (b)   What was the average speed of the cyclist from Dalton back to Cordy?

3   Which of these statements are correct?

       P   all isosceles triangles are similar   **R**   all parallelograms are similar

       Q   all squares are similar   **S**   all regular pentagons are similar   AQA

4   Calculate the size of an interior angle of a regular octagon.   AQA

5

    A

      $x°$

   O   *B*   *C*

      OBC is a straight line.

      AOB is an isosceles triangle with $OB = AB$.

      Angle $AOB = x°$.

      (a)   Write down, in terms of x,

            (i)   angle *OAB*,   (ii)   angle *ABC*.

      (b)   Angle *OBA* is $(x - 12)$ degrees.

          Find the value of x.   AQA

6   A toilet roll has 240 single sheets per roll.

   Each sheet is 139 millimetres long and 110 millimetres wide.

   Calculate the total area of paper on the roll.

   Give your answer in square metres.

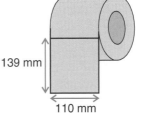

       139 mm

       110 mm   AQA

7   A hang glider flies 2.8 km on a bearing of 070° from *P* to *Q* and then 2 km on a bearing of 200° from *Q* to *R*.

   (a)   Make a scale drawing to show the flight of the hang glider from *P* to *Q* to *R*.

        Use a scale of 1 cm to 200 m.

   (b)   From *R* the hang glider flies directly back to *P*.

        Use your drawing to find the distance and bearing of *P* from *R*.

8   Calculate the area of a circle which has a radius of 9 m.

9   Solve the inequality $3x + 5 < 3 - x$.

10 (a) Draw and label the lines $y = x + 1$ and $x + y = 3$ for values of x from -1 to 3.

(b) The region R is satisfied by all of these inequalities: $x > 0$ $y > x + 1$ $x + y < 3$

Label the region R on your diagram.

11 Use a trial and improvement method to find a solution to the equation $x^3 + x = 57$.

Show all your working and give your answer correct to one decimal place.

12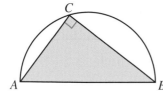

The diagram shows a semi-circle with diameter AB.

C is a point on the circumference.

$\angle ACB = 90°$.

$AC = 6\,\text{cm}$ and $CB = 8\,\text{cm}$.

Calculate the area of the shaded triangle as a percentage of the area of the semi-circle.

13 (a) Simplify the following.   (i) $e^4 \times e$ (ii) $f^7 \div f^3$ (iii) $(3hk^3)^2$

(b) Multiply out and simplify.   (i) $3p(p + 2)$ (ii) $(x - 7y)(x - y)$ AQA

14 The diagram shows a zig-zag path which joins the upper and lower gardens at a holiday resort.

The path DE is $25\,\text{m}$ long and $XE = 22\,\text{m}$.

(a) Calculate XD.

The path AC is $20\,\text{m}$ long and slopes at $24°$ to the horizontal.

(b) Calculate BC.

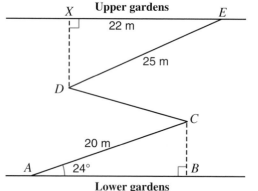

AQA

15 The volume of a cylinder is $75\,400\,\text{cm}^3$.

The height of the cylinder is $60\,\text{cm}$.

Calculate the radius of the cylinder.

16 (a) Solve the simultaneous equations $5x - 4y = -11$,

$\qquad\qquad\qquad\qquad\qquad\qquad\quad 3x + 2y = 0$.

(b) Factorise fully   (i) $3xy^2 + 6xy$,   (ii) $ma - nb - mb + na$.

(c) Solve the equation $x^2 - 7x + 12 = 0$.

17 A diagram shows points $A(2, 0)$, $B(0, 2)$ and $C(3, 5)$.

Find the equations of the line segments.

(a) AB,   (b) BC,   (c) AC.

18 A small tub of ice-cream weighs $50\,\text{g}$. The height of a small tub is $3\,\text{cm}$.

A large tub of ice-cream is a similar shaped tub that is $6\,\text{cm}$ high.

What is the weight of a large tub of ice-cream?   AQA

19 $ABCDEF$ is a triangular prism, $16\,\text{cm}$ long, as shown.

Calculate the size of the angle between AD and the base, $BCDE$.

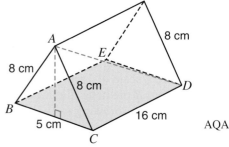

20 (a) Express as a single fraction $\dfrac{7}{3x} - \dfrac{2}{x}$

(b) Solve the equation $3x^2 - x - 5 = 0$.

Give your answers correct to two decimal places.

AQA

21 The dimensions of a rectangle are shown.
The rectangle has an area of 104 cm².
Form an equation for the area of the rectangle and show
that it can be written in the form $2x^2 + x - 105 = 0$.

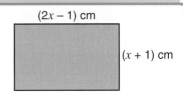

(2x − 1) cm

(x + 1) cm

22 A party hat is made from card.
The hat is made in two parts: a cone on top of a ring.
The cone has a height of 20 cm and base radius of 7.5 cm.

The ring has an internal radius of 7.5 cm and an external
radius of 10 cm.

(a) Calculate the area of the card used in making the
party hat.
Give your answer to an appropriate degree of accuracy.

A similar party hat is made in which the height of the
cone is 12 cm.

(b) Calculate the area of card used to make this party hat.

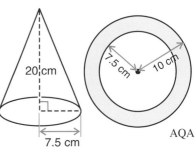

20 cm

7.5 cm

10 cm

7.5 cm

AQA

23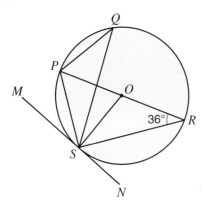

P, Q, R and S are points on the circumference
of a circle, centre O.
POR is a straight line.
The tangent MN meets the circle at S.

Given that $\angle PRS = 36°$, find

(a) $\angle PQS$,
(b) $\angle POS$,
(c) $\angle PSR$,
(d) $\angle PSM$.

Give a reason for each of your answers.

24 Solve the simultaneous equations $x = 2y + 4$ and $x^2 + y^2 = 5$.

25 (a) Draw the graph of $y = 3 \sin x° + 2$ for $0° \leqslant x \leqslant 180°$.
(b) Use your graph to solve the equation $3 \sin x° + 2 = 4.1$. AQA

26 A helicopter leaves a heliport, H, and its measuring instruments show that it flies 3.2 km on a
bearing of 128° to a checkpoint, C. It then flies 4.7 km on a bearing of 066° to its base, B.

(a) Show that angle HCB is 118°.
(b) Calculate the direct distance from
the heliport, H, to the base, B.

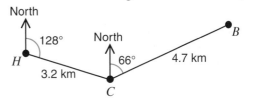

North

128°

North

66°

B

4.7 km

H

3.2 km

C

AQA

27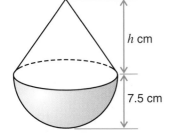

h cm

7.5 cm

A child's toy is in the shape of a cone on the top of a
hemisphere, as shown.
The radius of the hemisphere is 7.5 cm.
The volume of the toy is 1650 cm³.
Calculate the height of the cone. AQA

28 In triangle PQR, $\angle PRQ = 67°$, $PQ = 10.6$ cm and $RQ = 9.2$ cm.
(a) Calculate angle PQR.
(b) Hence, calculate the area of the triangle.

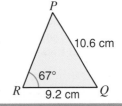

P

10.6 cm

67°

R

9.2 cm

Q

EP

Answers

SECTION ①

Exercise 1   Page 1

1. E.g. Students from one year group only.
   All students from the same class.
   More/less homework may be set on
   different nights.

2. (a) 15   (b) 13

3. (a) (i) Too personal.
   (ii) In which age group are you?
   Under 16 ☐ 16 to 19 ☐ Over 19 ☐
   (b) (i) Only students already using the
   library are sampled.
   (ii) Give to students as they enter
   (or leave) the college.

4. No.   Men: $\frac{180}{200} = 90\%$
   Women: $\frac{240}{300} = 80\%$
   Higher proportion of men can drive.

5. E.g. Two thirds of men are over 45.
   All women are aged 16 to 45.
   Twice as many women as men.

6. E.g. Divide the school population into year
   groups, and each year group into boys and
   girls, to create 10 subgroups.
   Choose 10 pupils, at random, from each
   subgroup.
   Sample could be taken by choosing every
   10th pupil from year group lists.

7. 4 managers, 5 secretaries, 9 other staff.

8. (a) A: 122, B: 78   (b) 72

SECTION ②

Exercise 2   Page 3

1. (a) £9   (b) £10.50   (c) £11.50
   (d) Median. Mode is the lowest price and mean
   is affected by the one higher-priced meal.

2. (a) 14.275
   (b) All values have increased by 1,
   so add 1 to mean.
   (c) 14.6
   (d) Mean.
   The highest value has been increased,
   so, median would not change, but mean
   would increase.

3. (a) 3   (b) 1.92   (c) Mode

4. (a) **B**   (b) 12   (c) 1.9

5. (a) 30.2 minutes   (b) $25 \leqslant t < 30$

SECTION ③

Exercise 3   Page 5

1. (a)
               0 | 7   means 7°C

0	7	9				
1	0	3	4	4	4	7	8
2	0	1	2			

   (b) 5°C or 24°C. Temperature can be either
   2°C above previous maximum, or
   2°C below previous minimum.

2.

Pet	Dog	Cat	Rabbit	Guinea pig
Angle	120°	75°	105°	60°

3. (a) (i) **C**   (ii) **B**   (b) **A**

4. (a) 60%   (b) 7 : 11
   (c)

Injury	Fatal	Serious	Minor	None
Angle	16°	28°	100°	216°

5. (a) $\frac{230}{360} = \frac{23}{36}$ or   0.64 (64%)
   (b) 1500

6. (a)

   Boys | | Girls   2 | 5 means 2.5 cm

Boys		Girls
	2	5
5 5	3	0 5 5 5
5 5 5 5 0 0	4	0 5 5
0 0	5	0 5

   (b) Girls have a larger range (3.0 cm) than
   boys (1.5 cm).

7. (c) (i) 3.8 m   (ii) 6.2 m
   (d) (c)(i) as estimated value lies between
   known values.

SECTION ④

Exercise 4   Page 8

1. (a) $80 \leqslant age < 90$
   (b) 40
   (c) (ii) Women:

Age (a years)	Frequency
$60 \leqslant a < 70$	1
$70 \leqslant a < 80$	5
$80 \leqslant a < 90$	13
$90 \leqslant a < 100$	6

   (iii) More men under 80 than women.
   Only women aged over 90.
   Women have greater range of ages.

2. 18

3. (a) (c)

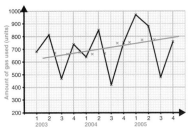

(b) 675, 665, 675, 662.5, 665, 747.5, 755, 772.5, 775

(d) Slight increase in units used.

4. (a) (i) Frequency densities:
6, 11, 10, 5, 1.5, 0.2
(ii) 3.25 km

(b) Mean: takes into account all journeys, **or** Median: as mean is affected by one extreme value.

5. (a) Frequency densities: 0.6, 4.2, 4.8, 3.1, 1

(b) 42

SECTION 5

Exercise 5 — Page 11

1. (a) (i) 66 m (ii) 16 m

(b)
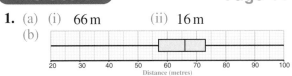

2. (a) (i) 10 kg (ii) 7 kg

(b)
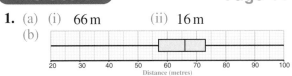

3. (a) 29 Median **A**: 70, Median **B**: 41

(b) (i) Group **B** (ii) 22 UQ: 55, LQ: 33

4. (a) 260 g (b) Cooking apples (c) 180 g

(d) The average weight of cooking apples is larger and they have a greater variation in weight than eating apples.

5. (b) (i) 100 (ii) 9

(c) (i) Joy. Lower interquartile range.
(ii) Laura. Lower median score.

SECTION 6

Exercise 6 — Page 14

1. (a) $\frac{2}{5}$ (b) 0.6

2. (a) $\frac{9}{20} = 0.45$

(b) 2, 3, 3, 4, 5. Numbers 2, 3, 4, 5 have occurred and 3 has occurred twice as often as other numbers.

(c) 100. Relative frequency of 5 is $\frac{1}{5}$.
$\frac{1}{5} \times 500 = 100$

3. (a) H H H, H H T, H T H, H T T
T H H, T H T, T T H, T T T

(b) $\frac{3}{8}$

4. (a) Missing entry is: 0.25

(b) Even. P(even) = 0.55 P(odd) = 0.45

5. (a) (i) $\frac{11}{30}$ (ii) $\frac{17}{30}$ (b) $\frac{7}{11}$

6. (a)

Train | Bus
0.4 late
0.7 late
0.3 not late
0.6 not late
0.7 late
0.3 not late

(b) 0.28 (c) 0.54

7. (a) $\frac{3}{5}$ (b) $\frac{3}{7}$

Exam Practice: Module 1

Non-calculator Paper — Page 16

1.

Pantomime	Angle
Aladdin	135°
Cinderella	105°
Jack and the Bean Stalk	75°
Peter Pan	45°

2. (a) Unequal intervals. Class intervals 3 to 6 and 6 to 8 overlap. No class greater than 8.

(b) Anna. Larger sample size.

3. (a)

	4	5 means 4.5 cm
4	5 8 8	
5	0 0 4 4 5 8	
6	0 2 4 5 5 5 6 8	
7	0 2 4	

(b) 2.9 cm

4. (a) $\frac{17}{75}$

(b) Yes. Female: $\frac{12}{50} = 24\%$, Male: $\frac{5}{25} = 20\%$

5. (c) (i) 120 hours (ii) 35 hours

(d) (c)(i) as it lies between known values.

6. (a) E.g. Sample size too small.
Sample likely to be biased.

(b) E.g. Much bigger sample.
Sample randomly selected from all parts of town.

7. (a) 110 cm - 120 cm (b) 118.5 cm

8. (a)

Relative frequency 0.3 0.2 0.1 0 — Number of trials 0 50 100 150 200

(b) 200.
As the number of experiments increases, relative frequency gets closer to 0.2.
$0.2 \times 1000 = 200$

9. (a) (ii) Median = 28 minutes,
Interquartile range = 11 minutes
(b) Median = 45 minutes,
Interquartile range = 8 minutes
(c) Times for male students have lower
average and more variation than those
for female students.

10. (a)

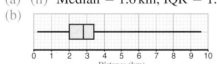

Hoopla   Darts

(b) (i) 0.42   (ii) 0.46

11. (a) (i) Frequency densities: 2.6, 6, 5, 3, 1.2
(ii) 36
(b) (i)

Age (y years)	$y < 20$	$20 \leqslant y < 50$	$\geqslant 50$
Male	8	48	12
Female	2	24	6

(ii) Both males and females from all age
groups will be represented in
proportion to membership.

12. (a) 90   (b) (i) 15.1%   (ii) 21.7 m

13. (a) $\frac{1}{30}$ (b) $\frac{1}{3}$

Exam Practice: Module   ①

Calculator Paper   Page 19

1. (a) 359.8 kg   (b) 58.6 kg
2. (a) **X 1, X 3, Y 1, Y 3**
(b) Numbers 1 and 3 are not equally likely.
3. (a) 6   (b) 3.55   (c) 3.5
4. (a) $\frac{1}{3}$ (b) $\frac{1}{6}$ (c) $\frac{1}{2}$
5. (a) 275 g
6. (a) (i) 0.8   (ii) 0.6   (b) 50   (c) 0.36
7. £75, £93
8. (a) $\frac{49}{100}$ (b) $\frac{21}{50}$
9. (a) (ii) Median = 1.6 km, IQR = 1.1 km
(b)

Distance (km) — box plot scale 0 to 10

(c) The average distance for primary pupils
is less and they have less variation in the
distances travelled.

10. 0.94
11. (a) Frequency densities: 2.5, 4.2, 2.4, 0.6
(b) 13.6 minutes   (c) 6
12. (a) $\frac{3}{22}$ (b) $\frac{34}{55}$
13. Child: 16, Adult: 23, Senior Citizen: 11
14. (a) (i) $\frac{3}{5}$ (ii) $\frac{3}{10}$ (b) (i) $\frac{4}{25}$ (ii) $\frac{1}{100}$
15. 63 leaves
16. 82.5%

SECTION   ⑦

Exercise **7**   Page 22

1. (a) 1 005 010   (b) 23 500
2. (a) 10 070   (b) 6685
    (c) 100 147   (d) 154
3. (a) (i) 9623   (ii) 2396   (b) 7227
4. £181 per month
5. 21
6. 13 301
7. (a) 3290   (b) 7 reams
8. (a) 770
    (b) (i) 19 coaches needed
      (ii) 9 empty seats
9. (a) 8   (b) 4   (c) 105   (d) 2
10. 150 cm
11. (a)

2	−3	4
3	1	−1
−2	5	0

(b) $(-12) + (18) + (-24) = 18 - 36 = -18$
12. (a) −7   (b) −3   (c) −6
13. Sue. Beth: 4, John: 12, Sue: 13
14. 98 304
15. £20 563 720

SECTION   ⑧

Exercise **8**   Page 25

1. (a) There are two figures after the decimal
points in the question but only one in
the answer.
(b) (i) 0.12   (ii) 0.06
2. $\frac{30}{0.05} = \frac{3000}{5} = 600$
3. (a) 2.64   (b) 12   (c) 0.0245   (d) 1360
4. 1.57 m
5. (a) 183.5 cm   (b) 155.5 cm
6. $\frac{7}{12}, \frac{5}{8}, \frac{2}{3}, \frac{3}{4}$
7. (a) $\frac{5}{12}$ (b) $\frac{2}{3}$
8. (a) $1\frac{4}{5}$ (b) $5\frac{1}{3}$ (c) 5
9. 54
10. (a) 0.167   (b) 1.7, 1.67, 1.66, $1\frac{1}{6}$, 1.067
    (c) $\frac{13}{20}$
11. (a) $6\frac{5}{12}$ (b) $1\frac{4}{5}$ (c) 4   (d) $1\frac{7}{10}$
12. $\frac{9}{20}$
13. £120
14. 98 pence per kilogram
15. 17.76792453

Exercise 9 — Page 27

1. (a) 630   (b) 626.5   (c) 600
2. 19 500
3. 50p × 800 = £400
4. (a) 100 is bigger than 97, **and** 50 is bigger than 49.
   (b) Smaller. 1000 is smaller than 1067, **and** 50 is bigger than 48.
5. (a) $\frac{9000}{10} \times 90p = £810$
   (b) 9000 is larger than 8873, 10 is smaller than 11, and 90 is larger than 89.9.
6. (a) 400.5 m   (b) 1598 m
7. No. For example, an answer of 0.01634… is 0.02 to 2 d.p. and 0.016 to 2 s.f. 0.016 is more accurate.
8. (a) 18.0952381   (b) 18.1
9. 9.2
10. (a) 31.28, correct to 2 d.p.
    (b) $\frac{90 \times 10}{20 + 10} = \frac{900}{30} = 30$
    So, answer to (a) is about right.
11. Lower bound 9.1 kg, upper bound 9.3 kg.
12. (a) (i) 4.605   (ii) 9.4409…
    (b) 278.2

Exercise 10 — Page 29

1. 8%
2. 28 marks
3. £40.80
4. 39 hours
5. £480
6. £333.70
7. 57.3%
8. Small bar.
   Large: 2.66 g/p
   Small: 2.78 g/p
9. 36%
10. 81
11. £11.52
12. £22 035
13. 3 years
14. (a) 40%
    (b) £960
15. 32%
16. 400
17. £950
18. (a) £4622.50
    (b) £480
19. £3.75
20. 19.1%

Exercise 11 — Page 32

1. (a) 1, 2, 3, 6, 9, 18
   (b) 35
   (c) 15 has more than 2 factors: 1, 3, 5, 15
2. 60
3. (a) (i) 125   (ii) 8   (b) 5 and 6

4. (a) 2   (b) 64
5. (a) $2^2 \times 3^2$ (b) $3^2 \times 5$
   (c) 9   (d) 180
6. No. $2^2 + 3^2 = 4 + 9 = 13$
   $(2 + 3)^2 = 5^2 = 25$
7. For example:
   $2^2 + 3^2 = 13$ and $3^2 + 5^2 = 34$.
8. (a) 5   (b) 0.25
   (c) $\sqrt{225}$, $\sqrt{225} = 15$, $2^4 = 16$
9. 30 seconds
10. (a) (i) 5   (ii) 3
    (b) (i) 75   (ii) 180
    (c) (i) a and b have no common factors.
        (ii) a is a factor of b.
11. (a) 72   (b) 225   (c) 32
12. $1\frac{1}{2}$
13. (a) $x = 9$ (b) $x = 3$
    (c) $x = 18$ (d) $x = 1$
14. (a) $\frac{1}{4}$ (b) 2
15. (a) 3   (b) $\frac{1}{8}$
    (c) 125   (d) $\frac{1}{8}$
16. (a) $\frac{7}{9}$ (b) 9
17. (a) $\frac{8}{5}$ (b) $\frac{1}{9}$ (c) $\frac{8}{25}$
18. 0.14
19. 4.25
20. (a) 47.1645…   (b) 47.2
21. (a) 2.02
    (b) $\sqrt{3 + \frac{6}{3} - \frac{9}{3^2}} = \sqrt{3 + 2 - 1} = \sqrt{4} = 2$
22. 1.1
23. (a) 1.9   (b) 5.9   (c) 11   (d) 0.025

Exercise 12 — Page 34

1. 1×10^6
2. (a) (i) 2.6×10^4 (ii) 26 000
   (b) (i) 8.9×10^{-5} (ii) 0.000 089
3. (a) 5.7×10^7 (b) 5.7×10^{-5}
4. (a) Uranus   (b) 5×10^3 km/h
5. (a) 5.6×10^4 (b) 3×10^8
   (c) 1.2×10^{-1}
6. (a) 2.34×10^6 (b) 9.6×10^{-3} cm
7. (a) 1.29×10^6 (b) 6.4×10^3
8. 300 people per doctor
9. (a) 1.6×10^9 (b) 0.000 79
10. £214.86
11. 9.47×10^{12} km
12. 0.000 008 5
13. (a) 2.15%   (b) 3.021×10^7 tonnes
14. 0.45%

Exercise 13   Page 36

1. 8 large bricks
2. 7.5 kg
3. (a) $\frac{3}{5}$ (b) 40%
4. 12 women
5. 750 red and 1250 yellow
6. £87
7. 250 disabled people
8. 25
9. £517.50
10. 4 days
11. £32.40
12. 1 : 20 000
13. Model A is 57.3 mm (or 57 mm) longer than Model B
14. Year 9: 360,   Year 10: 210,   Year 11: 180
15. 48 minutes

Exercise 14   Page 38

1. $1\frac{1}{2}$ hours
2. 165 km
3. 48 miles per hour
4. 3.6 km/h
5. 1 hour 36 minutes
6. 0924
7. (a) 40 miles per hour
   (b) 1116
8. Yes.
   $\frac{65}{80} \times 60 = 48.75$ mins.
   Arrives 1029.
9. 1.8 km
10. 28.8 mph
11. 28.8 km/h
12. 10 m/s
13. 1.27 seconds
14. (a) 12 seconds
    (b) 127.8 km/h
15. 9 g/cm³ ($9\,g/cm^3$)
16. 19 g
17. 259.3 people/km²
18. 106.6 people/km²

Exercise 15   Page 41

1. (a) $0.\dot{7}1428\dot{5}$ (b) $\frac{2}{9}$
2. (a) $5\sqrt{5}$ (b) 3   (c) 6   (d) $\frac{3}{4}$
3. (a) $100 \times 0.\dot{4}\dot{5} = 45.\dot{4}\dot{5}$
       $99 \times 0.\dot{4}\dot{5} = 45.\dot{4}\dot{5} - 0.\dot{4}\dot{5} = 45$
       So, $0.\dot{4}\dot{5} = \frac{45}{99} = \frac{5}{11}$
   (b) $\frac{7}{11}$
4. (a) $1000x = 378.378\ldots$ (b) $x = \frac{14}{37}$
5. $3\sqrt{2}$
6. (a) $4\sqrt{3}$ (b) 9   (c) $\sqrt{3}$ (d) 30
7. (a) $\frac{4}{5}$ (b) $5\sqrt{3}$ (c) $7\sqrt{3}$ (d) $2\sqrt{3}$

8. $5\sqrt{2}$
9. (a) $2 \times 2 \times 5$
   (b) (i) $a = 2$, $b = 5$ (ii) $x = -\frac{1}{2}$
10. $12\sqrt{3}$
11. (a) $3\sqrt{5}$ (b) 5
12. (a) $n = 12$ (b) 1
13. $\frac{2\sqrt{3} + 3}{3}$
14. (a) $x = -2.5$ (b) $4 + 6\sqrt{2}$

Exercise 16   Page 43

1. (a) (i)

x	-2	0	2	3
y	-3	1	5	7

   (c) $x = 1$
2. (a) Missing entries are: 3, 0, 3
   (b)
   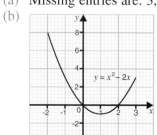
3. (a) Missing entries are: $-3, -5, 1, 7$
   (b)
   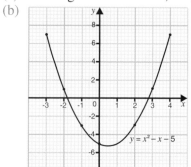
   (c) (i) $x = -1.8$ and $x = 2.8$
       (ii) $x = -2.7$ and $x = 3.7$
4. (a) (b)
   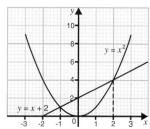
   (c) Rearrange $x^2 - x - 2 = 0$
   to give $x^2 = x + 2$.
   To solve $x^2 - x - 2 = 0$,
   read the values of x where the
   two graphs intersect.
   $x = -1$ and $x = 2$
5. $y = 2x + 1$

6. (b) Draw the graph of $y = 1 - x$.
$x = -2.4$ and $x = 0.4$

7. (a) Missing entries are: 6, −4
(c) $x = -1$ and $x = 4$
(d) Rearrange $x^2 - 4x - 1 = 0$
to give $x^2 - 3x - 4 = x - 3$.
Draw the graph of $y = x - 3$.
$x = -0.2$ and $x = 4.2$

8. Rearrange $x^2 - x - 11 = 0$
to give $x^2 + 2x - 7 = 3x + 4$.
Draw the graph of $y = 3x + 4$.
$x = -2.9$ and $x = 3.9$

SECTION 17

Exercise 17 Page 45

1. (a) $\frac{0.6}{0.4} = \frac{9}{6} = \frac{16.5}{11} = 1.5$, so, $m = 1.5n$
(b) (i) $m = 2.7$ (ii) $n = 8.4$

2. (a) $y = \frac{2}{x}$ (b)

x	0.4	2.5	100
y	5	0.8	0.02

3. $x = 5$
4. $R = 4$
5. (a) $m = \frac{2\sqrt{n}}{3}$
(b) (i) $m = 4$ (ii) $n = 225$
6. £16
7. (a) 500 metres (b) 356 kHz
(c) 548 metres
8. (a) (b)

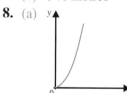

9. $n = -\frac{1}{3}$
10. (a) $y = 640$ (b) $z = 4$

Exam Practice: Module 3

Non-calculator Paper Page 46

1. (a) 3 is a factor of 15 and 27.
(b) 27
(c) (i) 15 and 27 (more than 2 factors).
(ii) 35
2. (a) (i) 4.74 (ii) 0.08 (iii) 80
(b) £23.40
3. (a) $\frac{1}{2}$, $\frac{3}{5}$, $\frac{5}{8}$, $\frac{2}{3}$, $\frac{3}{4}$ (b) $\frac{9}{40}$
(c) (i) $\frac{13}{20}$ (ii) $\frac{1}{6}$ (iii) $\frac{8}{15}$
4. 8 hours 24 minutes
5. (a) $40 \times 5 \times 40 = 8000$ miles
(b) (i) 67% (ii) $12\,000 \times 40\text{p} = £4800$
6. £3.60
7. 48 pence

8. (a) 5^3. $3^5 = 243$ and $5^3 = 125$.
(b) (i) 288 (ii) 750
9. 40%
10. 10
11. 75 mph
12. (a) 34.7 (b) $\frac{100 \times 3000}{0.5} = 600\,000$
(c) 0.005
13. (a) £6.60 (b) (i) 745 (ii) 754
14. (a) (i) $2^3 \times 3^2$ (ii) $2^5 \times 3$
(b) (i) 288 (ii) 24
15. (a) 12.5 km (b) 109.5 minutes
16. 80 km/h
17. (a) 6×10^{-19} (b) (i) 0.6 (ii) 0.6060606
18. (a) $\frac{400 \times 3}{0.6} = \frac{1200}{0.6} = 2000$
(b) 2.4×10^{-6} (c) $\frac{8}{9}$
19. (a) (i) 3.86×10^7 (ii) 5.4×10^{-5}
(b) (i) 1×10^9 (ii) 4×10^{-3}
20. £60
21. (a) $2^4 \times 3 \times 5$ (b) 15
22. (a) $1\frac{11}{12}$ (b) $3\frac{1}{3}$ (c) $\frac{5}{6}$ (d) $1\frac{1}{2}$
23. 40
24. 20 male passengers
25. (a) $\sqrt{\frac{40\,000}{(10^2)}} = \sqrt{400} = 20$ (b) 1.5×10^4
(c) £500 000
26. (a) 0.4
(b) $\left(\frac{1}{4}\right)^{\frac{1}{2}}$, $\left(\frac{1}{2}\right)^2$, 5^{-1}, 2^{-3}, 3^{-2}.
(c) (i) $x = 7$ (ii) $x = 2$ (iii) $x = 1$
(d) $\frac{1}{27}$
27. 6 minutes less
28. (a) $B = 2h^3$ (b) 2 kg (c) 4 m
29. 7.25 m
30. (a) 9 (b) $2^{\frac{5}{2}}$ (c) 4 (d) $\frac{1}{27}$
31. (a) Missing entries are: 5, −9, 0
(c) Rearrange $2x^2 - x - 9 = 0$
to give $2x^2 + x - 10 = 2x - 1$.
Draw the graph of $y = 2x - 1$.
$x = -1.9$ and $x = 2.4$
32. (a) $T = 80$ (b) $M = 1.44$
33. (a) (i) $8\sqrt{3}$ (ii) 4
(b) 16 (c) $\frac{1}{3}$ (d) $\frac{7}{33}$

Exam Practice: Module 3

Calculator Paper Page 49

1. 24.1 kg
2. 50
3. (a) (i) 1.73 (ii) 0.216 (b) $m = 142.8$
4. 39 hours
5. Small.
Small: $\frac{180}{36} = 5$ g/p Large: $\frac{300}{63} = 4.76$ g/p

6. E.g. $2^2 + 3^2 = 4 + 9 = 13$, **not** even.

7. 0824

8. (a) 4   (b) 51.2

9. 12.5%

10. Numbers between 0 and 1.

11. (a) 1.92 kg   (b) 2.208 kg
    (c) 5 months

12. 20 and 32

13. 32 minutes

14. (a) £564.66   (b) 15.7625%

15. (a) (i) $2^3 \times 3^2$ (ii) $2^4 \times 5$
    (b) 12 minutes

16. 889.61 dollars

17. 0.45, correct to 2 s.f. All numbers given to
3 s.f., so, answer can only be correct to 2 s.f.

18. (a) £227.50   (b) £167.44

19. 3150

20. 126.3 people per square kilometre

21. (a) $\sqrt{6.9}$, 2.58, $2\frac{4}{7}$, 1.6^2
    (b) (i) 290   (ii) $\dfrac{600 \times 30}{80 - 20} = \dfrac{18\,000}{60} = 300$

22. (a) 1.728×10^7 (b) 1.85

23. £63.80

24. £1200

25. £27 385

26. (a) 7.3×10^6 tonnes   (b) 0.725%

27. (a) Missing entry is: 9
    (c) Draw the graph of $y = 4x - 1$.
      $x = 0.4$ and $x = 1.6$

28. (a) $1\frac{1}{8}$ (b) 7.1×10^9

29. (a) $7\sqrt{2}$ (b) $\dfrac{\sqrt{6}}{6}$

30. 2.6845×10^8

31. (a) $\dfrac{34}{99}$ (b) $\dfrac{314}{495}$

32. 10.5%

33. (a) $3\sqrt{5}$ (b) $\dfrac{\sqrt{10}}{2}$

34. (a) $R = \dfrac{18}{d^2}$
    (b) (i) $R = 0.125$ ohms   (ii) $d = 1.2$ mm

35. 3.9×10^{-2}

36. $V = 3.608275$

SECTION 18

Exercise 18   Page 52

1. (a) $(t + 5)$ years   (b) $(x - 5)$ years

2. $(3x + 2y)$ pence

3. (a) $6m$ (b) $m + 2$ (c) m^3

4. $(4x + 200)$ degrees

5. $(5d + 15)$ pence

6. | $2y$ and $y + y$ | $2(y + 1)$ and $2y + 2$ |
| y^2 and $y \times y$ | $2y + y$ and $3y$ |

7. (a) (i) $3x + 3$ (ii) $x + 2y$
    (b) (i) $2x + 6$ (ii) $x^2 - x$
    (c) (i) $2x - 5$ (ii) $13 + 3x$
    (d) (i) $2(a - 3)$ (ii) $x(x + 2)$

8. (a) £xy (b) £$y(x - 5)$

9. (a) $12 - x$ (b) $(d + 5)$ pence
    (c) $x(d + 5) + d(12 - x) = (5x + 12d)$ pence

10. (a) $7a + 2b + 4ab$ (b) $4x + 15$

11. $14x - 9$

12. (a) y^5 (b) x^3 (c) z^2 (d) $\dfrac{x}{y}$

13. (a) (i) $6a^7$ (ii) $4a^4$ (b) $3x(x - 3)$

14. (a) $12a^7$ (b) $3a^3$

15. (a) $8 - 6n$ (b) $6m^2$ (c) $2m(4n - 1)$

16. $4x - 1$

17. (a) (i) $6a^4$ (ii) $2x^6$
       (iii) $2mn^4$ (iv) $20x^5y^2$
    (b) (i) $9m^6$ (ii) $8a^6b^3$

18. (a) (i) $2x^2 - 6xy$ (ii) $9a^2 + 3a^3$
    (b) (i) $2y(2x - y)$ (ii) $3m(m - 4)$
    (c) $x^2 - x$

19. $3a^6b$

20. (a) $4xy - 2x^2y$ (b) $3pq(2 - q)$ (c) $3m^3$

21. (a) $4xyz^2$ (b) $\dfrac{1}{m^3}$

22. $81x^4y^8$

23. $\dfrac{a^2}{c}$

SECTION 19

Exercise 19   Page 54

1. (a) $x = 5$ (b) $x = 2$ (c) $x = 4$

2. (a) 5   (b) 4

3. (a) $x = 10$ (b) $x = 6$
    (c) $x = 6$ (d) $x = 11$

4. $n + (n + 3) + (2n - 1) = 30$
                  $4n + 2 = 30$
                        $n = 7$

5. (a) $x = 1\frac{1}{2}$ (b) $x = -1$

6. $x = 6$

7. (a) $x = 8$ (b) $x = 1$
    (c) $x = -4$ (d) $x = 2\frac{1}{2}$

8. (a) $x = 6$ (b) $x = 3$ (c) $x = 1\frac{1}{2}$

9. (a) $16x + 4(2x + 3) = (24x + 12)$ kilograms
    (b) $24x + 12 = 132$, $x = 5$

10. (a) $x = 2\frac{1}{2}$ (b) $n = 6$
    (c) $m = -1\frac{1}{2}$ (d) $x = -1$

11. (a) $x = -21$ (b) $x = 2\frac{1}{2}$
    (c) $x = \frac{3}{5}$ (d) $x = -12$

12. (a) $x = 17$ (b) $x = 1\frac{1}{5}$

13. (a) $x = 1$ (b) $x = -2\frac{1}{2}$
    (c) $x = 2\frac{1}{2}$ (d) $x = 6$

14. $3(x + 4) = 5x$ $x = 6$

15. (a) $x = 1$ (b) $a = -4$ (c) $x = 6\frac{1}{2}$

16. (a) $x = 1\frac{2}{5}$ (b) $x = -11$

17. $x = -\frac{1}{4}$

18. $x = \frac{4}{5}$

19. $x = 7\frac{2}{5}$

SECTION 20

Exercise 20   Page 56

1. (a) 2   (b) -8 (c) 8   (d) -15

2. (a) -60 (b) 6

3. $L = 8$

4. $A = -11$

5. 90

6. 24

7. $T = 100$

8. $S = -8$

9. $T = -12$

10. $M = 4$

11. (a) 260 cans   (b) $N = \frac{3T}{2} + 20$
    (c) 130 tickets

12. (a) $-1\frac{5}{8}$ (b) $-\frac{5}{8}$

13. $t = \frac{c + 5}{3}$

14. (a) $d = 62.8$ (b) $t = \frac{2d}{u + v}$
    (c) $t = 7.5$

15. (a) $v = 12.2$ (b) $a = \frac{v - u}{t}$

16. $r = \frac{ps}{g}$

17. (a) 48   (b) $-\frac{2}{3}$

18. $f = 9.6$

19. $P = \frac{V^2}{R}$

20. $s = 2.2$

21. (a) 3 750 000   (b) $h = \pm\sqrt{\frac{5g}{3}}$

22. $q = \frac{5p}{p + 1}$

23. $v = \frac{uw}{u - w}$

24. $m = \frac{3 + 5n}{n - 1}$

SECTION 21

Exercise 21   Page 58

1. (a) 17   (b) 81   (c) $\frac{1}{16}$

2. (a) -10
    (b) Subtract the next even number (-8).

3. (a) 14
    (b) No. Number must be (multiple of 3) -1.

4. 5, 6, $5\frac{1}{2}$

5. -2, -8

6. No. The sequence does not end.
    Sequence: 1, 6, 10, 8, 4, 8, 8, 0, 16, ...

7. (a) Pattern 20 has 58 squares.
    $3 \times$ (pattern number) -2
    (b) $3n - 2$

8. (a) 40. Add 7 to the last term.   (b) $7n - 2$

9. (a) $2n + 3$ (b) $4n - 3$

10. (a) 5, 8, 13
    (b) No.
    $102 \;(= 106 - 4)$ is not a square number.

11. (a) n^2 (b) $n^2 + 1$

12. (a) $\frac{5}{9}$, $\frac{10}{13}$ (b) 5th term.

13. (a) $3n + 2$ (b) $n^2 - 1$

SECTION 22

Exercise 22   Page 61

1. (a)

x	-3	0	3
y	7	1	-5

    (b)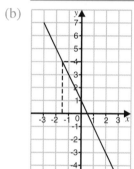
    (c) $y = 4$

2. (a)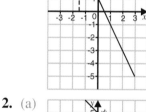
    (b) $x + y = 5$

3. (a) $P(0, 3)$, $Q(6, 0)$ (b) $m = 5.5$

4. (a) $y = 4$ (b) (i) $\frac{1}{2}$ (ii) $y = \frac{1}{2}x + 1$

5. 1: **R**,   2: **S**,   3: **Q**,   4: **P**

6. (a)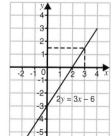
    (b) 1.5
    (c) $x = 3$

7. $y = -\frac{2}{5}x + 2$

8. (a)

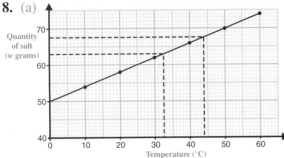

(b) (i) 32.5°C (ii) 67.6 grams
(c) (i) $a = 0.4$, $b = 50$ (ii) 88 grams

9. $B = \frac{1}{5}t + 12$

10. (a) $y = \frac{2}{5}x + 2$ (b) $y = \frac{2}{5}x - 1$

11. The line $5y = x + 4$ has gradient $\frac{1}{5}$.
The line $y = 6 - 5x$ has gradient -5.
$\frac{1}{5} \times (-5) = -1$, so lines are perpendicular.

12. $y = -2x + 2$

13. $P(-8, 0)$

SECTION 23

Exercise 23   Page 63

1. (a) 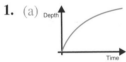   (b)

2. (a) Decreased (b) 70 minutes
(c) 8 mph

3. (a) 30 minutes (b) 4.8 km/h
(c) 3 km (d) 3.2 km/h

4. (a) 1.8 km/min² (b) 6.3 km

SECTION 24

Exercise 24   Page 66

1. (a) $x > 3$ (b) $x \geq -2$
(c) $x \leq 2$ (d) $x < -2$

2. (a)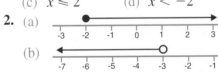
(b)
(c)
(d)

3. (a) $-1, 0, 1, 2$ (b) $1, 2$ (c) $-1, 0, 1$
4. (a) $x > 7$ (b) $-2 < x \leq 1$
5. $x < -2$
6. $x < 6\frac{1}{2}$
7. 1: Ⓑ, 2: Ⓒ, 3: Ⓓ, 4: Ⓐ

8. (a) (b)

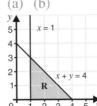

9. (a) (b)

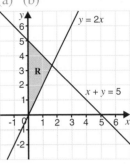

10. $x \leq 3$, $y \geq 1$, $y \leq x$
11. (a) (i) $-4, -3, -2, -1, 0, 1$ (ii) 16
(b) $x \geq 10$ and $x < 20$
12. (a) (i) $x \leq 4$ (ii) $x > 2$
(b) 3, 4
13. (a) $x < 6$ (b) $x > 0$

SECTION 25

Exercise 25   Page 68

1. 1: B, 2: C, 3: D, 4: A
2. (b) $x = \pm 2.2$ (c) $x = \pm 1.4$
3. (a)

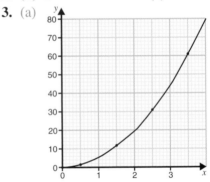

(b) 3.2 seconds (c) 80 m
4. (a) Missing entries are: 7, 2, -2
(b)

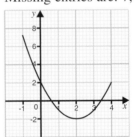

(c) $x = 0.6$ or $x = 3.4$
5. (b) (i) $x = 0$ or $x = 5$
(ii) $x = 0.7$ or $x = 4.3$
(c) $x = 2.5$, $y = 6.25$
6. (a)

(b) The graph does not cross the line $y = 0$.
(c) 0.9, correct to 1 d.p.

128

7. (b) If $y = 3x$ and $y = x^2 + 1$,
then $3x = x^2 + 1$, which can be
rearranged as $x^2 - 3x + 1 = 0$.
Solutions are given by the values of x
where the two graphs intersect.

(c) $x = 0.4$ or $x = 2.6$

8. Rearrange $x^2 - x - 8 = 0$
to give $x^2 + x - 5 = 2x + 3$.
Draw the graph of $y = 2x + 3$.
$x = -2.4$ and $x = 3.4$

9. (a) Table of values to draw graph.

-3	-2	-1	$-\frac{1}{2}$	0	$\frac{1}{2}$	1	2	3
-24	-6	0	0.375	0	-0.375	0	6	24

(b) $x = 2.3$

10. (a)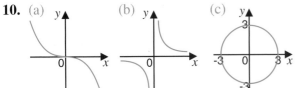
(b)
(c)

11. (a) Table of values to draw graph.

x	-2	-1	0	1	2
y	0.0625	0.25	1	4	16

(b) $x = 1.5$

12. $x = -3.4$, $y = -2.2$ **and** $x = 3.8$, $y = 1.4$

SECTION 26

Exercise 26   Page 70

1. (a) $x^2 - 7x$ (b) $x^2 + 3x - 10$
(c) $2x^2 + 5x - 3$ (d) $9x^2 + 12xy + 4y^2$

2. (a) $x(x - 6)$ (b) $(x - 3)(x + 5)$
(c) $(x - 1)(x - 3)$ (d) $(x - 3)(x + 3)$

3. (a) $x = 0$ or $x = -5$
(b) $x = 3$ or $x = -2$
(c) $x = -1\frac{1}{2}$ or $x = 1$

4. (a) $(x - 4)(x + 3)$ (b) $x = 4$ or $x = -3$

5. (a) $x = 0$ or $x = 3$
(b) $x = 1$ or $x = 2$
(c) $x = 2$ or $x = -3$

6. $x = -1$ or $x = 3$

7. $x = 4$ or $x = 7$

8. (a) $(2x + 3)(x - 5)$ (b) $(x - 5y)(x + 5y)$

9. (a) $(2x + 1)(x - 3)$
(b) $x = -\frac{1}{2}$ or $x = 3$

10. $x = -\frac{2}{3}$ or $x = 1$

11. $p = 3$, $q = -14$

12. (a) $(x - 2)^2 - 12$
(b) $x = -1.46$ or $x = 5.46$

13. $x = -4.19$ or $x = 1.19$

14. $x = -1.14$ or $x = 6.14$

15. $x = -0.58$ or $x = 2.58$

16. $x = 3.4$

17. (a) $x = \frac{1}{x} + \frac{1}{2}$
$2x^2 = 2 + x$
$2x^2 - x - 2 = 0$
(b) $x = -0.78$ or $x = 1.28$

SECTION 27

Exercise 27   Page 72

1. (a)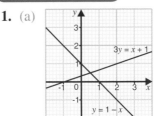
(b) $x = \frac{1}{2}$, $y = \frac{1}{2}$

2. (b) $x = \frac{1}{2}$, $y = 3\frac{1}{2}$

3. $x = 2\frac{1}{2}$, $y = \frac{1}{2}$

4. (b) The lines are parallel.

5. $x = 1\frac{1}{2}$, $y = 6$

6. $x = -2$ $y = 5$

7. $x = 1\frac{1}{2}$, $y = -1$

8. (a) $x + y = 40$ and $4x + 7y = 184$
(b) $x = 32$, $y = 8$

9. (a) $2x + 4y = 65$ and $x + 3y = 40$
(b) $x = £17.50$, $y = £7.50$

10. $x = \frac{1}{2}$, $y = -5$

11. $x = 2$, $y = -1$

12. (a) $x = 2$, $y = 0$ and $x = -4$, $y = 12$
(b) $x = 1$, $y = 5$ and $x = 4$, $y = 8$
(c) $x = 2.24$, $y = 4.48$ and
$x = -2.24$, $y = -4.48$

13. $x = -2.5$, $y = -2.4$ and $x = 6$, $y = 1$

14. (a) $x = -1$, $y = -12$ and $x = 2$, $y = -9$
(b) $x = -1$, $y = 4$ and $x = 4$, $y = -1$
(c) $x = \frac{1}{2}$, $y = 2$ and $x = 1$, $y = 1$

SECTION 28

Exercise 28   Page 74

1. $12x$

2. $2x(x + y) - (x + y)^2$
$= 2x^2 + 2xy - x^2 - 2xy - y^2$
$= x^2 - y^2$

3. (a) $(3x + 4)^2 - (3x + 2)^2$
$= 9x^2 + 24x + 16 - 9x^2 - 12x - 4$
$= 12x + 12$
(b) $x = 3.25$ or $x = -1$

4. (a) $x - 3$ (b) $\frac{x}{2}$ (c) $\frac{x+1}{x-3}$ (d) $\frac{x}{x-1}$

5. $\frac{2}{2x+1}$

6. (a) $\frac{3}{2x}$ (b) $\frac{5x+1}{2(x+1)}$ (c) $\frac{4x-1}{(x+2)(2x-5)}$

7. $x = -5.77$ or $x = 2.77$

8. $x = -2\frac{1}{2}$ or $x = 1$

9. $x = -1.62$ or $x = 0.62$

10. (a) (i) $(3p+1)(p+5)$ (ii) $\frac{p-5}{3p+1}$

(b) $x = 1\frac{1}{3}$

11. (a) $x^2 + 2 + \frac{1}{x^2}$

(b) (i) $\left(x - \frac{1}{x}\right)^2$ (ii) $x = 1$ or $x = -1$

12. (a) $2x^2 - 3x - 10 = 0$ (b) $x = 3.1$

13. $x = 6.4$

SECTION 29

Exercise 29 — Page 76

1. (a)    (b)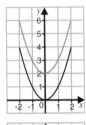

(c) 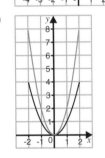   (d)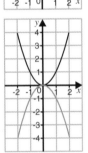

2. (a) $y = f(x-2)$
(b) $y = f(x) - 2$
(c) $y = -f(x)$

3. (a) $y = 2\cos x$ (b) $y = \cos x + 1$
(c) $y = \cos(x + 45°)$

4. (b) $y = 0.2x + 4.5$, $x = 77.5$

5. (a)

x	1	2.5	3	4	6	10
$\frac{1}{x}$	1	0.4	$0.\dot{3}$	0.25	$0.1\dot{6}$	0.1

(b) $a = 7.5$, $b = 4$

Algebra

Non-calculator Paper — Page 77

1. (a) $5x$ (b) $3a - 4b$ (c) $3m^2$

2. (b) $(-1, 1)$

3. (a) 30
(b) 50th term is an odd number.
All even terms are odd numbers.

---

4. (a) 6   (b) 12

5. -11

6. (a) $(x-3)$ years   (b) $4x$ years
(c) $x + (x - 3) + 4x = 45$, $x = 8$
Louisa: 5 years,   Hannah: 8 years,
Mother: 32 years

7. $t = 5$

8. $x = 1.5$

9. (a) (i) $3(a-2)$ (ii) $k(k-2)$
(b) (i) $m^2 - 4m$ (ii) $3x^2 + 15x$
(c) (i) $x = 3$ (ii) $x = -1$ (iii) $x = \frac{1}{2}$

10. (a)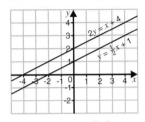

(b) Lines are parallel, same gradient.

11. (a) $x < 5$

(b) $-1, 0, 1$
(c) $x = 1$, $y = -2$

12. (a) $3n - 5$ (b) $x = \frac{y+5}{2}$

13. (a) Missing entries are: 4, 1
(c) (i) $x = 1$ (ii) $x = -0.4$ or 2.4

14. (a) 20
(b) (i) $(x-2)(x-3)$
(ii) $x = 2$ or $x = 3$

15. (a) (i) $\frac{1}{2}$ (ii) $-1\frac{1}{2}$ (b) $\frac{3}{4}$

16. (a) (i) a^4 (ii) a^6 (b) $q = \pm\sqrt{p-r}$

17. (a) $x \leqslant 7$ (b) $y^2 - 14y + 49$
(c) $6x^7$ (d) $(p+4)(p-3)$

18. (a) $27x^6y^3$ (b) $2a^4b^2$

19. (a) $3(x-5)(x+5)$ (b) $(3x-5)(x-1)$

20. (a)   (b)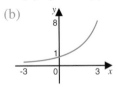

21. $x(19 - x) = 78$
$x = 6$ or $x = 13$,   so, length $= 13\,\text{cm}$.

22. (a) $(2x+3)^2 - (2x+1)^2$
$= 4x^2 + 12x + 9 - (4x^2 + 4x + 1)$
$= 8x + 8$
$= 8(x + 1)$
(b) $x = -1$ or $x = 9$

23. (a) $2(x-2)$ (b) $a = \frac{c}{1-c}$
(c) $a = 9$, $b = 2$, $c = -5$

24. $y = \frac{3x+5}{x+1}$

25. $y = 2x - 7$

26. (a)   (b)   (c)

27. $x = 1$, $y = 3$ and $x = -1\frac{1}{2}$, $y = -2$

28. $(2x - 1) - 3(x + 1) = 2(x + 1)(2x - 1)$
$2x - 1 - 3x - 3 = 4x^2 + 2x - 2$
$4x^2 + 3x + 2 = 0$

Algebra

Calculator Paper   **Page 79**

1. (a) 30 minutes   (b) 16 mph
(c) From C to D. Steepest gradient. (d) 4 pm

2. (a) 7   (b) (i) $x + 3$ (ii) $3n - 1$

3. (a) $(x + 45)$ pence
(b) $3(x + 45) + x = 455$, $x = 80$
Glass of milk costs 80 pence.

4. $x = 2.6$

5. (a) (i) $t = -1$ (ii) $x = -\frac{1}{5}$
(b) (i) $7x - 3$ (ii) $y^2 - y - 20$
(c) (i) m^6 (ii) n^5

6. (a) **A**: $x = 2$, **B**: $y = 1$, **C**: $x + y = 2$
(b) $x \leq 2$, $y \leq 1$, $x + y \geq 2$

7. (a) 1, 2, 3   (b) $x = 5$, $y = 2\frac{1}{2}$
(c) $y(x - y)$ (d) $x = 2$ or $x = 5$

8. (a) 0.012   (b) $x = \frac{5y^2}{2}$

9. $x = 6.75$

10. (a) 2 and 3   (b) $x = 2.84$

11. $x = -3.45$ or $x = 1.45$

12. (a) $3x(x + 2) = 4(x + 3)$ (b) $x = 1.7$
$3x^2 + 6x = 4x + 12$
$3x^2 + 2x - 12 = 0$

13. (b) (i) $x = -1.2$ or $x = 1.2$ (c) $y = 1 - x$
(ii) $x = -1.5$ or $x = 1$

14. $x = 0.22$ or $x = 2.28$

15. $n = -\frac{3}{4}$

16. (a) $\frac{x + 3}{x + 1}$ (b) $y = \frac{x}{x - 1}$
(c) $a = 4$, $b = 1$, $c = -4$

17. $x = 1$, $y = 3$ and $x = -4$, $y = 8$

18. (a) $p = -2$, $q = 3$ (b) $x = \frac{3y + 1}{y - 2}$

19. $x = -1.56$ or $x = 2.56$

SECTION   30

Exercise 30   **Page 83**

1. (a) $a = 48°$, $b = 44°$
(b) $c = 117°$, $d = 117°$
(c) $e = 42°$, $f = 76°$, $g = 62°$

2. (a) $x = 150°$ (b) $y = 123°$ (c) $z = 108°$

3. (a) E.g.   (b) E.g.

4. $\angle ABC = 114°$

5. $\angle ADB \neq \angle DBC$

6. (a) 140°
(b) Number of sides $= \frac{360°}{20°} = 18$
Sum of angles $= (18 - 2) \times 180°$
$= 16 \times 180°$
$= 2880°$

7. (a) $\angle PQR = 139°$ (b) $\angle LMX = 141°$

8. 12 sides

SECTION   31

Exercise 31   **Page 85**

1. (a) $a = 65°$ (angle in semi-circle = 90°)
(b) $b = 48°$ (angles in same segment equal)
(c) $c = 110°$ (angle at centre = 2 × angle at circumference)
(d) $d = 70°$ (opposite angles of a cyclic quad add to 180°)

2. $x = 37°$

3. (a) $\angle BCO = 31°$
(b) $a = 100°$, $b = 40°$, $c = 50°$

4. (a) $\angle ADB = 53°$ (b) $\angle ACD = 32°$
(c) $\angle ADC = 95°$ (d) $\angle BAD = 95°$

5. $\angle ABC = (x + 90)°$

6. $x = 52°$, $y = 76°$, $z = 58°$

7. (a) $x = 65°$ (b) $y = 130°$ (c) $z = 50°$

SECTION   32

Exercise 32   **Page 87**

1. 17 cm²   **8.** $YP = 4.8$ cm
2. $b = 6$ cm   **9.** 754 cm²
3. 27 cm²   **10.** 297 m²
4. 8.6%, correct to 1 d.p.   **11.** (a) 220 cm
5. 52.5 cm²   (b) 47.7 cm
6. 7 m   **12.** 16π cm²
7. (a) 81.7 cm   **13.** 796 cm²
(b) 19.6 cm²

14. Yes. Semi-circle $= \frac{1}{2}(\pi \times 10^2) = 50\pi$ cm²
Circle $= \pi \times 5^2 = 25\pi$ cm²

15. $(4\pi + 18)$ cm

16. (a) 150 cm²   (b) 129°

17. (a) 12π cm²   (b) $(12 + 4\pi)$ cm
(c) Point P lies on the arc AB.
$\angle BOA = \angle BPA = 120°$
reflex $\angle BOA = 240° = 2 \times \angle BPA$,
angle at centre = 2 × angle at circumference.

SECTION 33

Exercise 33 — Page 90

1. (b) (i) 250° (ii) 1530 m
2.
3.

   Lawnmower can reach

   Part of house

   P
4.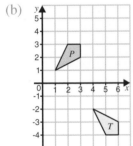

   L — M

   … equidistant from L and M
5. (a) (b)

   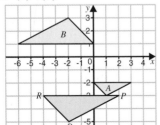

   (c) $PX = 3.9$ cm

SECTION 34

Exercise 34 — Page 92

1. (a) (i) $x = -1$ (ii) $\begin{pmatrix} -1 \\ 2 \end{pmatrix}$

   (iii) Centre $(0, 2)$, scale factor 2.

   (b)

2. (a) Translation with vector $\begin{pmatrix} 4 \\ -3 \end{pmatrix}$.

   (b) Enlargement, scale factor $\frac{1}{3}$, centre $(0, 0)$

   (c) Enlargement, scale factor -2, centre $(0, -1)$.
3. Reflection in $y = x$.
4. (a) $Q(1, 3)$

   (b) (i) $S(4, -2)$ (ii) $\begin{pmatrix} -1 \\ 3 \end{pmatrix}$ (c) $X(1, -1)$
5. (a) (b)

   (c) Enlargement, scale factor -2, centre $(0, -1)$.

SECTION 35

Exercise 35 — Page 93

1. $BC = 13$ cm
2. 6 km
3. 28.7 cm
4. 9.85 units
5. $3.4^2 = 11.56 \quad 2.1^2 + 2.8^2 = 12.25$

   Since $3.4^2 < 2.1^2 + 2.8^2$, $\angle PQR < 90°$

   So, ΔPQR is an acute-angled triangle.
6. (a) 19.2 km (b) 9.8 km
7. 63.4 cm²
8. $AB = 22.9$ cm
9. 34 cm²

SECTION 36

Exercise 36 — Page 96

1. $MN = 6.4$ cm
2. (a) $x = 49.4°$ (b) $QR = 5.45$ cm
3. 4.2 m
4. 286°
5. (a) 9.7 cm (b) 53.9°
6. 18.4°

SECTION 37

Exercise 37 — Page 98

1. (a) 4 (b) 1
2. (a) (b)
3. (a) **B** has larger volume.

   A: Volume $= 2 \times 6 \times 2 = 24$ cm³

   B: Volume $= 3 \times 3 \times 3 = 27$ cm³

   (b) **A** has larger surface area.

   A: Surface area $= 56$ cm²

   B: Surface area $= 54$ cm²
4. 145 cm²
5. 180π cm³
6. No. $h = \dfrac{1000}{\pi \times 7^2} = 6.5$ cm

   Total depth $= 9 + 6.5 = 15.5$ cm

   15.5 cm < 18 cm
7. 90 cm³
8. 180π cm³
9. (a) 32 673 cm² (b) 10 cm
10. (a) 4 712 389 cm³ (b) 4 594 579 cm³
11. (a) 219.8 cm² (b) 374 cm³
12. (a) 3811 cm³ (b) 1143 cm²
13. 11.2 cm

132

Exercise 38 — Page 101

1. 36.25 km
2. Debbie is taller.   5 ft 4 in = 160 cm
   Joyce is heavier.   9 st 2 lb = 58.2 kg
3. £813
4. (a) 1.35 m²   (b) 200 000 cm³
5. (a) 18.5 cm   (b) 17.25 cm
   (c) Only accurate to 1 d.p.
6. 220.5 kg
7. (a) $\sqrt{(a^2 + b^2)}$ (b) $\dfrac{abd}{2}$
8. (a) 2.5 cm ≤ width < 3.5 cm
   (b) 11.25 cm² ≤ area < 19.25 cm²   (c) $x = 4$
9. 67.0766… cm³
10. 1142
11. 4.98 cm ≤ radius < 5.03 cm, to 2 d.p.

SECTION 39

Exercise 39 — Page 103

1. (a) Ratio of widths = 1 : 2 **but**
   ratio of lengths = 5 : 7.
   (b) 7.5 cm
2. (a) $XY = 10$ cm   (b) $AC = 1.2$ cm
3. **B** and **D** (ASA)
4. (a) QRS, TUP
   (b) (i) $\angle PTU = 30°$ (ii) 21.6 cm
5. (a) 81 cm³   (b) 4.5 cm
6. 20 cm

SECTION 40

Exercise 40 — Page 104

1. (a) $\overrightarrow{XY} = \mathbf{y} - \mathbf{x}$ (b) $\overrightarrow{QP} = \frac{1}{2}(\mathbf{x} - \mathbf{y})$
2. (a) $\overrightarrow{AB} = \begin{pmatrix} 6 \\ -4 \end{pmatrix}$ (b) $D(2, 6)$
3. (a) $\overrightarrow{PQ} = \mathbf{a} + 3\mathbf{b}$
   (b) (i)   (ii) $\overrightarrow{RP} = -5\mathbf{a} - \mathbf{b}$
   (c) (i) Parallel and equal in length.
       (ii) Parallelogram
4. (a) (i) $\overrightarrow{AB} = 4\mathbf{b} - 4\mathbf{a}$ (ii) $\overrightarrow{PQ} = 2\mathbf{b} - \mathbf{a}$
   (b) $\overrightarrow{QR} = 4\mathbf{b} - 2\mathbf{a} = 2(2\mathbf{b} - \mathbf{a})$ and
   $\overrightarrow{PQ} = 2\mathbf{b} - \mathbf{a}$
   So, vectors $\overrightarrow{QR}$ and $\overrightarrow{PQ}$ are parallel and,
   since Q is a common point, P, Q and R
   are colinear points.

5. (a) (i) $\overrightarrow{AB} = \mathbf{b} - \mathbf{a}$ (ii) $\overrightarrow{RA} = \mathbf{a} - 3\mathbf{b}$
       (iii) $\overrightarrow{BQ} = 4\mathbf{a} + 2\mathbf{b}$
   (b) $\overrightarrow{AS} = 3\mathbf{a} + 1\frac{1}{2}\mathbf{b}$

SECTION 41

Exercise 41 — Page 108

1. (a) (i) $x = 300°$ (ii) $x = 120°, 240°$
   (b) (i) 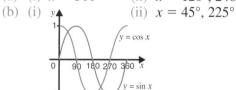   (ii) $x = 45°, 225°$
2. (b) $x = 116°$ (c) $x = -64°$, $x = -116°$
3. (a)
   (b) $\cos x = \dfrac{\sqrt{5}}{3}$ (or 0.745 to 3 d.p.)
   (c) $y = 138.2°$
4. (a) $\angle QRP = 28.6°$ (b) 103 cm²
5. (a) $\angle BAC = 48.5°$ (b) 15 m²
6. 177.3 m
7. $ZY = 11.8$ km. Bearing of Z from $Y = 282°$.
8. (a) $\angle BAC = 62.7°$ or $\angle BAC = 117.3°$
   (b) $BC = 12.9$ cm

Shape, Space, Measures — Section Review

Non-calculator Paper — Page 109

1. (a) $a = 126°$ (b) $b = 95°$, $c = 55°$
   (c) $d = 55°$
2. $30 \times 20 \times 10 = 6000$ cm³
3. (a) 060°   (b) 300°
4. (a) Greatest: 20.5 kg,   least: 19.5 kg
   (b) 1.15 kg
5. (a) (b)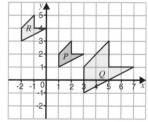
   (c) Enlargement, scale factor $\frac{1}{2}$, centre $(-7, 7)$.
6. (a) (b) (c)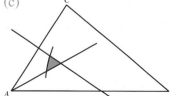

7. (a) $1440°$ (b) 12 sides

8. $14\pi\,\text{cm}$

9. (a) abc has dimension 3(volume)
(b) πa, $\sqrt{a^2 - c^2}$ and $2(a + b + c)$

10. (a) $AC = 6\,\text{cm}$ (b) $PR = 1.5\,\text{cm}$

11. (a) $\overrightarrow{PQ} = 6\mathbf{a} - 6\mathbf{b}$

(b) $\overrightarrow{OR} = \mathbf{a} + \mathbf{b}$

(c) $\overrightarrow{OS} = 5\mathbf{a} + 5\mathbf{b}$

(d) Points O, R and S lie on a straight line.
$\overrightarrow{OS} = 5\overrightarrow{OR}$

12. (a) $w = 30°$
ΔOBD is isosceles. $\angle ODB = \angle OBD$
(b) (i) $x = 80°$
(ii) $y = 40°$, $\angle AOD = 2 \times \angle OCD$
(c) $z = 20°$

13. (a)

(b) (i) $x = 333°$ (ii) $x = 153°$, $207°$
(iii) $x = 63°$ (iv) $x = 63°$, $117°$

14. $14.5\,\text{cm}^2$

Shape, Space, Measures — Section Review

Calculator Paper — Page 111

1. Height $175\,\text{cm}$, weight $70\,\text{kg}$.

2. E.g. $a = 4\,\text{m}$, $b = 6\,\text{m}$; $a = 3\,\text{m}$, $b = 7\,\text{m}$; etc.
$(a + b = 10)$

3. (a) (i) Ext. $\angle = \frac{360°}{6} = 60°$.
$a =$ int. $\angle = 180° - 60° = 120°$
(ii) $b = 15°$
(b) No. Only equilateral triangles, squares and hexagons tessellate.
Interior angle must divide into $360°$ a whole number of times.

4. $(2.5, -1)$

5. (b) (i) $215°$ (ii) $17\,\text{km}$

6. (a) $540\,\text{cm}^2$ (b) $AC = 39\,\text{cm}$

7. $769\,690\,\text{cm}^3$

8. $x = 52.1°$

9. Footpaths HX, XS, shorter by $171\,\text{m}$.
Footpaths $850\,\text{m}$, Waverly Crescent $1021\,\text{m}$.

10. (a) $AP = 7.5\,\text{cm}$ (b) $AC = 2.4\,\text{cm}$

11. (a) $\angle QRS = 75°$
(b) Reflex $\angle POS = 360° - 80° = 280°$
Reflex $\angle POS = 2 \times \angle PXS$
(Angle at centre $= 2 \times$ angle at circum.)
So, $\angle PXS = \frac{1}{2} \times 280° = 140°$.

12. $21.7\,\text{km}^2$

134

---

13. (a)

(b) Enlargement, scale factor $-\frac{1}{2}$, centre $(-1, 2)$.

14. (a) Perpendicular distance $= 4.77\,\text{m}$
Area $EFCB = 40.5\,\text{m}^2$
(b) $\angle EMN = 69.7°$

15. (a) $74.4\,\text{cm}^2$ (b) $2.43\,\text{cm}$

16. (a) $\overrightarrow{OX} = 2\mathbf{b}$, $\overrightarrow{AX} = 2\mathbf{b} - \mathbf{a}$.
(b) $\overrightarrow{BM} = \mathbf{b} - \frac{1}{2}(2\mathbf{b} - \mathbf{a}) = \frac{1}{2}\mathbf{a}$
$\overrightarrow{OA} = \mathbf{a}$ and $\overrightarrow{BM} = \frac{1}{2}\mathbf{a}$
(multiples of the same vector, $\mathbf{a}$)
So, BM is parallel to OA.

17. $x = 194.5°$, $345.5°$

18. $115.935\,\text{m}^2$

19. (a) $27.6\,\text{cm}^2$ (b) $BD = 11.5\,\text{cm}$
(c) $\angle BCD = 154°$

20. (a) $1.1\,\text{m}^3$ (b) $0.326\,\text{m}^3$

21. $BC = 10.9\,\text{cm}$

22. Upper bound $= 4.7782\ldots\,\text{cm}$
Lower bound $= 4.7186\ldots\,\text{cm}$

Exam Practice: Module 5

Non-calculator Paper — Page 114

1. (a) $5x + 15$ (b) (i) $x = 6$ (ii) $x = 1.5$

2. $8.1\,\text{cm}^2$

3. $3t + 2(t + 5) = (5t + 10)$ pence

4. $6.5\,\text{cm}^2$

5. (a) $x + (2x - 1) + 3x = 41$
(b) $x = 7$ Numbers on cards: 7, 13, 21

6. $36\pi\,\text{cm}^2$

7. Greatest: $11.5\,\text{kg}$, least: $10.5\,\text{kg}$

8. (a) $x = 112°$ (corresponding angles)
(b) $y = 50°$

9. $3n - 4$

10. (a) (i) $5(a - 2)$ (ii) $x(x - 6)$
(b) (i) $8a + 2$ (ii) $x^2 - 6x + 8$
(c) $t = \frac{S + 1}{3}$
(d) m^5

11. (a) $p = 30°$ (b) $d = 150°$

12. (a) (b)

(c) Rotation, $180°$, about $(3, -1)$.

13. $V = 3 \times 4 \times 4 \times 8 = 384\,\text{cm}^3$

14. (a) Missing entries are: 5, −1, 1

(b)
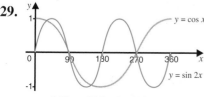

(c) $y = -1.25$ (d) $x = 0.4$ or $x = 2.6$

15. $\sqrt{a^2 + b^2}$ and $4(a + b + c)$
Both have dimension 1.

16. (a) 1, 2, 3, 4, 5   (b) $x = 5$, $y = -1$
(c) $n(n - 1)$ (d) $6a^5b^2$

17. (a) $BC = 12$ cm   (b) $CD = 10.5$ cm

18. (a) $a = 35°$ (angles in same segment)
$b = 145°$ (opp. angle of cyclic quad)
(b) $c = 61°$ (angle in a semi-circle = 90°)
(c) $x = 60°$ (tangent meets radius at 90°)

19. (a) $3x(x - 2)$ (b) $3x^2 - 10x - 8$
(c) $t = \dfrac{4W - 3}{5}$

20. (a) $\angle PQR = 120°$ (b) $BC = 3$ cm
(c) $1 : 0.64$

21. (a) $y = x^2 - 1$ (b) $y = 2^x$
(c) $x^2 + y^2 = 9$ (d) $y = \dfrac{1}{x}$

22. (a) $(n - 3)^2 - 2(n - 3)$
$= n^2 - 6n + 9 - 2n + 6$
$= n^2 - 8n + 15 = (n - 3)(n - 5)$
(b) $x = 2$ or $x = -5$

23. 3.865 m

24. (a) $9a^6$ (b) $x = 0$ or $x = 3$
(c) $n = \dfrac{2m - 3}{m + 3}$

25. (a) $\overrightarrow{BA} = -2\mathbf{b}$ (b) $\overrightarrow{BC} = 6\mathbf{b} - 2\mathbf{a}$

26. $y = 2\frac{1}{2}x$

27. (a) $a = 3$, $b = 12$
(b) $x = -\sqrt{12} - 3$ or $x = \sqrt{12} - 3$

28. (a)   (b)

(c)

29.

$x = 30°$, $90°$, $150°$, $270°$

30. (a) $\dfrac{15}{x} + \dfrac{11}{x - 2} = 4$
$15(x - 2) + 11x = 4x(x - 2)$
$15x - 30 + 11x = 4x^2 - 8x$
$4x^2 - 34x + 30 = 0$
$2x^2 - 17x + 15 = 0$
(b) $x = 1$ or $x = 7.5$
So, Zarig's average speed is 7.5 mph.

31. $\dfrac{2x}{x + 4}$

Exam Practice: **Module** 5

Calculator Paper   Page 117

1. (a) 14   (b) 53
2. (a) Between 10.50 and 11.10. Steepest slope.
(b) 12 km/h
3. **Q** and **S**
4. 135°
5. (a) (i) $\angle OAB = x°$ (ii) $\angle ABC = 2x°$
(b) $x = 64°$
6. 3.6696 m²
7. (b) 2.15 km, 295°
8. 254 m²
9. $x < -0.5$
10. (a) (b)

11. $x = 3.8$
12. 61.1%

13. (a) (i) e^5 (ii) f^4 (iii) $9h^3k^6$
(b) (i) $3p^2 + 6p$ (ii) $x^2 - 8xy + 7y^2$
14. (a) $XD = 11.9$ m   (b) $BC = 8.1$ m
15. 20 cm
16. (a) $x = -1$, $y = 1\frac{1}{2}$
(b) (i) $3xy(y + 2)$ (ii) $(m + n)(a - b)$
(c) $x = 3$ or $x = 4$
17. (a) $x + y = 2$ (b) $y = x + 2$
(c) $y = 5x - 10$
18. 400 g
19. 25.1°
20. (a) $\dfrac{1}{3x}$ (b) $x = -1.14$ or $x = 1.47$
21. $(2x - 1)(x + 1) = 104$
$2x^2 + x - 1 = 104$
$2x^2 + x - 105 = 0$
22. (a) 640 cm²   (b) 231 cm²
23. (a) $\angle PQS = 36°$ (angles in same segment)
(b) $\angle POS = 72°$ ($\angle$ at centre = 2 × $\angle$ at circum.)
(c) $\angle PSR = 90°$ (angle in a semi-circle = 90°)
(d) $\angle PSM = 36°$ (angle in alternate segment)
24. $x = -0.4$, $y = -2.2$ and $x = 2$, $y = -1$
25. (b) $x = 44°$, $134°$
26. (a) $\angle HCB = (180° - 128°) + 66° = 118°$
(b) $HB = 6.82$ km
27. 13.0 cm
28. (a) $\angle PQR = 60°$ (b) 42.2 cm²

135

Index ●●●●●●●●●●●●●●●●●●●●●●●●●●●●●●●●